HEGEMONY AND STRATEGIES OF TRANSGRESSION

SUNY Series, Postmodern Culture
Joseph Natoli, editor

Hegemony and Strategies of Transgression

ESSAYS IN CULTURAL STUDIES AND COMPARATIVE LITERATURE

by
E. San Juan, Jr.

STATE UNIVERSITY OF NEW YORK PRESS

Published by
State University of New York Press, Albany

For information, address State University of New York Press,
State University Plaza, Albany, N.Y., 12246

Production by Cathleen Collins
Marketing by Nancy Farrell

Library of Congress Cataloging in Publication Data

San Juan, E. (Epifanio), 1938–
    Hegemony and strategies of transgression : essays in cultural
studies and comparative literature / E. San Juan, Jr.
        p.   cm. — (SUNY series, postmodern culture)
    Includes bibliographical references and index.
    ISBN 0–7914–2527–4. — ISBN 0–7914–2528–2 (pbk.)
    1. Literature, Comparative—History and criticism.   2. Culture
conflict in literature.   3. Developing countries in literature.
4. Literature and history.   I. Title.   II. Series: SUNY series in
postmodern culture.
PN871.S26   1995
809—dc20   94–34540
                                                                        CIP

10 9 8 7 6 5 4 3 2 1

The weapon of criticism cannot, of course, replace criticism of the weapon, material force must be overthrown by material force; but theory also becomes a material force as soon as it has gripped the masses. Theory is capable of gripping the masses as soon as it demonstrates *ad hominem*, and it demonstrates *ad hominem* as soon as it becomes radical. To be radical is to grasp the root of the matter. But for man the root is man himself.

—Karl Marx

Unrelenting revolutionary activity coupled with boundless humanity—that alone is the real life-giving force of socialism. A world must be overturned, but every tear that has flowed and might have been wiped away is an indictment; and a man hurrying to perform a great deed who steps on even a worm out of unfeeling carelessness commits a crime. . . .

From this contradiction between the sharpening of the problem and the lack of prerequisites to its solution in the initial stage of revolutionary development it follows that the individual skirmishes of the revolution may end in *defeat*. But revolution is the sole form of "war"—and this is its special law of life—where the final victory can be prepared only by a series of "defeats"!

—Rosa Luxemburg

CONTENTS

Contents

PART THREE: INTERVENTIONS

ACKNOWLEDGMENTS

Every task necessarily involves a community or at least a solidarity of workers and helpmates for its fulfillment. Whatever small degree of success I have achieved here, can be credited to the cooperation and support of numerous collaborators and friends. I have the pleasure to thank the following for contributing in one way or another to the completion of this task: James R. Bennett (University of Arkansas), Alan Wald (University of Michigan), Robert Dombroski (Graduate Center, City University of New York), Sam Noumoff (McGill University), and Roger Bresnahan (Michigan State University). For solidarity over the years I have benefited from the friendship of Norman and Nancy Chance, Bruce Franklin, Fredric Jameson, Paul Buhle, Sylvia Mendez-Ventura, Elmer Ordoñez, and Emmanuel T. Santos.

I am grateful to my colleagues at Bowling Green State University for their assistance and encouragement, especially to: Karen Gould, associate dean of the Graduate College; Ellen Berry, director of Women's Studies; Louis Katzner, Associate Vice President for Research and Dean of the Graduate College; and especially Robert Perry, chairman of the Department of Ethnic Studies, and Charles Cranny, dean of the College of Arts and Sciences.

I am also taking this opportunity to express my gratitude to John Gatta, chairman of the Department of English, University of Connecticut, and other colleagues for their recognition of the value of the work I have been doing.

For giving me valuable insights and sustenance in every way, Delia Aguilar, professor of Ethnic and Women's Studies, Bowling Green State University, deserves more credit than I can ever acknowledge here. The same goes for Karin Aguilar-San Juan, editor and martial artist, who is enrolled in the sociology graduate program at Brown University; and Eric San Juan, formerly with Hale and Dorr, Boston, and now in graduate studies in anthropology at the University of Chicago, both of whom provided joy and wisdom.

The raw materials in this book, now thoroughly reprocessed and reshaped, first appeared in articles published in the following journals to whose editors I am grateful: *Nature, Society, and Thought, Revue de litterature comparée, Orbis litterarum, North Dakota Quarterly, Border/lines, New Orleans Review, MELUS, Left Curve,* and in my recent book *From the Masses, to the Masses: Third World Literature and Revolution*. Finally I want to thank the editorial and production staff of the State University of New York Press whose intelligence, care, and expertise have made this work materialize in its present form.

INTRODUCTION

Scenes of carnage in Somalia, East Timor, Haiti, in the occupied territories of Palestine and in all the fragments of what was once Yugoslavia. . . . Images of violent confrontations in South Africa, and not too long ago in Los Angeles, and now in Yemen and Rwanda. . . . The year 1994 opened with the uprising of the Indian communities led by the Zapatista National Liberation Front in Chiapas, Mexico, just after the signing of the North America Free Trade Agreement. Signs of the apocalypse? Or of the long-awaited devolution from the age of the super-powers? In the prologue to *The Rules Are No Game*, Anthony Wilden (1987) has given us a background to this landscape of horrendous waste, disfigurations of pieties and *ressentiment*. Connecting "local knowledges" with their overarching reality, Noam Chomsky (1991) has rendered in bold strokes the lessons of the par-adigmatic First World (United States)–Third World (Vietnam) encounter in our time, recalling what Mark Twain (1992), in his "To the Person Sitting in Darkness," did for his audience at the turn of the century.

Faced with this multitudinous reality, the practitioners of "humane letters" in the United States—quite a separate tribe from the aforementioned disturbers of the peace—have displayed erudition and ingenuity in theorizing but have failed to engage with crude, sublunary happenings. Why? Because all (except for those skeptics on the fringe and other scandalous but marginalized *conscienticizers*) have refused to understand exactly what is meant by the dominant, expansive, and vir-tually inescapable stranglehold of the United States—its economic, political, and cultural hegemony—over the world system in terms of the everyday lives of masses of people in what is called the "Third World." Although the term "cultural impe-rialism" has been domesticated for ideology-critique (Tomlinson 1991) and token criticism of certain government policies is the standard fare for liberals, still the majority of U.S. intellectuals and arbiters of taste function today without any thought of how their words and actions, whether they know it or not, "represent" the claims to (cultural/racial) superiority of a nation-state whose interventions in Latin America, Asia, and the Middle East have brought disaster and misery to mil-lions since the nineteenth century. Edward Said's recent *Culture and Imperialism* is just one reminder of that record. Unless there is some sophisticated criticism and

1

disavowal of this complicity, I am afraid that the activities of U.S. academics can only serve to advance transnational capital's ascendancy for now and throughout the next century.

Confronted with that wholesale charge, the reader might expect a dossier of proofs and other substantiating material in what follows. But no such file will be found here except obliquely, by way of a protracted meditation on ideas, topics, and issues that I think have supplied the alibis for that refusal to acknowledge overt/covert collusions with hegemony. Eschewing myths of transparency and self-evidence, we are left with the hieroglyphs of mediations. The last four chapters of this book seek to decipher those mediations in the micropolitics of racial relations, the irreducible value-measure in the "general economy" of the United States vis-à-vis people of color. On the whole, this collection strives to respond to hegemony by a detour through reflections on the theoretical consensus, hermeneutic exercises, "misprisions" of writers' ethical and political stances, and the now monumentalized affects of postmodernism—in one version, "how the world dreams itself to be American." In this context, I address the vicissitudes of "hegemony" (here used in the original Gramscian sense) extrapolated from the refractions of certain posthumanist and postfoundationalist trends both in critical discourse and in dissenting speculations on postmodernism and the Third World/"postcolonial" situation.

Platitudes about "globalism," world citizenship, and the supposedly benign rule of planetary corporations abound today amid reports of intensifying nationalist-ethnic strife and racial violence everywhere. With the celebration of instantaneous and omnipresent differences, the subtending "hyperreal" has truly arrived. Regardless of one's view on these disparate phenomena, I think there can be no worthwhile exchange on culture and art today without a sense of the capitalist world system as its condition of possibility, its enabling complex of presuppositions and theorems. In other words, one cannot theorize on culture in the United States (or in Europe) without being implicated in its geopolitical resonance in what dependency scholarship refers to as the "periphery," that excess called the "Third World" which threatens market stability but makes sublimation possible. A minor digression: I prefer to use the somewhat dated term "Third World" despite its problematic status today in order to evoke the milieu of Fanon, C.L.R. James, and Che Guevara (Hadjor 1993). I should define "Third World" here (the binary South/North is more geographically restrictive) as a convenient label for the not fully modernized or still unindustrialized regions of the world, formerly colonized territories and spheres of influence, which are not homogeneous by any means—my survey of the diversity of themes, styles, and sensibilities of Third World writers easily confirm this—but which all share "a community of fate" (Otto Bauer's terms) in their being subordinated in varying degrees, then and now, to the power of the imperial centers and/or transnational corporate interests.

The contingent nature of First World and Third World cultural transactions, the range of its schisms and interdictions, may be exemplified by my own personal history with all its untypical and perhaps even "inscrutable" characteristics. Whatever the liabilities may be, the intent here corresponds to Deleuze's (1993) definition of ethics: "not to be unworthy of what happens to us."

Perspectives by incongruity then: when I began graduate studies in the discipline of "English literature" in 1960, a time of "sweetness and light," the people of Havana had just welcomed Fidel Castro with his victorious column of guerillas from the Sierra Maestra. It was also a time when African, Latin American, and Asian liberation struggles were beginning to be preempted by Western outrage at oppression in "actually existing socialism," otherwise known as Solzhenitsyn's "Gulag archipelago." In the fifties I was trained as a "New Critic" by the salvific, disciplinary regimes of a neocolonial outpost, the Philippines, virtually a dependency of the United States. This neocolonial "tutelage" continued at Harvard University. After the passage of years of upheavals (including the catastrophic reign of the Marcos dictatorship and its traumatic aftermath, the Aquino restoration of oligarchic rule), I still recall I. A. Richards' memorable course in "Poetics" where the venerable sage descanted on the "esemplastic" power of the imagination, according to the scriptural dicta of Coleridge's *Biographia Literaria* (now far removed from the decentering of subjectivity in *Mencius on the Mind*). Ensconced then in the cloister of Widener Library, I participated vicariously in the resurgence of the anti-imperialist, national-democratic struggle in the Philippines. While still influenced by the ingratiating formalist apparatus of the New Criticism (somehow conflated with the archetypal utopianism of Northrop Frye and Marcusean psychoanalysis), my exposure to the "thickness" of reality came by way of research into the Victorian aesthetic movement, in particular the careers of such *fin-de-siècle* prophets as William Morris and Oscar Wilde. Perhaps my interest in oppositional renovation dates back to this concern with the complex and dynamic linkages between culture and society, with what Raymond Williams (1977) would call the sociohistorical contexts for "structures of feeling" that anchored the ambiguities, ironies, and paradoxes of language in the socially active processes of writing and reading. Artist, text or performance, and audience are all dialectically imbricated in any specific cultural event. Writing is "always already," as I discovered anew (with the help of Sartre and the cunning of radical existentialists), complicit with and immersed in the world.

Scarcely could I foresee then what turns and leaps would transpire in the uneven formation of a Third World/Filipino sensibility caught in "the belly of the beast," to use Jose Marti's double-edged phrase. When the structuralist movement arrived in the 1970s, followed by the nihilistic transvaluation of most received doxa and conformisms, I was already a product of that whole unprecedented molar/molecular transformation called "the sixties" (Jameson 1984; Howard 1977). The Indochinese Revolution and resistance to imperialist "business as usual" in the "treacherous" hinterlands, combined with the civil rights and the women's liberation movements, provided a supplementary education to the one I received, courtesy of philanthropic largesse. The itinerary of my intellectual adventure did not immediately lead to that wonderful zone of hybridity, syncretic melange, and cosmopolitan eclecticism imagined by Lyotard, Baudrillard, and their followers. It pursued a detour, as it were, in the process of which I encountered again the worldliness—how could it not have been disenchanting?—of what the hieratic gatekeepers of the sanctuary called "literariness." As a poet, fictionist, and essayist in two languages, English and Pilipino, I registered this worldliness in quotidian lived experience in the untamed boondocks (from the Tagalog word *bundok*) and in the urban headquarters of the colonial suzerain. I experienced literariness not through the optic of Foucault's archaeology but through the polemics of Frantz Fanon, the letters of George Jackson, the speeches of Malcolm X, and the diary of Che Guevara. *Ejagham nsibidi*, "cruel letters," one might say (Thompson 1983). The genealogy of this volume may be traced from this engagement with the contestatory narratives of the disturbers of the peace of the status quo, a plot that now proceeds through moments of "interrogation," "reconfiguration," and "intervention" (rubrics I use here to mark the stages of a certain wayward trajectory).

Given this background, one can understand how it is possible to discern in the interstices of the essays here elements of a traditional humanist orientation juxtaposed with a stance valorizing the ideal of national liberation or self-determination for people of color. This concretely epitomizes the axiom and operation of "uneven and combined development," a phase of my education in which the struggle to free the homeland releases transgressive impulses in the migrant's milieu. For an exile interpellated by the U.S. racial Imaginary (including its institutions and officials), neither "pessimism of the intellect" nor "optimism of the will" offers any genuine alternative. Better to ruminate on Matthew 25.45: "Inasmuch as you did it not to one of the least of these, you did it not to me." What the stranger/alien (as categorized by bureaucratic surveillance) needs is a guidebook or exemplum for negotiating the passage from the place of deracination to the site of estrangement and back. Inscribed in these liminal circuits where self-coincidence is impossible, the forging of a conscience for the embattled community makes the exile's predicament bearable and even of some consequence.

At this point I want to draw up a rough inventory of what is circumscribed by the uneven contours of this metamorphosis outlined above. In part one, I grapple with the challenge of the deconstructive machine and its privileging of a "rigorously unreliable" ontology (Paul de Man, Miller) by counterposing to it the emancipatory vision of Walter Benjamin. As an exercise in construing discourses as events, the first essay opens the field for examining what is at stake in the complicity between modes of critical enunciation and their ethico-political repercussions. While for many scholars the refunctioning of Mikhail Bakhtin and the historicizing precept of dialogism have been salutary in releasing them from the fetishism of *écriture* and closure of textualist indifference, I argue in chapter 2 that an alternative approach may be more heuristic in clarifying the crisis of representation and its historical determinations: Antonio Gramsci's hypothesis on the intertextuality of the hegemonic process. In chapter 3, I explore touchstones in the Marxist archive (from Lukacs to Caudwell, Brecht, and Gramsci) in order to elucidate the liaison between the aesthetic and the ethico-political concerns of a historical materialist project, a linkage made problematic by the triumph of modernism over classic realism, as instanced by Adorno's recuperation of art's agency or power of transcendence (Larsen 1990). This review then prompts the occasion in chapter 4 for the Althusserian moment of conceptualizing literature as a mode of ideological production, exemplified chiefly by the work of Pierre Macherey. In the next chapter, I attempt a modified symptomatic reading of Hemingway's novel *For Whom the Bell Tolls*.

As a complement to the contestatory mode of part one and the reconstructive ambition of part two, I offer in chapter 6 a survey of selected poems by Hugh MacDiarmid, the great epic intelligence of the Scottish "Third World," to elicit what is missing in the subtle positings of deconstruction, the protocols of symptomatic reading, and the subversive construction of the "national-popular." This route then becomes the pretext for part three where the geopolitical filiations and ethico-political resonance of texts become the framework for inaugurating a "world cultural studies" quest antithetical to the Establishment model.

It will now be obvious to the reader how the format of this book replicates the unbalanced and asymmetrical development of the world system just as it images the uneven profile of my own intellectual formation. Part three, however, introduces a substantive departure from the usual schematism of the field. In chapters 7 and 8, I examine the differential practice of racial and colonial subject-ification as crystallized in certain episodes in Baldwin's career and in selected texts by Asian-American authors. My appraisal of the diasporic imagination participates in the general project of canon revision now under way. It is grounded in the history of the deracination of whole migrant communities and the contingent modalities of their incorporation in the sociolibidinal/political economy of the United States. Questions of frames of reference, reification of boundary coding, displacements of meaning into the power-knowledge constellation, the emergence of cheap Third World labor as the new decentered subject, and so on, are foregrounded here. In examining the textualization of migrant bodies/minds by the U.S. racial Imaginary, I remind the reader of my original proposition that in general all U.S. intellectuals are implicated in the racial politics of the capitalist state, still the salient if not central instrumentality through which commodity-fetishism and corporate hegemony are reproduced daily, reinforced and reaffirmed.

Articulated with the constitution of racialized subjects and the comprador/elite politics of sublimation in late capitalism, the mapping of the uneven, unsynchronized terrain of dependent societies is pursued further into the realm of postmodern aesthetics and social theory in chapter 9. Finally I return to my opening theme: the fraught convergence of Third World transgression and Western late-modern techniques of recontainment (Anderson 1988). My focus here is the interrogation shared by other dissenters to the postmodernist dispensation: we ask whether parody, hybridity, pastiche, syncretic heterogeneity, ironic metafabulations, and so on, can be catalyzing or enabling concepts in assessing the seemingly incommensurable modalities of cultural production and the subjugation of bodies-minds in the Third World. As a riposte to postmodern elite populism, I try here to investigate the possibilities of contextualizing specific Third World writers in the theater of antagonistic forces and practices that constitute the present world system. In the interface with Western theorizing, these committed writers conceive their art as both representational and signifying practices, not simply mimicking a spontaneous "politics of identity" but mobilizing energies for large-scale, thoroughgoing transformations. No longer anarchic spectacles nor ludic simulations, their writing organizes a politics of desire with reason grounded in self-reflexive experience, maneuvering bodies and memory against the hegemonic Leviathan.

In the last chapter, I resume certain arguments in the disputes concerning identity and representation set forth in my book *Racial Formations/Critical Transformations* and provisionally sum up the intent of part three: the proposal for a new inquiry called "World Cultural Studies." Perhaps the epithet "World" is superfluous since this new research program posits the eventual "withering away" of nation-state boundaries. Unfortunately the travelling U.S. authority on theory carries his "national" burden in his psyche: when and if these nomadic experts happen to interest themselves in the history, society, and culture of their former colonies—say, the Philippines, or Puerto Rico (I suspect these areas are avoided or evaded because they don't command the scholarly exchange-value associated with older traditional cultures like those of China, India, Japan, etc.), they unwittingly repeat the "civilizing mission" of their forebears. This is where the vocation of cultural studies can perform an advisory role. Stuart Hall recalls the original inspiration of this inquiry: aside from assaying the power/knowledge nexus, and anticipating social change, cultural studies assigns priority to the analysis of the kaleidoscopic structures and dynamics of racism, especially now that contemporary racism inheres in "the fear—the terrifying, internal fear—of living with difference," making our lives and societies "profoundly and deeply antihumane in their capacity to live with difference" (1992b, 17–18). One of these fears is directed toward feminism in general and its uncanny undoing of patriarchy (Ebert 1993). In this volume I have only been able to address women writers from the racial minorities (Asian American, Native American); a fuller and substantial appreciation of socialist feminism regarded as the "fulfillment of the Western Marxist project" (Gottlieb 1989, 22) is reserved for another occasion.

Perhaps the emblem for this emerging "world cultural studies" I have in mind, an enterprise that will speak truth to power and foreground the collective historic agency of masses of people—in particular, peasants, women, and other sectors declassed by the Manichean delirium Fanon so poignantly diagnosed—is the life and work of the great Caribbean revolutionary C. L. R. James. In *The Black Jacobins* and essays like "Dialectical Materialism and the Fate of Humanity" and "From Toussaint L'Ouverture to Fidel Castro," James (1992) analyzed the dialectic of power and difference which generated the fear Hall spoke of and thereby unleashed those subterranean energies circulating in the exchange between "native" creativity and Western hegemony. In 1953, James was banished from the United States after writing his critical masterpiece, *Mariners, Renegades, and Castaways*. Perhaps John Berger had James in mind when he wrote about modern homelessness and the incarnation of millennial dreams: "This century, for all its wealth and with all its communication systems, is the century of banishment. Eventually perhaps the promise, of which Marx was the great prophet, will be fulfilled, and then the substitute for the shelter of a home will not just be our personal names, but our collective conscious presence in history, and we will live again at the heart of the real. . . . Meanwhile, we live not just our own lives but the longings of our century" (1984, 12).

As his prodigious life-work testifies, James endeavored to live "at the heart of the real" and often succeeded. One proof of this is that in James's synthesis of global trends since the Bolshevik revolution up to the fall of Nkrumah and the crisis of the postcolonial state in the newly independent Third World countries, we can find penetrating insights into the phenomena called "postcolonial" as manifested by certain Caribbean and African politicians and intellectuals who, in refusing a revolutionary Marxism outlook, succumbed to the blandishments of bourgeois pluralism and the seductions of careerism (Henry and Buhle 1992).

The new fashionable trend called "postcolonial criticism" (Bhabha 1992) is, in my judgment, the name of a symptom produced by poststructuralist theories (Derrida, Lacan, Foucault) when regurgitated and worked over by intellectuals from the former colonies disclaiming *inter alia* homeland, origins, foundations, telos, history, reason, and objective reality (Dirlik 1994). But postcoloniality (like the Indian subcontinent) has no ideal-typical essence—as its practitioners claim—so this portrait I delineate becomes simply a shadowy persona in the larger allegory of multiculturalism I elaborate in chapter 10. Prejudiced against foundational scripts by racial "minorities" or aborigines (such as Leslie Marmon Silko or Toni Morrison), the postcolonial critic usually begins with the critique of Western logocentrism/identitarian metaphysics, at once a compromising and teleological move. Unless she wants to sanction the permanence of Eurocentrism, she must prefigure in the same move of inversion and distanciation her autonomous trajectory. She thus needs to expose and repudiate the constitutive effects of the intellectual division of labor in the world system that she has just erased from her account. In this catachrestic performance, the "post" in "postcolonial" which replicates First World conservatism, is thus sublated to a stance of displacement begging recognition from—not the masses in Africa, Asia, or Latin America—but their tutors, Western master-theoreticians of the "sublime." The postcolonial then turns out to be the new comprador of disorganized accumulation. Postcoloniality is thus one of those language-games of positionalities or subject-positions whose rules transnational capitalism has set up and deployed in order to refurbish its worn-out ideological apparatus for subjugating people of color and service its new flexible disposition (Callinicos 1989).

World cultural studies tackles postcoloniality as a case to be evaluated within the framework of world-system analysis I suggested earlier. What is at stake here is not just discourse but the value of practical reason (employed by Third World activists) in questioning its limits and potential in relation to the agenda of progressive social transformation in the uneven global arena. Hence the research perspective I adopt here, grounded maybe in a cruder but not mechanical materialism, goes beyond Habermas' commitment to salvaging critical reason from its instrumental subservience to transnational profitmaking (Heller 1984). Here I introduce the qualification that in the intractable and recalcitrant hinterlands where Lyotard's eclectic consumer either resides in the policed enclaves of the comprador elite, or exists only as a blur in the television screen, the struggle is chiefly for bread, land, shelter—for the integral and organic conditions of possibility for rational communicative actions free from the violence of capital, and more—for a significant measure of dignity appropriate for love and the needs of the species-being (see, for example, the powerful modernist realism of the Vietnamese writer Nguyen Huy Thiep [1992]).

By this detour of "world cultural studies," I envisage the transition from Western "hegemony" to the transformative and oppositional practices of all those "others" inhabiting margins, pariah zones, quarantines, detention and deportation centers, internal colonies in North America and in Europe; this transition epitomizes the itinerary of this author's journey through the terrain called Western *litterae humaniores* now reconceived as the deterritorializing style of critical praxis. In this practice of conflating outside and inside (evinced more in my *Writing and National Liberation* and *From the Masses, to the Masses*), what occupies center-stage are the creative and critical powers of people of color who have been victimized by transnational capital while producing/reproducing social wealth. Irrecusably, the future of over two-thirds of the planet's inhabitants is indivisible from their unremitting struggle for democratic empowerment, national self-determination, popular justice, and dignity. Their variegated, tortuous modes of combatting class exploitation and national oppression comprise heterogeneous projects of resistance that ultimately reproduce the "Third World" as a permanent political-cultural agency of local as well as intercultural transformation. Whenever there is imperial-racial domination in any form, historical experience teaches us that there will always be a "Third World" subject of resistance and dialectical transcendence.

When in February 1989 Salman Rushdie's novel, *The Satanic Verses*, drew a death-sentence from the Ayatollah Khomeini of Iran, the event marked a historic turning-point in the vicissitudes of postmodern theorizing, a field of philosophical inquiry characterized by the celebration of "*différance*," simulacra, and the disappearance of objective "reality" under the incessant free play of signifiers. Here an artifice, a construct of the imagination, erupts into the world of pain, violence, and death. What hurts is the real, no doubt, but the fetishist (of language, ideas, tropes) denies and affirms this at the same time. Exiled from the habitat of the intelligible by Western neoliberal pragmatism, totality returns—it seems—with a vengeance. Meanwhile, writers and intellectuals all over the world have rallied to Rushdie's defense in the name of freedom of expression, an anthropomorphic ideal as old as Aesop's fables, Socrates' sacrifice, and Milton's *Areopagitica*. In the process, the supremacy of the West is implicitly reaffirmed. This controversy opens the space for exploring the fundamental reality of the uneven and unequal development of the world system, a geopolitical set-up which arguably began with Europe's colonization of Africa and the "New World." This reality dictates the continuing global hegemony of Eurocentric knowledge/power of which U.S. intellectuals (with very few exceptions) are the most resourceful guardians, purveyors, and apologists.

Entering the threshold of transnational corporatism (Miyoshi 1993) and a putative globalization-from-below which repudiates nation-state sovereignties (Brecher 1993), we are besieged with recurrent, urgent questions that skirt the fringes of polite conversation in the North some of which I rehearse here randomly:

Can a liberal democratic dispensation still claim moral legitimacy when its complicity with transnational corporate exploitation is witnessed daily? Is nationalism no longer valid, no longer a viable project for subalterns only now emerging (as flexible labor, traffic of exported bodies) into the arena of world history? Are "peoples without history" forever condemned to "postness" and the *Nachträglichkeit* of the unrelenting forces of Western finance/knowledge capital? Is writing at the border/margin—always at the mercy of "Cartesian imperialism" ("I invade you, therefore you exist")—a mode of collective resistance to reification and the religion of free trade? Or is it a symptom and effect of postmodern avantgardism, of "the incredulity toward metanarratives"? In the world of nearly universal commodity fetishism, is the vernacular speech of people of color (not yet postcolonized by e-mail) an alter/native idiom that can catalyze the "political unconscious" of the silent majority in the metropolitan centers? Can the ideals of pluralism and individualistic liberty in industrialized civil society suffice to empower the victims of racist/sexist power? Should we ("natives" of internal/external colonies, Fanon's "wretched of the earth") repudiate both the Enlightenment paradigm and its

antithesis, the ludic play of cyborgs and nomads, in favor of autochtonous programs enacted by "specific intellectuals" and the *testimonios* of indigenous sur-
vivors? In the diaspora of the bearers of labor-power, can we not find a new
strategic vantage-point for resistance where "sovereignty" (Bataille) can be seized?
Can we devise a new problematic of relations based on a Brechtian mode of distancing and estrangement, juxtaposing incommensurable and heterogeneous elements, that may clarify for us the antinomic configuration of triumphalist
capitalism? Brecht reminds us: "The changeability of the world insists on its con-
tradictoriness. There is something in things, people, events, which makes them
what they are, and at the same time something which which makes them different"
(Tatlow 1980, 25). Should we settle for the ethos of multiculturalist consensus
grounded on a telos of consumption? Who are "we" anyway to dare formulate
here an allegory of the quest for identity, equality, and justice? Aren't we guilty of
"totalizing"?

     Such questions, though far from being innocent, fall short of making up a dif-
ferentiated and overdetermined totality. They remain abstract, lacking the syncopated mediations needed to make them concrete. However, they may be said to
approximate the central themes and preoccupations of certain currents of "critical
theory," articulated with the reservations—"Yes, but . . ."—of those excluded and
silenced, voiced here by a witness from Southeast Asia (the Philippines). They are
meant to provoke a rehistoricizing of conventional wisdom and received opinions.
They also hope to instigate further reflection on the predicament of dissident reason paralyzed not only by the opportunist logic of various pragmatisms but by the
naturalized morality of a consensual "racist culture" (Goldberg 1993). Such reflection, however, can be fruitfully conducted only in mutual or reciprocal exchange
with the discourses/acts of people of color which, I submit, necessarily define the
limits of Western theory inscribed in the hierarchical power relations of the world
system. In this exchange, the validity-claims of the interpellations of those "others"
who ultimately constitute our own selves shall then be recognized and appreciated.
As Dante said in *Purgatorio* XV: "By so much more there are humans who say
"ours," so much the more of good does each possess."

     But even so, in my judgment, these claims may be redeemable only beyond
the exorbitant scene of writing, in the locus of a range of conflicts where the "literary" becomes a collective if heterological practice with determinate and decisive
effects. At that point then we don't need to assert the political outlook as the
"absolute horizon of all reading and interpretation," since events shall have overtaken us and made "hope practical," reconfirming once more the Filipina insurgent Salud Algabre's conviction that "No uprising is ever defeated; each one is a
step in the right direction" (Sturtevant 1976, 296). Anticipating such an eventual-
ity, we hope to witness the return of the moment of totality when the actions of
lord and bondsman—to evoke the legendary protagonists of Hegel's *Phenomenology
of the Spirit*—intersect and collide, at which conjuncture the imagination whether

in the North or the South takes its appropriate place in the battlefronts of history. This is at last the stage of "permanent cultural revolution" which Henri Lefebvre (1971) first envisioned in 1967, a festival in which the concept of Fate—"*Verweile doch, du bist so schön!*"—shall finally be displaced by the awareness of a possible happiness for everyone on this earth.

Part One

Interrogations

1

"To Read What Was Never Written"

FROM DECONSTRUCTION TO A
POETICS OF REDEMPTION

In one of his less well-known ambidextrous fables, "The Translators of The 1001 Nights," Jorge Luis Borges (1981) captures in its tone and design the vicissitudes of poststructuralist critical theory as it negotiates its rite of passage from modernism to postmodernism. If we have no access to the source text, can we trust the interpreter? The problem of translation, of hermeneutics in general (subsuming the family of language games called interpretation, exegesis, commentary, and so forth), inheres in the ordeal of a choice that critics are compelled to face in a time when the author's death, for some his protracted obsolescence, has been celebrated (by Roland Barthes and Michel Foucault, among others) at the same time as the birth of the reader and the sacrifice of her innocence. This ordeal, now probably a banal exercise for the heirs of deconstruction and neopragmatism, was initially posed by Jacques Derrida as a choice between assuming the truth of an origin (the prototypical or paradigmatic text, founding vessel of the unitary cogito, the autonomous subject) and affirming "free play" beyond humanism, beyond metaphysics, beyond the dream "of full presence, the reassuring foundation, the origin and the end of the game" (Derrida 1988, 122). We are urged to choose not "suspension of disbelief" nor "the best that is known and thought," but *jouissance*, the dance of the negative, desire, *différance*—the temptation to think the unthinkable, to be seduced by the sirens of undecidability.

In Borges' intertextual game, the competing translators of the Arabian nights resolved by their stance of naive mastery the tension between fidelity to an origin and premeditated betrayal: they did not hesitate to improve the original. It was the path followed by an illustrious predecessor, Edward FitzGerald, the author/translator of the *Rubaiyyat*. No doubt the code of "Orientalism" (Edward Said's term) and its decorum saved them from the imperative of honoring the original script; hence Borges praises the "happy, creative infidelity" of Mardrus. How can one be faithful if the original is "a confusion of mirrors, the mask is beneath the face, so

15

that no one knows which is the true man and which his idols"? The text our translators would "bear across" (the literal sense of *translatus*) is a space where "Chance has played at symmetry, at contrast, at digression" (1981, 86). "Always already" treacherous, the original can no longer be traduced nor betrayed. At this juncture, we find ourselves trapped in a labyrinth of mirrors, re-inscribed as it were in Lacan's register of the Imaginary.

Borges attempts to diagnose the idiosyncrasies of each translator by adducing the influences of race, nationality, cultural milieu, individual temperament (Hippolyte Taine's coordinates), and accidental conjunctures of society and artist; their reciprocal dynamics would explain the peculiarities of each translation. But in his tone of mock erudition and serio-comic judiciousness, Borges only succeeds in parodying his philological pretext: he presents miniature encyclopedias of each author, a foretaste of the pastiche each would replicate in turn. But no betrayal has been committed, it seems, for after all the putative original (how can it be authenticated?) was itself an intriguingly puzzling game. And, to compound the imbroglio, each translator—Galland, Lane, Burton, Dr. Mardrus and Enno Littman—seems to be prematurely suffering from Harold Bloom's "anxiety of influence"! In the course of anatomizing the translator's dilemma, Borges historicizes the dualism but in the same gesture pronounces it a mirage:

> The elegant Newman-Arnold debate (1861–62), more memorable than its two interlocutors, has argued extensively the two general ways of translating. Newman in it defended the literal mode, the retention of all verbal singularities; Arnold, the strict elimination of distracting or hindering details. This proceeding may furnish the pleasures of uniformity and gravity; the other, continuous small wonders. Both are less important than the translator and his literary habits. To translate the spirit is an intention of such enormity, so phantasmal, that it can well turn out to be inoffensive; to translate the letter, a precision so extravagant that there is no risk in attempting it. (1981, 76)

If translating the spirit is phantasmal and mimicking the letter futile or superfluous, then the effort of reading or making sense, interpretation in general, becomes (to echo Sartre) a vain if not useless passion.

One wonders how, in the process of contextual evocation, Borges' translators have so uncannily become Dickensian creatures who are soon to metamorphose into Kafkaesque characters, caught in the toils of an alien narrative whose form/substance they have tried to render in their own native language. (Without knowing it, they have themselves been "translated," so to speak, by Borges.) It might be that the etymological, archaic force of the verb "to translate"—to transfer or move relics, or a saint's body, from one place (of internment) to another; to entrance or enrapture; to cause to remove one disease from one part of the body to another (Webster 1972)—has exercised a spell on our archival guide so that a psychoanalytic transference may be said to have transpired. No compromise (such as that made by Schlegel-Tieck with Shakespeare) between original and mimicry was reached. In any case, if translation is an impossible and futile task, is the hope for a correct reading a delusion?

The controversy in contemporary critical theory over meaning and the problem of valid interpretation (re-writing: iterability, the repetition *problematique*) pivots less on the circularity of the hermeneutic method, which has been debated in the West from Schleiermacher to Heidegger, Gadamer, Hirsch, and Rorty, than on questions of how language or textuality connects with history, society, and power. Feminism, the new historicism, and various postmodernist schools (Lyotard, Baudrillard) are all contesting the terrain which Borges' translators have left desolate. Translation construed as mediation of the horizons of discourse becomes the key issue.[1] Derrida's wager of choices I alluded to earlier, its refusal of history and the phenomenology of experience, may be concretized by glossing an exemplary text of the major deconstructionist of our time, Paul de Man (1986): his commentary on Walter Benjamin's 1923 essay "The Task of the Translator."

De Man begins his lecture by citing the advance of philosophic comprehension attested to by Gadamer's concept of modernity centered on language and the historicity of understanding. In contrast to the pragmatic view, Benjamin's dismissal of the importance of the reader or audience (in the first paragraph of his essay) represents for de Man a prophetic and antimodernist position (for a contrasting approach, see Jameson [1971]). Benjamin is credited with a gnostic historicism based on apocalyptic remembrance, a secularized epiphany blasting "the continuum of history"—the empty homogeneous time of bourgeois commodity fetishism (1969, 261). De Man points out that this ambivalent image of Benjamin has repercussions in the blindness of his translators who misread the original, and whose failure is for that reason heuristic. For de Man, the failure of the translator is the object lesson: "The translator has to give up in relation to the task of refinding what was there in the original" (1986, 80). Benjamin distinguishes between the poet and the translator: the poet seeks to convey a meaning (a statement of something outside language), whereas—de Man paraphrases—"the relationship of the translator to the original is the relationship between language and language," whereby the translator vanishes and *langue* occupies the site vacated by *parole*: "Translation is a relation from language to language, not a relation to an extralinguistic meaning" (1986, 82). Translation resembles philosophy in that it is not an imitation of the world as we know it; it also resembles criticism or theory of litera-

---

1. I concur with Jacobs' view that for Benjamin, "translation functions as a metaphor both for the potential text-ness of a text and also as a metaphor for that which Benjamin calls 'criticism' . . . in which the textness of the text is given full play" (1978, xvi–xvii).

ture (following the tenets of Friedrich Schlegel and Jena Romanticism). De Man generalizes the ironic thrust of translation for Benjamin when it "undoes the stability of the original by giving it a definitive, canonical form in the translation or in the theorization." Just as for Borges' translators, so here the original is neither definitive nor canonical: "The translation canonizes, freezes, an original and shows in the original a mobility, an instability, which at first one did not notice" (1986, 82). What a speculative reader like de Man does is what a translator for Benjamin does: the original is not imitated or reproduced but "put in motion, de-canonized, questioned in a way which undoes its claim to canonical authority." Further, translation resembles history (assumed here as a non-organic process) in being the perspective from which natural changes are understood; the original can be understood only from the perspective of the translation.

The translation then does not put across (*ubersetzen*) or imitate the original. Like philosophy, critical theory and history, translation disarticulates and undoes the original; it reveals that the original was "always already disarticulated." All these acts of dismantling and transporting, de Man elaborates, "kill the original, by discovering that the original was already dead. They read the original from the perspective of a pure language (*reine Sprache*), a language that would be entirely freed of the illusion of meaning—pure form if you want; and in doing so they bring to light a dismembrance, a de-canonization which was already there in the original from the beginning. . . . Translation, to the extent that it disarticulates the original, to the extent that it is pure language and is only concerned with language, gets drawn into what he calls the bottomless depth, something essentially destructive, which is in language itself" (1986, 84). Relative to this "pure language" unconcerned with meaning, translation discloses "the suffering of the original language." (At this point, de Man illustrates the failure of the translators to reformulate precisely Benjamin's meaning—and therefore reveal the "suffering" of the original?) Translation reveals the death of the original, but more crucial it reveals the *"mise en abyme* structure" which the text in the same breath enacts. So de Man concludes that Benjamin's text dramatizes an untranslatability "which inhabits its own texture and will inhabit anybody who in his turn will try to translate it, as I am now trying, and failing, to do." This untranslatable text "is an example of what it states, it is a *mise en abyme* in the technical sense, a story within the story of what is its own statement" (1986, 86).

Undismayed by this failure which betokens success on another level, de Man next summarizes Benjamin's theory of language, the contradistinction between logos, what is meant (*das Gemeinte*), and lexis, the way language means (*Art des Meinens*). Here de Man insists on a distinction between the phenomenological intentionality of meaning and the non-human (in effect, structural or semiotic) mode of meaning. While the former requires hermeneutic labor, the latter demands poetics; they are mutually exclusive. De Man erroneously thinks that they are purely linguistic for Benjamin. Benjamin postulates a disjunction between word and sentence, between grammar and meaning. Translation puts the compatibility between grammar and meaning (or rhetoric, for de Man) in question. In a literal translation (like Holderlin's translations of Sophocles), de Man says that the meaning completely disappears because the translation is unintelligible. This slippage of meaning cannot be controlled by grammar (like the word *Aufgabe* "which means task, also means something completely different, so that the word escapes us. What is being named here as the disjunction between grammar and meaning, *Wort* and *Satz*, is the materiality of the letter, the independence, or the way in which the letter can disrupt the ostensibly stable meaning of a sentence and introduce in it a slippage by means of which that meaning disappears, evanesces, and by means of which all control over that meaning is lost"[1986, 89]). Here is de Man's familiar motif of the vertigo of "referential aberration," the aporia or undecidable moment—not to be confused with the indeterminacy of *Rezeptionsaesthetik*—presided by the governing trope of irony (1979, 10).

The concluding part of de Man's lecture concentrates on the disjunction between symbol and what is symbolized, between trope and "the meaning as a totalizing power of tropological substitutions." Benjamin uses tropes that convey the illusion of totality, thus contradicting his premise, so that the text "seems to relapse into the tropological errors that it denounces." For example, the text uses analogies whose validity it disclaims: "Whenever Benjamin uses a trope which seems to convey a picture of total meaning, of complete adequacy between figure and meaning, a figure of perfect synecdoche in which the partial trope expresses the totality of a meaning, he manipulates the allusive context within his work in such a way that the traditional symbol is displaced in a manner that acts out the discrepancy between symbol and meaning, rather than the acquiescence between both" (1986, 89). The passage at issue is this:

> Fragments of a vessel which are to be glued together must match one another in the smallest details, although they need not be like one another. In the same way, a translation, instead of resembling the meaning of the original, must lovingly and in detail incorporate the original's mode of signification, thus making both the original and the translation recognizable as fragments of a greater language, just as fragments are part of a vessel. (1969, 78)

De Man corrects Zohn's version of the last sentence by inserting "broken" before "part of a vessel" so as to prove (by this gesture of emendatory intervention) that fragments remain fragments and will never constitute a totality because they only "follow each other metonymically." Notice how a slippage from referent (object language) to metalanguage renders the line of reasoning suspect. Undisturbed by this, de Man goes on to insist that Benjamin's original intention is to express the totality of fragments (the greater language) but his use of metonymy in the discourse undermines his literal or grammatical predication.

Nor is this supererogatory gesture enough. De Man even goes on to contend that the translation breaks the fragment (itself) further, so the vessel (if ever there was one whole thing) never appears—"we have no knowledge of this vessel, or no awareness, no access to it, so for all intents and purposes there has never been one" (1986, 91). By a stroke of verbal wish-fulfillment, de Man has made Benjamin's vessel disappear! Accordingly de Man infers from this "the unreliability of rhetoric as a system of tropes which would be productive of a meaning" and the meaning ideally intended by Benjamin is never reached. The freedom of the translation— why not this faulty translation of Zohn too?—may be discerned in its success in disclosing the instability of the original (the linguistic tension between trope and meaning). Trope and meaning cannot coincide or be adequate to each other; and Benjamin demonstrates this by "by displacing them in such a way as to put the original in motion, to de-canonize the original, giving it a movement which is a movement of disintegration, of fragmentation" (1986, 92). The movement of the original is like a permanent exile except there is no homeland (no *reine Sprache*), for de Man. This errancy of language constitutes history; the disjunctive and figural power of poetic language should be distinguished from sacred or pure language. The political and historical spheres exist for purely linguistic reasons. Extrapolating from Benjamin's "Theological and Political Fragment," de Man paradoxically ascribes to Benjamin a non-messianic and non-dialectical conception of history and politics rooted in the stasis of rhetoric and the poetical structure of language (for an antithetical view, see Rosen [1988], Davies [1970]). By this completely unwarranted genealogy, de Man affiliates Benjamin's dialectical nihilism with Nietzsche's perspectivism.

Following this outline I have sketched, de Man's pretext of a commentary turns out to be an argument for the primacy of a quasi-Nietzschean theory of language-use as a form of will to mastery, more exactly a theory of reading that would privilege the rhetorical or tropological dynamics that the critic perceives operating in the text. The reader is the ideal site for the unfolding of aporias, that is, between the performative and constative functions of discourse, between metalinguistic statements and tropological praxis, between synchronic and diachronic permutations. What de Man's analytic style constructs is the rhetorical reader, the ideal subject (according to Ellen Rooney [1989]) of the pluralist problematic of "general persuasion." Given the impossibility of unequivocal meaning and the futility of aiming for a verifiably accurate translation free from "rigorously unreliable" tropes, one might ask then what is the effect of this specific form of reading that relentlessly, even granted its surplus yield of pleasure, pursues its own dissolution, or at least the phantasy of its own death?

I submit that de Man's strategy of reading as epitomized here (a project traversing his career from "Crisis and Criticism" in *Blindness and Insight* to *Allegories of*

Reading) reveal more his ethical and political agenda than the problems and needs Benjamin was grappling with in 1921 when his preface to his translation of Baudelaire was composed. When he deems it expedient, de Man forsakes all contexts—biographical, historical, cultural, and so forth—in the obsessive pursuit of undecidability, a problematic that Benjamin himself tried to resolve in the redemptive or "rescuing" critiques of *Der Ursprung des deutschen Trauerspiels*, "The Work of Art in the Age of Mechanical Reproduction," the Arcades project, and his essays on Baudelaire, Proust, Brecht, Leskov, and others. (The British critic Terry Eagleton [1981], among others, provides a Marxist articulation of Benjamin's utopian materialism in opposition to the Nietzschean/nihilistic and religious construal.) A few facts about Benjamin's situation and his intellectual development would show that de Man's argument is not only an arbitrary superimposition but in effect confirms one thesis of Benjamin concerning the return of a long-submerged mimetic faculty (see Habermas 1988).

During the early period of his career, Benjamin went through the intellectual crisis of responding to the catastrophe of World War I by struggling to formulate an ethics that would transcend the symbolist mysticism of Ludwig Klages and the Stefan George circle. He already felt that Kant's epistemology conceded too much to the claims of a positivist scientism. His crucial 1916 essay "On Language as Such and on the Language of Man" postulated a sacred language inherent in the power of naming (God's creative word) as contradistinguished from the profane language of communication (language as signs). Humankind's expulsion from paradise signified a fragmentation of the pure, original language into an impure plurality of languages. With the breakup of this edenic unity of nature and humans, the need for knowledge and interpretation was born. While human language shares the creative, naming function of divine language, it is largely confined to a receptive/cognitive use. This profane use of language for communication springs from the requirements of analytical judgment which obtains after the hierarchy of languages has displaced the "idolatry of nature" present in magical/mythical thought and symbolism; this notion in turn prompted Benjamin to formulate a theory of monadic ideas and the doctrine of anamnesis elaborated in the "tractatus," the literary form designed for the revelation of divine truths (Roberts 1983).

Now it may be observed that the essay on translation conceives language as symbolic only when it performs a naming function (*nennendes Wort*), thus communing with the creative word of God (*schaffendes Wort*); the divine *Ursprache* is immanent in the ontological fate of humans as giver of names. For Benjamin, therefore, the symbolic function, the mimetic iconicity of signs, participates in the divine/sacred language. When humans use language, they translate or give voice to the speechless anonymity of the fallen object world; they transpose the lower language of things (found in sculpture, painting, etc.) into the higher one: the pure, original, seamless totality of linguistic expression. Even literal translation elevates a lower tongue because it sublates it from its degraded communicative level to the naming sphere of pure language. What de Man calls "meaning" (conventional sign system utilized for judgment, a kind of pragmatic nominalism) is displaced in translation by the "creative word" participating in the realm of what Benjamin (1969) calls *"Lehre"* (doctrine, truth). Translation or commentary preoccupied with the work's subject matter mediates between poetry (naive, intuitive) and *Lehre*, while criticism (*Kritik*) engages with the truth content of the work.

Within this theoretical framework, Benjamin's concept of translation performs not an epistemological but an ethical function in mediating between the sacred and profane, between language as formal individuation through naming and language as signs or even prattle (*Geschwatz*). Situated within Benjamin's notion of "rescuing critique," it seeks to generate a coalescence of subject and object by the utopian, micrological project of deciphering the concealed script (the lost paradisiac language) of redeemed life in the profane texts of art, landscapes, ordinary objects. The ethos of reading and interpretation is thus premised on the historicity of human existence. History, as Benjamin construes it, "is the subject of a structure whose site is not homogeneous time, but time filled by the presence of the Now (*Jetztzeit*)." Surrealism embodied this ethos of writing through the praxis of rereading. In deciphering the world as a sacred text and decoding the utopian impulse threading the heterogeneous, disconnected instances to trigger a profane illumination, André Breton and Louis Aragon, for example, practised a form of translation whose ethics is for Benjamin (1978) authentically revolutionary.

Both as a reading of what has been written but forgotten, and as a writing-remembrance (anamnesis), translation for Benjamin may thus be conceived as a mode of discovering the secret hieroglyph of a promised happiness—the Messiah's advent, Now-Time—immanent in the historical process. Here we encounter Benjamin's technique of mortification. The significance of an artwork unfolds itself in its afterlife, "a transformation and a renewal of something living" whereby the original undergoes a change—"a maturing process comprehended only from a historical standpoint." Of all literary forms, Benjamin writes, translation "is the one charged with the special mission of watching over the maturing process of the original language and the birth pangs of its own" (1969). Following the principle of mortification applied in the analysis of baroque allegory in *The Origin of German Tragic Drama*, where truth is captured in the decaying *memento mori* of once beautiful objects, Benjamin suggests through Biblical allusion the difference between commentary and translation:

> Commentary and translation stand in the same relation to the text as style and mimesis to nature: the same phenomenon considered from different aspects. On the tree of the sacred text both are only the eternally rustling leaves; on that of the profane, the seasonally falling fruits. (1978, 68)

In "The Task of the Translator," Benjamin posits the telos of writing in their "perpetual renewal" through translation as an act of re-reading and re-writing mediated through the rhythm of temporality and death. Translation envisages tracking hidden correspondences and analogies that adumbrate "the predestined, hitherto inaccessible realm of reconciliation and fulfillment of languages," that is, the dissolution of Babel and the messianic restoration of the Divine Kingdom. This is anticipated in the 1916 essay on language: "The language of things can pass into the language of knowledge and name only through translation—as many translations, so many languages—once man has fallen from the paradisiac state that knew only one language" (1978, 326). By ignoring Benjamin's complex thinking on language, de Man can thus easily erase the key concept of *reine Sprache* (figured as an unbroken vessel) in a gesture of insinuating his own nihilism into the text, thus precipitating the fall which he accuses Benjamin's translators (in their guise as commentators) of being guilty.

The paramount aim of translation and, by implication all interpretation, is the recovery of that sacred language of naming, the fusion of cognition and creation, which lies embedded in all phenomena viewed as signs, indices, or icons. Benjamin defines the task of the translator as, in essence, the articulation of intertextuality (what Bakhtin/Voloshinov calls "utterance" as event with polyphonic or dialogic resonance) that registers the "echo of the original." The translator aims at the totality of the languages he is dealing with; he aims for that "single spot" where the reverberation of the original can be generated in his own. Whereas the intention of the poet is "spontaneous, primary, graphic" in that he confronts "specific linguistic contextual aspects," the translator's intention is "derivative, ultimate, ideational." The ultimate and ideational burden of translation depends not on the reproduction of the sense (ideas, judgment, meaning) but on its detailed and loving "incorporation of the original's mode of signification." This mode is the naming power of prelapsarian *Ursprache*. Not exactly surrogates of one another, both original and translation are fragments of the "one true language" before the "Breaking of the Vessels" (marking the entry of evil in the Kabbalah). The rhetorical figure Benjamin uses is infelicitous not because it is masquerading as metaphor, contrary to what de Man alleges, but because the fragments are supposed to be harmonized (note the valorization of sound over sight), losing their isolated existence as parts. Immediately Benjamin shifts to the musical trope: "as regards the meaning, the language of a translation can—in fact, must—let itself go, so that it gives voice to the intention of the original not as reproduction but as harmony, as a supplement to the language in which it expresses itself, as its own kind of *intentio*" (1969, 78–79). Hence literalness or faithfulness to the materiality of the signifiers betokens the work's "great longing for linguistic complementation." The succeeding passage refutes de Man's thesis that word, the materiality of the letter, can disrupt the stable meaning of a sentence, when it points out that the "literal rendering of the syntax" makes the real translation transparent: "it does not cover the original, does not block its light, but allows the pure language, as though reinforced by its own medium, to shine upon the original all the more fully."

In its refusal to reproduce the sense or paraphrase the cognitive content of the original, the literal translation seizes only the mode of a text's temporal existence, its "magical immanentism." In the 1933 text "On the Mimetic Faculty," Benjamin propounds his concept of language as rationalized mimesis which fills in the gaps of the 1923 essay (see Rabinbach 1979):

> For if words meaning the same thing in different languages are arranged about that thing as their center, we have to inquire how they all—while often possessing not the slightest similarity to one another—are similar to what they signify at their center. . . . In brief, it is nonsensuous similarity that establishes the ties not only between the spoken and the signified but also between the written and the signified, and equally between the spoken and the written. . . . Script has thus become, like language, an archive of nonsensuous similarities, of nonsensuous correspondences.
>
> This aspect of language as script, however, does not develop in isolation from its other, semiotic aspect. Rather, the mimetic element in language can, like a flame, manifest itself only through a kind of bearer. This bearer is the semiotic element. Thus the coherence of words or sentences is the bearer through which, like a flash, similarity appears. For its production by man—like its perception by him—is in many cases, and particularly the most important, limited to flashes. It flits past. It is not improbable that the rapidity of writing and reading heightens the fusion of the semiotic and the mimetic in the sphere of language. (1978, 335–36)

Literalness or the focus on what Brecht would call the "gestic" dimension of language, Benjamin suggests, is "the arcade into the language of the original" surrounded by the wall of the sentence. Literalness which abjures direct transcript of denotation yields freedom in a perfectly straightforward sense: "For what is meant by freedom but that the rendering of sense is no longer to be regarded as all-important?" Literalness then is not the exchange of cognitive, semantic content but a hermeneutic deciphering where nonsensuous similarities (the presence of the mimetic in the semiotic) can be registered. This inflects St. Jerome's classic rule of nonliteralness: *"Non verbum e verbo, sed sensum exprimere de sensu"* (Frenz 1973). Human language, for Benjamin, constitutes the world as a context of meanings; human language is only a particular form of universal "language as such" which embodies all essences. Translation is then the polylogue or colloquy of various expressions—art, dancing, astrology, and so on—that incarnate the immanent but also transcendent logos.

This is the point where Benjamin's messianic agenda surfaces, underscored in the concluding paragraph of "The Task of the Translator" where the Holy Writ reconciles language and revelation, where the text is identical with truth or dogma, where servitude to the original and loose adaptation coalesce in the interlinear version of the Scripture, the prototype of all translation. Holderlin's translation where meaning "is touched upon only fleetingly, like the aeolian harp by the wind," resembles the tangent (described earlier) that "touches the original lightly and only at the infinitely small point of the sense, thereupon pursuing its own course according to the laws of fidelity in the freedom of linguistic flux." This conjunction of freedom and fidelity, however, can lead to the gates of language enclosing the translator with silence. Another way of restaging this enigmatic denouement may be found in Benjamin's characterization of Holderlin's translations of Sophocles: "in them meaning plunges from abyss to abyss until it threatens to become lost in the bottomless depths of language."[2] While the trope here may be read as dramatizing the notion that pure language "inhabits linguistic creations only in symbolized form," Benjamin is not rehearsing the *mise en abyme* of an astute rhetorical demystification; rather, the figure of flux anticipates the idea of the secret mimetic potency of language posited in "On the Mimetic Faculty," an idea "strongly reminiscent of the "dialectical image" researched in Benjamin's *Passagenarbeit* (Wolin 1982).

We can now return to de Man's reading with the judgment that it not only instrumentalizes Benjamin's text but also inflicts a calculated violence on its ideas and words. In a typical maneuver, de Man fragments his source text when he thematizes the disjunction of Being and meaning, what is symbolized and the symbol, a cleavage which he claims to see in the text and whose rationale he attributes to the author's indecisiveness, a vacillation of motives between what he intends (hypothetical) and what the text enacts.[3] For example, de Man argues that for Benjamin, the symbol and what it symbolizes do not correspond. The passage in question, however, pursues in a subtle dialectical manner the mediations between these two polarities since languages are not self-contained differential systems (as one version of Saussurean linguistics asserts) but "media of varying intensities" in "a continuum of transformations." It stresses, in particular, the necessary ethical imperative of a totalizing vision—the philosopher's task of comprehension through a historical remembrance, the critic's quest for redemptive meaning inscribed in the "flashing image" that signals the reconciliation of man and nature:

---

2. Compare the erotically invested imagery here with Adorno's portrait of Benjamin: "Subjectivity, plunging into the abyss of significances, 'becomes the ceremonial guarantee of the miracle because it announces divine action itself' " (1967, 231).

3. Both Juhl (1984), Ray (1984), and Seung (1982) discern certain effects of the hermeneutic circle in de Man's reading practice. For more sympathetic appraisals, see Leitch (1983), Culler (1982), and Norris (1988) who all mount a spirited defense of de Man's "linguistics."

In all language and linguistic creations there remains in addition to what can be conveyed something that cannot be communicated; depending on the context in which it appears. It is something that symbolizes or something symbolized. . . . While that ultimate essence, pure language, in the various tongues is tied only to linguistic elements and their changes, in linguistic creations it is weighted with a heavy, alien meaning. To relieve it of this, to turn the symbolizing into the symbolized, to regain pure language fully formed in the linguistic flux, is the tremendous and only capacity of translation. . . . It is the task of the translator to release in his own language that pure language which is under the spell of another, to liberate the language imprisoned in a work in his re-creation of that work. For the sake of pure language he breaks through decayed barriers of his own language. (1969, 79–80)

What is at stake here is the liberation of "pure language" under the magic spell of a decaying one, the emancipation of repressed energies contained in the source text. The polemical, even moralizing tenor, of the tropes here strongly repel the contagion of vertiginous irony. Here the antinomy of freedom and necessity (fidelity) is played out when pure language is conceived as the locus where the profane world of thinking and communication is extinguished, an extinction brought about by the demand of fidelity (the index of an ethical vocation) which dissolves sense/meaning. Allegorizing translation, for Benjamin, performs a redemptive vocation: to release the pure language imprisoned in the original, and in doing so destroy also the "decayed barriers" of the target language. This converts the symbolized form reified in "finite linguistic products" into the fragmentary and concealed symbol active in life. Pure language inheres in linguistic elements in the diverse tongues, while in art it is submerged in alien meaning. To turn the symbolizing process (in the natural realm) into the symbolized, what Benjamin calls the end/purpose of life in the "representation of its significance," is the task of the translator. Here, ultimately, the translator is the messianic figure whose problematic text is "unconditionally translatable" and whose release from the spell of aporia, the impasse of indeterminacy, marks the watershed for the flow of revelation's utterance.

What calls for close scrutiny is the key exhibit de Man presents for converting Benjamin into a precursor of deconstructive reading, namely, this passage where texts are likened to fragments of a vessel:

Wie nämlich Scherben eines Gefäässes, um sich zusammenfügen zu lassen, in den kleinsten Einzelheiten einander zu folgen, doch nicht so zu gleichen haben, so muss, anstatt dem Sinn des Originals sich ähnlich zu machen, die Übersetzung liebend vielmehr und bis ins Einzelne hinein dessen Art des Meinens in der eigenen Sprache sich anbilden, um so beide wie Scherben als Bruchstuck eines Gefässes, als Bruchstück einer grösseren Sprache erkennbar zu machen. (1972, 18)

Fragments of a vessel which are to be glued together must match one another in the smallest details, although they need not be like one another. In the same way a translation, instead of resembling the original, must lovingly and in detail incorporate the original's mode of signification, thus making both the original and the translation recognizable as fragments of a greater language, just as fragments are part of a vessel. (1969, 78)

De Man corrects Zohn's translation of the first sentence by preferring Carol Jacobs' translation of "fragments of a vessel, in order to be *articulated* together must follow one another in the smallest detail." "Articulated together" instead of "glued together" or "join together" insinuates a differential or diacritical connotation, while "follow" instead of "match" allows de Man to assert that the text displays "a metonymic, a successive pattern, in which things follow, rather than a metaphorical unifying pattern in which things become one by resemblance." What this translation seeks to avoid, de Man alleges, is "a convincing tropological totalization." De Man further insists that what Benjamin says in the last sentence is that the fragments "are the broken parts" of a vessel: "he says the fragments are fragments, and that they remain essentially fragmentary. They follow each other up, metonymically, and they will never constitute a totality" (1986, 91). Not only are all translations fragments, but the vessel is constantly breaking—in fact "there was no vessel in the first place"! This pronouncement of closure signals a breakdown in the coherence of de Man's argument since, in the first place, he acknowledges the scriptural reference to the "Breaking of the Vessels" in the lore of the Lurianic Kaballah only to set it aside. And, second, the term "fragments" does not constitute metonymy nor synecdoche by itself. What the passage presents obviously is a simile or comparison: the whole phrase "broken parts of a vessel" concretizes "broken parts of the greater language." So that for de Man to acknowledge the "broken parts" and ignore the whole of which they are parts is to refuse the evidence of metaphor and its drive toward synthesis, correspondence, totality, via remembrance or anamnesis. It is a telling evidence of (to use de Man's own terms) the blindness of his insight, a blindness to what Benjamin would later conceive as "nonsensuous similarity" apprehended by a topological (not tropological) mapping of the configuration of appearances that may cut the fissure for the "instantaneous flash" of messianic grace (Wohlfahrt 1979).

Is this simply a careless misreading on de Man's part caused by an attitude heedless of contexts, oblivious to Benjamin's intentionality of understanding and beliefs, caught in the hubris of a transcendental skepticism (my phrase) which he, as if through a mirror-image, imputes to others in "The Resistance to Theory"? I don't think so because this pattern of premeditated or doubled misunderstanding may be found replicated by his erstwhile colleague at Yale University, J. Hillis Miller, whose reading of the same text evokes a similar adventurism, a strategic maneuvering that aims to sabotage any project with epistemological claims and semantic determinations.

In *The Ethics of Reading*, Miller notes that the figure of the broken parts of the vessel is unintelligible as "description of a physical phenomena, though its impossibility as literal description may be what makes it work as a figurative description of a linguistic fact" (1987, 124). On second thought, Miller applies a scholastic standard of adequation between thing and word when he judges that the image "does not correspond" to Benjamin's concept of "a pure language." In other words, there is a discrepancy between what Benjamin wants to convey, namely, that both original and translation are bad translations of a lost original, and the image which is "an impossible metaphor." Miller thus concludes: "It fails to carry the meaning that is entrusted to it, since the fragments must fit and not fit, and they must both be parts of a greater vessel and not part of that vessel. That vessel has no shape and no meaning, since it is the place where all information, all sense, all shape, and all intention are extinguished in the expressionless word (or Word)" (1987, 125–26).

It is remarkable how Miller's mystifying and mystified attitude to the vessel repeats de Man's terror at its presence, or its putative existence. Both surreptitiously deploy an apparatus of linguistic axioms that erases history or reduces it to another text, a modality of performative figuration. Unlike de Man, however, Miller confesses bafflement at the meaning of "*reine Sprache*," compelling him to reduce it to "the equivalent, the translation into another idiom, of what Henry James means by "thing" or "matter." Then he reconceives it as the "paradox of a wordless word" generating an effect of unreadability or undecidability. Is this not evidence of a reductive will on the part of the deconstructionist to thematize and so instrumentalize the testimony of Benjamin's disclosure? Given our understanding of Benjamin's conception of the difference between sacred and profane languages, Miller's interpretation is starkly inadequate not because it is profane language (thus inadvertently validating Benjamin's theory) but simply because it dispenses with Benjamin's horizon of intentionality, in particular his controlling narrative of the fragmentation of languages in man's fall into knowledge—the genesis of the communicating word, "a parody . . . of the expressly immediate, the creative word of God"—and the possibility of recuperating the "intensive totality of language" incarnate in man as namer. Miller's ethics of masterful reading is rendered suspect by Benjamin's affirmation of a metanarrative or totalizing vision of the communication process:

> [I]n man God set language, which had served *Him* as medium of creation, free. God rested when he had left his creative power to itself in man. This creativity, relieved of its divine actuality, became knowledge.

Man is the knower in the same language in which God is creator. God created him in his image, he created the knower in the image of the creator. Therefore the proposition that the mental being of man is language needs explanation. His mental being is the language in which creation took place. In the word creation took place, and God's linguistic being is the word. All human language is only reflection of the word in name. . . .

Translation attains its full meaning in the realization that every evolved language (with the exception of the word of God) can be considered as a translation of all the others. By the relation, mentioned earlier, of languages as between media of varying densities, the translatability of languages into another is established. Translation is removal from one language into another through a continuum of transformations. Translation passes through continua of transformation, not abstract areas of identity and similarity. (1978, 323–25)

In the latter passage, translation as a continuum of transformations spans the whole spectrum from literal fidelity to free translation or "imitations" (such as those witnessed by Borges' translators, by Robert Lowell's or Ezra Pound's practice). This idea qualifies the contested notion of translation as producing fragmentary copies of an unmediated or self-identical, homogeneous text.

Given Benjamin's conception of the disparity between sacred and profane languages, it now becomes clear how de Man's interpretation proves starkly inadequate if not wayward because it dispenses with Benjamin's horizon of intentionality, in particular his controlling narrative of the fragmentation of languages in man's fall into knowledge, the event which inaugurates the genesis of the communicating word. Benjamin believes in the possibility of recuperating the "intensive totality of language" incarnate in man as namer. Therefore translation is possible and every translation is successful, given the communion of tongues projected in the utopian ideal of a plenitude of meaning (for example, poetry as naming) recuperable from the *Jetztzeit* incarnate in ruins, relics, fragments, traces—precisely the waste and detritus of social life taken by de Man and Miller as tokens of undecidability. Phrased another way, in the wake of the Lacan-Derrida exchange (Johnson 1981), Benjamin's "letter" always arrives at its destination. To appreciate what this implies, it is necessary that the hermeneutic circle be broken by a kind of reading which revitalizes a decayed mimetic faculty—the matrix of Benjamin's poetics of redemption:

"To read what was never written." Such reading is the most ancient: reading before all languages, from the entrails, the stars, or dances. Later the mediating link of a new kind of reading, of runes and hieroglyphs, came into use. It seems fair to suppose that these were the stages by which the mimetic gift, which was once the foundation of occult prac-

tices, gained admittance to writing and language. In this way language
may be seen as the highest level of mimetic behavior and the most complete archive of nonsensuous similarity: a medium into which the earlier
powers of mimetic production and comprehension have passed without
residue, to the point where they have liquidated those of magic. (1978,
336)

Reading as mimesis or creative reproduction: for Miller and de Man, Benjamin has
just invented another trope, the figure of representation, that will ineluctably self-
deconstruct "under the laborious task of a scrupulous slow reading."

In a programmatic essay "The Search for Grounds in Literary Study," Miller
judged that every "conceivable representation of the relations of words to things,
powers, persons, modes of production and exchange, juridical or political systems"
will be revealed as another figure of speech. Ideology, for example, turns out to be
anamorphosis for Miller, "a species of affirmation by denial, abnegation, what
Freud called *Verneinung*" (1989, 823). It would be instructive to sketch in passing
how Miller illustrates the pitfall of this rhetorical reading in his statement that "In
Marxist theory, for example that of Louis Althusser in *For Marx*, ideology is the
name given to the imaginary structures, whereby men and women resist facing
directly the real economic and social conditions of their existence." From
Althusser's vantage point of symptomatic reading, Miller's ascription of resistance
to humans which is absent in the original definition betrays an unconsciousness of
his own motives.[4] The specter of "false consciousness" always attached to a vulgarized version of Marxism exposes the limits of a rhetorical critique of ideology. This
claim to deserve our trust based on the assumption of a hegemonic liberal pluralism
that casts a patronizing aura of tolerance enables deconstruction to interrogate all
foundations—except the linguistic—and uphold the fetish of an unconceptualizable arche-writing which legitimates itself. But, as Paul Ricoeur (1978) has noted,
this closure of the universe of signs by dispensing with the referent, bypassing the
decisive event of enunciation (the upsurge of the speaking subject), and confining
oneself to the effects of a system of internal differential relations, "an autonomous
entity of internal dependencies," only succumbs to that metaphysics of reification
which the deconstructive skeptics are purportedly trying to avoid in the first place.
Clearly the reductive simplification of this reading, and its privileging of antinomies and interminable equivocations which induce infinite regress in a timeless
synchrony, has the singular virtue of escaping the methodical doubt of its practitioner. Meanwhile, naive readers outside the circle of the enlightened presumably
continue to suffer as victims of a metaphysical fallacy: that of confusing the repre-

---

4. Althusser's definition of ideology cited by Miller is found in the essay "Ideology and Ideological
State Apparatuses" (1971), not in *For Marx*.

sentational function of language with phenomena, things, meanings, signifieds—all illusory presences.[5]

In a manifesto of his later period, "The Resistance to Theory," de Man negates the validity of literature's mimetic and epistemological claims and questions "its authority as a model for natural or phenomenal cognition." What literary theory should be concerned with, according to De Man, is the refusal of historical and aesthetic signification so that it can address not "the meaning or the value but the modalities of production and of reception of meaning and of value prior to their establishment—the implication being that this establishment is problematic enough to require an autonomous discipline of critical investigation to consider its possibility and its status" (1986, 7). Here De Man privileges the vocation of the theorist as one who somehow salvages "a knowledge" from ideology by unmasking it, stressing that "it is no longer possible to ignore the epistemological thrust of the rhetorical dimension of discourse."

An excess of theory soon transgresses the boundaries of the disciplinary regime. The ethical imperative surfaces in de Man's riposte to his critics when he arrogates to his methodology a salvific mission:"What we call ideology is precisely the confusion of linguistic with natural reality, of reference with phenomenalism. It follows that, more than any other mode of inquiry, including economics, the linguistics of literariness is a powerful and indispensable tool in the unmasking of ideological aberrations, as well as a determining factor in accounting for their occurrence" (1986, 11). The definition of "ideology" here, in a replay of Miller's obsession, evinces a pathetic naivete and poverty reminiscent of the "false consciousness" of vulgar Marxism which deconstructionists are fond of attacking. Despite the self-defensive assertion at the end that theory contains within itself the "language of self-resistance," a compensatory move to ward off any charge of being self-uncritical or unreflexive, de Man all the same valorizes the performative, the rhetorical displacements that language wreaks on grammatical cognition, speech act-oriented theories, reader response, and so on, including the claim of language to be a perfect model of anything.

We now begin to suspect, without thoroughly unpacking our dossier of queries and reservations, that de Man's rhetorical methodology and criteria of judgment premised on the "linguistics of literariness" are ultimately sustained by a Nietzschean perpectivism and by the logic of a nominalistic relativism armed with self-reflexive irony. It implies an ideological closure diametrically opposed to

---

5. Foley (1985) summarizes previous criticisms by Lentricchia, Said, and others. She seems to follow Brecht's advice (recorded by Benjamin) to mobilize "*das plumpe Denken*" in her vigorous polemic against the claims of deconstruction; but her notion of Marxism is undialectical and suffers from a lack of thick historical mediations—an inadequacy that Adorno noticed also in certain writings of Benjamin. But Benjamin's own "Marxism" is still a contested topic, perhaps ultimately undecidable?

Benjamin's practice of immanent critique, of critique as "mortification." While it may be shown quite convincingly that de Man is not really demonstrating anything true or false—just as Fish, caught in a tighter hermeneutic circle of shifting interpretive communities, is also persuading his co-believers of nothing really substantial in his perlocutionary rituals—I would prefer to endorse Julia Kristeva's critical stance, her caveat that "there is an *other* besides the irony of the learned man; there is . . . *rhythm, death,* and *future*" (1980, 27). With such an ethical commitment entailed by one's inescapable accountability to others, Benjamin conceived of the critic's responsibility "to brush history against the grain" by considering in a dialectical fashion every text to be read and translated as a document not only of civilization but also of barbarism.

But can this duplicity be extended to cover the scandal of the Belgian Nazi sympathizer of 1940–42? By hindsight, Jonathan Culler (1988) explains that the mature de Man's repudiation of aesthetic ideology, totalizing metaphors, and anthropomorphizing organic unity may be interpreted as lessons gained from that wartime experience and the distance of time. Of course this is to posit that impossible self-coincidence, the reconciliation of incompatibles, already ruled out by de Man's insistence on our temporal predicament. De Man himself has endeavored to expose all claims to self-possession and unmediated identity as some kind of unwarranted violence on the "human condition." But logocentrism seems to take its disingenuous revenge here. Witness to this is Alasdair MacIntyre (1990), who points out that the attempt by de Man's apologists to vindicate the moral credibility of his later standpoint has been made on the basis of a conception of moral accountability "deeply at odds" with de Man's genealogic authority. Invoking de Man's dictum that language "dissociates the cognition from the act" (1979, 277), can we then accept a plausible narrative of the rift between the young fascist sympathizer and the old allegorist of irony? And if we deconstruct the hierarchy between the ironic antihumanist and the romantic nationalist, assuming that those personae can be ascribed to the same persisting body, shall we obtain an equalizing "difference" of presence/absence? And what do all these propositions signify if play, trace, and the abyss deprive us of any ground for a consensus of judgment; and, more portentously, whatever we say and do now becomes unsaid and undone in the same breath?

What is ultimately at stake lies in the space/time permitted for articulating those questions: the freedom or violation of the speaking/reading subject, its subordination to coercive agencies or its liberation. Perhaps Kristeva would then ask: what then is the ethics of deconstructive irony? We arrive at this crossroad where it is indeed difficult to resist the position that this "exorbitation" of the linguistic model (however seminal and provocatively challenging the insights that Derrida, de Man, and their epigones might gather in their textual explorations) has not only liberated us from the curse of origin, presence, God, the subject, reason, history, and truth—ideals long cherished as the blessings of Western civilization. It has also released us from the responsibility to the claims of the multitudes and their suffering, bewitched as we are by the seductive illusions of this subaltern science called tropological reading, grammatology, or textual archaeology to which the old-fashioned Benjamin, ever the believer that translators (even the outlandish fabricators imagined by Borges) cannot betray, alludes in a letter to the poet Hugo von Hofmannsthal: "every truth has its home, its ancestral palace, in language, that it is erected from the oldest *logoi*, and in face of a truth established in this way the insights of the individual sciences remain subaltern, as long as they, so to speak, nomadically here and there make use of the realm of language, preoccupied with that view of the sign-character of language whose irresponsble arbitrariness impresses itself on their terminology" (Wolin 1982, 41).

2

From Bakhtin to Gramsci

INTERTEXTUALITY, PRAXIS, HEGEMONY

Ecriture, arche-writing, trace, *lisible*, and *scriptible* texts—a scene of writing, primordial and "always already" iterable, confronts us everywhere after the critical interventions of such "strong" readers as Barthes, Derrida, Foucault, and de Man. We have learned how "writing degree zero" banishes origin, self-presence, the perceiving consciousness, and the "expressive substance" or "reality" of the public *doxa* that serves as the pretext of discourse. With the disappearance of the writer/author, we are supposed to revel in "the joyous affirmation of the world and of the innocence of becoming." Perhaps Franz Kafka's (1961) unforgettable tale, "In the Penal Colony," can rehearse the truth-claim of grammatology and release us from "the prison-house of language."

In the deliberately contrived theatrical scene of the narrative where the officer of the penal colony demonstrates to the traveller (also labelled explorer) the operation of a fabulous killing machine, we encounter writing as a mode of transmitting justice and truth. Unfortunately the receiver/addressee dies in the process. "Whatever commandment the prisoner has disobeyed is written upon his body by the Harrow," explains the officer, who also believes that "Guilt is never to be doubted" (197-98). Only through this lethal inscription on his body does the condemned prisoner learn his sentence. What is the evidence for this? At the height of his suffering, the officer shares his expertise with gusto:

> Enlightenment comes to the most dull-witted. It begins around the eyes. From there it radiates. A moment that might tempt one to get under the Harrow onself. Nothing more happens than that the man begins to understand the inscription, he purses his mouth as if he were listening. You have seen how difficult it is to decipher the script with one's eyes; but our man deciphers it with his wounds. To be sure, that is a hard task; he needs six hours to accomplish it. By that time the Harrow has pierced him quite through and casts him into the pit, where he pitches down

upon the blood and water and the cotton wool. Then the judgment has
been fulfilled, and we, the soldier and I, bury him (204).

Such punishment triggers "the look of transfiguration on the face of the sufferer," a
revelation that in turn brings ecstasy to the audience/readers of this performance.
Only then does the script displayed earlier in manuscript by its guardian-keeper
become legible to the traveller and, by implication, to us readers.

Writing as access to law, justice, and knowledge translates into torture, violence, and death; on the obverse side, reading becomes acquisition of truth, orgas-
mic bliss, the "pleasure of the text." Focusing on the entire process of execution as
a "travesty of copulation," Clayton Koelb (1989) interprets the Harrow as a male
body, a phallocentric precision instrument, designed to rape its victims. Ironically,
the victim here turns out to be the officer, the dispenser of justice; the inter-
preter/reader of the text inscribed on the bodies of malefactors offers himself as a
sacrifice, a mnemonic testimony to the truth of tradition—the linkage of past, present, and future (Thiher 1990). The writing-machine, however, self-destructs in
the process. Is this a comic parody of the fall of the textualizing apparatus? We
detect a satiric gloss on writing as bearer of a forgotten truth when the narrative
closure depicts the traveller discovering the former Commandant's tomb mocked
by its location, its inscription prophesying the messianic return of the
Commandant ignored by everyone. What lesson then can we glean from Kafka's
exemplum? Perhaps our reading will only repeat the figure of attraction/repulsion
manifest in the traveller's behavior, a sado-masochistic pattern whose oscillation
will confirm our eventual fall into the absymal trace of arche-writing, from which
there is no redemption.

However, if Kafka's narrator is also a traveller/explorer who at the end
quickly departs from this harrowing "scene of writing," we can infer that an escape
from the penal colony or prison-house of *écriture* is just possible, a route I explore in
this chapter.

In the crisis of Western hermeneutics and epistemology intimated by Kafka's
"parable," the guardians of the liberal marketplace of ideas have sought to remedy
the discontent of their clientele and entrepreneurs by a re-appropriation of the
margins (Borges is only one of those commodified imports) and their accommoda-
tion into the center. The "masters of suspicion" (Marx, Nietzsche, Freud) are
domesticated to revitalize old New Critical maxims and reinforce the dualism of
ends and means implicit in pragmatism and administrative-technocratic culture in
general. In this process of reconstituting the hegemony of idealist aesthetics, the
work of Mikhail Bakhtin construed in an instrumental, selective fashion has so far
proved efficacious. For example, Wayne Booth (1982), in his well-known essay
"Freedom of Interpretation: Bakhtin and the Challenge of Feminist Criticism,"
deploys the key notions of polyphony, dialogism, and heteroglossia to argue for a

new, more all-encompassing pluralism that would even expose the androcentrism, that egregious flaw, in Bakhtin's book on Rabelais in accord with current feminist thinking. The term "ideology," which before would be terribly offensive to neo-Aristotelian sensibilities, now becomes an honorific marker when Bakhtin's pronouncements are invoked. Booth quotes Bakhtin: "Human consciousness does not come into contact with existence directly, but through the medium of the surrounding ideological world. . . . In fact, the individual consciousness can only become consciousness by being realized in the forms of the ideological environment proper to it" (Bakhtin and Medvedev 1978, 14). The novel then becomes the model genre because it employs the techniques of dialogized heteroglossia, that is, "it represents the co-existence of socio-ideological contradictions between the present and the past, . . . between different socio-ideological groups in the present, between tendencies, schools, circles and so forth, all given a bodily form." In spite of Bakhtin's blindness to his male-centered discourse, Booth believes that Bakhtin's "version of dialectical thinking" is peculiarly useful, although in the end he calls on the thoroughgoing skepticism of David Hume to account for the eternal differences between men and women, old and young, and so on. Nonetheless, the perspectivism of Bakhtin is congenial in that it demonstrates our freedom to take in (as Booth puts it) "the many voices we have inherited and discovering, in our inescapably choral performance, which voices must be cast out of our choir." Thus the "chaotic" politics of interpretation is prevented by Booth's timely prophylaxis from disturbing the polite conversation of predominantly white males in the elite academies of the Empire.

From another angle, David Lodge finds Bakhtin's alternative to Saussurean linguistics heuristic and catalyzing. He cites Bakhtin's definition of the word as a "two-sided act. . . . It is determined equally by whose word it is and for whom it is meant. . . . A word is territory shared by both addresser and addressee, by the speaker and his interlocutor" (1973, 85–86). Lodge values Bakhtin's theory of the novel as the carnivalized, antinomic genre par excellence and Bakhtin's approach to it "via the typology of discourse rather than via the Aristotelian categories of plot and character, or the Romantic concept of 'style as the man'" (1987, 92). He prizes, above all, Bakhtin's belief that the privileged quality of the novel (the reference is to Dostoevky's works) is its foregrounding the unfinalizable nature of life: "the world is open and free, everything is still in the future and always will be in the future." Consequently a "Galilean" consciousness of plural languages conveying truths emerges with the novel's orchestration of heteroglot voices in an open-ended polyphony. What grounds this conception of the novel as the archetypal genre embodying a vision of unfinalizable becoming is Bakhtin's refusal of "theoretism" and instantiational models of understanding where abstract systems of norms ignore the complex "prosaics" of everyday life (Morson and Emerson 1994, 64–65). Bakhtin holds that while the mathematical and natural sciences aim for mastery of "reified objects," the epistemology of the human sciences facilitates the production of knowledge by interpreting the discourse of others. The critic or literary scholar "is forced to engage in talk not only about discourse but with discourse in order to penetrate its ideological meaning, which is attainable only by a form of dialogical understanding that includes evaluation and response" (Todorov 1984, 16). The object of inquiry of the humanistic disciplines is the text, or humans as producers of texts constituted by a fugue of "form-shaping ideologies" or habits of vision; "the real object is social man speaking and expressing himself through other means." By "text," Bakhtin refers to utterance or discourse as language in its "concrete and living totality," a "concrete sociolinguistic horizon" whose theme or meaning can only be apprehended by an "active" understanding through dialogue or conversation (exchange of interacting horizons of interlocutors) which is "always historical and personal." The person generating utterance poses a question to what is knowable, seeking not accuracy or propositional veracity but depth of insight: "The object of the human sciences is *expressive* and *speaking being*. Such a being never coincides with itself, that is why it is inexhaustible in its meaning and significance" (1986, 162).

The prime enabling concept of Bakhtin's "sociological poetics" is utterance first introduced in *Marxism and the Philosophy of Language* (I take Voloshinov and Bakhtin as co-authors) and elaborated most fully in a later essay, "The Problem of Speech Genres." Utterance is the basic unit of linguistic communication with fluid, ever-shifting boundaries. Its three aspects—thematic content, style, and compositional structure—only acquire import when they inhabit particular spheres of communication and, through usage, engender relatively stable styles called "speech genres." Utterance occurs always in a social process of communication, in a shared context ("in-betweenness") of multiplicity and struggle. Against the humanist view that meaning inheres in the unique personal consciousness and the deconstructionist view that meaning resides in the unconceptualizable "trace" of differentiality, Bakhtin locates meaning in social exchange, in the relay of tangled and meshed signifying chains. Clark and Holquist paraphrase Bakhtin's core insight: "I can mean what I say, but only indirectly, at a second remove, in words that I take and give back to the community according to the protocols it observes. My voice can mean but only with others," in chorus or dialogue (1984, 12). Both the internal and external expressions of the speaking subject are "wholly the product of social interrelations." All utterance then is grounded in specific sociohistorical ecologies, in intersubjectivity, in a community that is not homogeneous but heterogeneous, a complex differentiated unity.

One central principle informs Bakhtin's theory of writing, the principle of "social and historical localization": "Human personality becomes historically real and culturally productive only insofar as it is part of a social whole, in its class and through its class," which then "determines the content of his personal and cultural creation" (1976, 31). That observation may sound like a routine recapitulation of Marx's fundamental insight that "the human essence is no abstraction inherent in

each single individual [the error of Enlightenment humanism]. In its reality it is the
ensemble of the social relations" (1975, 423). The mainstream exponents of
Bakhtin's dialogism inveterately downplay or dismiss the influence of Marxist
thought on Bakhtin, such as the idea of the imbrication of language and consciousness in critical-sensuous praxis found in *The German Ideology*:

> Man also possesses "consciousness"; but, even so, not inherent, not
> "pure" consciousness. From the start the "spirit" is afflicted with the
> curse of being "burdened" with matter, which here makes its appear-
> ance in the form of agitated layers of air, sounds, in short, of language.
> Language is as old as consciousness, language *is* practical consciousness
> that exists also for other men, and for that reason alone it really exists for
> me personally as well; language, like consciousness, only arises from the
> need, the necessity, of intercourse with other men. Where there exists a
> relationship, it exists for me: the animal does not enter into "relations"
> with anything, it does not enter into any relation at all. For the animal,
> its relation to others does not exist as a relation. Consciousness is, there-
> fore, from the very beginning a social product, and remains so as long as
> men exist at all (1978, 158).

The sociohistorical contextualization of utterance or discourse elaborated by
Bakhtin exhibits close affinity with the Marxist idea of revolutionary praxis found
in the "Theses on Feuerbach"—the dialectical reciprocity between human sensibility and concrete circumstances pivoting around the determinant process of (economic, political, ideological) production.

In "Discourse in Life and Discourse in Art," Bakhtin defines utterance as verbal exchange transpiring on shared sociocultural terrain. It is dependent on extra-
verbal contexts: the common spatial horizon of the interlocutors, their knowledge
and understanding of the situation, and their common evaluation of that situation.
Discourse is always oriented to the other person: " 'I' can actualize itself in discourse only by relying upon 'we.' In this way every quotidian utterance appears as
an objective and social enthymeme" (1976, 100). Hence the fundamental reality of
language is verbal interaction characterized by participation in a unitary language
(centripetal tendency) and by sociohistorical heteroglossia (centrifugal stratifying
forces). The theme of an utterance is always "the concrete historical situation that
engendered the utterance." "Intonation" is the term Bakhtin gives to the gestic
expression or embodiment of values, the axiological or ideological horizon, in
which the verbal and non-verbal boundaries intersect. The three-role drama in
Bakhtin's notion of discourse or speech-event proceeds through three coordinates:
its orientation to the speaker, the addressee or listener, and the "hero" or the topic,
the third decisive participant. In this model of communication, the relations
between speaker and listener are always in a process of transformation. Unlike the

structuralist model, there is no ready message to be transmitted but one which is constructed in verbal transactions. What is meaning then but "the *answers* to the questions" posed by a process in which language metamorphoses into voice: "Language is not a neutral medium that passes freely and easily into the private property of the speaker's intentions; it is populated—overpopulated—with the intentions of others. Expropriating it, forcing it to submit to one's own intentions and accents, is a difficult and complicated process" (1981, 294). All discourses are therefore intertextual, that is, they enter into a dynamic semantic field where constant negotiation, conflict, compromise, collaboration, and permanent tension prevail—the condition of possibility of meaning.

Underlying this theory of the utterance is Bakhtin's philosophical belief that knowledge of one's self can only be obtained through the mediation of others. Alterity and exotopy ("an elsewhere beyond integration or reduction") determine the possibility of self-knowledge:

It is only in another human being that I find an aesthetically (and ethically) convincing experience of human finitude, of a marked-off empirical objectivity. . . . I achieve self-consciousness, I become myself only by revealing myself to another, through another and with another's help. The most important acts, constitutive of self-consciousness, are determined by their relation to another consciousness (a "thou"). Cutting oneself off, isolating oneself, closing oneself off, those are the basic reasons for loss of self. . . . It turns out that every internal experience occurs on the border, it comes across another, and this essence resides in this intense encounter. . . . The very being of man (both internal and external) is a *profound communication. To be* means to *communicate*. . . . To be means to be for the other, and through him, for oneself. Man has no internal sovereign territory; he is all and always on the boundary; looking within himself, he looks *in the eyes of the other* or *through the eyes of the other*. (Todorov 1984, 95–96).

This principle of radical alterity premised on the notion of subject-position as "inbetweenness" is translated by Bakhtin's poststructuralist followers as infinite relativity, carnivalizing improvisation, or antinomian perspectivism. Social life is conceived as an unfinished, open-ended colloquy.

On this point, Paul de Man (1986) considers Bakhtin's exotopy (for example, the otherness of the prisoner to the officer, the "outsidedness" of the officer to the traveller, in Kafka's "In the Penal Colony") as less a hermeneutic than a metaphysical theorem, an ontological thesis flawed by its "metaphysics of presence." For Bakhtin, however, Dostoevsky's novelistic universe is not paralyzed by aporia; it is in fact highly volatile, where there is "a plurality of consciousnesses, with equal right and each with its own world, [that] combine but are not merged in the unity of an event" (1984, 6). Overshadowing his affirmation of the populist, subversive carnival of Rabelais, Bakhtin's praise of Dostoevsky is generally taken as an endorsement of a liberal democratic system that privileges tolerance and individual rights. Bakhtin unwittingly becomes the heir of Locke, Mill, and free-enterprise utilitarianism.

To test Bakhtin's usefulness for literary analysis and judgment, suppose we ask what would be the consequences of applying dialogism to a reading of, for example, Leroi Jones' celebrated play *Dutchman*?

Readers will no doubt recall the explosive climax of that confrontation between Lula, the white woman who functions as the seductive provocateur, and Clay, the middle-class suburban black youth, in the labyrinth of the New York subway. Lula has been taunting him for being "just a dirty white man," and tempting him to break out," calling him "Ol Thomas Wooly-Head" who "Let the white man hump his ol' mama, and he jes' shuffle off in the woods and hide his gentle gray head." What would Bakhtin say of Clay's discourse—monologic, answerable, heterological? Here is an excerpt:

> Don't you tell me anything! If I'm a middle-class fake white man . . . let me be. And let me be in the way I want.
>
> (Through his teeth) I'll rip your lousy breasts off! Let me be who I feel like being. Uncle Tom. Thomas. Whoever. It's none of your business. You don't know anything except what's there for you to see. An act. Lies. Device. Not the pure heart, the pumping black heart. You don't ever know that. And I sit here, in this buttoned-up suit, to keep myself from cutting all your throats. I mean wantonly. You great liberated whore! You fuck some black man, and right away you're an expert on black people. What a lotta shit that is. The only thing you know is that you come if he bangs you hard enough. And that's all. The belly rub? You wanted to do the belly rub? Shit, you don't even know how. You don't know how. That ol' dipty-dip shit you do, rolling your ass like an elephant. That's not my kind of belly rub. Belly rub is not Queens. Belly rub is dark places, with big hats and overcoats held up with one arm. Belly rub hates you. Old bald-headed four-eyed ofays popping their fingers . . . and don't know yet what they're doing. They say, "I love Bessie Smith." And don't even understand that Bessie Smith is saying, "Kiss my ass, kiss my black unruly ass." Before love, suffering, desire, anything you can explain, she's saying, and very plainly, "Kiss my black ass." And if you don't know that, it's you that's doing the kissing. (1964, 34–35)

Here we confront the intensity of logomachia, utterance as the battleground or site of racial war, corresponding to Bakhtin's perception that "each word is a little

arena for the clash of and criss-crossing of differently oriented social accents." Take
the illocutionary force of expressions like "belly rub," "Uncle Tom," "I love
Bessie Smith," whose counterhegemonic resonance is captured by their intonation; their libidinal charge exposes from its dark recess in the nation's archive the
whole blood-soaked history of black-white relations since the days of slavery. For
Bakhtin, intonation or tonality configures the interface between the life-situation
(the unsaid, the absent context) and the signifiers themselves, so that it condenses
all the political-ideological forces locked in struggle, even as the whole speech registers the nuances of antagonistic motifs, connotations, and allusions. One can ask,
in this spirit, "Whose words are those Clay is hurling around, and for whom are
they meant?"

Following the cardinal precepts of Bakhtin's "The Architectonics of
Answerability" in which one's personal life is conceived as an action suffused with
ethical responsibility, Clay's utterance reveals its symbolic import as a collective
response to a recurrent emergency, assuming the form of a prophecy of what
would happen if blacks lose their "otherness" and become assimilated as "stand-up
Western men." We know that the play's denouement answers this with Lula's violent murder of Clay. Initially Clay's utterance reflects back Lula's image or phan-
tasm of blacks, a condensation of white pathology vis-à-vis blacks. His reaction also
defines Lula who is here less an individual than an allegorical rendering of the racist
and sexist ethos of the dominant society. It is Lula's reified image of the black male
that Clay recuperates, inflects, articulates. So far this aligns with Bakhtin's rhetoric
of answerability: I exist only insofar as the Other listens or speaks to me, and vice
versa. It presumes a principle of cooperation (prescribed by speech-act theory)
amid dissensus and dissidence. Valorizing the "surplus of humanness," loopholes,
and the surprising inconclusiveness of events, Bakhtinian "prosaics" tends to concentrate on the unique existential depth of the speaker's personality (Bakhtin's paradigm of the speech genre brings to mind Lacan's mirror-stage of the Imaginary) so
that addressivity and polyphony may even be used to fabricate autonomous selves
resisting authoritarian, official discourse. Whereas, I submit, Jones' project is to
invent the multi-accented, embattled speech of the black petty bourgeoise fraction
in a moment of crisis. Jones' theater enacts the black man's ordeal of attaining self-
consciousness via the mediation of popular memory and its habitus of resistance. In
addressing both the oppressor who manipulates a coercive, disciplinary code and
the libidinally invested black bodies whose awakening still lies in the future, Jones
refuses a resolution like the unfinalized fugue of Dostoevsky's novels by aiming for
what Bakhtin calls a naive, "objectivized, finalizing form," even a programmatic
manifesto drawn from the palimpsest of double-voiced words, that would spell
freedom from racist subjugation coinciding with the protagonist's death.

Bakhtin proposed the notion of "creative understanding" as the ideal situation where one recognizes the other without surrendering one's "outsidedness."
Although multiple contexts and communities are presupposed in Bakhtin's staging

of the utterance, the thrust of the dialogic scenario is toward self-knowledge even though in principle the self can never coincide with itself. On the evidence of biographical accounts, Bakhtin shifted his focus alternatively on either the process or product of the speech-situation. Heteroglossia, after all, implies the contrapuntal movements of centralization and dispersal, standardization and variation. Similarly, the eventfulness of *parole* cannot be appreciated without the systemic ground of *langue*, just as the surprising realization of human potential and its defamiliarizing impact are lost without the relatively static background of a persisting structure to sustain them.

It is notable that for all of Bakhtin's emphasis on sociohistorical contexts and limits, he never actually theorizes the concrete multiple determinations that would circumscribe the specific locations of his speech-performers (except in his discussion of grotesque realism and the carnivalesque in Rabelais). Mary Russo reminds us that Bakhtin "fails to acknowledge or incorporate the social relations of gender in his semiotic model of the body politic, and thus his notion of the Female Grotesque remains, in all directions, repressed and undeveloped" (1986, 219). Convinced of one's "non-alibi" in life, Bakhtin (1993) regards history as an unanswerable constraint that can be voluntaristically transcended; but one might ask if the surplus of human potential guaranteeing unfinalizability remains inexhaustible?

One can argue then that Bakhtin's humanism precipitates a fall into the flux of heteroglossia and the fetishism of incompleteness. What is chiefly lacking in dialogism is precisely what we find in the critical dialectics of Lukács and Gramsci, namely, the concept of totality or complex of structural determinations that render any utterance or linguistic form intelligible in a milieu dominated by the power of capital. Lukács, for example, would connect *Dutchman* to the underlying social antagonisms and ethical dilemmas, particularly the overdetermined racial conflicts in U.S. society in the 1950s and early 1960s, that are represented in the "typical" physiognomies of Clay and Lula. Aesthetic forms (expressionist drama, realist novel) are defined by their mimetic function conceived not as one-dimensional reflection of facts but as selective arrangement intent on providing a critical understanding of causal mechanisms and internal contradictions immanent in social processes. For Lukács, the most crucial factor that catalyzed the metamorphosis of the bourgeois novel from archaic epic and drama is the growing complexity of the division of labor in the transition from feudalism to capitalism, a development that has also generated the split between public and private spheres. This is the epochal disintegration of the rationalist episteme that heralds the advent of the decentered, schizoid subject in late modernity. I might add here that this alienation of labor, the negation of human species-being, entails the divorce of civil society (family, sexuality) and the state (politics). Lukács cites Marx's analysis of the dichotomy between "the personal individual" and "the class individual" engendered by competition in the marketplace (where the selling and alienation of labor-power as commodity, in bourgeois society, defines freedom) which then produces "the accidental character" of individual lives: "Hence, in imagination the individuals under the rule of the bourgeoisie are freer than before, because their conditions of life are more accidental for them; in reality, they are naturally more unfree, because much more subsumed under material power" (1973, 289).

In *History and Class Consciousness*, Lukács (1971) examines the nature of modern social totality defined by reification, a state of affairs in which human relations takes on the character of relations between things, assuming "a phantom objectivity" that obstructs cognition and transformation of reality. In this context, the novel is assigned the task of representing how the direction of a social tendency or a determinate historical necessity manifests itself "in the small, imperceptible capillary movements of individual life," whereas in drama, the social contradictions are crystallized in "world-historical individuals" or types in whose personalities "the essential social-moral determinants" are concentrated. Historical praxis of individuals as types instead of the act of verbal exchange between individuals occupies center stage in Lukács' thought. From this perspective, we can describe Jones' play as the "typifying" expression of the racial contradictions (overdetermined by class and gender) in U.S. society at a specific conjuncture, conflicts that energize and limit Lula's and Clay's utterances. This is a thematizing strategy that is itself confirmed by the playwright's confession in his autobiography: "Drama proliferates during periods of social upsurge, because it makes real live people the fuel of ideas. . . . During this period, I was struggling to be born, to break out from the shell I could instinctively sense surrounded my own dash for freedom. I was in a frenzy, trying to get my feet solidly on the ground, of reality" (Baraka 1984, 187, 194). Jones here anticipates what Gramsci calls Ibsen's "theater of ideas" with its singular anti-Aristotelian (but pre-Brechtian) catharsis.

While Lukács subsumes language in a structural homology or correspondence between artistic form and social totality, Gramsci pays closer attention to signs and writing practices as manifestations of cultural power. Gramsci considers language a basic element in the constitution of subjects, of humans as "intellectuals" or self-aware individuals. He defines language as "a totality of determined notions and concepts and not simply and solely of words grammatically void of content. Every level of language or utterance is permeated with definite concepts of the world; in every person one finds a bundle of contradictory notions, what is called 'common sense,' notions imposed mechanically by various social groups" (1957, 58–59). Here, unlike Bakhtin's triad of speaker-context-addressee, the whole speech-act situation and its constituents are already articulated as elements of a synthesizing worldview. Communication is then grasped as the conflict of ideologies which are temporarily stabilized in a hegemonic process. Hegemony refers here to the ascendancy of a historic bloc of social forces, with its moral-intellectual leadership directing the energies of the whole society (Sassoon 1980). For Bakhtin, however, hegemony would establish monologism, prohibit the free play of heterogeneous voices and impose an abstract system of normative rules.

One cannot help but sense an aestheticist, formalizing tendency in Bakhtin to valorize dialogue for its own sake and sidetrack the absence of an environment where reification will not congeal utterance. Gramsci, for his part, opposes any mystification of praxis, of speech or action. The question for Gramsci is how the project of freedom for the masses—that is, of forging one's conception of the world "critically and consciously"—can be realized in the face of the compulsive pressures toward mass conformity in class-divided societies. In other words, how can the individual become free in the process of making himself through participation in changing society? Speaking is, for Gramsci, a constituent of revolutionary praxis; discourse can only be authentically conceived as transformative action. The act of evaluating the multiplicity of voices/languages that interpellate the individual from outside implies also, for Gramsci, criticizing multiple conceptions of the world so as "to make [them] coherent and unified," to discriminate and assay those layers or imprints inscribed by historical determinants: "The beginning of the critical elaboration is the consciousness of what one really is, that is, a 'know thyself' as the product of the historical process which has left you an infinity of traces gathered together without the advantage of an inventory" (1971, 324). The self here is a locus of converging manifold forces, not a static essence or unfinalizable interiority endowed with a plenitude of "surplus humanness."

Gramsci's usefulness for oppositional critique lies in his grasp of language as the specific material site in which signification (ideology) occurs. Thus language can serve to realize the cultural hegemony of the democratic will and its unification provided one takes into account how, in language itself, social distinctions and cultural inequalities have become ossified. Christine Buci-Glucksmann lucidly formulates this Gramscian analysis: "The strata of language subsist in each individual, the trace of cultural worlds that are now fossil remains, but still capable of reappearing. Critical understanding of oneself, and the struggle between old and new, the struggle for hegemony, consist in locating onself within language, since language itself, through a particular social milieu, situates us in it as subjects" (1980, 368). Language then is the medium, not the source, that gives determinate form to our attitudes, beliefs, and actions; exposing their transitory metaphorical nature, and in the process dissolving the "intuition-expression" linkage of ideology at the heart of Crocean aesthetics. The source for drawing up a critical inventory is the collective praxis (social will acting on structures) that informs all verbal interaction.

Following this line of reasoning, one can read Clay's acts of enunciation which I quoted earlier as a passionate attempt to compile and critique this inventory, to transvalue it by means of parody, hyperbole, reflexive irony, and other devices. It is also a struggle to counter the pressures of hegemonic discourse by sublimating the voice of the oppressor (internal and external) so as to generate an exorcism of the Dutchman's (or, on second thought, the Dutchwoman's?) curse. We can interpret this curse suggested by the title as Clay's unreflecting obedience to the former slave-master's ideal of rationality which, if pushed to its logical con-

clusion, spells murder, even destruction of that order which paradoxically identifies him as human under erasure, that is, subject to racist dehumanization. What
Clay's speech enacts is therefore not just a reproduction, an echoing of multiple
voices drawn from the archive of his race. What his utterance performs in the
drama is the criticism and hierarchical ordering of that inventory Gramsci refers to
so that his life as commodified object can metamorphose into a conscious, acting
subject. The praxis of communication is thus invested with an emancipatory force,
an agency geared to mobilize the potential of Clay's species-being in order to
change his character and with it the black people's position in U.S. history.

It becomes clear then that the basic disparity between Bakhtin and Gramsci
involves the problematization of speech acts and their effects. Bakhtin privileges
the verbal performance as value-producing. For Gramsci, the understanding of any
cultural text or practice cannot begin from an undue privileging of the speech-situation in its unique unrepeatability, as Bakhtin tends to do, because then the complex relation between the speakers' changing positions and the equally mutable
sociocultural contexts would be preempted by some apriori assumption of a sovereign consciousness in control, an idealist "Reason" owned by its proprietor, a
coherent deontological subject. A proper theorization of ideology (manifested in
varied cultural forms of expression, texts) vis-à-vis the contingencies of social existence, the drawing up of a research strategy studying the intertextuality of utterances, for Gramsci, would begin with mapping a specific milieu in which the
subject finds herself inserted. "Languages are social products, the cultural expression of a given people," Gramsci writes; but that does not imply a homogeneous
linguistic community because a common language reflects sociohistorical differences and divisions by class, region, gender, and so on. Each social group or sector
produces its specific ways of thinking, feeling, linguistic usages, that is, elements of
a worldview that can enter into the construction of a dominant or hegemonic culture. Language stratification prevails with the coexistence of cosmopolitan,
"national-popular," provincial or folkloric, religious languages, and so on (1986,
164–87). Language then serves as a microcosm of a determinate existential reality,
embedded in the action of mutually reciprocal forces that comprise the mode of
production and the ideological superstructure of any social formation.

Since Gramsci's project is the all-sided emancipation of the Italian nation-
people through their transformation into creative, conscious agents of history, the
linguistic question—the struggle for a national-popular literature, for example
(Dombroski 1989)—enters into the shaping of a "socio-cultural unity where dispersed aims and wills can be unified by a single purpose, a common world view."
For Bakhtin, this would mean a progression toward imposing an authoritarian discourse, dogmatism *tout court*. But for Gramsci the producers of utterances, especially organic intellectuals and their communities, can only be grasped within the
category of a totalizing worldview:

Language also means culture and philosophy (although at the level of common sense) and, therefore, "language" as a fact is actually a multiplicity of more or less organically coherent and coordinated facts. . . . Every cultural expression, every moral and intellectual activity, has its historically specific language: this language is also called "technique" and "structure". . . . The work of art, though, also contains other "historical" elements besides its specific emotional and cultural world. These pertain to language meant not only as a purely verbal expression that can be grammatically photographed in a given time and place, but also a sum total of images and modes of expression that are not included in grammar (1985, 120, 122).

Here Gramsci avoids the structuralist trap of synchronicity, the closed circuit of signifier-signified, by an implied semiotics of language use analogous to Wittgenstein's notion of "language games," techniques for purposes dictated by varying "forms of life": " 'Literary' language is strictly tied to the life of a nation's masses and is only developed slowly and molecularly" (1985, 120). Clay's language, from Gramsci's viewpoint, participates in a complex force-field of colliding worldviews: those of the white middle class, the black petty bourgeoisie, the folkloric disenfranchised masses, the black proletariat, and so on. What the play reveals particularly in the idioms, mannerisms, syncopated or stylized rhythms, and rhetorical figurations is the dialectic of hegemonic and counterhegemonic impulses coexisting in a historic bloc. "Bloc" denotes the moment of a multilayered struggle of forces when economic infrastructure and cultural superstructure organically coalesce. In *Dutchman*, the sexual and erotic innuendoes are overdetermined by vocabularies inflected according to orientations by race, class, and gender. It is easy to detect how Clay's speech (like spirituals, minstrel plays, other signifying rituals of the black people) harnesses "raw materials" from the dominant consensus to shape a counterhegemonic articulation of the subaltern race, deploying hortatory eloquence, invective, scatological imagery, and coded messages, in an ideological "war of position" aimed at seizing political power.

One should add here that in the heterogeneous milieu of *Dutchman* where politicization of sexuality, fantasy, and the unconscious saturates the style and plot, distancing is attained by "black humor" and "street-smart" idiom. Affirmation of group identity takes precedence over everything else. Jones identifies himself as a committed African-American artist who refuses to accept the schizoid predicament of the writer in mass consumer societies of late capitalism. The New York subway train—and by extension the urban metropolis—becomes simultaneously the womb of insurgent popular consciousness and the tomb of hegemonic programs for the assimilation of the "internal colonies" of people of color.

Now, for Gramsci, *Dutchman* would be considered a highly mediated reflection of the ensemble of contradictions and discordant elements in U.S. society. Its dramatic form is not dialogic but polemical and didactic as befits the strategy of an emergent group consciousness locked in struggle against the hegemonic order. What is needed is critical demystification, not pathos. The qualitative leap of Clay from a status of passive recipient/object to one who initiates a symbolic verbal assault stages a transvaluative, conversion process envisaged by Gramsci as "catharsis" which he elaborates thus:

> The term "catharsis" can be employed to indicate the passage from the purely economic (or egoistic-passional) to the ethico-political moment, that is the superior elaboration of the structure into superstructure in the minds of men. This also means the passage from "objective to subjective" and "from necessity to freedom." Structure ceases to be an external force which crushes man, assimilates him to itself and makes him passive; and is transformed into a means of freedom, an instrument to create a new ethico-political form and a source of new initiatives. To establish the "cathartic" moment becomes therefore, it seems to me, the starting-point for all the philosophy of praxis, and the cathartic process coincides with the chain of syntheses which have resulted from the evolution of the dialectic. (1971, 366–67)

Whereas for Bakhtin this moment of catharsis is either initially assumed to be given in each of the protagonists in a many-tongued, relativizing *agon*, for Gramsci it is the project of mobilized agency in a party or political alliance where each individual metamorphoses into a conscious, responsible participant. This process unfolds within the totality of the class struggle operating in multiple levels, overdetermined by manifold intentionalities. Jones' play seeks to transcribe one moment of this process.

Within this radically historicist framework, the modalities of writing can be understood as ideological forms of social consciousness that forfeit their neutrality when they function as effective organizers of the subaltern masses, creating "the terrain on which men move, acquire consciousness of their position, struggle," in specific conjunctures ultimately circumscribed by the existing constellation of productive forces and relations. Thus speech genres and utterances are both acting and acted upon, mediated by a variety of social practices and institutions (political, economic, ideological) distributed in space. Bakhtin's category of utterances with their heteroglotic instability cannot really alter normative circumstances. Confronted by these normative structures, Gramsci assigns to intellectuals (in the broad sense of organizers of group mentalities) the task of actively intervening in the ideological class struggle. These organic intellectuals serve the classes or groups to which they are attached by mobilizing art and other cultural practices to accomplish the project of winning hegemony, that is, freedom of the national-popular bloc from bourgeois oppression together with the destruction of the bases for reproducing class hierarchy, exploitation, and reification.

Compared to Gramsci's theory of language use, Bakhtin's dialogism appears limited in its tendency to hypostatize difference and alterity. In Bakhtin's universe of discourse, we become spectators to a theatrical spectacle of difference, a new ethical sublime (Dunn 1992). While Bakhtin's ideas of answerability and utopian absence of closure, evolved within the repressive atmosphere of the Stalinist period, may be able to release us from the seductive spell of poststructuralist nihilism and assorted opportunist utilitarianisms to which I have alluded earlier, they lack the enabling critical resources one can find in Gramsci's concepts of "catharsis" and "hegemony," a pragmatics of relational positionality (Holub 1992) that can aid in the construction of a hermeneutics of utterances, speech acts, and geopolitical intertexts within the "untranscendable horizon of history."

Such horizon seems to have been blocked temporarily by the transgressive theater of victimization, Kafka's "In the Penal Colony," which opened this chapter. Each word in that narrative, indeed, "tastes of the context or contexts in which it has lived its socially charged life" (Bakhtin 1981, 293). Yet instead of savoring those words, the traveller's reticence, his morbid attentiveness to the officer's monologue, the spectacle of ritualized violence, and the final disillusionment all conspire to send us fleeing from such a godforsaken place. But, on second thought, this allegory is nothing but an assemblage of words, a revolutionary "minor" writing, to be sure (Deleuze and Guattari 1986). It is a *scriptible* text, no doubt, but still a series of utterances bound in syntagmatic and paradigmatic chains of signification—*écriture* incarnate.

Such chains may be entangling and burdensome unless we remind ourselves again that language is, in Marx's words, "communal being speaking for itself." Gramsci's insistence on the social constitution of speech-acts needs to be supplemented by Ferruccio Rossi-Landi's innovative inquiry into the homology between linguistic and material production, language as work and trade, and the function of linguistic capital in reinforcing hegemony. Rossi-Landi recapitulates the guiding insights of Bakhtin/Voloshinov and Gramsci:

> Language and languages, as its products, are formed *within* the dialectic of the satisfaction of needs, that is, within the process of the institution of work and production relationships; language is also human work and languages are its necessary objectification. . . . The production of signs *is* an institution of work and production relationships, just as these relationships *are* signs. Language is a form and an expression of the society; it is in language, or more broadly speaking in the sign, that society *manifests itself.* (1983, 38, 41, 63)

Within a historical-materialist problematic, Rossi-Landi extends Wittgenstein's ideas on "language games," their relevance to "forms of life," and the criterion of language use to elucidate the phenomenon of linguistic alienation and the semiotic production of ideology in the service of capital. Kafka's penal colony will certainly not be spared from the transformative and deterritorializing power of this critique.

3

Arguments within Marxist Critical Theory

> The world, which is the same for all, has not been made by any
> god or man; it has ever been, is now, and ever shall be ever-
> living fire, kindled by measures, quenched by measures.
> —Herakleitos
> No one has hitherto laid down the limits to the powers of the
> body.   —Benedict Spinoza

In the *Grundrisse*, Marx (1973) asked why Greek art, though born from an economically backward society long extinct, still continues to exercise "an eternal
charm." Since then, his unsatisfactory answer has sparked a history of argumenta-
tion—not only in the humanities but in cultural politics, in general—to which this
chapter belongs. Both Mikhail Lifshitz (1973) and Max Raphael (1979) gave plausible and substantial explanations to Marx's "unsatisfactory" answer, but their
works have been swallowed up in the anticommunist maelstrom.

In this century marked by the birth and demise of the "socialist" experiment
in the Soviet Union and elsewhere, Marxism's crises have been much belabored by
its enemies. But such periods of encountering limits and discordance—prefigured
here by Marx's puzzlement—are integral to its character as "incomplete, fallible, a
tradition in process" (Mulhern 1991), though without doubt still the unsurpassable
horizon of thought in our time. Meanwhile language, textuality, structure have
shrouded that horizon and preempted any real engagement with Marx's original
puzzlement.

In the wake of the poststructuralist transvaluation of texts as the ceaseless play
of *gram*, of the unchoreographable dance of signifiers, which one may interpret as a
historically specific reaction to dogmatism in its various manifestations—economistic, sectarian, mechanical, empiricist, and so on—I would like to reaffirm the
axiom that art's condition of possibility inheres in the concept of praxis: creative,
non-alienated labor. Enunciated by Marx in the *1844 Manuscripts* and *The German
Ideology*, this theorizing of the aesthetic as a value in/of transformative action is
recast in *Capital* in the figure of the architect, the epitome of human activity:

> We are positing labor of a form that is exclusively characteristic of man.
> . . . The poorest architect is categorically distinguished from the best of

51

bees by the fact that before he builds a cell in wax, he has built it in his head. The result achieved at the end of a labor process was already present at its commencement, in the *imagination of the worker, in its ideal form*. More than merely working an alteration in the form of nature, he also *knowingly works his own purposes into* nature; and these purposes are the law determining the ways and means of his activity, so that his will must be adjusted to them. (Marx and Engels 1973, 53–54).

Adolfo Sanchez Vasquez extrapolates from this the idea that the interplay between objective necessity (nature) and human needs is what begets this teleological praxis: "Human needs characterize man as an active being, and his activity consists of creating a human world that does not exist by itself, outside of him" (Vasquez 1973, 61; 1977).

Art and labor are therefore creative acts that express humanity through the objects man makes and endows with purposes, objects that satisfies his needs. These needs together with the sensory organs undergo historical changes. Henri Lefebvre suggests that we call *poiesis* activities that give human form to the sensuous, and praxis all interhuman relations, thus subsuming *poiesis* (Rudich 1965). Lefebvre uses "praxis" to denote the "dialectical relation between man and nature, consciousness and things . . . if every praxis is content, this content creates forms; it is content only by virtue of the form born of its contradictions" (1968, 45–46). Within the framework of a Marxian social ontology, Agnes Heller (1972) identifies "value" as one of the primary categories of social praxis (cooperative labor), a category oriented to the measure of "species-being" as the groundwork of a revolutionary (that is, anticapitalist) ethics and aesthetics.

In retrospect, this "scientific socialist" perspective is now considered heretical or even vulgar and reductive. *Homo faber* has been displaced by *homo ludens* and *homo loquens*. In the New Left testament on this subject, *The Aesthetic Dimension*, Herbert Marcuse attempts to posit and validate the crucial divorce between aesthetics and politics in monopoly capitalism by suggesting that Lenin, and the Bolshevik revolutionary tradition originating from Marxism-Leninism, rejected the transcendental and liberating "truth of art" (1978, 56–57). Somehow the bourgeoisie followed suit. Most literary historians treat Lenin's dialectical conception of art as outmoded, narrowly concerned with "the popularization of culture" and guilty of "utilitarianism" (for balance, see Shcherbina 1974). This also applies to the dicta of Mao Tsetung, Ho Chi Minh, Kim Il Sung, Fidel Castro, and so on. Although a rhetorician like Hayden White (1980) can refunction "reflection theory" to judge the activist claims of Marxists themselves, it remains the case that "reflectionism" still serves as the favorite whipping horse of bourgeois scholarship. This ranges from academic Marxologists like Peter Demetz (1967) to celebrated pundits like Edmund Wilson (1948) and George Steiner (1967). Their own "damaged" opinions are recycled today in more fashionable idioms suitable to what is called a "postrevolutionary" milieu.

With the renaissance of Marxist critical theory in the late 1960s and early 1970s, especially the recovery by Louis Althusser of certain fundamental insights into the constitution of the subject by ideology, it seems appropriate to resituate the necessary task of Marxist theorizing on literature within a more engaged, interventionist strategy of cultural politics. This reconfiguration would not simply be a scholastic reading of texts to disclose their metaphysical fallacies or rhetorical virtues, a practice inspired by leftist followers of Derrida. It would also not be a revival of a prophetic-anarchist strain in Marxism as an alternative to bureaucratic conservatism or social-democratic opportunism, an approach exemplified by Maynard Solomon's *Marxism and Art* (1973). What this rethinking (amid the impasse of the 1980s) hopes to stimulate is the active intervention of the committed intellectual in the social practices of everyday life.

In Lenin's critical practice of interrogating texts, particularly in his appraisal of Tolstoy's works, we can discern the model of an activist hermeneutic. Lenin focuses on the organic yet mediated linkage between knowledge and action, cognition and organized will—a new radical conception of textuality and signifying practice which would be elaborated later on in their distinctive, unconventional ways by Christopher Caudwell (1937), Antonio Gramsci (1971), and Bertolt Brecht (1964). As Pierre Macherey (1978) has pointed out, Lenin demonstrated the internal conflict in Tolstoy's writings between the critical-realistic protest embodied in the texts and the quietist reactionary doctrines of the author. He showed how these contradictions foregrounded in the narrative form spring from the ideological position of the artist himself and the inherent limitations of such a position. Such distancing between elements of the work opens up a space for critical intervention, whereby Lenin seizes the "tendentiousness" of history itself revealed by the text:

> But the contradictions in Tolstoy's views and doctrines are not accidental; they express the contradictory conditions of Russian life in the last third of the nineteenth century. The patriarchal countryside, only recently emancipated from serfdom, was literally given over to the capitalist and the tax collector to be fleeced and plundered. . . . Tolstoy is original, because the sum total of his views, taken as a whole, happens to express the specific features of our revolution as a *peasant* bourgeois revolution. (1967, 30; 48–62)

Tolstoy's landlord/patriarchal ideology, distinguished by a sharp awareness of class conflict and a specific resolution proposed for this conflict, finds itself objectified and disrupted by the structure of his texts. In this process, the ideology is internally redoubled, thereby exposing its limits and inadequacies (for example, the social framework of beliefs informing the protagonists in *Anna Karenina*). For these limits and inadequacies to reveal their presence, a dialectical reading is required.

Lenin offers us an analysis of the historical contradictions in Tolstoy's class position vis-à-vis the 1905 bourgeois democratic revolution, focusing on the advocacy of Christian quietism, an ethico-political position which hides the complex totality of the material contradictions. In the same breath, the intrinsic lack in the text expresses the insufficiency of the historical situation, namely, the ambiguous role of the peasantry in the emerging socialist revolution. One can perceive this problematic of Tolstoy's ideology being demystified (its false claims to totality and naturalness exposed) in "The Death of Ivan Ilyich" where the existential anguish suffered by Ivan exceeds the social corruption afflicting his petty bourgeois stratum.

While the symptomatic diagnosis that Macherey recommends tends to privilege the text as a displacing mechanism that reveals the limits of ideological incorporation, I would like to stress here that Lenin's practice operates within and outside these hermeneutic strictures. By situating Tolstoy's texts at the conjuncture of class alignments (Gramsci's constellation of historic forces) and foregrounding the ambiguous role of the peasantry in the revolutionary process as a whole, Lenin anatomizes the contingencies of literary form itself. He succeeds in grasping what Lukács (1970) calls "intensive totality" as well as that oxymoronesque quality called "the partisanship of objectivity." Lenin does not deviate from Marx and Engels' example; both grasped the profound tendentiousness of history captured in realistic art when they took into account the artist's will and power of discrimination (Morawski 1973). Lenin treats the text as articulated by multiple determinations, not just by the purely linguistic or rhetorical. In effect, Lenin decenters the organic formal unity of texts, elucidating their "political unconscious" in the conflicted historical totality subsuming them. With a more acute feel for circumstantial texture, Galvano Della Volpe chides Plekhanov and Lukács for not learning from Lenin to define "realism" more broadly; Lenin showed how Balzac saw "his (progressive) enemies not less but more truly than those on his own side," while Tolstoy saw "his own side and his own (unprogressive) ideas more truly" (1978, 237). Paradoxically, both artists avoided a spurious tendentiousness by simply describing the image of the world from their own biased, colored optics.

Our argument here posits the textual production of meaning, the discursive process of signification, as a dialectical transaction in which ideology is cognized as a social practice, not a transcribed "false consciousness." This is not Lenin's innovation; his substantive contribution takes the form of articulating a conjunctural theory of revolutionary strategy and tactics outlined in *What is to be done?* It is actually Marx's, specifically in his critique of religion where the notion of what Lukács (1971) later on calls "reification" as derived from commodity-fetishism is first broached. In general, religion as an "inverted world-consciousness" provides the heuristic model for the unity-in-conflict of the real and the illusory. Marx associates praxis with discourse in his critique of Hegel's *Philosophy of Right*:

> Religion is, in fact, the self-consciousness and self-esteem of man who has either not yet gained himself or has lost himself again. . . . It is the fantastic realization of the human being because the human being has attained no true reality. . . . The wretchedness of religion is at once an expression of and a protest against real wretchedness. Religion is the sigh of the oppressed creature, the heart of a heartless world and the soul of soulless conditions. It is the opium of the people.
>
> The abolition of religion as the illusory happiness of the people is a demand for their true happiness. The call to abandon illusions about their conditions is the call to abandon a condition which requires illusions. Thus, the critique of religion is the critique in embryo of the vale of tears of which religion is the halo. (1970, 131)

Here Marx grasps the superstructure (religion) not as epiphenomenon but as a constitutive element in all social practice, just like that enigmatic object in *Capital*, the commodity. In conceptualizing the contradictory relation between intellectual objectification and social reality, he laid the groundwork for the versatile and dynamic intervention of transformative agents. Such agency, relative to varying historical sites, can be located in Lenin's party, Gramsci's "organic intellectuals" functioning in the ideological apparatuses of civil society. Or it can assume the guise of Brecht's interrogative gesture aimed at destroying the habitus of idealist thinking and its roots in Nature, custom, the self-evident doxa of bourgeois institutions.

Before pursuing the ramification of this "Leninist" moment of cultural politics in the Brecht-Lukács debate over socialist realism and its implications, it might be instructive to summarize here Caudwell's thesis presented in *Illusion and Reality*. For Caudwell, art is a specific mode of production of "historically necessary forms of social consciousness," in short, of literature as a politically valorized signifying practice.

Caudwell's controlling insight that the norm of bourgeois freedom is based on the occlusion of social relations stems from the Marxist principle of the dialectical interaction of subject and object. This idea is implied in Marx's concept of the subject as sensuous-practical activity, "theory as the outcome of practice on the object" (1978, 143). Marxist theory is oriented toward "concrete living," toward the realization of freedom (development or fulfillment of man's species-being) by society, collective or associated producers, mastering and directing the forces of nature. Engels conceived of freedom as lived in the appreciation/recognition of the necessary inscription of humans in the interface of nature and society. Caudwell reformulates this by locating the core of experience in the tension between man and nature, instinct and environment, affect and cognition. Caudwell seems to equate art and emotion, annulling the distinction between aesthetic and non-aesthetic effects, and thus exposing him to the vagaries of psychology or immediate pragmatic contingencies.

What is original and relevant for us in this context is Caudwell's elucidation of the aesthetic function. For him, art is not just a mere transcription of subjectivity (as in formalist idealism), nor a representation of objective reality (as in mimetic naturalism) but a production of a "mock world" where the "I," the transindividual subject of culturally determinate discourse (not the self-present "I" of phenomenology)—the "I" as a socially constituted ego of the "common affective world"—actualizes itself in comprehending and transforming the real world. "Poetry is . . . the sweat of man's struggle with Nature" conducted in history: "the phantasy of poetry is a social image" (1937, 130, 194; see Duparc and Margolies 1986, 27).

For Caudwell, individual consciousness always appears as a social product. Since the phantasy in art unfolds itself as the mobilizing of collective energies in which human thought and will (the genotype) act on the objective world, subject and object are posited as interacting dialectically. Poetry functions through the "conditioning of instinctive responses by the relations of society. . . . Because it must use the collective world of language, it focuses all the emotional life of society in one giant 'I' which is common to all" (1937, 72). Consequently, "poetry is public . . . for consciousness is a social construction" (1937, 244). Francis Mulhern distills Caudwell's poetics of collective dream in one proposition: "Poetry is the *psychological* agent in a general *historical* movement: by harmonizing *instinct* and *environment*, it facilitates the struggle of *man* against *Nature*" (1974, 47).

In the concluding chapter of *Illusion and Reality*, Caudwell translates the ethical and practical implications of his poetics as a call for petty bourgeois artists to "take the difficult creative road—that of refashioning the categories and technique of art so that it expresses the new world coming into being and is part of its realization" (1937, 289). This new world is socialist society where the poet, conscious of internal as well as external necessity (causality), serves as a figure for the fulfilled will and freedom of each social individual. The radicalization of the petty bourgeois artist, for Caudwell, occurs through proletarian cultural hegemony, a synthesis of the progressive elements in bourgeois art and a transitional, evolving revolutionary art (see chapter 9). For his part, Leon Trotsky distinguishes between socialist art (still to be fashioned in the future when classes shall have been abolished) and revolutionary art charged with partisan hubris. Proletarian art doesn't exist yet because, Trotsky explains, "proletarian individuality has not been sufficiently formed and differentiated" (1960, 225). Clearly Trotsky values the bourgeois intelligentsia and its masterpieces way above the uncouth workers and peasants he is trying to save (Laing 1978).

Caudwell's analysis confronts directly the mystifying effect of bourgeois ideology, its positing of a coherent autonomous ego. He tries to decenter this subjectivity through positioning it within the reciprocal interaction of society and nature, a praxis mediated by historical sedimentation and changing human needs. What Caudwell does not clearly spell out is the praxis of change on the level of art's content: "A revolution of content [in poetry], as opposed to a mere movement of technique, now begins, corresponding in the social sphere to a change in productive relations as opposed to a mere improvement in productive forces" (1937, 127). This presupposes the start of the dissolution of exchange-value together with money, the source of "socially necessary false consciousness."

Caudwell rejects the modernist resolution of the crisis in art's function—"the tragedy of the will of Joyce's *Ulysses* and Proust's 'I' living in a world wholly of personal phantasy"—because this is merely symptomatic of an escape from "content" and "social form" into the privatized sphere of dream. In its systematic upholding of individual freedom as a transcendence of necessity (reversing Engels), surrealism fetishizes technique and thus legitimizes the bourgeois notion of freedom which conditions it. This is also the basic thrust of Caudwell's (1971) criticism of George Bernard Shaw, D. H. Lawrence, and H. G. Wells. Upholding the primacy of social determinations over aesthetic choice, Caudwell notes that in the final capitalist crisis, "the question of form now tends to take a second place until the problem of social relations has been solved poetically" (1937, 297; Margolies 1969).

It remained for Brecht, in his contestation with Lukács over the methodology for achieving the goal of socialist realism, to identify not so much the objective moment—for example, the historicity of modes of production—as the subjective moment or pole of the dialectic. In the context of fascist barbarism, Brecht theorized the mental and perceptual categories through which, in the artwork and in the audience, the social totality is mediated and with it the "weak links" for mass intervention. In the meantime, the standard of nineteenth-century realism endorsed by Plekhanov, Mehring, and Lukács may be said to have discouraged the exploration of other alternatives to influence the drift of middle-class consciousness in the post–World War I era.

The agenda hinges on charting the dialectic of modernism and realism. How can a revolutionary practice of writing combat the seduction of bourgeois "culinary" art if it employs the mode of expressive realism? Such realism is the obverse of aestheticism. The office of such realism is precisely to conceal the historical specificity of the production of meaning and the reality-effect of codes of representation that interpellate individuals into subalterns. Realism generates the mirage of a subject as a given presence without history, self-identical, homogeneous, unchanging: the bourgeois illusion Caudwell tried to exorcise. If subjectivity is a discursive construct and the forms of discourse vary relative to specific formations and class positions, then the key to producing politically effective art lies in a creative practice where the signifying process is foregrounded and interrogated. Is the code of realism itself an immutable formal criterion? Or are the means of unfolding social totality and enabling access to it a matter of conventions determined by concrete historical conjunctures—the convergence of ideological, political and economic instances to which Althusser called attention? Is there just one realist style or form? Or is realism the epistemological grid and cognitive template within which a variety of forms (semiotic styles, signifying practices) can be explored?

While it is obligatory to contextualize the famous Brecht-Lukács debate in order to account for Lukács' privileging of the "intensive totality" of critical realism (evinced in Thomas Mann's novels) and Aristotelian catharsis (Lukács 1970), and for Brecht's historicizing of modalities of representation, it would be economical simply to rehearse the nodal points in this exchange (Arvon 1973). In all fairness, I would confess my partiality for Brecht's stance and its usefulness for consciousness-raising and strategic mobilization in Third World environments, as witness Augusto Boal's (1979) adaptation of *Verfremdungseffekt* in the "Joker" system. On the other hand, my work on Lukács (San Juan 1973) testifies to his protean value as a heuristic guide to comprehending the dynamics of "class consciousness," reification, and totality. From Lukács' highly compressed essay on *Lenin* alone, one can extrapolate a genuinely dialectical organon for a materialist criticism that tackles the issues of typicality, class equivalents of forms, conjuncture, alienation, and foresight—the central, enduring themes of the Marxist tradition (Baxandall 1983).

As everyone knows, Lukács privileges the neo-Hegelian criterion of typicality, the fusion of essence and appearance, suggested by Engel's comment on a now forgotten novel by Margaret Harkness (Rieser 1957). In applying this, Lukács often displays a mechanical one-sidedness that hypostatizes the "organic, rounded and closed" form of 19th-century realism as the permanent model for an emergent socialist realism. I concur with Werner Mittenzwei, who sharply exposes Lukács' formalist error. Mittenzwei argues that this ideal of typicality contradicts the principle in materialist dialectics that the contradictory character of essence and appearance, not their relative unity, functions as the determining force within the complex totality (1973, 225). Lucien Goldmann's structural-genetic method and its use of homology inspired by Lukács also commits this mistake (for a positive view, see Wolff 1981). In this regard, Lenin himself stresses the primacy of contradiction in *Philosophical Notebooks*: "In the strict sense, dialectics is the investigation of the contradictions *in the essence* of the things themselves; it is not only the appearances which are ephemeral, mobile, flowing, limited only by certain milestones, but also the essences of things" (Selsam and Martel 1963, 131).

Precisely in focusing on contradiction as the dynamic motivation behind any materialist theory of reflection, Brecht refuses the contemplative temper of Lukács' cognitive rationalism (see Lovell 1980, 68–76; Jameson 1971, 160–205). Brecht follows Lenin in situating the text (literary form, technique, genre) within the practical exigencies of the class struggle (Lang and Williams 1972). Using concrete (concrete = unity of the manifold) analysis to disaggregate the parts of what appears like a fixed solid complex of circumstances, Brecht devises a dramaturgy of anti-

Physis which poses the question: "What is to be done in such a situation?" In this concern for collective learning and action, Roland Barthes (1972) suggests, lies Brecht's virtues of responsibility and intelligence.

While the poststructuralist critic may discount Brecht's preoccupation with alienation-effect as merely an offshoot of his project of unfolding the causal nexus, "the network of social relationships," constituting any event, I think Brecht cannot be classified simply as an exponent of "epistemological conventionalism." He certainly does not subscribe to the theorem of the undecidability of meaning entailed by the alleged disappearance of the referent. Brecht's aesthetics includes a rhetorical or pragmatic moment within the cognitive: because what is represented in theater is not empirical montage of phenomena but the laws of social motion, to accomplish the task of provoking the audience to rational action, it is necessary to enforce critical distance. Techniques of defamiliarization and displacement are deployed to break routine and undercut habits of "common sense" that hide the possibilities for change in the nexus of events and actors (Brecht 1964). The knowledge induced by this syncopated or stylized realism involves the recipient's perception of such possibilities, a perception indistinguishable from a learning process where pleasure coincides with the questioning of reality. This critical response involves a desire to experiment and transform the given situation. Brecht thus rejects organic art that reconciles everything into an illusory self-contained whole. After describing the non-organic character of avant-garde art in which elements are not neutralized by being swallowed in a structure divorced from the praxis of life, Peter Burger (1984) highlights Brecht's method of breaking up the unified structure of plot or imagery by means of distancing/estranging performance. In this way Brecht allows the political-ethical potential of the work to produce its impact on the audience, no longer paralyzed by art's narcosis.

It is clear that Brecht's overriding purpose is to mobilize individual energies for organized, directed intervention in changing society, a goal to which the choice of forms or technical means is subordinate. Exposing the mutability of social relations, disclosing institutions and reflexes as artificial or constructed, revealing the process of justification behind legitimacy claims—all these require the will to subvert one-dimensional, fetishizing, and commodified "forms of life." The strategy also calls for the differential production of meaning through the act of demythologizing public consensus and demystifying received norms. Historicizing texts—making visible the dynamics of ideological-material production in shaping them—demonstrates and confirms the capacity of humans to collectively shape their world and realize man's unique species-being. Brecht's materialism reinscribes the reader/spectator as a type of potential revolutionary agency in the interstices of a conflicted totality, a society in process of transformation.

In what I consider a "touchstone" manifesto, "The Popular and the Realistic" (circa 1938), Brecht proposes a definition of realism admirable for its lucidity and latitude:

> Our conception of *realism* needs to be broad and political, free from aes-
> thetic restrictions and independent of convention. *Realist* means: laying
> bare society's causal network / showing up the dominant viewpoint as
> the viewpoint of the dominators / writing from the standpoint of the
> class which has prepared the broadest solutions for the most pressing
> problems afflicting human society / emphasizing the dynamics of devel-
> opment / concrete and so as to encourage abstraction. (1964, 109; see
> Bloch 1977, 68–85)

While the semantics of realism is chiefly conditioned by class and historic conjuncture, "popular" here may be construed as an interpellation of a united front or historic bloc somewhat analogous to Gramsci's notion of "national-popular culture"
(which I discuss later) catalyzed in the conquest of hegemony. Three years before
he died, Brecht reiterated his demand for art's "broad intelligibility," its harnessing
of the progressive elements in a national tradition, and its project of socialist realism
as "a deeply human, earth-oriented art which will liberate every human capacity."
Polemicizing against the pontifications of party bureaucrats, Brecht summed up his
conception of socialist realism which may be profitably contrasted to Zhdanov's
dogmatic caricature (Morawski 1974). Socialist realism, for Brecht, embraces two
central themes: first, socialist realist works reveal characters and events as contradictory, plastic, and alterable, laying bare "the dialectical laws of movement of the
social mechanism" so that the "mastering of man's fate" is made easier. And second, socialist realist works provoke "pleasure at the possibility of society's mastering man's fate," pleasure confluent with "socialist impulses." Underlying this
second proposition is the primacy of a working-class outlook that strives "to raise
human productivity to an undreamt-of extent by transforming society and abolishing exploitation" (Lang and Williams 1972, 226–27).

What Brecht adds to Caudwell's notion of the genotype (the collective
impulse of human desire) and to Lukács' axiom of typicality is a more thorough
dialectical grasp of contradiction as the driving force behind social processes (see
"A Short Organon for the Theater," section 45). Brecht also puts a premium on
socially shared pleasure, a move which transposes the utopian vision (Marx's sense
of "becoming" and "disappearance" of contradictions) into a sensuous, "earthly"
performance. Brecht seems to re-articulate in his own language Lenin's hermeneutic discovery of the lacunae and discrepancies in Tolstoy's texts when Brecht foregrounds the pleasure-yielding effect of experiencing the ordeals of solidarity and
struggle. Brecht's "Organon" concludes with the accent on process while evoking
the portentous advent of the Marxian "sublime":

> our representations must take second place to what is represented, men's
> life together in society; and the pleasure felt in their perfection must be
> converted into the higher pleasure felt when the rules emerging from

this life in society are treated as imperfect and provisional. In this way the theater leaves its spectators productively disposed even after the spectacle is over. Let us hope that their theatre may allow them to enjoy as entertainment that terrible and never-ending labor which should ensure their maintenance, together with the terror of their unceasing transformation. Let them here produce their own lives in the simplest way, for the simplest way of living is in art. (1964, 77)

The antinomies of form and content, style and theme, the popular and the realistic qualities in artworks, which took center stage in the debate between Lukács and Brecht, can be traced in the fractured and unresolved texts of Marxist cultural politics—from Trotsky's *Literature and Revolution* (1936), the "negative dialectics" of Frankfurt critical theory, Mao's influential *Talks at the Yenan Forum on Literature and Art* (1942), Sartre's existentialist inflection of praxis, and Fidel Castro's "Words to the Intellectuals" (1961), not to mention the substantial contributions of C.L.R. James, Roque Dalton, Cesar Vallejo, Ngugi Wa Thiongo, and many others. Questions about which element has primacy—form or content, authorial will or audience reception, political correctness or technical efficacy, and so on—can perhaps be clarified by examining next Gramsci's theory of hegemony as a political-ideological strategy founded on a recovery of Marx's idea of "praxis" noted earlier.

Let us recall that in "Theses on Feuerbach" Marx not only stressed the centrality of "human sensuous activity, practice," which defines the substance of social life; he also stated that "the human essence is not an abstraction inherent in each single individual" but is in fact indivisible from "the ensemble of social relations." No longer "civil society" and its foundation in private property, but "socialized humanity" is the point of departure as well as telos of revolutionary action. Contrary to the one-sided culturalist reading of Gramsci's thought which gives pride of place to ideology above the political, I submit that the site of hegemony is not just civil society but the totality of social relations where production and the state, economic base and ideological superstructure, constitute an ongoing process of shifting power alignments; in short, class subordination and dominance (Merrington 1977; Mercer 1978; Mouffe 1979; Sassoon 1980).

We can define Gramsci's concept of hegemony as a totalizing revolutionary strategy motivated by his emphasis on Marxism as "the philosophy of praxis," "the historicist conception of reality," which Gramsci elaborates in reaction to the Crocean problematic of art as intuition:

If one cannot think of the individual apart from society, and thus if one cannot think of any individual who is not historically conditioned, it is obvious that every individual, including the artist and all his activities, cannot be thought of apart from society, a specific society. Hence the artist does not write or paint—that is, he does not externalize his phantasms—just for his own recollection, to be able to relive the moment of creation. He is an artist only insofar as he externalizes, objectifies and historicizes his phantasms. Every artist-individual, though, is such in a more or less broad and comprehensive way, he is "historical" or "social" to a greater or lesser degree. (1985, 112)

By contextualizing the artist in a historically specific milieu, Gramsci qualifies all aesthetic questions as ultimately political in essence insofar as they are inscribed in culture grasped as a lived cross-section of social life, not an abstract or simply functional institution. Raymond Williams conveys to us the physiognomy of Gramsci's idea by conceiving hegemony as "a whole body of practices and expectations, over the whole of living: our senses and assignments of energy, our shaping perceptions of ourselves and our world. It is a lived system of meanings and values—constitutive and constituting—which as they are experienced as practices appear as reciprocally confirming" (1977, 110). But this process of establishing hegemony is not a spontaneous phenomenon. It is mediated by a new category of organic (as opposed to traditional) intellectuals whose command over material and intellectual knowledge endows them with a "directive" power to fashion ideologies that gradually become "common sense" through a complex network of consensus formation. Public and private spheres thus fuse in the project of cultural mediation where critical intervention—what I call "the Leninist moment"—transpires.

Gramsci's purpose in articulating the prospect of proletarian hegemony is connected with his goal of creating a national-popular culture where the moral-intellectual leadership of the proletariat is exercised. This culture serves as the key to translating "the philosophy of praxis" into common sense. Conversely, such a project also organizes and refines common sense into a scientific worldview. Put in orthodox terms, the hegemonic drive for a national-popular culture will eliminate the division between mental and manual labor, between city and countryside, which Marx envisioned in the *Manifesto*, the *Critique of the Gotha Program*, and elsewhere. Two passages indicate how Gramsci envisions the act of transposing the purely aesthetic problem into a cultural-ideological mode of radical transformation:

The premiss of the new literature cannot but be historical, political, and popular. It must aim at elaborating that which already is, whether polemically or in some other way does not matter. What does matter, though, is that it sink its roots into the humus of popular culture as it is, with its tastes and tendencies and with its moral and intellectual world, even if it is backward and conventional. (1985, 102–3)

Concretely "genuine" and "fundamental" humanity can mean only one thing in the artistic field: "historicity," that is, the "national-popular" character of the writer, but in the broad sense of "sociality," which can also be taken in the artistic sense so long as the social group that is being expressed is historically alive and the social connection not of an immediate "practico-political" nature. In other words, it must not be predicatory and moralistic, but historical and ethico-political. (Boelhower 1981, 585)

In the first quote, Gramsci grounds the terms "historical, political, and popular" in the realm of everyday life, of "common sense" however corrupted or distorted by unjust and exploitative social relations. In the second quote, he equates "historicity" with "national-popular" and "sociality," underscoring the mimetic or representational task of the artist who "realizes" the immanent direction of the historical process—realism here implying partisanship, tendentiousness. In this way he avoids the recalcitrant form-content dualism of traditional aesthetics I have alluded to earlier. By means of the category "national-popular" as applied specifically to Italian conditions, Gramsci historicizes the concept of hegemony by liberating it from class essentialism or economistic simplification. He sutures the theory of hegemony with the long-range project of nation-building peculiar to Italy's condition. Gramsci envisages the task of national liberation against foreign occupiers, or its spiritual counterpart, cosmopolitanism, as one that pursues its fulfillment via the formation of a popular historic bloc of various classes—in another context, the route of the Frente Sandinista in Nicaragua, for example.

From this point it is only a short step to reconceptualizing the dialectical linkage between form and content by their thorough historical grounding in specific conjunctures. The metaphysical problematic of Kant, Hegel, and Croce is thereby displaced or resituated in the site of specific predicaments. Gramsci contends for a dialectical interpretation of the polarity: "Can one speak of a priority of content over form? One can in this sense: the work of art is a process and changes of content [ways of thinking] are also changes of form [language]. . . . Therefore, 'form' and 'content' have a 'historical' meaning besides an 'aesthetic' one" (Boelhower 1981, 586). Caudwell's dilemma of how to correlate technique and content is resolved here by Gramsci's translation of abstract terms into concrete, group-based practices.

What unfolds in Gramsci's reflection is a materialist contextualization of the content-form duality in a process of discursive production: "historical form signifies a determinate language, while 'content' signifies a determinate way of thinking" (Dombroski 1984, 52). For Gramsci, then, the objectification or historicization of what is imagined (phantasy activity, for Caudwell) not only proceeds in the mind but, more decisively, coincides with the "forming" process (*poiesis*) which necessarily operates with material, sensorily apprehensible media, channels, devices, etc. Not only are forms of thinking already structured by socially determinate values, but forms of expression and representation are also given beforehand, that is, before creative appropriation begins. This is because techniques and other linguistic or formal elements are not pure schemata or empty categories but are in fact constituted by functional, culture-bound semantic values. In short, form is ideological in essence and thus political in its wider implication. For Gramsci, however, content is not the experience but the writer's attitude to it, an attitude that ultimately shapes style: " 'technical' stands for the means by which the moral content, the moral conflict of the novel, the poem, or the drama is made comprehensible in the most immediate and dramatic way possible" (1975, 943).

While Gramsci's performance of a dialectical reading of texts such as Manzoni's *The Betrothed* or canto X of Dante's *Inferno* can be upheld as a model for a historical-materialist *explication du texte*, I would rather focus here on what I call the moment of praxis in which the critic's theoretical intervention is not just hermeneutic but also transformative in effect. In the context of cultural politics, Gramsci effects a decisive change by anchoring the activity of the imagination in the intellectual's specific, concrete milieu as well as in the integrally hegemonic function that the knowing mind as creating mind enacts:

> An historical act can only be performed by "collective man," and this presupposes the attainment of a "cultural-social" unity through which a multiplicity of dispersed wills, with heterogeneous aims, are welded together with a single aim, one basis of an equal and common conception of the world, both general and particular, operating in transitory bursts (in emotional ways) or permanently (where the intellectual base is so well rooted, assimilated and experienced that it becomes passion). (1971, 349)

Ideologies or worldviews as lived experience or "passion," in Gramsci's felicitous phrasing, form the climax of a hegemonic process in which the function of criticism free of "unilateral or fanatical ideological elements" is that of grasping the contradictions in the critic's own position in society. That is to say, the critic committed to a revolutionary vision "not only grasps the contradictions, but posits himself as an element of the contradiction and elevates this element to a principle of knowledge and therefore of action." Praxis—unity of thought and action—results from this reflexive moment. The critic incarnates the historic task of the revolutionary class and activates a principle of transformation. This principle entails an inventory comprised of the systematizing and refinement of "common sense," together with the socialization of philosophical and scientific concepts that can move society forward by releasing suppressed human potential. Of crucial importance is Gramsci's imperative to educate and empower multitudes: "That the masses could be led to think about a current reality coherently and systematically is a philosophical fact much more important and 'original' than the discovery by a philosophical 'genius' of a new truth that becomes the property of small groups of intellectuals" (1971, 325).

Because Gramsci seeks to think through the complex oscillation of "identity" and "difference" in the density of worldly circumstances, especially those gravitating around the Italian conjuncture of an industrialized North and a predominantly rural South, his cultural theorizing takes as its point of departure the Marxist-Leninist category of unequal and combined development. This complex phenomenon obtains, according to Ernesto Laclau, "when a synchronic articulation occurs between stages which Marxist theory considers as successive (for example, the articulation between democratic tasks and the socialist leadership of those tasks)" (1987, 332). Given the fact of a dislocation in the normal development of society where the bourgeoisie fails to exercise its hegemonic mission, it devolves on the working class and its organic intellectuals (in alliance with the peasantry and the middle strata) to carry out the democratic tasks of national unity and development as a crucial flank of an all-encompassing socialist project, hence the national-popular thrust of the historic bloc. Laclau emphasizes the "logic of unevenness and dislocation," that is, the logic of the signifier which "presides over the possibility/ impossibility of the constitution of any identity."

While Laclau follows this metonymic pattern of ideological constitution of the subject to the point where all categories, being historically contingent, resist totalization in a higher rationality and remain fluid in their negativity and opaqueness, Gramsci opts for a different objective. He insists on fulfilling the necessary task of constituting or identifying the historical agent (the national-popular will, the historic bloc) that will release potential human energies stifled by repressive social relations. The mediating or catalyzing force in this project is the organic intellectual of the working class. History, for Gramsci, does not move in a linear one-dimensional fashion where base and superstructure always coincide, especially in dependent zones of the capitalist world system. Precisely because Gramsci perceives the diverse, uneven, and unstable mentalities that comprise any given social formation, he is compelled to postulate the mediating subject that will attempt totalization of the social process. I refer here to the hegemonic collective subject— in aesthetics, the revolutionary artist or dialectical critic—in whose action coalesce the economic, political, and ideological moments. We confront here the praxis of revolutionary transformation.

To illustrate the unique relevance of Gramsci's analysis to Third World formations where unequal and combined development obtains (as it did in Russia in 1917, China in 1949, Cuba in 1959, and Nicaragua in 1979), Gramsci differentiates between the sensibilities of the politician and the artist. Here he upholds the relative autonomy of the artistic from the programmatic desideratum of political action:

[T]he literary man must necessarily have a less precise and definite out-look than the politician. He must be less "sectarian," if one can put it this way, but in a "contradictory" way. For the politician, every "fixed" image is *a priori* reactionary: he considers the entire movement in its development. The artist, however, must have "fixed" images that are cast into their definite form. The politician imagines man as he is, and at the same time how he should be in order to reach a specific goal. His task is precisely to stir men up, to get them to leave their present life behind in order to become collectively able to reach the proposed goal, that is, to get them to "conform" to the goal. The artist necessarily and realistically depicts "that which is," at a given moment (the personal, the non-conformist, etc.). From the political point of view, therefore, the politician will never be satisfied with the artist and will never be able to be: he will find him always behind the times, always anachronistic and overtaken by the real flow of events. If history is a continuous process of liberation and self-awareness, it is evident that every stage (historical and in this case cultural) will be immediately surmounted and will no longer hold any interest. (1985, 110–11)

In discriminating between the political movement and the aesthetic (although it should be stressed that both are fused in the combined wars of "position" and "maneuver" of antagonistic social blocs), Gramsci distances himself from the sec-tarian elitism of the French communist Paul Nizan who condemned fellow-travellers like Malraux prior to the inauguration of the Comintern's Popular Front in 1932. Gramsci's predisposition for the necessarily heterogeneous, polychro-matic, temporally layered fabric of any society enables him to conceive of flexible strategies in achieving proletarian hegemony:

[M]oral and intellectual renewal does not develop simultaneously in all of the social strata. On the contrary, it is worth repeating that even today many people are Ptolemaic and not Copernican. There are many "con-formisms," many struggles for new "conformisms" and various combi-nation of that which already exists (variously expressed) and that which one is working to bring about (and there are many people who are working in this direction). It is a serious error to adopt a "single" pro-gressive strategy according to which each new gain accumulates and becomes the premiss of further gains. Not only are the strategies multi-ple, but even in the "most progressive" ones there are retrogressive moments. Furthermore, Nizan does not know how to deal with so-called "popular literature," that is, with the success of serial literature (adventure stories, detective stories, thrillers) among the masses, a success that is assisted by the cinema and the newspapers. And yet, it is this question that represents the major part of the problem of a new literature as the expression of moral and intellectual renewal, for only from the readers of serial literature can one select a sufficient and necessary public for creating the cultural base of the new literature. (1985, 101–02)

From this passage, one can ascertain what unifies Gramsci's ad hoc cultural reflections in prison, namely, the overriding task of moral and intellectual renewal of the whole society premised on the integration of the most highly developed philosophies (*Weltanschauungen*) with plebeian "common sense," folklore, and other disenfranchised and stigmatized forms of cultural production (for the "community in the aesthetic," see Haug 1987).

Gramsci's obsession is precisely the articulation of the intellectual's hegemonic vocation. This can be described also, following Debray's formulation, as the historical "implantation" of Marxism in a given national-popular tradition (1970, 48–52), the "translation" and at the same time transmutation of concrete life (common sense) into a constitutive and regulative philosophy: Marxism as the unity of the theory and practice of class struggle. This is the locus of synthesizing form and content, thought and action. Cognizant of the materiality of ideology and its specific modes of inscription, negotiation, and appropriation by social groups, Gramsci is not blind to initiatives originating from the petty bourgeois stratum. Witness his acclaim of Futurism as a decisive rupture in bourgeois hegemony generating a revolutionary effect which the socialists of his day refused to acknowledge because of their productivist bias and narrow-minded class reductionism. In this casual jotting on Futurism which I consider a benchmark-milestone in Marxist critical theorizing, Gramsci distinguishes between the rationally plotted seizure of state power and the kaleidoscopic convergence of various lines of transition which defies blueprint calculation. We watch here the performance of the theory of uneven/combined development:

> The battlefield for the creation of a new civilization is . . . absolutely mysterious, absolutely characterized by the unforeseeable and the unexpected. Having passed from capitalist power to workers' power, the factory will continue to produce the same material things that it produces today. But in what way and under what forms will poetry, drama, the novel, music, painting and moral and linguistic works be born? It is not a material factory that produces these works. It cannot be reorganized by a workers' power according to a plan. One cannot establish its rate of production for the satisfaction of immediate needs, to be controlled and determined statistically. Nothing in this field is foreseeable except for this general hypothesis: there will be a proletarian culture (a civilization) totally different from the bourgeois one and in this field too class distinctions will be shattered. . . . What remains to be done? Nothing other

than to destroy the present form of civilization. In this field "to destroy" does not mean the same as in the economic field. It does not mean to deprive humanity of the material products that it needs to subsist and to develop. It means to destroy spiritual hierarchies, prejudices, idols and ossified traditions. It means not to be afraid of innovations and audacities, not to be afraid of monsters, not to believe that the world will collapse if a worker makes grammatical mistakes, if a poem limps, if a picture resembles a hoarding or if young men sneer at academic and feeble-minded senility. The Futurists have carried out this task in the field of bourgeois culture. . . . [The Futurists] have grasped sharply and clearly that our age, the age of big industry, of the large proletarian city and of intense and tumultuous life, was in need of new forms of art, philosophy, behavior and language. This sharply revolutionary and absolutely *Marxist* idea came to them when the Socialists were not even vaguely interested in such a question. . . . In their field, the field of culture, the Futurists are revolutionaries. (1985, 50–51)

Except for his predilection for planning ahead, Brecht would be in complete sympathy with Gramsci's nuanced appraisal of a whole epoch in terms of the shifting relations of forces. After World War I, however, Futurism in Italy changed and broke up into different trends; it ceased to play a regenerative role. Gramsci informs Trotsky in a letter circa 1923: "The workers, who had seen in Futurism the elements of a struggle against academic Italian culture, fossilized and remote from the popular masses, had to fight for their freedom with weapons in their hands and had little interest in the old arguments" (1985, 54).

When we examine next Gramsci's assessment of Pirandello as another illustration of a dialectical mode of reading, we observe an analogous focus on the cultural rather than the narrowly artistic dimension of textuality. Maintaining his belief that "a national-cultural unity of the Italian people does not yet exist, that 'provincialism' and particularism are still deeply rooted in their customs and in the way they think and act," Gramsci contends that "Pirandello's importance seems to me to be more of an intellectual and moral, i.e. cultural, than an artistic kind. He has tried to introduce into popular culture the 'dialectics of modern philosophy, in opposition to the Aristotelian-Catholic way of conceiving the 'objectivity of the real' " (1985, 138, 145).

Viewing Pirandello's plays as organic extensions of the "physical personality of the writer," a personality which amalgamates the Sicilian, the Italian and the European, Gramsci apprehends the artist's self-conscious rendering of this multifaceted sensibility as the source of "his artistic weakness along with his great 'cultural' significance." The latter inheres in Pirandello's anti-Catholic (as opposed to the humanitarian and positivist bourgeois worldview) conception of the world and its fertile "dialectical conception of objectivity." Gramsci estimates highly the dramatist's educational impact. Because Pirandellian ideology is not bookish or tendentious but "linked to lived historico-cultural experiences," it succeeds in deprovincializing and modernizing the Italian public's taste (the petty bourgeois and philistine culture of the late nineteenth century) and combatting both Catholic idealism and bourgeois positivism. Gramsci thus judges any modernist or avant-garde impulse within the parameter of the hegemonic drive to invent and mobilize a national-popular identity: Pirandello "has done much more than the Futurists towards 'deprovincializing' the 'Italian man' and arousing a modern 'critical' attitude in opposition to the traditional, nineteenth-century 'melodramatic' attitude" (1985, 139).

"Humans make their history" but under the shadow of determinate constraints. And to these constraints of reification and alienation, one response in the archive is Lukács' humanist ethos and its "united front" impetus: the affirmation of totality and the typical, a modus operandi that sometimes courts the risk of downplaying the often incommensurable contradictions that blur the "mirror of social life" (Plekhanov). Another is Caudwell's machine of "collective phantasy" that channels libidinal investments toward materializing in actuality the dream of freedom and happiness. Art is indeed a form of spiritual production, but capitalism with its culture industry and the logic of private appropriation has imposed its own rigorous totality on this domain. In *Theories of Surplus Value*, Marx reminds us:

> Milton, who did the *Paradise Lost* for five pounds, was an *unproductive laborer*. On the other hand, the writer who turns out stuff for his publisher in factory style, is a *productive laborer*. . . . The literary proletarian of Leipzig, who fabricates books. . . under the direction of his publisher, is a *productive laborer*, for his product is from the outset subsumed under capital, and comes into being only for the purpose of increasing that capital. A singer who sells her song for her own account is an *unproductive laborer*. But the same singer commissioned by an entrepreneur to sing in order to make money for him is a *productive laborer*, for she produces capital. (Wolff 1983, 6)

Given the irony in which "consumption produces production" for capital, Brecht (like his friend Walter Benjamin) stressed the need to revolutionize the means and repertoire of artistic production, including the formal properties of theater, so as to release their power to radicalize the masses. Reception aesthetics and reader-response protocols are not innocent ventures; both are motivated by the exploitative interests not of interpretive communities but of the institutions that reproduce normality, the status quo, quotidian business; hence the need not only for critical-realist "reflection" but also a semiotics and pragmatics of distanciation. From this staging of reversal and disaffiliation, "organic" intellectuals need to induce in the people that moment of "catharsis" (in Gramsci's definition) in which the ethical-moral sensibility merges with political calculation in a revolutionary breakthrough. This itinerary of a certain historical-materialist vision of praxis is what I have tried to outline in this excursus.

One conclusion emerges from this necessarily selective and schematic review of the vicissitudes of Marxist inquiries into the politics of aesthetics: without the focus on the moment of praxis—the artist's or critic's intervention in the concrete arena of political struggle for hegemony, any rational analytic applied on art and its function will compulsively repeat the metaphysical idealism it seeks to overcome. In his sagacious study of the ideology of Western aesthetics, Terry Eagleton reminds us of Marx's inaugural insight that the emancipated senses are "theoreticians in their immediate praxis" (1990, 204). Gramsci echoes this in his idea that human consciousness or subjectivity can be fully grasped only in its overdetermined trajectory as a complex of material practices functioning in conserving or distintegrating a determinate conjuncture, a lived situation. Without positing this moment of rupture or opening for intervention, we shall reproduce the predicament of the bourgeois intellectual that Caudwell, Lukács, Sartre, and other Marxist thinkers acutely diagnosed: the division of mental and manual labor; the antinomy between subject and object, fact and value, nature and history—ideological reflexes of commodity production. These are the contradictions that praxis (somehow always revolutionary in translating the desire of multitudes) hopes to eventually resolve, despite setbacks and mistakes.

One way of blocking this compulsion to repeat mechanical or essentializing practices is to compose a totalizing but wayward narrative, a space (cognitive and pragmatic at the same time) where values/meanings compete within the framework of a self-reflexive socialist project—the vicissitudes of ideas in this essay somehow already anticipate the destination of this desire. This will also be the moment when a kind of Marxist self-recognition of its authentic vision may crystallize in the tension of juxtaposed practices consonant with facing the concrete political problems ushered by the era of late-modern global commodification with its more rabid capital accumulation and exhaustion of the ecosystem. Such a task commands priority in the agenda of democratic-socialist intellectuals everywhere.

Part Two

Reconfigurations

Transformation

4

Prospectus to an Aesthetics of "Imaginary Relations"

Almost three decades have now passed since the 1966 publication of Pierre Macherey's *Pour une theorie de la production litteraire* (*A Theory of Literary Production*, English translation published in 1978), a path-breaking theoretical achievement in literary and aesthetic theory within the overarching tradition of Western Marxism. This advance, however, remains hitherto unacknowledged. Except for Terry Eagleton's *Criticism and Ideology* and a passing reference to it in the guidebooks, Macherey's labor has been to a large extent neglected although there is some presumption that it has already been appropriated and even surpassed. The seminal importance of Macherey's reflections, its heuristic and pedagogical value, can be appreciated by its resonance in such works as diverse as Catherine Belsey's *Critical Practice*, Michael Sprinker's *Imaginary Relations*, Ellen Rooney's *Seductive Reasoning*, and Eileen Sypher's *Wisps of Violence*. Macherey and Etienne Balibar's essay, "On Literature as an Ideological Form," promises to be the definitive if controversial manifesto of the Althusserian revolution in the cultural politics of the last quarter of this century.

My purpose in this brief survey is not to eulogize one thinker's accomplishment—Macherey is only one of the many insightful critics inspired by Althusser's "structuralist" rethinking of classical Marxist doctrines—but to arouse anyone concerned in what is at stake in the contemporary debate on global cultural politics— questions pertaining to the subject in postmodernism; of the ethical/political implications of discourses on race, class, gender; the contextual pressures of global realignments on reading, interpretation, and the current revision of canons and disciplines. Ultimately, what underlies this attempt is my continuing project to rethink and perhaps renew an authentically creative, materialist critical practice in the zone where Third World popular-democratic struggles connect with the preoccupations of Western Marxism. This "return" to a Marxist practice in this domain of what I would call "world cultural studies," a field so far only intuited by students of Frantz Fanon and C.L.R. James, is being consciously attempted on the face of the current vogue (especially in elite intellectual circles) of skeptical relativism, pragmatic fundamentalism, and various forms of modish, obscurantist thinking that have grown to exercise a de facto hegemony in the wake of the collapse of "actually existing socialism" and the persisting weakness of resistance movements in the First World. The publication of *The Althusserian Legacy*, edited by E. Ann Kaplan and Michael Sprinker, as well as the continuing debates on the structuralist/poststructuralist transition, betoken an imminent "return of the repressed" even when both seem to be anachronistic in an age of surfaces and repetitions.

One way of presenting the originality of Macherey's work is by pointing to what is traditional in it. The cardinal principle in Marx and Engel's materialist conception of history inheres in the centrality of labor (practice, in general) around which the narrative of the revolutionary transformation of society pivots. In the 1857 *Preface to A Contribution to the Critique of Political Economy*, Marx foregrounds the decisive role of social production in shaping human nature and collective life. Engel's essay, "Labor in the Transition from Ape to Man," posits labor as "the prime basic condition for all human existence." Labor mediates consciousness and nature, thought and the physical environment. It generates culture and the condition required for actualizing human "species-being" in history. Though degraded by the alienation and reification in class societies, labor as self-activity, or sensuous critical practice (see "Theses on Feuerbach"), is the fundamental axiom of Marx's philosophy. Marx writes in *Capital*: "Labor is, in the first place, a process in which both man and Nature participate, and in which man of his own accord starts, regulates, and controls the material re-actions between himself and Nature. . . . By thus acting on the external world and changing it, he at the same time changes his own nature" (Solomon 1973, 22). The germinal insight privileging art as one kind of production was enunciated by Marx in the *Economic and Philosophic Manuscripts of 1844*:

> Conscious life-activity directly distinguishes man from animal life-activity. . . . In creating an objective world by his practical activity, in working-up inorganic nature, man proves himself a conscious species being, i.e., as a being that treats the species as its own essential being, or that treats itself as a species being. Admittedly animals also produce. . . . But an animal only produces what it immediately needs for itself or its young. It produces one-sidedly, whilst man produces universally. It produces only under the dominion of immediate physical need, whilst man produces even when he is free from physical need and only truly produces in freedom therefrom. An animal produces only itself, whilst man reproduces the whole of nature. An animal's product belongs immediately to its physical body, whilst man freely confronts his product. An animal forms things in accordance with the standard and the need of the species to which it belongs, whilst man knows how to produce in accor-

dance with the standard of every species, and knows how to apply everywhere the inherent standard to the object. Man therefore also forms things in accordance with the laws of beauty. (Solomon 1973, 25–26)

Consubstantial then with all transformative labor is an artistic impulse, a practice of fashioning beautiful artifices, that distinguishes the expenditure of energy by humans from that of animals.

Orthodox Marxism has habitually considered art as a superstructural phenomenon arising from its base in production relations, to use the familiar jargon. The two are associated in terms of correspondence, representation, homology or mechanical duplication. In this framework, art expresses a "definite form of social consciousness," a class-oriented ideology. This canonical proposition, vulgarized to "economic determinism" or positivist "reflectionism," has served as the foundational idea for all subsequent conceptualization of art in the Marxist archive. Both Plekhanov and Lukács applied Engel's criterion of the "typical" in their aesthetic judgment. Meanwhile, Christopher Caudwell stressed the utopian phantasy-work of poetry in his anthropological speculations in *Illusion and Reality*; and Lucien Goldmann focused on the homology between genres and collective worldviews. Althusser broke away from tradition by postulating the object of knowledge, art in this case, as a product that cannot be conflated with reality nor with the subject. The "relative autonomy" of the ideological level needs to be upheld. Macherey follows Althusser in conceiving art as a form of production with its own materials and means, a view that has been argued most forcefully by Walter Benjamin, Bertolt Brecht, and Ernst Bloch in their debate with the advocates of official "social realism."

A summary of Althusser's theoretical intervention is required in order to grasp the import and serviceableness of Macherey's contribution. It is also necessary in order to remind the reader that the still prevalent Cold War distortion of Marxism as a species of economic determinism and totalitarian terrorism—propagated by textbooks like *Literary Criticism* by William K. Wimsatt, Jr. and Cleanth Brooks, or *Critical Approaches to Literature* by David Daiches—still enjoys currency. Meanwhile, the deconstructionists are still trying to reduce "Marxist ideology" to a matter of tropes (anamorphosis), an error of a homogenized reading (Derrida 1981).

While the significance and validity of Althusser's recovery of the "authentic" Marx is still a topic of controversy, there prevails a consensus (Callinicos 1976; McLennan 1977; Hirst 1979; Geras 1986) that his key ideas—society as a complex differentiated whole structured in dominance; overdetermination, problematic, epistemological break, symptomatic reading—have clarified if not refuted to some degree certain distortions of Marxism. What empiricism (humanism, idealism) and essentialism (economism, historicism) have in common is their adherence to the notion of "expressive causality": one element in the system can account for every-thing. Empiricism refers to the view that knowledge is derived by the subject abstracting the essence from the real object; thought encounters reality without any mediation and derives from that the external guarantee of its truth. Knowledge is here conceived as vision, a perception and possession of the essence of an imme-diately given object. There is no separation of the object grasped in thought (con-crete-in-thought) and the object in reality (real-concrete). Empiricism underlies a theory of artistic realism which presupposes that reality can be immediately expressed or captured in the mirror of art provided the artist selects the essential elements of what is reflected.

Essentialism, on the other hand, holds that all phenomena in the linear con-tinuum of history can be reduced to an original essence, a totalizing Spirit/Mind, or a telos such as freedom or progress. The Hegelian dialectic of consciousness where various moments are conceived as externalizations of one internal principle (for example, Rome expresses the abstract legal personality) can be illustrated by various historicisms which reduce the knowledge of history to the self-conscious-ness of a subject, or by varieties of formalist criticism where a rhetorical mechanism (irony, paradox, aporia), or a universal *episteme*, is held to be the organizing princi-ple of the work. A recent version of this instantiation model is the categorization of postmodern art as pastiche, "incredulity to metanarratives," or preponderance of the simulacra. By confusing the object of knowledge with the real object and thus negating the differences in specific practices that constitute the complexity of any social formation, empiricism and essentialism have prevented any genuine under-standing of society as a decentered structure, a complex articulated whole with mutually determining levels or instances, each a necessary condition for the others. It has misconstrued the place of science and ideology (culture in general) within the concrete social formation.

Althusser's project of defining the specificity of Marxist philosophy as the the-ory of historical materialism that specifically deals with social formations and their history—that is, the theory of the history of the production of knowledge, the the-ory and history of science—hinges on the fundamental concept of practice. Knowledge, for Althusser, is not obtained through vision but through production, specifically in the form of theoretical practice occurring in the domain of thought. For Macherey, criticism as theoretical practice moves beyond ideology (unprocessed lived experience) in order to approximate the status of a science. "All levels of social existence are the sites of distinct practices," Althusser argues (1969, 229), with their specific effectivities that are mutually determining of each other and the whole configuration. This is an idea attributed to Marx's discovery of "a historico-dialectical materialism of praxis, . . . a theory of different specific *levels of human practice*" (economic, political, ideological, scientific) interacting with one another and with the totality they constitute.

"By practice in general," Althusser writes, "I shall mean any process of *trans-formation* of a determinate given raw material into a determinate *product*, a transfor-mation effected by a determinate human labour using determinate means (of 'production'). In any practice thus conceived, the *determinant* moment (or element) is neither the raw material nor the product, but the practice in the narrow sense: the moment of the *labour of transformation* itself, which sets to work, in a specific structure, men, means and a technical method of utilizing the means" (1969, 166–67). Each practice embodies the "structure of a production." Where art con-sists of the transformation of a given raw material (ideologically saturated experi-ence) into a specific product (text, art work) by means of a labor process and means/instruments of production (forms of linguistic practice, conventions), then art is properly understood as a mode of production with its distinctive processes, rhythms, and regularities. Macherey rejects the humanist conception of art as organic creation by an autonomous subject in favor of the view that art is a product shaped "*in determinate conditions.*"

Althusserian Marxism then revolves around this theorizing of distinct prac-tices and modes of production as the core of its epistemology and ontology. In the realm of epistemology, Althusser postulates three categories: Generality I desig-nates the concepts, intuitions, and abstractions that serve as the raw material of the-oretical practice; Generality II refers to the theory of science at a given moment (the problematic), the conceptual means for the production of knowledge brought to bear on the raw materials aforementioned and that sets limits to the posing of problems and their resolutions, in short, a distinct production process; Generality III refers to the product of the process described, a transformed theoretical entity: concrete scientific concepts embodying knowledge. What needs emphasis is the problematic associated with Generality II: the theoretical framework (paradigm) that correlates the basic concepts and presuppositions, specifies the nature and sig-nificance of each concept by its place and function in the system of relationships, and also enables the positing of certain propositions and the omission of others. The problematic in Marx's writings before 1857, according to Althusser, is the drama of human alienation and self-realization conditioned by the flawed ideology of humanism; the later Marx abandoned that problematic and so inaugurated the new, unprecedented science called "historical materialism."

One should not mistake the problematic with a worldview or *episteme.* This analytic organon cannot be equated with the essence of a thought, the "true ker-nel" extracted by an empirical reading of texts, since "it is centered on the *absence* of problems and concepts within the problematic as much as by their presence" (1970, 316). By determining what is to be included in a discourse, the problematic also thereby chooses what is to be excluded; hence the absences, lacunae, ruptures, silence. These elided questions, as well as those problems that are prematurely or not adequately posed (signalled by lapses, catachresis, fallacies), constitute the prob-lematic as much as those questions and concepts present. Given the nature of the problematic as the "unconscious" structure of theoretical discourse, a literal or empirical reading cannot apprehend it. A problematic can only be grasped by a symptomatic reading, not by an empiricist or idealist hermeneutics grounded on a myth of direct communication or identification with the logos. A symptomatic reading is peculiarly sensitive not only to the "sightings" but to the oversights, omissions, occlusions, interruptions; it analyzes, not merely records, the textual mechanisms that produce the oversights, omissions, and erasures.

In describing the differential and uneven structure of the social formation, Althusser (1970) deploys concepts derived from Freudian psychoanalysis, such as displacement, condensation, and overdetermination. They operate to characterize the effects of multiple contradictions in each practice and on the formation as a whole, and vice versa. A symptomatic reading would be precisely attuned to register those intricate process of mutual determinations—the pattern of dominance and subordination, antagonism and non-antagonism of the contradictions in the structure in dominance—at any given historical conjuncture (all elements are asymmetrically related but autonomous and contradictory, though one level of the social formation—either political, economic, ideological, or theoretical—acts as dominant, with the economic functioning as an absent determinant "in the last instance," its causality only grasped in its effects). To avoid reductionism, it is imperative to grasp society in its full complex mutations, as a decentered historical process—"a process without a subject." In this "ever pre-given complexly structured whole," individual subjects serve as supports or "bearers" of the structures and relations of the social formation.

Aside from this theory of specific practices inscribed in a multilayered dynamic whole (the synchronic dimension interfaced with the diachronic axis), Althusser's notion of symptomatic reading, which is partly modelled after the psychoanalytic deciphering of the patient's utterances, provides the rationale for Macherey's refusal of empiricist hermeneutics and normative criticism, its idealist sublimation. Macherey contends that interpretation, explication, "pure" or slow reading, is inadequate because the text which is overdetermined by multiple contradictions cannot spontaneously yield the object of cognition:

> We should speak of the work by moving it beyond itself, by establishing it in the knowledge of its limits. The question is then no longer one of commentary . . . but one of explanation—explanation which dislodges the work internally, just as it was obliged to deviate from its intentions in order to realize them. . . . What is the principle of the work's *disparity*? . . . It is this differential relation which will define the area of the problematic; and it is this which will enable us to present the work simultaneously in its reality and in its limits, taking into account the conditions of possibility and impossibility which make it visible. (1978, 161–62)

Macherey argues that the critic's obligatory task is to explain the principle of diversity caused by the work's relation to ideology (Eagleton 1983). Lacking any postulated unity deducible from it, the work is characterized by insufficiency, gaps, incompleteness "betokened by the confrontation of separate meanings, which is the true reason for its composition"; this incoherence demarcates the locus of the work. And this determinate complexity, the dissonant structure of the text born from the internally excluded determinations, can only be explained by a symptomatic reading:

> The structure of the work, which makes it available to knowledge, is this internal displacement, this caesura, by which it corresponds to a reality that is also incomplete, which it shows without reflecting. The literary work gives the measure of a difference, reveals a determinate absence, resorts to an eloquent silence. . . . What begs to be explained in the work is not that false simplicity . . . but the presence of a relation, or an opposition, between elements of the exposition or levels of the composition, those disparities which point to a conflict of meaning [and] reveals the inscription of an *otherness* in the work. . . . To explain the work is to show that, contrary to appearances, it is not independent, but bears in its material substance the imprint of a determinate absence which is also the principle of its identity. (1978, 79–80)

By disclosing the problematic of the text (the semantic and historical conditions of its possibility), the critic uncovers the presence of ideology that prohibits certain things from being said or represented. Therefore the critic must make those ruptures and absences speak in much the same way as the writing itself already exhibits the limits of ideology (what it cannot say) by figuration, by distancing and objectifying it through generic conventions and other devices.

In his nuanced reading of Balzac's *Les Paysans* and Verne's *The Mysterious Island*, Macherey demonstrates a theoretical practice of reading: the text is deciphered as a mode of transforming ideological materials into the objective figuration of fiction (compare Lukács' thematic exegesis of this same novel [1964]). This fictionalization is a distanciation of ideology from within, a demystification of its power by marking its limits. After sifting the raw materials—linguistic practices, generic and stylistic techniques of characterization, the conflict between the ideological project of representation and the figurative mode which thematizes it—the critic subjects them to a process of critical labor. Labor power is expended in the task of unfolding the unconscious of the text (the problematic) in order to produce Generality III: a special kind of cognition that art yields. What we know is not a reality fissured by contradictions and replicated in the text; our knowledge concerns the signifying enterprise of the text as it articulates the ideological and its operations.

Criticism achieves scientific rigor when it succeeds in explaining the work in terms of the ideological repression that constitutes it, elucidating in particular what connects and distanciates it from ideology. Criticism produces a knowledge of meaning-effect that "is an *effect* of those specific ideological-discursive strategies encoded in or produced as the text, being actively registered or productively consumed ["read"] according to, or as different ideological-discursive strategies" (Kavanagh 1982, 36). We thus attain a comprehension of the intricate and subtle mechanism of ideology, of the "imaginary relations" in which lived experience is mediated (Althusser 1971). Since the mediation of aesthetic codes and signifying conventions transforms the ideological raw materials (intuitions, beliefs, attitudes, feelings, rituals) in historically concrete ways, criticism needs to engage the two mutually constitutive moments of art as ideological form and as aesthetic/textual practice.

Given the novelty of this approach, crucial questions have been posed, among them: Is art ideology or truth? What role does this kind of critical practice play in elucidating the distinctions between art, ideology, and scientific knowledge? What are the political and ethical implications of these distinctions? Althusser's inquiry into the confluence of epistemology and aesthetics may provide clues to a general response. In his essay "The 'Piccolo Teatro': Bertollazi and Brecht," Althusser speculates on the idea of a materialist theater as a staging of an epistemological break with the ideological through various techniques of distanciation. In "A Letter on Art in Reply to André Daspre," Althusser commends in particular Macherey's reconstruction of Lenin's symptomatic reading of Tolstoy's writings. In this letter, Althusser enunciates cryptically his formula of what kind of knowledge or comprehension of society art affords through the intercession of criticism: "I believe that the peculiarity of art is to 'make us see,' 'make us perceive,' 'make us feel' something which *alludes* to reality. . . . What art makes us *see, and therefore gives to us in the form of 'seeing,' 'perceiving'* and *'feeling'* (which is not the form of knowing), is the *ideology* from which it is born, in which it bathes, from which it detaches itself as art, and to which it *alludes*" (1971, 204). Artistic practice then performs ideology, translates it into a vehicle capable of eventually producing concepts that would help construct a scientific knowledge of the lived experience refracted by ideology. Michael Sprinker succinctly encapsulates the rationale for Althusserian aesthetics: "The Althusserian science of art commences by giving the concept which would correspond to the phenomenon of the alienation-effect, since this effect is that which distinguishes the purely ideological from the aesthetic. . . . But the alienation-effect can also serve as a means for ideological interpellation, so that the work of art can therefore be said to function in two different ways: as the distantiation of ideological materials and as the production of a new ideology" (1987, 282).

Here I enter a parenthesis to call attention to the striking affinity between Althusser's argument and Brecht's program of inventing "alienation" effects that would destroy or displace the illusion of representation in bourgeois art. In plotting the strategy of the epic theater, Brecht aimed to destroy the fetishism (the imaginary coherence of the subject) in capitalist art and society that conceals the material structures (production process, institutions) underlying bourgeois legitimacy and the prevailing power relations. Inspired by the modes of juxtaposition and positioning in Chinese painting and theatrical performance, Brecht concentrated on the problem of how to achieve distanciation and displacement—what Stephen Heath (1992) designates as the "overturning movement between representation and production"—in order to promote a restructuring of perspective and induce revolutionary action. Althusser reads the Brechtian theater as an allegory of the critical practice he and Macherey are advocating:

> The play itself *is* the spectator's consciousness—for the essential reason that the spectator has no other consciousness than the content that unites him to the play in advance, and the development of this content in the play itself: the new result which the play *produces* from the self-recognition whose image and presence it is. Brecht was right: if the theater's sole object were to be even a "dialectical" commentary on this eternal self-recognition and non-recognition—then the spectator would already know the tune, it is his own. If, on the contrary, the theatre's object is to destroy this intangible image, to set in motion the immobile, the eternal sphere of the illusory consciousness's mythical world, then the play is really the development, the production of a new consciousness in the spectator—incomplete, like any other consciousness, but moved by this incompletion itself, this distance achieved, this inexhaustible work of criticism in action; the play is really the production of a new spectator, an actor who starts where the performance ends, who only starts so as to complete it, but in life. (1969, 150–51)

In a prescient way, Brecht has formulated exactly what Althusser and Macherey intend to accomplish in their theory of criticism: "the *dialectical* transformation of the totality of subjects into a *permanent crisis*," transforming "finished works into unfinished works" (Heath 1992, 255).

I return to Macherey and his exposition of Lenin's attempt to put Tolstoy's writing into a "crisis." Here Macherey offers us clues on how one may arrive at a knowledge of the radical otherness of structure, its differential but determinate irregularity, through a series of displacements. When Lenin employs the metaphor of mirror to designate the "truthfulness" of Tolstoy's rendering of historical reality, the metaphor functions not to copy or replicate (in facsimile) the real but to select from and even distort it. The reason lies in Tolstoy's personal and ideological point of view, necessarily limited and spontaneous, a class position which does not know itself as such. Lenin then inserts the writer's situation into the overdetermined totality of a revolutionary process which "is not a single conflict but a struggle articulated by a multiplicity of determinations" so that (following Althusser) "the historical process unfolds at several levels simultaneously" (1978, 121). This follows from the necessarily uneven development of the various practices in any society, with their unsynchronized tempo and rhythm. Circumscribed by the writer's class position and his contradictory beliefs, Tolstoy's work registers only partial glimpses of the whole revolutionary process; but in doing so, his art's mirror paradoxically makes "visible its own blindness without actually seeing itself" and so cannot help but reveal the whole in which it is inscribed. Lenin as critic deciphers the problematic or the "unconscious" of the text by a symptomatic reading focused on the dissymmetry between the text and its ideology. The key conflict involves Tolstoy the writer's impassioned protest against social injustice versus Tolstoy the landlord obsessed with Christ and quietist renunciation; the writer's uncompromising realism countervails the preaching of passivity and non-violence. While the first antithesis embraces the text and the contradictory site of its production, the second structures the content of the work itself: it places ideology in a relation of difference with itself, alluding to the "insufficiency" of the historical situation. In construing Tolstoy's texts as "an indirect figuration which arises from the deficiencies of the reproduction," given the incommensurable forces at play summarized by Lenin, Macherey contends that the disparities are not a reflection of the historical contradictions but rather "the consequences of the absence of this reflection." Such absence arising from the dialectic between the texts and the historical process defines the singular architectonics of Tolstoy's work.

Macherey discusses next how Lenin isolates Tolstoy's ideology of the "patriarchal naive peasant" as the cause for such absence, rift, or lack in the text. Following Althusser's thesis of ideology as the "imaginary relations" between humans and their world, the source of an imaginary unity that effaces all contradictions in actual life, Macherey points out how its presence in Tolstoy's texts is interrogated in order to make it speak "its own absences": "The text constructs a determinate image of the ideological, revealing it as an object rather than living it from within as though it were an inner conscience" (1978, 132). Tolstoy's text deconstructs ideology, turns it inside out, breaks it apart, converts its myths and mystifications into "visible objects" in order to reveal their limits.

> Even if the [specific] form of the text is itself ideological there is an internal displacement of ideology by virtue of this *redoubling*; this is not ideology contemplating itself, but the mirror-effect which exposes its insufficiency, revealing differences and discordances, or a significant incongruity. . . . Science does away with ideology, obliterates it; literature challenges ideology by using it. If ideology is thought of as a nonsystematic ensemble of significations, the work proposes a *reading* of

these significations by combining them as signs. Criticism teaches us to read these signs. (133)

While the text is contextualized in a determinate network of relationships, this analysis does not eliminate any space for the reader's (or writer's) contestation, contrary to the notion that Althusserian structuralism rules out agency. In fact the opposite is true: the emphasis here is on active participation—production of a knowledge (aesthetic science) of the text as production of knowledge (transformative critique). The critic's job is necessary and cannot be deferred if we want to transcend the seductive fetishism of the text and gain a scientific understanding of its historical conditions of possibility.

John Frow has summed up Macherey's innovative procedure as the "displacement of the problematic of an expressive or representational relation between two disparate realms" (21): on one hand, the text is inscribed as a component in the general system of social production, its "institutional conditions of existence"; on the other, the text is conceived as "a distinct practice of signification which is related not to a nondiscursive truth but to other practices of signification" (1986, 21). On the whole, Macherey has cogently argued the case that literary production demands recognition as an autonomous mode of practice irreducible to an origin, ground, or cause.

My purpose here is not to establish at this late date another sectarian orthodoxy but the humble one of trying to mark the frontier at which a scientific criticism initiated by Althusser's "discoveries" has so far advanced. Macherey's research program indicates a route for further exploration. Along this route, this pertinacious question often comes up: If the textual production of fiction, which unmasks by objectifying ideological mirages, yields us knowledge through the mediation of criticism (symptomatic reading), what is the status of this knowledge compared to that attained in science? Note that this is a knowledge produced by critical practice or discourse, not by the literary text. David Forgacs observes that what we get from Macherey is a descriptive and non-evaluative theory because Macherey "does not see literary works as containing a *knowledge* of reality which the critic can judge as being either correct or not. He sees them rather as productions or workings of things in reality, and knowledge in his approach is something the *critic* brings to bear on them" (1982, 182). One way of responding to this is to echo Althusser's assertion that symptomatic criticism is the enactment of class struggle in the field of literary criticism, an intervention whose ultimate political effects depend on the complex field of interacting practices. More challenging is the charge that Macherey's theory is one more version of conventionalism (Terry Lovell [1980] indicts Althusser for this deviation in the context of reviewing the debates between Lukács and modernists like Brecht). Answers to these objections may be found in our effort to ascertain the "logic" of responsibility, even the ethics of conceptualizing agency, that informs Balibar and Macherey's (1981) synthesis of Althusser,

Freud, and Gramsci (I invoke the last thinker as the unacknowledged presiding spirit of their essay) in "On Literature as an Ideological Form."

What Balibar and Macherey have set out to do here is precisely to supply the missing link between the scientific critical practice envisaged in *A Theory of Literary Production* and the arena of political mass struggle. They seek to clarify two questions integral to the articulation of first principles in aesthetics: first, how to explain the specific ideological mode of art (contradictory class positions of author and of text); and second, how to produce a scientific and historical analysis of aesthetic effects "within the ideological class struggle." To understand the ideological mode of literature, its class position, what is required is "a theory of the history of literary effects," their material condition of existence, their progressions and "tendential transformations." Logically prior to the political appraisal is the preliminary groundwork of elucidating the aesthetic effectivity of the artwork.

Before investigating the production of aesthetic effects in literature, however, Balibar and Macherey install their problematic within the materialist category of reflection. After upholding the ontological status of literature as material reflection of objective reality (reality existing independent of thought), they aver that the question of under what historical conditions can literature provide an accurate reflection hinges on "the relatively autonomous process of the history of science." "Reflection," in their construal, rejects empiricism by dispensing with the "mirror." In order to avoid the false debate between "formalism" (which valorizes the form of reflection detached from its material determinants) and "realism" in its normative usage—this debate is resurrected in many anthologies (Lang and Williams 1972; Craig 1975; Adorno 1977)—it is necessary to adhere rigorously to the necessary constitutive order of the two successive problems addressed by Lenin in *Materialism and Empirio Criticism*: first, the priority of the objectivity of reflection and the material reality of thought as reflection determined by the real which precedes and is irreducible to it; second, the exactitude of reflection or the form of reflection at issue that has a materialist implication only after the first problem, the objectivity of reflection, has been affirmed. The mistake of Lukács and others is to subordinate the first problem (the material reality of the reflection) to the second (the form or exactitude of its "thought-content"), a reversal of the materialist order.[1] Consequently, we need to separate in a constitutive order the two aspects of (1) literature as an ideological form, and (2) the specific process of literary production.

In examining literature as an ideological form (not a system of ideas or mental reflections of external data), Balibar and Macherey invoke Althusser's thesis in

---

1. The importance for Marx of this distinction between the real object and the object of knowledge as a guarantee against falling into nominalism (conventionalism) and idealism is stressed by Althusser (1990) in "Is it Simple to be a Marxist in Philosophy?"

"Ideology and Ideological State Apparatuses." In that essay, Althusser (1971) anchors the materiality of ideology to concrete institutional practices. He argues that the conditions of capitalist production are reproduced through the mediation of forms of political-ethical subjection embodied in material practices/ideological apparatuses of the state (ISA): family, church, school, laws, parties, trade unions, and so on, all of which transform individuals into concrete subjects through inter-pellation. Ideology involves then not just ideas or beliefs but practices, action in time/space, the activity of institutions. Its primary motivation is practico-social: the reproduction of social relations of domination/subordination in class society (note that this idea differs from the epistemological status of ideology discussed earlier; see McLennan 1977; Therborn 1980).

Within this new framework, the material objectivity of literature and its ideological potency can be grasped only "through the workings and history of determinate practices in determinate social relations," specifically through the workings of the ISAs. The ideological impact of literature can be spelled out through its linkage with an ensemble of social practices determining it: linguistic, pedagogic, and fictive. Literature's status as a historic ideological form vis-à-vis the class struggle is revealed when it denies its objective base in, among others, "the contradictions of linguistic practice in schooling." Balibar and Macherey underscore the centrality of the educational ISA in reproducing bourgeois hegemony. Within the mechanism of the schooling system, literary production is based on "the determinate processes and reproduction of the contradictory linguistic practices of the common tongue, in which the effectivity of the ideology of bourgeois education is realized" (86). Such contradictory practices are internalized through the labor of fiction, a mode of constitutive repression that reproduces bourgeois norms as dominant and thus testifies to class struggle pervading the structure of texts (for example, the repression/resistance oscillation involving Midland dialect used by Nottingham miners and the formal English of the textual apparatus in D. H. Lawrence's novels). When literature is presented as the work of individual genius, or the triumph of a homogenizing/synthesizing creativity and style (the axiomatic repertoire of formalist interpretation), we confront the "ideological form of literature" in this very process of distorting if not concealing altogether the political struggle inscribed in the linguistic, pedagogical, and fictive practices which determine its production.

We encounter finally the schema of a materialist analysis premised on the axiom that literature is "a practical, material process of transformation" (Macherey 1977, 3). Questions about "ideological form" cannot be divorced from an exploration of the specificity of ideological effects—not unifying effects but signs of historically determined contradictions generating these effects and "which appear as unevenly resolved conflicts in the text." As noted earlier, the text is a reworking of the class contradictions manifest in linguistic, pedagogical, and fictive practices; the last refers to the identification effect of interpellation. Here Balibar and Macherey deploy Althusser's formulation (ideology = representation of the individual's imaginary relationship to their actual conditions via social apparatuses) by defining texts as "imaginary" resolutions of irresolvable contradictions that constitute it. Using the mechanisms of symbolic figuration, displacement, condensation, and the like, the text displaces superimposed and discrepant ideological positions by redoubling or "substituting imaginary contradictions soluble within the ideological practice of religion, aesthetics, psychology" in a "language of compromise" (88–89). In this way the text stages the limits of an ideology in its inability to subsume or erase completely an antagonistic ideology. "Style" (synonymous with F. R. Leavis' "life" or Henry James's "thickness") is the result of this displacement or compromise.

Since a Marxist science of criticism is not concerned with "realism" (a model and its representation) but with materialism, Balibar and Macherey define literature as a complex process or production of fiction-effects, more precisely "the provider of the material means for the production of fiction-effects." Why "fiction effects"? Here is the crux of their argument. Granting that ideology (social practices attached to institutional apparatuses) functions as a mode of interpellating individuals into subjects (class subjects chiefly with rights, duties, etc.) "so that they perceive themselves as such," literature as an ideological practice "produces simultaneously a reality effect and a fiction effect, emphasizing first one and then the other, interpreting each by each in turn but always on the basis of their dualism [complicity]" (91). The literary discourse itself "projects the presence of the 'real' in the manner of an hallucination" (in other words, an imaginary referent) but in doing so it unleashes a power of seduction sufficient to transform concrete individuals into subjects by endowing them with "a quasi-real hallucinatory individuality" (Belsey 1980). Bourgeois ideology requires the relation between a "subject" and objects outside it, the basis of the "reality effect" on which interpellation—the identification effect—pivots. Without the reality effect, it would appear that the fiction effect would degenerate into what Benjamin calls "aura," a reflex of commodity fetishism and reification characterizing market-oriented society.

As a particular kind of ideological effect, the literary effect transpires within determinate social conditions; as a moment in the reproduction of the dominant ideology, it can be characterized as an ideological domination effect inserted within the reproduction of other effects: religious, juridical, political, and so forth. Proceeding from the textual labor expended to forge an imaginary resolution of lived contradictions, this domination effect (whereby subjects are engendered through interpellation by the textual apparatus) coincides with the process of literary consumption and other rituals such as interpretation, criticism, readings, and so on. The canonical text functions as one versatile agency for the reproduction of the dominant ideology in its ramifications. Through the domination effect, the text induces the proliferation of "new" discourses that reproduce the hegemonic consensus in its audience of readers; in this context, "subjection means domination and repression by the literary artifice of a discourse deemed 'inarticulate' and 'faulty' and inadequate for the expression of complex ideas and feelings" (96). With specific reference to liberal democratic society, Balibar and Macherey locate the basis of the production of the literary domination effect in the structure and historical role of the dominant ISA of schooling insofar as the text "moves tendentially via the effects of literary 'style' and linguistic forms of compromise." In foregrounding the dialectical movement of contradictions in a complex articulated whole, Balibar and Macherey not only answer the ubiquitous question of form versus content but also locate the space for the critic's political intervention. In this problematic, I think, one can find an analogy to the "weak link" discerned in the text, that "risk" of constantly negotiated compromise where a strategy for counterhegemonic resistance can be mounted: "The effect of domination realized by literary production presupposes the presence of the dominated ideology within the dominant ideology itself. It implies the constant 'activation' of the contradiction and its attendant ideological risk—it thrives on this very risk which is the source of its power. . . . Class struggle is not abolished in the literary text and the literary effects which it produces" (97).

With this argument that one inescapable effect of a text is its constant activation of ideological conflict, the practice of critical analysis not only produces knowledge (of the text's disruptive processing of its raw materials) but also gestures toward a distanciating judgment of the mystifying power of aesthetic experience— a twofold effect that can then interpellate individuals to be agents of a revolutionary rupture. Acts of transgression are always possible if this "activation of contradiction"—the agenda of Brecht's theater of narrative "estrangement," of Gramsci's "organic" intellectuals—is seized by a historic bloc to mobilize the masses and transform the prevailing hierarchy of power. Otherwise, it will only induce a catharsis that reproduces the status quo.

Without foreclosing any options, we have yet to deal with the issue of whether the discrimination of aesthetic value forms an integral part of a materialist critique, a "science of the text" within historical materialism, which has been raised by several commentators (Eagleton 1976; Bennett 1979). This evokes again the contentious problem of the relation between theoretical and political practice, that is, between the role of committed Marxist intellectuals in the West and the exigencies of a global revolutionary movement against capitalist domination.[2] Ultimately, the research program envisioned by Balibar and Macherey seeks to address not so much the appreciation of aesthetic value as the legitimacy of the normative order that privileges, among others, literary texts and works of art as enduring monuments of world civilization. Are questions like "Should the surplus

---

2. One recalls how Balibar and Macherey (1982), interviewed by two American experts on Althusser, disavowed "Althusserianism" and appealed—in a revealing symptomatic gesture—for a return to Marx's texts!

value of socialized labor continue to be expropriated by the corporate elite?" put into crisis by texts or normalized? We also cannot completely ignore the naive, unmediated query from our "spontaneous" and scandalized alter ego: Can a controversy over tropes, interpellation, or symptomatic reading trigger a crisis of systemic legitimation?

Seen from the perspective of traditional critical inquiry, Balibar and Macherey's claims may seem outrageously ambitious. But whether we like it or not, Althusser's intervention has radically altered the terrain of contemporary critical theory. Given the continuing debate on the nature of ideology, textual structure, and kindred topics, Balibar and Macherey's approach cannot be dismissed as ingeniously eclectic, a mere bricolage of elements gathered from the Enlightenment archive. Nonetheless I think what is needed—Balibar and Macherey implicitly recognize this in a 1982 interview—is the insertion of "theoretical practice" into the current world-system conjuncture so as to test and gauge its practical efficacy, its precise contribution to enhancing popular movements for radical transformation everywhere. This is probably what Fredric Jameson, the brilliant practitioner of an unashamedly totalizing metacommentary which acknowledges the value of Althusser, had in mind when he wrote in *The Political Unconscious*:

> [T]he Althusserian/Marxist conception of culture requires this multiplicity [of discrepant elements] to be reunified, if not at the level of the work itself, then at the level of its process of production, which is not random [like the semiotics of Barthes, for instance] but can be described as a coherent functional operation in its own right. The current poststructural celebration of discontinuity and heterogeneity is therefore only an initial moment in Althusserian exegesis, which then requires the fragments, the incommensurable levels, the heterogeneous impulses, of the text to be once again related, but in the mode of structural difference and determinate contradiction. (1981, 56; see Dowling 1984)

Without this theorem of a differentiated and complex whole (which Althusser claims is Marx's original discovery), it is difficult to theorize the reciprocal play of the specific effectivities of practices on one another and on the whole social totality, and in the same breath also identify the conjuncture in which cultural institutions, critical practice, and ethico-political calculation might converge. Such a convergence would of course witness the long-awaited revolutionary crisis that, to our postmodern sensibilities, appears only in the shape of the litterateur's nostalgic desire for the millennial apocalypse.

For Gramsci, the study of language and literature served as an index of history, a testimony anticipating the advent of a genuine popular-democratic, emancipatory future. It can be a point of departure for a personal or collective "inventory" of differences, especially in the contemporary world where the universal reign of the commodity—liberal pluralism, computerized mass consumption, the U.S.-ordained "New World Order"—threatens to reduce everything into an intolerably tedious repetition of the Same. Such a point of departure nonetheless will have to risk learning the lessons of the theoretical adventure begun by Althusser, Balibar, and Macherey.

5

Ideological Form, Symbolic Exchange, Textual Production

A READING OF HEMINGWAY'S
FOR WHOM THE BELL TOLLS

Criticism of Hemingway's *For Whom the Bell Tolls* (hereafter *FWBT*) for the last fifty years has been dominated by charges that the writer falsified facts and ignored truths. These indictments belong to the species of normative, empiricist criticism that seeks to impose an extra-aesthetic model or standard of propriety which claims that its access to an empirical "real" can judge whether the work is adequate to what it reflects.[1] Other critics who conceive of the work as a reservoir of unlimited meanings, universal themes or "essences" replicated in myriad forms, practice what has become the dominant academic genre of interpretive criticism. Like the normative type, hermeneutic criticism operates within the assumption that the intrinsic formal (linguistic, rhetorical) qualities of the text can serve as a guarantee of its ultimate, quintessential meaning.

In contrast, the theoretical approach I would like to explore here tries to take into account both aesthetic qualities and their historical grounding in its singular conceptualization of ideology as form. Instead of being construed as another interpretation of the text's meaning, this approach views the production of ideology— the lived relation of humans, their imaginary linkage to their "real" conditions (in Althusser's definition [1971, 152–56])—as the project of the text. "Ideology" here

---

1. Praised by Dorothy Parker, Howard Mumford Jones, Robert Sherwood, Edmund Wilson, and Carlos Baker, among others, and condemned by Dwight MacDonald, Lionel Trilling, Maxwell Geismar, Alfred Kazin, and other critics whose modalities of discrimination serve as inverted mirror-images of Alvah Bessie's trenchant denunciation of Hemingway's novel in his 1940 review (Baker 1972, 90–94), *FWBT* may have confirmed the opposite of its homiletic message: diverse islands of taste and opinion will never find themselves merging into a continent. For whom indeed is the bell tolling? In their wake, the body of criticism on this novel replicates the original partisan scruples and divisions (see Meyers 1982, 316–60).

designates not a set of ideas, false consciousness, or *Weltanschauung*, but rather an unconscious "system of representations," practices, and institutions, whereby humans live their relations to their historical circumstances by way of phantasy. What a text like *FWBT* does is to work on elements of the spontaneously lived experience, in particular the sense of selfhood as the matrix of identification and coherence, as raw textualized materials, endowing them with aesthetically gratifying expression and in the process demystifying them, that is, exposing the limits of their claims and effectivity. The ideology of the text materializes in that process. What the text performs is a transformative labor on an ensemble of representations, images, tonalities, so that by generating a formed sensuous concreteness, "structures of feeling" which distance and foreground their own constituents, the text would be able to reveal the complex relations of various ideologies in play to their grounding in history (interlocked modes of production, conjunctures of stratified social formations) which is their condition of possibility.

In "Literature as an Ideological Form," Pierre Macherey and Etienne Balibar propose that analysis of the ideological specificity of a text can avoid both intrinsic (essentialist) and extrinsic (functionalist) fallacies—versions of the empiricist problematic I've referred to earlier—by elucidating the conditions of its production. This requires analyzing the historically determinate contradictions that have produced the text and that manifest themselves in it as unevenly resolved conflicts. This approach rejects in principle the premise of organic unity or immanent self-sufficiency of the work. Because the work is the effect of certain contradictions that cannot be solved within a specific ideology, "it is materially incomplete, disparate and incoherent, since it is the conflicted, contradictory effect of superimposing real processes which cannot be abolished in it except in an imaginary way" (1981, 49–50). What this implies is that the text, instead of formulating a solution, provides a *mise en scène* where the contradictions can be distanced and displaced in a "language of compromise," a fiction-effect of their reconciliation. Comprised of fiction-effects bound with reality-effects, the form of the text stages the nature and limits of the ideological project of the writer insofar as it is unable to subsume the diverse contradictions which are its conditions of possibility. The form of the text's ideology can further be clarified in terms of the mechanism of identification it deploys and its "ideological domination-effect"—the subjection of individuals to the dominant ideology of the ruling class (1981, 51–58)—attested to by the uses to which *FWBT* has been harnessed by critics positioned in the ideological apparatuses of a given social formation (state plus civil society).

One such critic who "uses" Hemingway's novel for a clearly judicial intent is Lionel Trilling, who charges Hemingway for reducing political facts and moral judgment to physical pain and courage, thus subverting the ostensible purpose of the novel: "Hemingway's mind . . . cannot exemplify in art the idea of the community of men . . . ; he is wholly at the service of the cult of experience and the result is a novel which, undertaking to celebrate the community of men, actually glorifies the isolation of the individual ego" (Meyers 1982, 336).[2]

I would argue that instead of glorifying the isolation of the solitary ego and elevating the "cult of experience" to a moral or ethical norm, *FWBT* in its "deep structure" may be read as an allegory of the difficulties, perhaps the near impossibility, of creating through the fiat of individual example a heroic society where the classical virtues of courage, fidelity, and so on, imbue human actions with a telos, an intelligible significance. In unfolding the encounter and clash of contradictory practices, beliefs, and attitudes ultimately rooted in diverse social formations, the narrative problematizes "the cult of experience" and the code of sportsmanship or stylized decorum associated with it. What the text materializes is the aesthetic of self-consciousness, of the monadic gendered subject formed in the industrialized milieu of alienated labor and the competitive market during the crisis of the first three decades of the century, as it undergoes testing in what we would now call a Third World formation: a Spain torn by the regressive forces of the Church and the feudal landlord class represented by the "nationalist" military machine and the popular forces of peasants, workers, and elements of the petty bourgeoise strata, all these overdetermined by the global conflict between fascist Germany and Italy on the one hand and the anti-fascist camp including the Soviet Union and international volunteers. To conceptualize this dynamic relation between what Jordan represents and its inscription in the overdetermined scenario of the Spanish Civil War, is the task of a theoretical inquiry seeking a knowledge of the ideological form of the novel.[3]

In general, most readings of Hemingway's novel concentrate on the education of the protagonist Robert Jordan conceived as a reliable intellectual center of the narrative action. Most critics have ascribed to him a "moral pragmatism" which supposedly informs his commitment to the Republican cause. His character is defined by a professional devotion to work, to the public display of a skill, which evokes in turn the artisanal ethos characterizing the guild stage of mercantile capi-

---

2. Compare Edmund Wilson's opinion that the novel "is not so much a social analysis as a criticism of moral qualities" gravitating around "the common human instincts that make men both fraternal and combative" (in Meyers 1982, 320–23).

3. As contradistinguished from an analysis extrapolating diverse themes, ideas, notions, or motifs from the plot, character, style, or genre of the novel—the preoccupation of the conventional mainstream scholarship on Hemingway's work.

Most critics focus on Jordan's character in the hope of discerning some consistency of motivation or purpose. For example, Cooper asserts that Jordan affirms "American beliefs in democracy and opportunity" when he talks to himself: "You're not a real Marxist and you know it. You believe in Liberty, Equality and Fraternity. You believe in Life, Liberty and the Pursuit of Happiness. Don't ever kid yourself with too much dialectics" (1987, 59, 102). Qualified here by the unstable drift of the interior monologue, the appearance of capitalized abstractions in a Hemingway text always warrants an ironic gloss.

talism. He upholds the instrumental value of discipline, "absolute loyalty" to Golz's order, which entails the subordination of personal desire to the imperative of political obligation; his duty—fulfilling the mission that he accepts—acquires meaning only within the totality of the collective effort to save the Republic. But that belief, framed within the morality of a long-range, perfectionist "consequentialism" (Lukes 1987), is gradually rendered unstable by reservations, doubts, aleatory swerves of impulses, to the point where often Jordan has to remind himself repeatedly to suspend thought, to put his mind in abeyance while engaged in action. Undeterred, critics continue to praise Jordan for his "romantic idealism" which affirms the solidarity of the guerrillas despite betrayals, the nada of bureaucratic muddle and indiscriminate killing on both sides, unresolved moral questions (Young 1952; Meyers 1985; Lynn 1987; Warren 1974). When Jordan is asked about social class and property relations back home, his understated reply concerns inheritance taxes and the parcelling of frontier lands alienated from the Indian nations. At one point he contrasts the idea of a planned society with an axiom of a laissez-faire economy: "all people should be left alone and you should interfere with no one" (Hemingway 1940, 163). If there is any controlling conviction that would unify these incompatible strands in Jordan's character, it would be the fundamental assumption that guarantees the "truth" of symbolic exchange (the "I" as generalized equivalent in the economy of the text [Goux 1990]) between reader and narrator: "nobody owned his mind, nor his faculties for seeing and hearing" (Hemingway 1940, 136). This, I submit, is the foundational apriori of the text which is eventually sanctioned by death. In the end, Jordan's summing-up before he dies aims to transcend all partisanship by a totalizing aestheticism (misrecognized as truth-telling) empowered by its own self-cancelling futility: "The world is a fine place and worth the fighting for and I hate very much to leave it. . . . There's no one thing that's true. It's all true. The way the planes are beautiful whether they are ours or theirs. The hell they are, he thought" (Hemingway 1940, 467). Unless one were to privilege any of these scattered statements, the only judgment one can make about Jordan's character is that it is dispersed or fissured, hence susceptible to varying interpellations.

Instead of being centered on Jordan's subjectivity oriented by a *laissez-faire*, populist ethos of the literary artisan, the text works out an articulation of the ideologemes I have sketched earlier of which the character-system, focalizing technique, and linguistic style are but diverse mediations. I propose to view the novel as the textual fabrication of an internally complex ideology unsynchronized by multiple contradictions: between the disciplinary code of duty/fidelity to the Republic and the will of monadic egos, between the totemic minotaur of fascist technology and self-transcendence through erotic love and a neo-Nietzschean affirmation of worldly life. This is schematically represented in figure 1, a *combinatoire* with further ramifications.

FIGURE 5.1

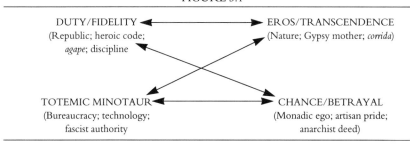

Transposed into various syntagmatic lines of development in the narrative, these opposing ideologemes are played out in the events of three days, a sequence given causality by Jordan's mission behind enemy lines, in the field of negations. This "holding action" bridges the gap between civic and personal motivations. By its superfluity it displaces value or its cathexis onto the privileged moments of erotic nihilism, the irruption of death and the sacred, in the site of what Bataille calls psychic expenditures, which may strike many as scandalous and accidental phenomena in this compressed time-space conjuncture where feudal, capitalist, and archaic formations collide. In the tensions arising between Jordan and the guerillas, between unrepeatable historical pasts and imagined futures, the text charts the terrain of conflict among overlapping social formations and attendant values: the sedimented archaic mode (*corrida* and mystique of death/erotic fulfill-ment), the residual slave and feudal mode (religion, the patriarchal regime), the emergent and dissonant capitalist (Jordan's professional ethic), and socialist modes (Republican/collective ethos). In this terrain we find dramatized the wide-ranging crisis of an uneven, overdetermined social formation, Spain of the 1930s, where Western liberalism collides with its archaic past and emerging future. What results is an absence figured by the text, an illusion of conflicts resolved: a problematic reaffirmation of an artificial heroic code salvaged from fragments of the historical past (ancient, artisanal modes) but lacking any organic social foundation in the pre-sent, with a universalizing aestheticism—the glorification of self-renouncing love and sensory pleasures—concealing that lack or compensating for its absence (more on this in Sections III and IV).

I would now like to examine the processing of these ideologemes, elements of the semiotic combinatory, that informs the text's production and critique of ide-ology, as manifested in three cruxes: El Sordo's resistance in chapter 27, Pilar's account of the insurrection in chapter 10, and Maria's violation in chapter 31. These episodes yield chronotopes that structure the energies of the narrative action. "Chronotope" is the heuristic category theorized by Mikhail Bakhtin to describe how events acquire representability and figuration in the convergence of temporal and spatial relations in novelistic discourse, "materializing time in space" and "permitting the imaging power of art to do its work" (1981, 84–85, 250).

II

What we have in chapter 27 is the chronotope of a beleaguered detachment of soldiers perched on a "chancre," El Sordo's metaphor punctuating some organic excess, an exception, which presages its negation. Their annihilation by scientific machinery epitomizes modern mass destruction (as in Guernica). This chronotope can perhaps be regarded as emblematic of the whole course of the Spanish Civil War from Hemingway's viewpoint, with the defeat of the Loyalists explained by their lack of disciplined coordination and by Franco's technological superiority. The illusion of a hill as refuge (such topography focused charismatic energies in archaic societies) dissolves to give way to the landscape of a chancre, matter foregrounded as antithesis to the lethal idealism of "mechanized doom." The guerrillas' sacrifice compensates for nature's disfigured anatomy. Reversing the morally charged asymmetry of highland and plain in the Hemingway canon, the concluding image also deflates any romantic idealism or aura of "pastoral elegy" which might inhibit the reality-effect of the fiction.

Like the dignified peasant Anselmo, who values the sanctity of human life so much that he hopes a collective civic penance will be held after the war to purge everyone's guilt, El Sordo functions here as a normative standard: his valor and fidelity to the Republic, his hunter's cunning and humor, his paternal concern for his "flock," his acceptance of the inevitability of fate, his enjoyment of sensuous life—all these qualities counterpoint the fascist's authoritarian folly, their cowardly reliance on technology, Captain Mora's hubris, and Lieutenant Berrendo's tribal piety. With his "hooked nose like an Indian's," El Sordo is the responsible herdsman who resembles the mythical frontier hero of the U.S. West.[4] Following the code of the ancient warrior-patriarch, El Sordo wins a moral victory (the general equivalent form of value in the economy of the text) but his physical destruction renders hollow the humanist life-affirming vision which he shares with Jordan: "But living was a field of grain blowing in the wind on the side of a hill. . . . Living was a horse between your legs and a carbine under one leg and a hill and a valley and a stream with trees along it and the far side of the valley and the hills beyond" (Hemingway 1940, 312–13).

---

4. El Sordo's nickname evokes Spain's patron saint as well as Goya, the painter of *Disasters of War* which Hemingway admired highly; it alludes also to the period of the Napoleonic Wars when the Spanish craft of guerrilla warfare was first fashioned. For the antithesis between modern technology and the American pastoral sensibility, see Guttmann (1962).

We can easily identify the presence of authorial ideology in operation here. Sight more than hearing functions as the privileged sensorium mobilized by the narrative to reconcile the disparity between the Loyalist guerillas and the fascists when El Sordo registers in his interior monologue the ritualized nuances of Captain Mora's ascent up the hill, with the enemy christened as a "Comrade Voyager" equal to his enemies in death. In the rhetorical gusto of El Sordo's verbal capture of his victim in motion, we perceive the operation of exchange on the level of the elementary form of value found in precapitalist economy. Later, El Sordo mockingly echoes the dead captain's taunt: incorporation of the voice of the Other establishes a specular relation in the imaginary register. What qualifies this archaic economy of simple exchange is the mock suicide staged by El Sordo, a form of absence which lures the fascist captain to the sacrifice. But this exchange is cut off by fascist bombs, negating Joaquin's invocation to any matriarchal mediator (from La Pasionaria to the Virgin Mary). A gap opens up when fascist technology (subsumptive and sovereign) "castrates" the organs of sensory pleasure.

What the narrative unfolds here—the contradiction between El Sordo's performance of his *arete* (skill) and the technological supremacy of fascism—may seem to question the validity of his example. Fascism in the person of Lieutenant Berrendo and his sectarian compassion for his dead friend seems a mirror-image of El Sordo's. However, the uneasy resolution of this contradiction in favor of the guerillas is immediately displaced by the last scene when Lieutenant Berrendo, surveying the carnage and ordering the beheading of the guerillas (the reality-effect), pronounces the banal thought—*Que cosa mas mala es la guerra*. Pathos as fiction-effect induces reader identification with this officer, obscuring the brutality of fascism and blinding us to its authoritarian rigidity, bureaucratic arrogance, and so on. Such ironical resonance is not a betrayal of Hemingway's surface intention but a consequence of the humanist aestheticism informing this chronotope.

But if we look closely, we shall find that what the text has really exposed is the limit of the humanist episteme that ends in the blanket condemnation of war and an undue equalizing of both victim and victimizer. Lieutenant Berrendo's prayer and melancholy reflection won't be able to smooth over the carnage inflicted by fascist bombs. Although bound to registering the consciousnesses of both parties in a gesture of universalizing empathy, the narrative finds itself decentered by the shift from El Sordo's camp where the power of the senses is extinguished to Lieutenant Berrendo's order to decapitate the bodies and his mechanical prayers. Given the discrepancies unfolded in this chronotope of physical defeat and spiritual victory, we see the text "spoken" by contradictions and trying to displace what it is incapable of resolving to a level which suspends it through a magical fiction-effect: Lieutenant Berrendo's ritual of unquestioning obedience to a power "from above."

At this point I would like to elaborate the concept of the text as production of ideological form reflecting precisely the dynamics of exchange that is the historical genesis of value. By means of a symptomatic reading, we can articulate the text's radical otherness, the space where the circuit of exchange is marked by determinate absences, ruptures, and gaps in the signifying chain, as the force that shapes the *problematique* of the text. By *problematique* (Althusser and Balibar 1970) we refer to the ideological framework, the system of exclusions and inclusions, deployed by the narrative to transcode into apprehensible images the "lived relations" which are its basic raw material.

Earlier I have proposed a hypothesis which thematized the authorial project of *FWBT*: the affirmation of an individualizing heroic code whose internal contradictions stem from its context, the overdetermined and uneven social formation of Spain in that historic conjuncture marking the crisis of global capitalism in the period of imperialism (finance capitalism). This hypothesis can be reformulated another way (following the argument of Jean-Joseph Goux's *Symbolic Economies*) in which the text is constructed by the trajectory of an exploration of various solutions (astheticism is one) to the predicament of Western liberal individualism intersecting with the crisis in a peripheral formation (Spain). While individualism can only nostalgically look back to the pre-industrial past of the U.S. Civil War, in Spain the force of centralization—the dominance of a generalized equivalent form of value operative in the market and commodity-production—is blocked by vestiges of older forms of economic and symbolic exchange (the ancient elementary value form overlayered by the feudal extended value form) that inform the cultural practices of both fascism and its antagonist, the Republic. On a more abstract plane, one can express the *problematique* underlying *FWBT* as Hemingway's fable of the genealogy of the value form, its vicissitudes and destiny. Since all value originates from exchange (in the spheres designated by Lacanian psychoanalysis as the imaginary, the symbolic, and the real)—substitution, replacement, or supplementation of what is lost, damaged, violated, or forbidden, the question of the novel's politics and ethics summed up in the term "ideology" hinges, I suggest, on the narrativization of the problem of searching for the universal equivalent form of value.[5]

By virtue of their annihilation, El Sordo's band with their courage, discipline, humor, and solidarity has incarnated for the first time in the narrative the most positive model of a universal equivalent form of value intelligible to all. It is the standard against which one measures the worth of all substitutes, supplements, compensations, and indemnities. El Sordo's loss, an excess beyond normal expectations, constitutes the equivalent value form in which others (the actions of Anselmo, Jordan, etc.) are reflected. It marks a significant stage in the emergence of a power of idealization or representation that transcends those heads (the fetishized

---

5. Cognizant of the antinomies and equivocations pervading the novel, Thorne (1980) and Kastely (1988) fail to connect them with the uneven, overdetermined historical contexts—the conditions of possibility of the narrative. On Hemingway's fascist tendencies, see Burgum (1950).

reflex of a regressive, animistic mode of exchange) appropriated by the enemy as spoils. In this sense, death or a particular way of dying is conceived as an exclusion, an excess, that triggers the circulation of meaning governed by the presence of a universal equivalent (like the money form in bourgeois economy) realized in its ideal form. I think this is what the silence after the bombing, the incisions on the earth's surface, and the headless bodies ultimately reveal.

III

Using this mode of ascertaining what the text with its empiricist problematic cannot possibly know and the text's foregrounding of conflicting modes of exchange that hinders such a knowledge, let us consider next a key section of the novel that has been judged crucial in legitimizing the charge of Hemingway's political indeterminacy. I refer to the interpolated account of the uprising in Pablo's village near Avila, a recollection by the gypsy Pilar, an idyllic interlude. A bond of shared knowledge between Pilar, Maria, and Jordan is thus established that creates a community and also a reference point, an anchorage in the historical "real" to demonstrate what, for Jordan, "we" did to them and not just what was done to us.

What is puzzling here is the outcome of what many critics consider an inaugural moment of revolutionary change when the subalterns of a feudal order wake up and challenge the long-entrenched power of the ruling gentry of the town: Pilar's sense of hollowness, shame, and sense of wrongdoing ("a great feeling of oppression and of bad to come") even though she assented to the crowd's killing of Don Faustino, a consensus that intimates the advent of a general equivalent form of value. But note Pablo's disillusionment: the priest died "badly," without sufficient dignity, not because Pablo expected priests to die with dignity but because the priest happened to be Spanish: national pride is what is at stake. There is no discernible sense of glory or heightened cathexis attending Pablo and Pilar's concluding reflections.

The ideological apparatus of the narrative here is the focalizer Pilar from whose perspective we watch the unfolding of a chronotope of power reversal, a threshold event. From the beginning to the end of this episode, Pablo's quest is for a universal equivalent form of value crystallized in the phrase "how to die." This decorum of dying as the law of symbolic exchange would centralize the social organism and unify the body politic now torn asunder. But a contradiction thwarts the quest: this goal of grasping a universal equivalent, an abstract form like money, is fixated to the code of an archaic order where the warrior's prowess, the bullfighter's skill, or the hunter's technique, for example, is the measure of valid substitution. What we next behold is Pablo turned into a priest-like figure in a rite of collective revenge; accession to power is preceded by excommunication, exclusion, and sacrifice. This is dramatized by the breach of the barracks and the execution of the *civiles*. After Pablo's exercise of defining the surplus, what can be removed from circulation, "No one said anything"—a telling silence at the overthrow of centuries-old taboos, a transitional moment that opens a gap before the substitution is made.

We are aware that rather than being a popular-democratic movement of self-conscious and militant revolutionaries, this uprising is a kind of putsch spontaneously erupting, with one overriding tendency directed by Pablo and his followers. According to Pilar, our informant and chronicler of the genesis of the value form, it is Pablo who organized the peasants armed with flails for a *capea* (the peasant gauntlet often interpreted as a parody of the art of the corrida, a sign of Pablo's *ressentiment*) so that everyone will participate, "that each man should have his share in the responsibility" (1940, 106). We hear them express divergent views in this episode. In this polyphony of voices (eventually the heteroglossia deteriorates inside the Ayuntamiento), the logic of symbolic exchange has metamorphosed to the extended value form where there is no single unitary form of value but rather fragmentary equivalent forms that are mutually exclusive; hence the ambivalence and reversible polarities that abound here as well as throughout the narrative, in incidents and protagonists alike, checked only at times by the text's ideological strategy of containment.

A large part of this killing ritual, however, is devoted to the collective ridicule of the cowardly, pretentious Don Faustino Rivero. The duty of abolishing the gentry's political power, its power of representation, is here replaced by a motive of revenge occasioned by personal insult—a regression to the logic of simple exchange: barter, an eye for an eye. What follows is entailed by the refusal to acknowledge a general equivalent form, thus the arbitrary and anarchic chaos of bodies indulging in pure use-value. Pilar explains the mob's cruelty in killing Don Guillermo Martin as a result of drunkenness; "drunkenness" then becomes the name of what is unrepresentable which, at the risk of paradoxically representing it, points to that passage of exorbitant mass delirium that violates taboo and ushers in the sacred. What is significant is that it is precisely at this traumatic moment of Pilar's scruple that we encounter the scission in the weave of memory charged with the most pregnant libidinal investment, an interruption (a caesura within a caesura) that hints at the not-said, the unthought, of the discursive economy of the text:

> "Is it not so in your country, *Ingles*?"
> "It is so," Robert Jordan said. "When I was seven years old and going with my mother to attend a wedding in the state of Ohio at which I was to be the boy of a pair of boy and girl who carried flowers—"
> "Did you do that?" asked Maria. "How nice!"
> "In this town a Negro was hanged to a lamp post and later burned. It was an arc light. A light which lowered from the post to the pavement.

And he was hoisted, first by the mechanism which was used to hoist the arc light but this broke—"

"A Negro," Maria said. "How barbarous!"

"Were the people drunk?" asked Pilar. "Were they drunk thus to burn a Negro?"

"I do not know," Robert Jordan said. "Because I saw it only looking out from under the blinds of a window in the house which stood on the corner where the arc light was. The street was full of people and when they lifted the Negro up for the second time—"

"If you had only seven years and were in a house, you could not tell if they were drunk or not," Pilar said.

"As I said, when they lifted the Negro up for the second time, my mother pulled me away from the window, so I saw no more," Robert Jordan said. "But since I have had experiences which demonstrate that drunkenness is the same in my country. It is ugly and brutal."

"You were too young at seven," Maria said. "You were too young for such things. I have never seen a Negro except in a circus. Unless the Moors are Negroes."

"Some are Negroes and some are not," Pilar said. "I can talk to you of the Moors."

"Not as I can," Maria said. "Nay, not as I can."

"Don't speak of such things," Pilar said. "It is unhealthy. Where were we?" (1940, 116–17)

This passage functions as a substitute clarification of, a mock attempt to explain, that phenomenon of "drunkenness" which Pilar's testimony cannot fully comprehend. It is a difficulty promptly displaced here by analogy with an incident involving Jordan and his mother. What is foregrounded by the interruption is the absence, the lapse, that defines the problematic associated with Pilar's visual rendering of the events where Pablo is supposed to have acquired the charisma of revolutionary leadership. The allusion to a childhood experience suggests regression; the racist lynching by a mob seen by mother and son intrudes into a wedding ceremony (an integrating force) while the description of the hanging is displaced by the phenomenon of the arc-light mechanism, an index of its historical anchorage and the technological sophistication which counterpoints the lynchers' "drunkenness." But what I think is more suggestive here is the vulnerability of the point of view, in this case the loss of vision—of discovering a certain knowledge—marked by the mother's surrogate exercise of "paternal" authority. This knowledge involves more integrally the function of the U.S. Civil War and the subsequent Indian Wars in articulating a general equivalent value form for Jordan (for U.S. society as a whole) inasmuch as Jordan's grandfather, the totem figure in his personal history, metonymically invokes a logic of exchange premised on exclusion of nations and racial groups.

The linkage between Moors (Franco's Moorish troops and the historical obsession of Spanish Catholicism with the Islamic Other, gypsies, and other pariahs are not far behind this allusion) and Negroes is made by Maria but is immediately suppressed by Pilar. A prohibition is installed: victimization becomes the matrix for valorization. What the frame of the narrative consciousness cannot name, its condition of possibility and the enabling power of its reality-effect, the hallucination of truth it engenders, is nothing else but the historical genealogy of sovereign power (the homogeneous nation state, racialized absolutism) in the process of symbolic exchange. Both fascist authoritarianism and the Republic's ideal of discipline gestures toward a general equivalent form of value that can only be realized through political struggle. The civil war then becomes a kind of trial by ordeal where use-value (immediate pleasure, the aesthetic-humanist norm) is sublated by a logic of exchange (interiorized moralizing, *pietas* converted to corporate will) embodied here in the massacre of the fascists and the lynching of the literally invisible Negro. The primary struggle in which guerrilla partisans and fascists are engaged may be described as a semiotic maneuvering across boundaries of sentiments, memories, and wills to occupy that position defining the universal equivalent form of value necessary to synthesize/unify the social totality. A parallelism between the histories of Spain and the United States is signalled here but quickly interrupted, resumed only fleetingly in Jordan's meditations on his father's cowardice and its compensating substitute, his grandfather's heroic performance in the Civil War and the Indian Wars.

Having formulated at the risk of hermeneutic superimposition what presides at the boundary of what is said and what is not said, I would like to focus on the charade inside the Ayuntamiento and the subsequent mayhem when Pablo (as surrogate for the slain mayor) allows the riotous crowd to enter the building. Just as an exchange occurs between the positions of the gentry (bull into bullfighter) and the peasantry (bullfighter into bull) in the public square where the victims are still individualized, the interior happenings in the Ayuntamiento offer us the spectacle of an exchange between a generalized body of victims and an amorphous force whose uncontrolled violence deprives the priest of any opportunity for exhibiting dignity in death, as Pilar believes. On Pablo's accession to power, the empowerment of the masses, the text is silent—a constitutive, telltale silence.

I have noted how Pilar's memory recital segments itself between the demarcated spaces of the barracks, the plaza, and the interior of the Ayuntamiento—the loci of traditional power and social hierarchy—but as soon as this inverted fertility ritual of flailing bodies evolves into some kind of propitiation of a river god, her narrative line becomes fractured, wobbles, drifts, calling attention to itself, to its status as a discursively constructed subject dependent on a contextual frame where paternal authority still dominates. The text exposes the narrator's inadequacy in explaining the indiscriminate killing as a result of "drunkenness" when that partic-ular syntagmatic chain is broken to yield a space for the fragment of a subtext, the continuing acts of racial oppression in U.S. society (involving primarily blacks and American Indians)—I submit that this is the resurrected "political unconscious" of the text—as a possible betrayal of the emancipatory ideals of the Civil War. Such telescoping implies the intertextual horizon of the novel's ideology, the effective-ness of its normalizing of events as obvious and "true" being premised on the nec-essary repression of prior historical texts.

The apparatus of focalization is the site of the inscription of authorial ideology mediated through a participant-observer, the gypsy's maternal sensibility which is muted for a while but surfaces again at the end. This struggle for the right of wit-nessing may be conceived as the artist's right to know everything, the Flaubertian godlike omniscience; but the narrator's passion for possessing the truth is a ruse, a fictive mediation, managed to displace the contradiction between the claim of rev-olutionary justice, of collective responsibility embodying the birth of freedom expressed by Pilar earlier, and the vindictive thirst for blood. Pablo's quest for a general equivalent value form is sidetracked to the obsession with national honor. While the move from the outside to the inside (from which the woman is signifi-cantly excluded) signals the condensation of energies required for an assault on the structure of traditional power, the lack of any directive will or structure of author-ity to replace the feudal elite is left unremarked. Use-value, direct gratification of needs, supervenes: no exchange transpires, no substitutions are accomplished except in the position of eyewitness. Pilar's vision, however, is cut off just as the priest is about to be killed, a hiatus that betokens the vulnerability of the woman/gypsy's testimony as well as its threatening refusal to sanction the doings of patriarchal power. The resolution here of the manifold oppositions I have sug-gested, particularly the contradiction between the logic of feudal/archaic exchange that fetishizes a heroic style of behavior and the logic of general equivalence that reifies human relations, assumes a libidinally charged figuration in the person of Don Guillermo's wife whose lament is captured by Pilar after the satire on plebeian anarchy. Pilar describes the plaza drenched in the moonlight and the sombre calm-ness of the landscape that is broken only by the "splashing of the water in the foun-tain." The pathos resonant in the narrator's sensorium neutralizes the provocative effect of this episode with a compromise image, an illusion that guarantees the acceptance and eventual sublimation of all the losses, interruptions, omissions, and inexplicable horrors into the figure of *pietas*, the Madonna grieving over the dead Christ.

Notwithstanding this fiction-effect of reconciliation, one should emphasize Pilar's heterogeneous position, her gypsy marginality, and her access to mystical lore. She poses a challenge to both the customary patriarchal domination of reli-gious, chauvinist-fascist Spain and also the bourgeoise rule of exchange-value which measures everything by the abstraction of money as the reifying universal equivalent value form. Pilar is the excess that condenses the negative and preserves difference in terms of subverting the homogenizing force of the Virgin Mother as ideological compromise and deferring the apotheosis of male honor crystallized in tauromachy through the counterexample of Pablo's degeneration. Finally, Pilar's artistry here—Hemingway's art of sentence-production—may be read as stand-in, understudy, or replacement, for the universal equivalent form of value underpinning the rule of imperialist capital against whose hollow and fraudulent, legitimizing slogans Hemingway's craft has been self-consciously mobilized.[6]

IV

So far I have remarked on the internal otherness, the constitutive absence inscribed in the text, that arises as effects of necessary determinations implied by the mode of representing ideology as the form symbolic exchange assumes. This configuration of effects, a mapping of the conflicted diachrony of the ideologemes I have mentioned earlier, is what a historical materialist inquiry seeks to delineate. These effects are glimpsed in what the text tries to occlude—the blind spots, elisions, lacunae, and silences that a symptomatic reading enables us to apprehend and, to some extent, decipher. In the case of Pilar's account, we have suggested that what the narrative viewpoint does not see is not what she does not see, but what she sees. One episode, the embedded account of Maria's rape, may further substantiate the hypothesis of the incomplete and dis-integrated form produced by the text as an index of the layered historical contradictions immanent in "lived relations."

In Maria's retrospective account of her victimization by the Falangists, the narrator who combines the functions of witness/participant refuses to evaluate what is really going on. While narration tries to impose the ideology of the subject

---

6. The shift of positions in public space is overdetermined by gender conflict. After separating herself from the peasant mass, Pilar has to contend with a foul-smelling drunkard embracing her, shouting "Open up! Open!" so that she feels "as though the mob were on my back as a devil is on your back in a dream" (1940, 122). Intoxicated by the spectacle but somehow metaphorically imprisoned, this man pushes Pilar away; only when Pilar hits his groin does he relent and allow Pilar to gaze at the scene of slaughter, the scopic drive of this now nearly androgynous figure investing the rite with the collective memory attached to a folk primal scenario. The accession to truth, to the circulation of supplements and substitutes through the bars of patriarchal rule, comes about with a blow at the male genitals as Pilar wrestles with her unnamed antagonist and wrests her right (*derecho*) to witness this engendering of superfluity that then becomes translated into the mother's unilateral gift to her children (Maria and Jordan).

(the daughter defined by father/mayor), focalization disrupts this imposition and transcribes opaque outlines:[7]

> I saw my face in the mirror of the barbershop and the faces of those who were holding me and the faces of three others who were leaning over me and I knew none of their faces but in the glass I saw myself and them, but they saw only me. (1940, 351)

As a synecdoche of fascist violence, this outrage can only be captured by a mirror that positions a specular subject (the focalizer who experiences) dissociated from the speaking subject, an alterity conveying the misrecognition entailed by the ideology of the self-identical subject in classical liberal thought. Metonymy (the apparatus of bourgeois realism) overcomes the metaphoric substitution typical of the fetishizing mechanisms of feudal society. And the spatial rift that intervenes eludes verbalization, fabricating that unintelligible rupture which hollows the authority of the narrator and her self-validating testimony.

Unable to totalize the scene, the spatializing grid that the text manipulates captures phenomena refracted into so many serial notations which can be taken as symptomatic of a breakdown of the traditional indigenous code and the incapacity of a transplanted atomized sensibility to replace it. The limitations of Hemingway's narrative mode, his economy of the signifier and its confinement to a transcription of the bare image of things, has been often noted. Paul Goodman, for example, acutely detects an internalized passivity, events as happenings-to-one, denoted by the sweet but passive style, a passivity characteristic of life in contemporary society with "high technology and centralized organization" (1974, 154). A craft of omission, a minimalist strategy of evoking the unrepresentable, was indeed Hemingway's response to the crisis of representability, "the legitimation crisis" of public discourse and the decay of civic virtues which contaminated hypostatized abstractions like "sacred," "glorious," "sacrifice," in the period before and after World War I, the Wall Street crash, and the 1930s Depression. Such a deliberate choice of negotiating the gap between the speakable sign and the unspeakable meaning, according to Robert Weimann, depends on the historical situation and the writer's choice whether to meet some existential challenge (to represent war, for example) by closing the links and gaps of representation: "In Hemingway, the signifier is held in a state of uncanny balance between its capacity for releasing and its ability to obliterate meaning" (1989, 44). Even when Hemingway's style and

---

7. Note that the analogical conversion of the fascists into Indians makes Jordan's partisanship a continuation of the genocidal pacification of the Indian nations in the North American continent after the U.S. Civil War, an idea reinforced by Jordan's worship of his grandfather whose participation in the pacification of the natives overshadows his role in the Civil War (see *FWBT* 338).

rhetoric in *FWBT* have become more exuberant, sometimes even baroque, as critics like Beach and Stephens have noted, "the fear remains, and its register is the sheer amount of silence and invisibility, affecting the whole range of information, insight and emotion which, in the rupture between the simple signifier and the difficult signified, is darkly withheld" (Weimann 1989, 45).

Rewriting ideology as style allegorizing modes of production, Fredric Jameson ruled out the validity of searching for any ideological message in Hemingway's texts because "their deepest subject is simply the writing of a certain type of sentence, the practice of a determinate style" (1971, 409).[8] This echoes the conventional consensus that Hemingway the artist is a function of the textual economy of the "objective correlative," a puritanical signifying practice geared to purge cant and sentimental illusion from prose. Performative more than constative in design, Hemingway's direct, spare style which many consider the artist's graceful response to the pain of the ubiquitous nada, the futility of modern life, supposedly mimics the ritual of the hunt and the bullfight—models of collective performance in pre-capitalist societies. The type of sentence Hemingway wanted to write seeks to achieve a "neutral *compte rendu* of external displacements," registering the movements in the external world of objects and also the tension between people. Moreover, Hemingway's texts embody the experience of sentence-production as non-alienated work, writing as a skill comparable to hunting and bullfighting "which project a total image of man's active and all-absorbing technical participation in the outside world." In the wake of U.S. industrial transformation after World War I, Jameson contends that Hemingway's valorization of efficient technique "satisfies the Protestant work ethic at the same time that it glorifies leisure; it reconciles the deepest and most life-giving impulses toward wholeness with a status quo in which only sports allow you to feel alive and undamaged" (1971, 411–12).[9] Since the complex fabric of U.S. social reality is inaccessible to the type of sentence Hemingway practices, it is necessary to exile/expatriate his

---

8. In the novel, Hemingway uses Jordan as his persona to express his vow to write "about the things he knew, truly," not the way things were supposed to be. This is the writer's doctrine of truth-telling (more precisely, bullshit-detecting) not as realistic or simple mimetic transcription but as a labor of invention: "A writer, if he is any good, does not describe. He invents or *makes* out of knowledge personal and impersonal. . . . [F]rom all the things that you know and all those you cannot know, you make something through your invention that is not a representation but a whole new thing truer than anything true and alive, and you make it alive." (Plimpton 1963, 237, 239). If FWBT is an invention of what is known and not known yielding a more authentic knowledge, truer than the reality the critics invoke, how exactly can we describe this text as a production of a peculiar kind?

9. Aside from the *locus classicus* of Hemingway's aestheticism, *Death in the Afternoon* (1932) and his subsequent book *Green Hills of Africa* (1935) provide validation for my thesis on Hemingway's doctrine of artisanal individualism, for example: "The work was the only thing, it was the one thing that always made you feel good, and in the meantime it was my own damned life and I would lead it where and how I pleased" (1932, 72).

characters to the reality of foreign cultures where, Jameson believes, "the individual comes before us not in the density of a concrete social situation in which we also are involved, but rather with the cleanness of objects which can be verbally circumscribed" (1971, 412).

Despite its cogency, Jameson's historicizing insight may not apply to this particular novel whose complex process of discourse production successfully projects its milieu's thickness and density in the drama of symbolic exchange, in the historic crisis of value, authority, and representation.[10]

The crisis of representability in *FWBT* cannot be divorced from the antagonisms between archaic, feudal, and capitalist forms of value as reflected in the distortions of chronotopes, ambivalent attitudes, and shifting point of view. A tendency toward spatial reduction typical of the early stage of merchant capitalism is partly replicated but also undermined, for example, in Pilar's story of the matador Finito's last day. The entire movement of this episode may serve as a microcosmic emblem of what some readers consider a tragic peripeteia; on the other hand, the banquet is a success in dramatizing the impossibility of recuperating the virtues of courage, fidelity, and intelligence which comprise the good in classical heroic society by way of aristocratic self-assertion. We confront again the ideological project motivating the narrative: lacking the appropriate social structure and its general equivalent form of value where individuals are given clear roles defining what they owe to others and what is owed to them, specific rights and duties which allow one's peers to confer honor on a man, can the individual living in modern society still uphold those virtues by sheer personal will-power and stoic determination?[11]

Alasdair MacIntyre (1981) believes that it is out of the question because our atomistic, liberal society where language games predominate cannot comprehend the organic connection in ancient society between the concept of courage and its allied virtues with the concepts of friendship, fidelity, and honor predicated on accountability to household and community. Action, morality, and social structure in heroic society are all inextricably coalesced so that individuals are able to perform actions required by their specific roles without the existential anguish ironi-

---

10. For the novel's exploitation of "language magic," see Stephens (1974).

11. Critics of various persuasions seem to agree that *FWBT* celebrates the heroic virtues of courage and competence enabling one to display "grace under pressure," a style of confronting death which would confirm that "life is worth living and that there are causes worth dying for" (Young 1952, 16–17). Those virtues are associated with *pietas* and love (Scott 1966, 29); the collective spirit of personal pride and integrity binding the guerillas (Waldhorn 1972, 172); partisanship for basic social ideals, "belief in man's noblest possibilities" (Benson 1969, 154). Mark Schorer's comment that FWBT is a "nearly poetic realization of man's collective virtues" (Meyers 1982, 340) as well as Carlos Baker's exposition of the novel as an epic with a tragic pattern (1972, 245–59) diverge from the contention of others that the narrative foregrounds the code of anarchic individualism, a charge echoed by most critics subscribing to an orthodox liberalism or a vulgar and caricatural "Marxism."

cally inflected in Jordan's ruminations. Virtue or *arete* has meaning in relation to the everyday conduct of a household and a community; glory is the recognition by his community of an individual's performance in sustaining the public and cosmic order. (In contrast, "La Gloria" in the novel signifies a mystical dissolution of separate consciousnesses akin to what Bataille [1985] calls the homogeneity of the sacred.) Both Jordan and the guerrillas value trust and friendship, but in heroic society trust and fidelity which underwrites friendship can only spring from a task-oriented courage. Courage then is not just the capacity to face any particular harm or danger as in safari hunting; rather, it is the capacity to face a particular pattern of danger where the individual's role, his accountability to a local community, is fully assayed and comprehended. While the guerrilla camp to which Jordan attaches himself (but not fully because his inner life is bifurcated by the negative figure of his father and the positive image of his grandfather, by the flux of his internal monologue) via Maria, Pilar, and Anselmo is torn by dissension and betrayal, the larger world of the Republic suspends accountability and blurs roles despite the fabled Communist discipline. Lacking the necessary social foundation, Jordan has to calculate in an instrumental or pragmatic fashion a code of professionalism that elevates his minor mission to a status on which presumably humanity's future turns—an inflation that owes more to his desire to transform his grandfather as vehicle of the phallic law than to any viable communal ethos of rights and obligations. If anything, it is the identity of the Republic conceived as the general equivalent form of value and its hegemonic destiny that is at issue in the whole novel. For Jordan, El Sordo, Anselmo, and others lacking any orthodox religious belief, the Republic represents an emergent discourse of humanist individualism in conflict with a still dominant discourse of religious collectivism and sub-ensembles of other discourses: romantic egotism blended with male camaraderie, atheistic naturalism, the dualism between GayLord Hotel and International Brigade, and so forth. What complicates the humanist discourse is its conflation with a discourse of mystical self-renunciation where narcissism is finally conquered by eroticized death and cyclical nature: recall that earth and forest frame Jordan's killing of Berrendo as prelude to his own extinction.

But the heroic virtues in ancient societies are always tied to organically integrated communities, not to a bureaucratic State or sovereignty transcending localities. Fate is a social reality, not a naturalistic event, because it is embedded in the synthesizing framework of an enacted epic narrative which accords destiny and death their due. While the fact of human fragility and vulnerability is duly acknowledged by the novel, it is articulated via the ethic of artisanal professionalism whose paradigm or archetype is the art of tauromachy. Meanwhile, the glorification of death (loss in *jouissance*, castration, the father's suicide, etc.) may draw its rationale from Walter Benjamin's insight that "Death is the sanction of everything that the storyteller can tell. He has borrowed his authority from death" (1969, 94), by which Benjamin refers to death immanent in natural history, as in Hemingway's satiric exemplum "A Natural History of the Dead" in *Death in the Afternoon*.

But here we encounter a crucial nuance in the novel's hybrid ideology meant to correspond to a general equivalent form of value: the obsession with self-destruction as an act of conspicuous wastage so as to enable a tacit plenitude of meaning to be installed in its place. We recall that Jordan celebrates the bravery of his grandfather in his participation in the Civil War (the crucible testing his man-hood) and the Indian wars (the natives like El Sordo, Pilar, and her gypsy tribe function as analogues to the indigenous American Indians) as against his father's cowardly suicide. For the guerrillas, Jordan is the alien or stranger with a gift of secret knowledge. Finding himself excluded both from the guerrilla band and betrayed by his father and metonymically by the commercial inanity of bourgeois society, Jordan tries to mediate his connection with a larger, this time interna-tional, community by invoking his grandfather's pre-industrial heroism. This tran-sitional stage of of Jordan's maturation is placed in "undiscovered country" behind enemy lines, an enclave in lost or alienated territory, where Jordan enacts a tactical "holding operation" for an offensive that is already doomed or compromised before its actual launching. This American professor of Spanish, volunteer partisan, and grandson of a Civil War veteran later on, after his involvement with Maria, Pilar, Pablo and El Sordo, comes to inhabit for three days the borderline, a "zone of occult instability," between the native and the stranger (see his equivocal but totalizing judgment of the Spanish character, [1940, 355]). Inserted in territory where his presence spells death, Jordan dislocates the guerrillas' lives, uprooting them, causing death for some; he is the bearer of a signifier whose meaning remains enigmatic despite the attempts to thematize its politics.[12]

Whatever its final significance, Jordan's intrusion into contested terrain cre-ates a disturbance of the space-time equilibrium of that social formation and signals a transitional crisis from the primitive and feudal stages of exchange to a more cen-tralized form. In any case, the problem of which equivalent form of value will become the hegemonic standard for Spanish society remains central to any inquiry about the novel's invention of ideology. In chapter 23, Jordan meditates on the Spanish "extra-sacrament," the old religion taken from the "far end of the Mediterranean" which erupts in wars and inquisitions: "the act of faith" immanent in the ecstasy of killing. Edward Stanton elaborates on the mystical aura surround-ing Maria and Pilar, as well as the nexus of love and death in religion, in the corrida ritual and its pagan/folk provenance (1989, 166–79). Characterizing the novel as a pastoral elegy which centers on the fused or suspended time of the Now, Earl

---

12. Warren French is the only critic so far who has interpreted this positioning of Jordan behind enemy lines as synecdoche of Hemingway's "separate war" (1971, 56–70). See also Broer (1973, 88–97).

Rovit and Gerry Brenner focus on Jordan's self-realization, the "immortality of becoming other" (1986, 126). But this otherness is predicated on translability, on the presence of a hegemonic law of equivalence operating in the symbolic, imaginary, and "real" registers. And that law springs from sacrifice, victimization, and the promise of transcendence in a heroic death which grounds the dynamics of symbolic exchange and ideological form in *FWBT*.

Nothing of this is entirely implausible to the canonical standards of Hemingway criticism. However, I think the mystique of heroic death and the obsession with a ritualized violence—together with its erotic libidinal charge insofar as it affects the narrative strategy of positioning subjects—can only be understood properly when it is seen as a negation of earlier forms of symbolic exchange predicated on simple equivalence (revenge) or relative forms (fetishism). For, as Bataille points out, it is human sacrifice that founds the sacred, in secular terms the universal equivalent form of value undergirding any polity: "But the development of knowledge touching on the history of religions has shown that the essential religious activity was not directed toward a personal and transcendent being (or beings), but toward an impersonal reality. Christianity has made the sacred *substantial*, but the nature of the sacred . . . is perhaps the most ungraspable thing that has been produced between men: the sacred is only a privileged moment of communal unity, a moment of the convulsive communication of what is ordinarily stifled" (1985, 242). From this perspective, we can qualify the ideological project of *FWBT* I have sketched earlier as the struggle to salvage the sacred from the ruins of progress, to elaborate a discourse of the universal equivalent form of value, by a transformative reworking of the privative, subjectivized point of view distinguished by its claim to rational (visual/spatial) control and its deconstruction in the affective intensities of such lived experience as those involving the erotic liaison of Maria and Jordan, the apocalyptic catastrophe inflicted on El Sordo's guerilla band, the massacre of fascists relived by Pilar, and so forth. It is in Pilar's unforgettable evocation of the smell of coming death (1940, 136–37) that we see the limits of the focalizing apparatus, together with its ideological drive to subsume everything in a constellation of monads, severely tried and finally betrayed with the metonymic slippage of signifiers suspended by a reifying metaphoric impulse. What is epiphanic here is the connotative import of the odor of death-to-come, which sutures the folds of birth and of death; the evocation of this odor by Pilar, the gypsy prophet of what's to come and chronicler of the past's *Nachtraglichkeit*, recuperates the historical genesis of the sacred itself, that lost unity of social life intimated by so many fragments, traces, and constellations of nostalgic hieroglyphs and ideograms, to whose absence the narrative is constantly gesturing.

It would of course be obviously reductive to equate the novel's ideological form with any single thematic cluster. But it is equally indubitable that the narrative structure of *FWBT* inheres not only in its setting and atmosphere, dialogue, manipulation of point of view, and mode of characterization but more crucially in the handling of time, especially the dialectic between story-duration and text-duration. It would be too lengthy to detail the textual exploitation of ellipsis, descriptive pause, summary, and scene; the variation of frequencies (singulative, repetitive, iterative) and other techniques whereby the text's ideological closure is disrupted. Bakhtin's concept of the chronotope I have touched on opens up again the question of the historicity of Hemingway's narrative strategy as a textualizing of absences and omissions—what has been pejoratively named "the metaphysics of the text." My argument is that the text interrogates this metaphysics when it puts on trial the problematic of aestheticism and the anachronistic proxy of heroic individualism as the novel's answer to the profound transitional crisis of Western civilization focused in the peculiar social formation of Spain in the 1930s.

One of the most profound changes characterizing the transition from the feudal or tributary formation to market capitalism in Western society involves the phenomenon of time-space compression, the conquest and rigorous control of space as the totalizing thrust of Enlightenment thinking. In *The Condition of Postmodernity*, David Harvey explains how the rational ordering of space through scientific cartography required by bourgeois commerce, the determination of property rights in the utilization of land for capitalist agriculture, and so on, also entailed the contraction of the time horizon "to the point where the present is all there is" (1989, 241)—schizophrenic time fusion. By fragmenting the spatial order and homogenizing it, capitalist production could accelerate the flow of time for the generation of surplus-value in the process of primitive accumulation. All these complex developments have registered themselves in modernist art, particularly in the experimental syncopation of time into space and in the privileging of a subjectivized or psychologized point of view.

The economy of time-space compression in *FWBT* finds itself realized not only in the seventy hours' span of the diegetic sequence (story duration) but more decisively in the aestheticist-romantic orientation of the structure and Jordan's rationalization of the brevity of his life. I have already discussed Pilar and Maria's interpolation, traumatic "spots of time," and nodes of cathexes where a plenitude of meaning seems to halt temporal progression. I have also provided a metacommentary on the episode of El Sordo's last stand where the flow of time is markedly decelerated to coincide eventually with the utterance of Joaquin's prayer to the Virgin Mary. But it is in the erotic union of Maria and Jordan (1940, 73, 158–59, 263, 379) where apocalypse (time collapsed into space) erases the schism of public and private, inside and outside, in order to restore a full presence.[13] The "full word" is thus recuperated through a deliberate mimicry of the language of Catholic prayer as the sexual climax is reached in chapter 37: "this was what had

---

13. Spilka's new book (1990, 246–55) may qualify the traditional conception of Hemingway's "machismo" and reinforce the centrality of Pilar in the textual production of ideology.

been and now and whatever was to come . . . oh, now, now, now, the only now, and above all now, and there is no other now but thou now and now is thy prophet" (1940, 379). Routine time of alienated work in a secular world is overthrown by the sacramental instant of "dying" in the love act, a calculation of pleasure which finds its philosophical sanction in the theory of marginal utility as the measure of value in circulation (Goux 1990). We can discern in this fusion of erotic love and loss of self a version of the universal equivalent form of value whose absence is the burden of the ideological production of the text. This loss of self, the catharsis of psychic duplicity which Jordan thinks has been accomplished in the almost religious passion of the International Brigade, is what valorizes Jordan's work done "alone" and "coldly in the head" (1940, 172). It is the aim of the self-transcending experience of sexual union the remembrance (substitution) of which enables Jordan to endure the pain of mutilation during the retreat, avoid suicide, and uphold his commitment to his grandfather's example as the overarching standard of exchange.

Through a symptomatic reading of *FWBT*, we can gain a knowledge of the textual production of fiction-effects such as the syncopation of time-space, gaps and silences that I have detailed here which renders the form of ideology apprehensible. However, since the power of ideology cannot be thoroughly grasped without investigating how the text constitutes, motivates, and transforms readers (including critics, reviewers, and scholars) as social subjects—for ideology is that by which individuals are interpellated as subjects fitted to perform specific tasks in a lived relation to a given sociohistorical project, that is, the text's "ideological domination effect" (Young 1981), our task will not be complete until we have assessed the whole rich corpus of glosses, exegeses, and commentaries on Hemingway's novel. This essay announces a call for others to help accomplish this task.

ADDENDUM

A survey of previous "Marxist" approaches to Hemingway's works[14] will reveal that most of them take a mechanical or non-dialectical approach based on a one-dimensional reflectionist theory, casting serious doubt on their proclaimed "Marxism." Maxwell Geismar's (1961) judgment of Hemingway as an isolated individualist is typical of "leftist" criticism of Hemingway in the three decades after *A Farewell To Arms* appeared. From a slightly different angle, the Soviet critic Ivan Kashkeen (1961) takes off from Geismar's liberal, orthodox conception of Hemingway as a profoundly ambivalent, tragic writer. But unlike Geismar, Kashkeen, less tied to the specific historical coordinates of U.S. society (the Depression, the New Deal, and so on), is able to illuminate the oscillation between the positive, "humanistic" elements and the decadent, reactionary elements in Hemingway's corpus. In the same volume of assessments edited by Carlos Baker where Kashkeen's article appeared, Deming Brown's survey of Soviet opinion entitled "Hemingway in Russia" (1961, 145–61) doesn't reveal much except that official Soviet critics follow a rigid Party line. So what else is new?

Overall, what has been claimed to be the orthodox Marxist view turns out to be a crude, mechanical commentary that subordinates aesthetic values to empirical or positivist sociological criteria—a throwback to the worst of Taine or Zola (see also Bessie 1974).

In this brief note I suggest a new historical-materialist appraisal, taking as a point of departure the theoretical framework proposed by Louis Althusser and other "revisionists." Fredric Jameson (1972), among other innovators, has ventured a historicist reading of Hemingway by a metacommentary on the now legendary prose style. Using ideas developed by recent formulations (especially those influenced by Gramsci) induced by the challenge of Third World critiques of "Western Marxism," I would like to propose a contextualizing approach to *For Whom the Bell Tolls* that would suggest possibilities for a genuine dialectical articulation of form and desire inscribed in Hemingway's signifying practice.

From the standpoint of a historical-materialist hermeneutics, Hemingway's novel may be taken as an exemplary textual paradigm of cultural overdetermination. Succinctly put, it is as if Hemingway had constructed a narrative *combinatoire* intended to demonstrate how a heroic male will-to-discipline and its protean displacements can effect a reconciliation of the complex, multilayered contradictions of the modern world, specifically the interwar conjuncture of the 1930s, between the collapse of the global market in 1929 and the outbreak of World War II. Such

---

14. This short article was written as a propaedeutic guide prior to composing the essay above.

a reconciliation in the sphere of modernist fiction is essentially ideological, a form of illusory but effective closure.

Of the manifold contradictions or "raw materials" the text works on, the most fundamental or primary is usually formulated as that between fascism (Franco, the Axis powers) and parliamentary democracy (the constitutional Republic). From the orthodox view, these two antagonistic systems span the extremes of the ideological spectrum of bourgeois society in its historical development in a Western context: from liberal to statist corporatism. However, Hemingway's text is precisely different from other radical critiques of fascism construed as the most reactionary form of bourgeois hegemony in that it attempts to articulate the intertextuality of a social formation (Spain as index for the antithesis between Third World and Western metropolis) to unfold the various codes or subtexts that produce the thematic contradictions regularly inventoried by the traditional formalist evaluation of Hemingway's work.

I suggest the following series of subtexts that overdetermine Hemingway's rendering of the fascism–Republic polarity: anarchist individualism (Pablo) and bureaucratic discipline (e.g., Marty), private sensibility (Jordan) and communal responsibility (El Sordo), rational perception and intuitive decision, Eros (Maria) and Agape (Anselmo). Such categories may be conceived as hypothetical rubrics for moments or stages of the narrative development unfolded in the text. They make up the binary oppositions embedded in the diachronic movement of the plot, structuring the sequence of incidents in a teleological fashion so that they are ultimately invested with morally qualitative and philosophic significance.

One way of expressing the dialectic between the synchronic and diachronic axes of the text is to re-inscribe them into a larger but more concretely differentiated site of material practices subsumed in the concept of "mode of production." This concept organizes in a dialectical fashion the three interacting instances of the political, the economic, and the ideological. It is precisely within this synthesizing concept of the crisis of historical modes of production within a concrete social formation that one can define the unprecedented originality and power of Hemingway's novel.

I submit that what *For Whom the Bell Tolls* renders, in the interweaving of its various codes (in *S/Z*, Roland Barthes stipulates five: proairetic, hermeneutic, cultural, connotative, and symbolic), is the crisis of liberal thought (C.B. Macpherson's "possessive individualism") with its concomitant property relations and political institutions, as exemplified in the Spanish conjuncture of the early 1930s (see Colodny 1970). This hegemony of a historic bloc (an alliance of classes) over state and civil society is faced with two mutually irreconcilable possibilities or futures: the fascist organic/religious corporatism with its mystique of death and technology, or the socialist/collective egalitarianism, with all its tensions and ambiguities, illustrated in Robert Jordan's sojourn with the guerrilla outfits (Pablo's and

El Sordo's). Overdetermining this conjuncture between industrial monopoly capitalism (Franco's bureaucratic machine plus the high-powered technology associated with Germany and Italy) and the feudal apparatuses and practices linked with the Church, tributary landownership, and the double symbolic function of bullfighting (see *Death in the Afternoon*), is the utopian nostalgia for, and metaphoric allusions to, an artisan style and norm of activity—Jordan's professional concentration on his task of blowing up the bridge, the exaltation of bullfighting as *techne* or craft, Anselmo's hunting rituals, and so on. All these would reject the reified and alienating forms of capitalist society, particularly its instrumental rationality and its alienating, commodified work, which are both crystallized in the technocracy of war. They would in turn revalorize individual integrity as both a spiritual attribute of socialized personality and a commitment to the good of the community. This is the allegory of virtue distilled in the novel. In this utopian dimension, memorably dramatized by El Sordo's confrontation with death and his affirmation of life as sensuous apprehension, or by the erotic loss of ego in Jordan's love for Maria, lies Hemingway's characteristic gesture of reconciling the various contradictions described above.

One might contrast this strategy of resolution and its quasi-existentialist denouement with André Malraux's use in *Man's Hope* of what Kenneth Burke calls "frame of acceptance." In the famous scene of the wounded aviators' descent from the mountain in part three just before the Republican victory in the Guadalajara front, the pain and suffering of the combatants are evinced as testimony of an eternal human adventure. The cinematic angle of the narrative blends action and reflection, the details of the landscape orchestrated with ideas of a transcendent consciousness that ultimately imposes meaning on the whole scene:

> In the silence suddenly grown murmurous with the sound of rippling water, the ring of decaying fruit seemed to typify the passage from life to death that not only was the doom of men but was an immutable law of the universe. Magnin's eyes wandered from the tree to the ageless ravines. One after another, the stretchers were going past. . . . The solemn, primitive march of that line of stretchers had something as compelling about it as the pale rocks that merged into the lowering sky, something as fundamental as the apples scattered on the ground. . . . And the steady stream of their tread over the long, pain-burdened journey seemed to fill the vast ravine, down which the last cries still came floating from the birds above, with a solemn beat like a funeral drum. But it was not death which haunted the mountains at that moment; it was triumphant human will. (1938, 400–401)

This kind of montage that generates the pathos of a sublime archetypal event is ruled out by Hemingway's sensibility. For the American ethos of personalist virtue entails an aporia when juxtaposed with a collective struggle; the virtuoso performance of the deed redeems the protagonist and sanctions the legitimacy of a social order that values such individual act. Malraux, on the other hand, values "the infinite possibilities" of human destiny incorporated in art and thought in which heroic communal sacrifices find their just vindication.

What is peculiar to the Hemingway text in its transcoding of the historic crisis of bourgeois liberalism in a Third World hybrid formation like Spain, is its oblique ironic inflection. Hemingway's vision of transcendence is itself limited and conditioned by its internal contradiction, that is, by what it denies: the individual body's death, technological domination, and so on. For implicit in the typical Hemingwayesque glorification of the beleaguered, stoic, virile consciousness, with its aestheticized valorization of skill for its own sake, or Renaissance *virtu* drastically narrowed into specialized craft (blowing bridges, bullfighting), is the fascist doctrine of *Fuhrerprinzip*, elitist male/patriarchal supremacy, and power hierarchy as a natural given. This cluster of mystifications is coupled with the metaphysical idealism of the immediate present which Jordan's selfless commitment and consciously chosen sacrifice to the Republic's cause is meant to negate.

One may interpose here Elliot Paul's ethnographic account of Spanish society before and after Franco's revolt in 1936, *The Life and Death of a Spanish Town*, as an exemplary inversion of Hemingway's concern with individual male heroism. Paul's anatomy of the antagonistic political-ideological forces I have categorized is performed through a meticulous description of everyday life in Santa Eulalia and the scrupulous characterization of over fifty *dramatis personae* from all classes and walks of life. Unlike Hemingway, Paul's narrative is polyphonic: no single voice dominates—not even the "central intelligence" whose shifting gaze unifies the diverse characters—perhaps because Paul's empathy with the inhabitants is more adequate and his belief in the right of Spanish popular self-determination more genuine. Unlike Paul, Hemingway is less concerned with capturing the dynamics of the Spanish collective psyche than fighting his own war with the depersonalizing logic and mechanical uniformity of U.S. business society.

At the center of the aporia between the imagination and fetishized power which somehow the text is unable to transcend, even though it tries to sublimate or marginalize it, is the sexual politics reflected by the role of Maria as the emblematic victim/recipient of male power. She personifies the crucible of the male will to dominate nature and time—in effect, to sustain castration of the Other so as to assert the phallocentrism of Hemingway's art. In the process, however, this project of the phallocratic will is subverted by the ambivalent role of Pilar as surrogate patriarch/leader of the guerrilla band, and (with Maria) as the archetypal Demeter-

Kore construed by Carl Jung and Carl Kerenyi (1963) as the archaic embodiment of the libidinal forces manifest in different forms of violence described in the text.

A conflation of the Symbolic and Imaginary registers (as formulated by Lacan) may be perceived in Robert Jordan's personal dilemma of trying to organize his life, to give it meaning and direction, by sublating his father's suicide (the patriarch cognized as wounded and absent) and in the process reinserting an earlier historic model of cultural production (rural or pre-industrial America) as symbolized by his grandfather, a veteran of the Civil War and the subsequent campaigns of extermi-nating the Indians. The following passages in chapter 30 are symptomatic of the failure of Jordan's psyche to fully negotiate the process of evolving from the Imaginary (the myth of spiritual oneness with the world; the plenitude of union with the mother's body) to the Symbolic (history) without the mediation of a hegemonic patriarchal authority (the grandfather, Karkov, Golz) that seriously undermines the construction of a socialist project in which Jordan has chosen, albeit in his own terms, to participate:

> I wish Grandfather were here instead of me. Well, maybe we will all be together by tomorrow night. If there should be any such damn fool business as a hereafter, and I'm sure there isn't, he thought, I would certainly like to talk to him. . . . I had no right to ask before. I understand him not telling me because he didn't know me. But now I think that we would get along all right. I'd like to be able to talk to him now and get his advice. Hell, if I didn't get advice I'd just like to talk to him. It's a shame there is such a jump in time between ones like us.
>
> Then, as he thought, he realized that if there was any such thing as ever meeting, both he and his grandfather would be acutely embarrassed by the presence of his father. Anyone has a right to do it, he thought. But it isn't a good thing to do. I understand it, but I do not approve of it. . . . But you do understand it? Sure, I understand it but. Yes, but. You have to be awfully occupied with yourself to do a thing like that.
>
> Aw hell, I wish Grandfather was here, he thought. For about an hour anyway. Maybe he sent me what little I have through that other one that misused the gun. Maybe that is the only communication that we have. But, damn it. Truly damn it, but I wish the time-lag wasn't so long so that I should have learned from him what the other one never had to teach me. But suppose the fear he had to go through and domi-nate and just get rid of finally in four years of that and then in the Indian fighting, although in that, mostly, there couldn't have been so much fear, had made a *cobarde* out of the other one the way second generation bullfighters almost always are? Suppose that? And maybe the good juice only came through straight again after passing through that one?

I'll never forget how sick it made me the first time I knew he was a *cobarde*. Go on, say it in English. Coward. It's easier when you have it said and there is never any point in referring to a son of a bitch by some foreign term. He wasn't any son of a bitch, though. He was just a coward and that was the worst luck any man could have. Because if he wasn't a coward he would have stood up to that woman and not let her bully him. I wonder what I would have been like if he had married a different woman? That's something you'll never know, he thought, and grinned. Maybe the bully in her helped to supply what was missing in the other. And you. Take it a little easy. Don't get to referring to the good juice and such other things until you are through tomorrow. Don't be snotty too soon. And then don't be snotty at all. We'll see what sort of juice you have tomorrow. (1940, 338–39)

Buried in the palimpsest of writing, elided by the logocentric presence of the dramatic monologue, is the key enunciation around which a transformative critique would turn: "Because if he wasn't a coward he would have stood up to that woman and not let her bully him." Implied in this diagnosis of failure is an anarchic impulse that Hemingway's novel shares with George Orwell's *Homage to Catalonia*. But it is actually more in the anarchosyndicalist ideal of the key protagonist Samar, in Ramon Sender's *Seven Red Sundays*, that we find Jordan's profound motivation; an ideal of "sublime generosity" whose matrix Sender finds sedimented in the dream of a utopian order "in which all men are as disinterested as St. Francis of Assisi, bold as Spartacus, and able as Newton and Hegel" (12).

Perhaps the clarification of the above thematic crux, apart from a transcoding of the quoted interior monologue, hinges on a multiple reading of Pilar's function in the triangulation of desire, reason, and history. At this juncture we also confront the problematic of the subject (the narrator, the reader, the chief protagonist) as an effect of the suturing of text and speaking voice through the rhetorical strategies of castration and fetishism of the female, as theorized by contemporary feminist semiotics.

I would like to conclude by mapping out in a Greimasian semantic rectangle the thematic limits constraining Hemingway's text. In this formula, one can also apprehend the possibilities of establishing equations and reversals that the narrative explores in its quest for a harmonious and necessarily fictive resolution, the ideological closure I have alluded to earlier. The schema in figure 2 below, which it is the task of a new Marxian critique to historicize in the conflict of various modes of production and the struggle for hegemony, is a shorthand abbreviation of the dialectical energies informing Hemingway's novel. It is a schema that also attests to its versatile signifying power.

FIGURE 5.2

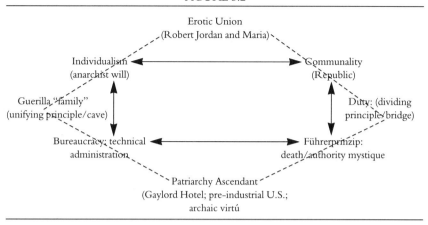

In *Death in the Afternoon,* Hemingway formulated the principle or motive force of his signifying practice thus: "I was trying to write then and I found the greatest diffficulty, aside from knowing what you really felt, rather than what you were supposed to feel, and had been taught to feel, was to put down what really happened in action; what the actual things were which produced the emotion that you experienced" (1932, 2). The ethics of veracity and sincerity implied by that assertion governs the style of *For Whom the Bell Tolls.* Coincidentally, it also informs this famous passage from *The German Ideology* by Marx and Engels: "We do not set out from what men say, imagine, conceive, nor from men as narrated, thought of, imagined, conceived, in order to arrive at men in the flesh. We set out from real, active men, and on the basis of their real life-process we demonstrate the development of the ideological reflexes and echoes of this life-process. . . . Life is not determined by consciousness, but consciousness by life, [by men's] actual, empirically perceptible process of development under definite conditions." Any viable Marxist hermeneutics necessarily seizes this as its ineluctable point of departure, as "the bell" that tolls also for all readers, scriptors, and genealogists of Hemingway's now monumental text.

6

Hugh MacDiarmid

TOWARD A MATERIALIST POETICS

Only through the objectively unfolded richness of man's essential being is the richness of subjective human sensibility (a musical ear, an eye for beauty of form—in short, senses capable of human gratifications, senses confirming themselves as essential powers of man) either cultivated or brought into being. For not only the five senses but also the so-called mental senses—the practical senses (will, love, etc.)—in a word, human sense—the humanness of the senses—comes to be by virtue of its object, by virtue of humanized nature. The forming of the five senses is a labor of the entire history of the world down to the present.

. . . The human essence is no abstraction inherent in each single individual. In its reality it is the ensemble of social relations.

—Karl Marx

Anyone daring for the first time to enter the massive and immense structure composing the entire oeuvre of Hugh MacDiarmid would do no worse, I feel, than take the poet's affirmation of his beliefs about his vocation at face value and see how they fare in our appreciation of his poems. One can at the outset suggest that the magisterial theme of MacDiarmid's poetry is the achievement of the fullest human freedom or self-fulfillment for everyone, what Marx and Engels in *The Communist Manifesto* called the free development of each individual predicated on the free development of all. MacDiarmid envisioned poetry as "human existence come to life." What complicates this outlook and makes it problematic for most commentators is MacDiarmid's now legendary if controversial nationalism and his lifelong crusade against British imperialism and its Scottish allies. In his self-commentary of 1952 he describes his paradoxical commitment: "if he is an extreme Scottish nationalist he is also one of the greatest internationalists even Scotland has ever produced" (1970a, 21).

Indeed, MacDiarmid was proud of his being "organically welded" with the working masses because he was rooted in the place of his birth, Langholm in Dumfriesshire, whose "tremendous proletarian virtue" saved him from the ordeal

of searching for his identity amid the religiosity, parochialism, and general alienation of the milieu. In this habitat he would celebrate how man "will flash with the
immortal fire" and "rise/To the full height of the imaginative act/That wins to the
reality in the fact"—life flaming in the vision of "the light that breaks/From the
whole earth seen as a star again/In the general life of man" (1970a, 36). It seems
that MacDiarmid's imagination grounds its truth, its enabling virtue, in the terrestrial, quasi-Manichean drama of a struggle between progressive and reactionary
forces; in this theater "whaur extremes meet," the spirit's *agon* performs its daily
ritual of incarnation. In effect, MacDiarmid strove to realize the harmony of affective and cognitive faculties in praxis, in practical sensuous activity, where thought
and feeling coalesced (Thomson 1974). Poetic utterance is this praxis of communication.

At the age of forty-six, MacDiarmid reflected on his career by assaying the
crisis that overtook poets like Keats, Wordsworth, and Rimbaud. In the process he
expressed the radical historicist foundation of his "method of being":

> —I am forty-six; of tenacious, long-lived, country folk.
> Fools regret my poetic change—from my "enchanting early lyrics"—
> But I have found in Marxism all that I need—
> (I on my mother's side of long-lived Scottish peasant stock
> And on my father's of hardy keen-brained Border mill-workers).
> It only remains to perfect myself in this new mode.
>
> (1978, 30)

What this "new mode" signifies is nothing else but the principle of dialectical
materialism that holds paramount the historical specificity of any cultural/ideolog-
ical practice. It also posits the reciprocal dynamics of human sensibility and the
multilayered social totality in which it is inscribed. Hence MacDiarmid situates his
own art concretely within the cultural heritage of Scotland. He disavows any tendency toward "purely hothouse proletarian literature" by addressing what Gramsci
calls the "national-popular" needs of the masses in Scotland, needs that provide the
energies for a socialist project of winning hegemony. While MacDiarmid's comprehension of Marxism may be revisionist from the perspective of orthodox
Marxism-Leninism, I think his practice is more revolutionary insofar as the construction of a poetic idiom geared to shaping a materialist/scientific consciousness
is concerned. Like Bertolt Brecht or Ernesto Cardenal, he wanted to communicate
to the masses and in the process educate (both teach and learn from) them. One
can argue that MacDiarmid's moral authority originates from the spontaneous
"creaturality" and ironic humor of plebeian Scotland, a lifeworld imbued with joy
and dignity, at once material and transcendental.

In "Aesthetics in Scotland," MacDiarmid outlines his militant stance: "I
regard the cultural question of supreme importance, and believe the function of

Literature and the Arts to be the expansion of human consciousness, or as my friend Sean O'Casey termed it, 'the sensitive extension of the world. . . .' My real concern with Socialism is as an artist's organised approach to the interdependencies of life" (1978, xxvii–viii). Perhaps the fundamental thesis crystallizing Mac-Diarmid's various formulations of his social responsibility as a Scottish poet, the "central passion that animates" his poetry, is this passage from the magnificent "Third Hymn to Lenin" which he quotes at the beginning of chapter 6 of his auto-biography *Lucky Poet*:

> Our concern is human wholeness—the child-like spirit
> Newborn every day—not, indeed, as careless of tradition
> Nor of the lessons of the past: these it must needs inherit;
> But as capable of such complete assimilation and surrender,
> So all-inclusive, unfenced-off, uncategorized, sensitive, and tender,
>
> That growth is unconditional and unwarped—Ah, Lenin,
> Life and that more abundantly, thou Fire of Freedom!
> Firelike in your purity and heaven-seeking vehemence,
> Yet the adjective must not suggest merely meteoric,
> Spectacular—not the flying sparks, but the intense
> Glowing core of your character, your large and splendid stability,
>
> Made you the man you were—the live heart of all humanity—
> Spirit of Lenin, light on this city now!
> Light up this city now!
>
> (1972, 312)

Immediately obvious here is the fact that the city, not rural landscape, becomes the privileged site of metamorphosis and "soul-making." Two themes are signalled in that passage—the theme of growth or process of renewal leading to a differenti-ated, innovative, and responsive wholeness; and the theme of enlightenment and the invention of a character, a heroic archetype or model forged in the fires of anti-imperialist class struggles. Both themes are dialectically integrated in MacDiarmid's aesthetic practice which aims not just to reflect reality or express personal idiosyn-cracies but actually produce necessary forms of social consciousness. In terms of Christopher Caudwell's (1946) theoretical framework, MacDiarmid's poetics jux-taposes mimesis, the contrivance of a phantasy "Mock World," and pragmatic socialization of affects where the "I" (the social ego) generates and experiments with new social possibilities. In this reckoning, poetry becomes an agent of histor-ical and psychological change.

Such controlling themes distilled here in schematic form, however, have to be mediated in a verbal design both *utile et dulce*. Aside from that twin Horatian dimension of classic art, what is desired above all is that the form should avoid "the irresponsible lyricism" of banal feeling MacDiarmid identifies with the narcissistic sentimentality that plagues capitalist society. In "Utterly a Creator," he conceives of the oscillation between idea and emotion, between passion and intellect, transpiring in the artistic process of inventing forms. He describes the process as one of "conflict/Between discipline at its most strenuous/And feeling at its highest—wherein abrasive surfaces/Are turned upon one another like millstones,/And instead of generating chaos/Refine the grist of experience between them." Art is thus conceived as a peculiar form of production, its product being "an intricately-cut gem-stone of myriad facets/That is yet, miraculously, a whole."

My favorite example of MacDiarmid's *ars poetica* is the poem "Crystals like Blood." Here the analogy of imaginative creation and the operation of a grinding machine is used to suggest the condition of possibility for experiencing grief coalesced with love for the memory of a departed loved one. The speaker begins with a recollection: he found "Crystals like blood in a broken stone" he picked up one day, one face of the broken chunk torn from the bedrock "caked with brown limestone." Then follows telltale notations of the "greenish-grey quartz-like stone/Faintly dappled with darker shadows" streaked with "veins and beads/Of bright magenta." From this tableau, the speaker shifts to another recollection, this time a scene in a factory where one precious mineral (mercury) is extracted from the red ore of cinnabar crumbled by iron piledrivers and lifted up into a kiln:

> And I remember how later on I saw
> How mercury is extracted from cinnabar
> —The double ring of iron piledrivers
> Like the multiple legs of a fantastically symmetrical spider
> Rising and falling with monotonous precision,
> Marching round in an endless circle
> And pounding up and down with a tireless, thunderous force,
> While, beyond, another conveyor drew the crumbled ore
> From the bottom and raised it to an opening high
> In the side of a gigantic grey-white kiln.
>
> So I remember how mercury is got
> When I contrast my living memory of you
> And your dear body rotting here in the clay
> —And feel once again released in me
> The bright torrents of felicity, naturalness, and faith
> My treadmill memory draws from you yet.

                                                      (1993, 231)

One cannot help perceiving in the brute force of the pile drivers performing one repeated motion over and over and its thunderous sound an intimation of feelings the speaker is struggling to control; such feelings are bound to the logic of an image taken from the realm of industrial technology. The elegy acquires an "objective correlative" for a melancholy that, if not displaced appropriately, would damage the ego. What enables the displacement is something Vladimir Mayakovsky (1972) once called the rigor of "the social demand." The spare, monosyllabic phrasing of the last stanza demonstrates a calculated mimesis of the process of extracting mercury itself, with the rapid flow of the line "The bright torrents of felicity, naturalness, and faith" capturing the moment of "release"—only to be reined in by the laconic tone of the last line. The modulation here contours poignantly the flow of mourning.

What is striking in this anti-elegy can be elucidated as a trope of analogy: the mercury of memory and the rotting body in the clay symmetrically evoke the two contrasting surfaces of the fragment of bedrock painted earlier. What is surprising, however, is not any supposed parallelism between the mill and the imagination but the proposition that the tension between the poet's "living memory" of the loved one and his full consciousness of her physical decay is what releases the radiant burst of vital life that sustains the speaker's mind. The point then is not loss as such but loss as a mode of recovery.

The theme of a mind in control and triumphant over time and death is refracted in "The Terrible Crystal." The poet addresses a white stone "formed in tragedy/And calcined in catastrophe." In the "white intensity of that single central radiance" found in the stone he contemplates, he glimpses "Visions of a transcendental country/Stretching out athwart the temporal frontiers." The crystal embodies "the cataclysm and central fires" of life kindled at those moments "When consciousness is crucified upon circumstance." Here, the Marxist axiom of the dialectic between matter and consciousness, social being and the psyche, is modulated to assign to thought (where concepts of relations are produced) an unexpected locus of agency:

Clear thought is the quintessence of human life.
In the end its acid power will disintegrate
All the force and flummery of current passions and pretences,
Eat the life out of every false loyalty and craven creed
And bite its way through to a world of light and truth.

(1967, 30)

Lest MacDiarmid be accused of philosophical idealism by sectarian partisans, I venture to remind them that thought, for Engels, is a modality of matter in motion. Here, the logical culmination of thought's adventure is the mystical "diamond body" MacDiarmid celebrates in the poem "Diamond Body in a Cave of the Sea," where "seeming deception prefigures truth" in his achieving knowledge that the earth ebbs and flows, the water remains steady—the revelation of the "Great Tao" of the world. The stones in "On A Raised Beach" deliver the same epiphanic epistemology.

In the Western tradition, one can valorize MacDiarmid's quest for a poetry of knowledge as a refunctioning of the classic humanistic ideal of art combining knowledge and pleasure in a context where everything is commodified. His affinity, however, is with Brecht's mode of teaching/learning via techniques of distanciation and restructuring. One example is MacDiarmid's resort to an image of technical process at the end of what began as a salute to the archaic past, "Lamh Dearg Aboo." He is concerned with how the meaning of Scotland's history, its ancient heroic greatness, can be captured by evoking the unified action of fifteen hundred men in battle. To convey this discipline and singleness of purpose, the poet abruptly shifts to a scene of machinery in motion acutely delineated—the foil to the "fog of oppression and cant" scattered by "fluent Gaelic sunlight":

> To see this is as when in a great ship's engine-room
> Through all the vastness of furnaces and clanging machinery is found
> The quiet simple thing all that is about—a smooth column of steel,
> The propeller shaft, in cool and comfortable bearings, turning round
>   and round with no sound
> —All the varying forces, the stresses and resistances,
> Proceeding from that welter of machinery.
> Unified into the simple rotation of this horizontal column,
> And conducted calmly along its length into the sea.

Conventional opinion attributes to MacDiarmid an obsession with the heterogeneous, with incompatibilities and incongruities. But further inquiry will show that the poet's drive for mastery of form and linguistic resources derives from a profound engagement with the political and social dynamic immanent in lived experience. In "The Terrible Crystal," the poet seeks a poetry with "the power/Of fusing the discordant qualities of experience,/Of mixing moods, and holding together opposites." The yoking of opposites and contradictions in his imagery and style is not just an exercise of multiplying metaphysical conceits, an exhibition of the proverbial "Caledonian Antisyzygy" (Bold 1988) for its own sake; rather, it is an integral part of the hybrid, decentered poetics he is trying to evolve. He longs for "an imaginative integrity/That includes, but transcends, sensibility as such," an integrity that struggles "through complexity to simplicity," a necessary and equally difficult task. After the organized gallimaufry of *A Drunk Man Looks at the Thistle*, MacDiarmid replaced the emblematic thistle with Cencrastus, the Curly Snake, which "represents not only all the sinuosities of ancient Celtic wisdom but also the devious resourcefulness of MacDiarmid himself, who has said of the winding path near Langholm called the Curly Snake: "It has always haunted my imagination and has probably constituted itself the ground plan and pattern of my mind" (1978, xv).

I suggest that MacDiarmid's protean and syncretic art be seen as one of those recurrent efforts in Western culture to reconcile classic and romantic polarities. Indeed, the precise term for this strategy of interrogating and transforming those polarities constituting the bourgeois art of representation is critical "dialectics." Underneath the poet's will to achieve encyclopedic scope is a passion for inventing multiple perspectives needed to overturn fixed positions and revealing their anchorage in practice and cooperative production. MacDiarmid valorizes the experience of change and the analytic discernment of shifting relations; he strives to dramatize process and mutability amid the illusions of stasis and permanence. His imagination traces its genealogy to the dialogue between Heraclitus and Parmenides at the dawn of Western science and cosmological speculation. In "Poetry and Science," MacDiarmid invokes Walt Whitman's call to conform to "the concrete realities and theories of the universe furnished by science." More crucial is his quote from the philosopher Santayana: "The heart and mystery of matter lies in the seeds of things, *semina rerum*, and in the customary cycles of their transformation" (1970a, 244). In "The Terrible Crystal," he pursues "the hidden and lambent core": "A teleology essentially immanent,/God's relation to the world being in some general way/Like the relation of our minds to our bodies."

MacDiarmid's conception of a scientific poetics inheres in a view of reality as process where facts are events, where phenomena enact the laws of motion. His predilection for description of perceptible surfaces (for instance, geological formations) or physical motions as vehicles for staging the evocation of felt thought may be illustrated in many of his longer poems, especially "On a Raised Beach." In a short one entitled "The Skeleton of the Future (At Lenin's Tomb)," the symbolic play of colors and the chiaroscuro of background/foreground elements function as tropological networks that compress a whole range of ideas and values about the permanence of a significant life, its precision and objectivity, vis-à-vis the transience of the body:

Red granite and black diorite, with the blue
Of the labradorite crystals gleaming like precious stones
In the light reflected from the snow; and behind them
The eternal lightning of Lenin's bones.

Characteristically, MacDiarmid's mind orbits around the sense of sight counterpointed by a fine instinct for the music of syntax and grammar: for instance, he refers to Lenin's "lizard eyes." He vows to revenge Lorca's death inspired by the poet's pupils "that had known how to see/Unique colours and foreshortenings of wonder." Sight recoils from ecological blurring: Edinburgh, like most cities, suffers from the dark "monstrous pall" of industrialism for which Lenin's clairvoyance would be a way out. Such clairvoyance is "the result of a profound and all-sided knowledge of life/With all its richness of colour, connexions and relations."

Sensitive to manifold and subtle linkages of intuition, MacDiarmid can apprehend the paradox of "Light and Shadow," of ignorance and knowledge fused in signifying practice. "Cross-lights of errors" share with "shadowy glimpses of unknown thoughts" a subliminal power to illuminate the limits of rationality so that the poet is led eventually to pray: "May I . . . never fail/To keep some shining sense of the way all thoughts at last/Before life's dawning meaning like the stars at sunrise pale." This humility, or more exactly materialist wisdom, serves to circumscribe a strong neo-Platonic or even quasi-Hegelian idealism in MacDiarmid ascribable perhaps to his faith in what Coleridge calls the "esemplastic" power of the imagination: "Know that thought is reality—and thought alone!—/And must absorb all the material—their goal/The mastery by the spirit of all the facts that can be known." That affirmation, however, is repeatedly undercut and qualified by the poet's intuitive mastery of what Engels designates as "the dialectics of nature."

Corollary to the exaltation of the poet's imagination is his conviction that such mastery is made possible only by the collective labor and sacrifice of working people. The creative impulse is now interpreted here as a refinement of the energy that circulates in the sociolibidinal economy of matter. In the haunting four lines of "On the Ocean Floor," MacDiarmid seems to counterpoint his belief in individual genius by discovering "what as a communist he should be aware of—the masses themselves, dying and falling anonymously like the foraminifera, but from whom something is going to rise up, a new society like the chalk cliffs rising from the depths of the sea" (Morgan 1976, 21):

> Now more and more on my concern with the lifted waves of genius
> gaining
> I am aware of the lightless depths that beneath them lie;
> And as one who hears their tiny shells incessantly raining
> On the ocean floor as the foraminifera die.

The foraminifera here may be deemed the microcosmic counterpart of the stones in "On a Raised Beach." Meanwhile, in the poem *In Memoriam James Joyce*, MacDiarmid expresses the cosmological aspiration of totalizing all the richness and diversity of phenomena in art. Again the drive is toward synthesis, the proof of interdependency, via distanciation or estrangement and transformative critique. The poet strives to make "a moving, thrilling, mystical, tropical,/Maniacal, magical creation of all these oppositions" under the pressure of circumstances. To absorb the "abysses and altitudes of the mind of man," he seeks for a language with "A marvellous lucidity, a quality of fiery aery light,/Flowing like clear water, flying like a bird,/Burning like a sunlit landscape." In effect, the production of poetic art involves the analytic of distinguishing materials and methods of articulation that engage "the central issues of life," "reality in motion." Or, as MacDiarmid puts it more precisely: the dialectics of the era expressed in "The class war, the struggles and ideals/Of the proletariat bent on changing the world,/And consequently on changing human nature" (1978, 67).

The most elaborate performance of MacDiarmid's aesthetics is found in two chapters, "The Kind of Poetry I Want," and "The Ideas Behind My Work," in his epic self-study *Lucky Poet*. In essence, McDiarmid's lifelong pursuit of comprehending the "interdependencies of life" compels him to orient his imagination toward "problems of value" embodied in quotidian experience and to do justice "to the disruptive as well as to the cohesive forces" in society. One of the finest illustrations of MacDiarmid's dialectical mode of mapping reality in motion is the poem "The Glass of Pure Water." Critics who fault MacDiarmid for his self-indulgence in polemical and propagandistic statements—never mind their failure to discriminate between mimetic, didactic, and allegorical genres—often ignore poems with a complex figural constellation that escapes the formulaic typology of academic pluralism. Such pedagogy, antithetical to MacDiarmid's avant-garde hubris, is afraid to take the risk of grappling with contingencies, particularly the risk of anticipating liberation in a future where repression, scarcity, and the state no longer exist.

What is at stake here is the vexed issue of the politics of the imagination and the complicity of art and power. In "The Glass of Pure Water," the problem of writing political poetry is posed most sharply: what is the relation between the poet-persona with his revolutionary vision and the oppressed masses sunk in mute suffering, the object contemplated, whom the poet wants to serve with his intellect? Is the emancipatory consciousness always inserted from the outside? Or is there a spontaneous impulse for change in the masses that poetry aims to channel and intensify to bring about their deliverance? In short, is the imagination a messiah for the nation-people, or is it an agitprop catalyst for radical transformation?

MacDiarmid begins with problematizing our capacity to discern "the essence of human life":

Hold a glass of pure water to the eye of the sun!
It is difficult to tell the one from the other
Save by the tiny hardly visible trembling of the water.

By our own unaided perception, we cannot grasp difference. But "the lives of these particular slum people . . . like the lives of all/The world's poorest" remind the poet less of the glass of water he delineated earlier than of the feeling they had "Who saw Sacco and Vanzetti in the death cell/On the eve of their execution." The reference to these exemplary anarchists victimized by a racist/capitalist state

introduces the observation that the language of bare hands, universally understood
by all, defies speech or utterance. "Hands" operate as simultaneously synecdoche
and metonymy for human labor, praxis, all transformative action. The Angel who
reports on the condition of human life to God exploits the infinite resources of
signs produced by the intricate movement of the hand:

> And look at the changing shapes—the countless
> Little gestures, little miracles of line—
> Of your forefinger and thumb as you move them. . . .
>
> The only communication between man and man
> That says anything worth hearing
> —The hidden well-water; the finger of destiny—
> Moves as that water, that angel, moved.
> Truth is the rarest thing and life
> The gentlest, most unobtrusive movement in the world.
> I cannot speak to you of the poor people of all the world
> But among the people in these nearest slums I know
> This infinitesimal twinkling, this delicate play
> Of tiny signs that not only say more
> Than all speech, but all there is to say,
> All there is to say and to know and to be.
> There alone I seldom find anything else,
> Each in himself or herself a dramatic whole,
> An 'agon' whose validity is timeless.
>
> Our duty is to free that water, to make these gestures,
> To help humanity to shed all else,
> All that stands between any life and the sun,
> The quintessence of any life and the sun;
> To still all sound save that talking to God;
> To end all movements save movements like these.

We confront here the nullity of speech, the futility of words; the imperative is
to fight the "monstrous jungle/of useless movement; a babel/Of stupid voices." So
the speaker calls for the oppressed subalterns under the rubric of "Gaeldom" to
"overcome the world of wrong" and terminate "the essential immorality of any
man controlling/Any other," in particular government with its "monopoly of violence." What follows this challenge, however, is not an anarchist's moral fable but
a satiric denunciation of corruption inflicted on millions by a system of property
relations (capitalism) that has confined the water's flow and shrouded the sun. First
things first. However, the poem's logic is more labyrinthine and its overall design

less transparent. The rhetoric of biblical indignation does not end in a fiery climax of retribution; rather, it urges solidarity with the poorest and lowest where truth ultimately resides because movement inhabits "the bottom of that deepest of wells" where presumably water (which cannot be owned or appropriated by a privileged few) abounds:

> For the striking of this water out of the rock of Capitalism;
> For the complete emergence from the pollution and fog
> With which the hellish interests of private property
> In land, machinery, and credit
> Have corrupted and concealed from the sun,
> From the gestures of truth, from the voice of God,
> Hundreds upon hundreds of millions of men,
> Denied the life and liberty to which they were born
> And fobbed off with a horrible travesty instead
> —Self-righteous, sunk in the belief that they are human,
> When not a tenth of one per cent show a single gleam
> Of the life that is in them under their accretions of filth.
>
> And until that day comes every true man's place
> Is to reject all else and be with the lowest,
> The poorest—in the bottom of that deepest of wells
> In which alone is truth; in which
> Is truth only—truth that should shine like the sun,
> With a monopoly of movement, and a sound like talking to God.

The assertions in the last three lines provoke more questions than they answer: Are the poor buried under "accretions of filth" and denied any power of speech capable of redeeming themselves? Will God descend to talk to them, to communicate the message of deliverance? Is the truth of being in the bottom, in the water associated with "the monopoly of movement," enough to destroy the apparatus of oppression that conceals the sun? Language indeed fails to discover the timeless regenerative "agon" in each person in the slums, the action of deconstructing the fetish of an ego-centered identity that equalizes everyone, yet still requires the Celtic peoples to unite and fulfill their world-historic mission. Is there a submerged, unintended irony here? It seems that at this juncture MacDiarmid's Scottish nationalism fuses with his proletarian internationalist conscience to engender a pathos of what I may call the "socialist sublime," that is, the vision of the oppressed in possession of truth, endowed with abundant energy for action, waiting for the moment of reckoning. On the other hand, this may be a realization of Rosa Luxemburg's notion of the spontaneous revolutionary instinct of the masses.

What is perhaps more challenging is Carl Freedman's argument that MacDiarmid's style of uneven and discordant idioms, overlaid with "idiosyncratic rhetorical overkill" and "unabashed didacticism" such as that exemplified by *The Battle Continues*, is a symptom of the poet's predicament: "an artist who refuses to temper his uncompromisingly militant stance, and yet who understands that this stance has no effectivity within any larger social collective" (1984, 53). Given the non-revolutionary conjuncture of Scotland in MacDiarmid's lifetime, his poetry assumes highly "individual" and "contingent" forms; and because he is not connected with any viable working-class insurgency, MacDiarmid supposedly fails to become an organic intellectual of the Scottish proletariat. On the other hand, precisely because of this failure, so it is alleged, MacDiarmid succeeds in composing a disjunctive, radically decentered postmodernist art, such as the first two hymns to Lenin. Freedman claims that MacDiarmid's political aesthetic responds to the absence of a mass revolutionary audience; it is "an art which, in its radical formal structures, comes to terms with its own frustration of immediate political effectivity without surrendering an explicitly revolutionary posture" (1984, 54).

Obviously this opinion doesn't take account of MacDiarmid's wide range of civic involvement that demonstrates his versatile talents, astute calculations, and ethical realism. While the argument may be germane to *The Battle Continues*, I don't think it engages with the twin aspects of MacDiarmid's vocation explored here: first, the critique of the ideological milieu of Scottish subalternity, and second, the prophetic or utopian disclosure of transformative possibilities, this latter being the magisterial task he has elected to fulfill. As for his not becoming an organic intellectual of the Scottish proletariat, so much the better: MacDiarmid has avoided this workerist and sectarian ambition. I submit that it is the hegemonic potential of the Scottish nation-people, not the corporatist working class, that is the raw material for the theoretical-poetic imagination operating on the terrain of ideological contestation. MacDiarmid's singular achievement in constructing a national-popular speech (both in Scots Lallans and English) with a radical democratic content cannot be facilely dismissed, especially in the context of what prevailed before and what has followed after his death. His influence, now incalculable, continues to grow around the world; the critical appraisal of his multifarious accomplishments has just begun. Surely, everything needs to be historicized once more! But more important, I contend that MacDiarmid's Scottish nationalism cannot be erased or preempted by proletarian vanguardism without forfeiting everything to the enemy. In the crucible of this popular-democratic nationalism, all pronouncements about MacDiarmid's inadequacy as a revolutionary writer must needs be assayed.

MacDiarmid's inventory of what is possible for "a single and separate person" as he would like to be springs from a well-tried sense of social responsibility. In "Reflections in a Slum," the poet returns to a more realistic calculation of empirical reality. He seems to register caution in responding to such scenes of misery:

"Alas! how many owe their dignity,/Their claim on our sympathy,/Merely to their misfortune." Suffering has no value in itself—unless it posits its antithesis or alternative. One explanation for this aporia between the socialist principle of mass action and a quasi-religious belief in the messianic destiny of the oppressed is MacDiarmid's concept of the "unconscious goal of history," the cunning of Reason which uses men's purposes for its own ends. As the poet of *To Circumjack Cencrastus* puts it:"By thocht a man mak's his idea a force/Or fact in History's drama: He canna foresee/The transformations and uses o' the course/The dialectics o' human action and interaction'll gie/The contribution he mak's" (1978, 5). While MacDiarmid concedes that humans (with their intelligence and integrity) make history under given circumstances, within determinate historic parameters, he concurs with the cardinal insight of historical materialism that the conditions determining our actions are not altogether willed by us but are in fact inherited from the past and reproduced by the inertia of received "common sense," by the inveterate routine of hegemonic practices and institutions. In effect, politics cannot be reduced to economics, nor revolution to an explosion of unruly crowds no matter how righteous the cause.

A final evidence of MacDiarmid's project of forging a materialist poetics can be found in "On a Raised Beach," considered by Alan Bold (1983) and others to be "arguably his greatest poem in English." Edwin Morgan is impressed by "its obstinate questioning of the unanswering—the million-year-old stones of a beach, which (like the eemis stane) could tell us so much about our prehistory if we had any means of unlocking their secrets—it brings out the most original, the most bleak, the most deeply speculative aspect of the author" (1976, 23). Whatever signs of metaphysics may be discerned in the texture of the poem, however, cannot warrant inferring from it (as Bold does) a "solipsistic credo" pivoting around a quest for formal essences, or a principle of individuation derived from the single reference to Duns Scotus' "hacceity" (*hacceitas*), that presumably structures this protracted meditation on life, death, and all creation. The paradigm is to be found elsewhere.

The poem begins by posing alternatives: "All is lithogenesis—or lochia": either the emergence of solid matter and all its manifold and distinctive heterogeneity, or the soggy cluttered discharge of blood, tissue, and mucus from the vagina after childbirth. Either a disciplined focus on the form-giving act, or the messy evacuation that attends all production. One observes how the first strophe presents the infinite variety of geologic formations observed in this beach (with a spatio-temporal referent), a diversity that defies one's capacity to discriminate and make things intelligible. But the speaker is not an idle empiricist obsessed with cataloguing sense data. Rather, he is concerned with the search for a historic/mythical event involving matter: "But where is the Christophanic rock that moved?" To loosely translate that line: Where is the achieved form that renewed life? The question links matter and motion, conjoins time and space, in exploring on "this shin-

gle shelf" the stones' resolve to thwart injury by iconoclasts and quacks (of which
more later). The perspective of the seer occasions a felicitous telescoping of stasis
and flux, center and circumference. It exhibits a point of view that affords a syncopation of locus and optic, object and subject: "Nothing has stirred/Since I lay
down this morning an eternity ago/But one bird." A play on the permanent openness of the bird's "inward gates" and the stones' follows; but through the stones'
gates "wide open far longer" no human can see. Why? The poet then compares
himself to the stones:

> I too lying here have dismissed all else
> Bread from stones is my sole and desperate dearth, . . .
> I am no more indifferent or ill-disposed to life than death is;
> I would fain accept it all completely as the soil does; . . .
> I must begin with these stones as the world began.
>
> (1993, 147)

Process and product coalesce in the stones. Matter then is imperishable even
as all organic life will perish and subsist in the soil and stones. "So these stones have
dismissed/All but all of evolution, unmoved by it." Their permanence seems to
belie humanity's "fleeting deceit of development" which has engendered "iconoclasts and quacks." What follows this is a reflection on how conflict and "psychological warfare" bring about "animal life's bolder and more brilliant patterns"—the
panorama of punctual, secular history—but "no general principle can be guessed"
from this evolutionary phenomena. What we apprehend doesn't give a clue to the
ultimate telos of life: "What the seen shows is never anything to what it's designed
to hide." And all these variegated forms and functions around us "all come back to
the likeness of stone." Is the stone then the paradigmatic form or monistic substance, or is it symbolic of the principle of matter-in-motion? The answer is an
affirmation of the presence of an elemental energy (a modality or inflection of matter) investing the forms of stone and all worldly phenomena:

> We must be humble. We are so easily baffled by appearances
> And do not realize that these stones are one with the stars.
> It makes no difference to them whether they are high or low,
> Mountain peak or ocean floor, palace, or pigsty.
> There are plenty of ruined buildings in the world but no ruined stones.
> No visitor comes from the stars
> But is the same as they are.
>
> (1993, 148)

More than the democratic or egalitarian aspect of the stones is in question here.
What establishes the correspondences is this energy that makes possible "an adjust-

ment to life" and allows spontaneity and "prelapsarian naturalness" to evolve into a "divine rhythm" harmonizing heaven and earth. Again it is the will to differentiate and homologize that enables the comprehension of appearances. The poet, however, rejects these illustrations and exhorts us to just accept the stones—the *thisness* or *hacceitas* of particular objects in the circumstantial world. But he doesn't end here.

Because of this single-minded concentration on the reality of the stony world, one commentator faults MacDiarmid for contriving a poetry of statement in which a rhetoric of persuasion and argument predominate so that in sum poetic intensity is lost (Smith 1980). Granted there are moments of brilliance and pathos in the poem, yet the deployment of ideas is supposed to distract because such ideas can only win intellectual assent and are often liable to stimulate dissent. In short, the poem is wrongheaded because it provokes thought! Moreover, our commentator goes on, the tendency to demonstrate belief in animism or a kind of pathetic fallacy that imputes life to stones somehow weakens the intuitive stoicism pervading the poem. Are these objections based on formalist dogma valid? Is there no latitude in our aesthetic theory for entertaining the classic genre of didactic art, logopoeia (in Ezra Pound's terminology), as a legitimate species? Pablo Neruda (1981), the Chilean poet, once averred that "political poetry is more profoundly emotional than any other" species of writing. In both East and West aesthetics, "lyricism is the matrix of didacticism" (Miner 1990, 129) as exemplified in the Chinese *Wen Fu* by Lu Qi which proclaims that poetry "is the means by which all principles are known"—a doctrine that conflates expressive, affective, and mimetic functions.

I submit that "On a Raised Beach" is not mainly about facts and ideas, but rather about the dialectical action between them. In brief, it is about the process of making meaning of the world, of renewing our apprehension of life and its interpendency with death or non-being. It is also about the re-affirmation of art's civic function in society and the integration of the artist with his public. Moreover, it seeks to define the complex responsibility of the imagination to the human community, an obligation that inevitably violates the canonical "touchstones" of traditional humanism espoused by Matthew Arnold, F.R. Leavis, and latter-day apologists for imperial "Western civilization."

We now confront the thematic core of the poem, "the imaginative act/That wins to the reality in the fact," as MacDiarmid enunciated it earlier. The stage of recognition arrives when the speaker refuses metaphor and symbol, language as such or more precisely rhetoric, as surrogates for what is apprehensible by the naked senses: "It is a paltry business to try to drag down/The arduous furor of the stones to the futile imaginings of men,/ To all that fears to grow roots into the common earth." Textuality is superseded by the terrestrial Ur-difference, decentering humanism and possessive individualism.

I think the last line drives home MacDiarmid's tellurian vision and needs to be underscored: the "common earth" as matrix and telos of an eternal process. The poet urges us: We need to learn infinite patience, the tact of controlling our emotions. We need to endeavor to "sustain a clear and searching gaze." What is privileged here is the will to discipline our bodies and minds, our instincts and desires, in order to grasp the cosmic telos or "ordered adjustments" in the material universe. It is the regimen of becoming a separate and singular person within the community:

> This is the road leading to certainty,
> Reasoned planning for the time when reason can no longer avail.
> It is essential to know the chill of all the objections
> That come creeping into the mind, the battle between opposing ideas
> Which gives the victory to the strongest and most universal
> Over all others, and to wage it to the end
> With increasing freedom, precision, and detachment
> A detachment that shocks our instincts and ridicules our desires.
> All else in the world cancels out, equal, capable
> Of being replaced by other things (even as all the ideas
> That madden men now must lose their potency in a few years
> And be replaced by others—even as all the religions,
> All the material sacrifices and moral restraints,
> That in twenty thousand years have brought us no nearer to God
> Are irrelevant to the ordered adjustments
> Out of reach of perceptive understanding
> Forever taking place on the Earth and in the unthinkable regions
>   around it;
> This cat's cradle of life; this reality volatile yet determined;
> This intense vibration in the stones
> That makes them seem immobile to us)
> But the world cannot dispense with the stones.
> They alone are not redundant. Nothing can replace them
> Except a new creation of God.
>
>   (1993, 149)

Lest this verse paragraph be construed as a mystical pantheist celebration of organic life, or a postmodern parody of Spinoza, I would like to underscore the phrase "this reality volatile yet determined" as key to the philosophical insights the poet registers in the next paragraph: he penetrates the stone world and perceives "a stupendous unity,/Infinite movement visibly defending itself/Against all the assaults of weather and water, . . . /The foundation and end of all life." Note here how the apparent immobility of the stone world is constituted by "infinite movement" contraposed against the flux of weather, water, and the poetic persona's consciousness.

In the next section, the poet pursues the theme of will and the imperative of self-discipline. The faith that builds mountains cannot be discovered by humans "unless they are more concentrated and determined,/Truer to themselves" and also inerrable and unshakable as the stones. So the poet urges: "It is necessary to make a stand and maintain it forever." The stones have gone through "Empires, civilizations, aeons"; and so "They came so far out of the water and halted forever," God's creation confronting the maker. Wisdom proceeds from understanding the process of determination and the moment of resolution; from this knowledge comes the acceptance of death and its interdependency with life:

> The moon moves the waters backwards and forwards,
> But the stones cannot be lured an inch farther
> Either on this side of eternity or the other. . . .
> These stones will reach us long before we reach them.
> Cold, undistracted, eternal and sublime.
> They will stem all the torrents of vicissitude forever
> With more than a Roman peace.
> Death is a physical horror to me no more.
> I am prepared with everything else to share
> Sunshine and darkness and wind and rain
> And life and death bare as these rocks though it be
> In whatever order nature may decree. . . .
> (1993, 150–51)

The polyphony of ideas is finely orchestrated here, with an unfinalizable resonance. We are not provoked to utilitarian counter-argument or Nietzschean skepticism, as others have warned us. The quest for a coincidence of individual psyche and cosmic law is attained here when the poet grasps the teaching of the stones as the emblem of energy-matter and its law-governed existence; the precept concerns a decision taken and carried out without hesitation because it concurs with nature's decree. Rationality, will, and feeling all converge. However, the acquiescence to death as part of the circulation of cosmic energy does not mean a submission to a nihilistic or fatalistic creed. On the contrary, the poet emphasizes: "It is reality that is at stake." I think we have touched here the nerve center of MacDiarmid's revolutionary commitment: death's logic doesn't introduce a reunification of what has been separated, of object and image, of the stormy beach and the speaker's self. It is a problem of subsuming our limited ego to the larger determinations that position us in the world: "What happens to us/Is irrelevant to the world's geology/ But what happens to the world's geology/Is not irrelevant to us." So we must reconcile ourselves to the stones, not the stones to us. Consciousness does not dictate the shape of the world; the world shapes the conduct and mutation of consciousness. We may ignore the world's limits, but they will not ignore us.

In the next quote we hear again the theme of conforming our lives to the
reality that, allegorized by the stones in this anonymous beach, assumes a rigor and
austerity mirroring a disciplined mind, a cohesive wholeness of will that enables
"great work" opposed to the alienated and commodified life of the "crowd."
Instead of dispersal, a gathering of elements and their centralization demand priority. What is at stake involves the maturation of a creative sensibility, of imagination
as praxis:

> Here a man must shed the encumbrances that muffle
> Contact with elemental things, the subtleties
> That seem inseparable from a humane life, and go apart
> Into a simple and sterner, more beautiful and more impressive world,
> Austerely intoxicating; the first draught is overpowering;
> Few survive it. It fills me with a sense of perfect form,
> The end seen from the beginning, as in a song. . . .
>
> But the kindred form I am conscious of here
> Is the beginning and end of the world,
> The unsearchable masterpiece, the music of the spheres,
> Alpha and Omega, the Omnific Word.
> These stones have the silence of supreme creative power,
> The direct and undisturbed way of working
> Which alone leads to greatness.
> What experience has any man crystallized,
> What weight of conviction accumulated,
> What depth of life suddenly seen entire
> In some nigh supernatural moment
> And made a symbol and lived up to
> With such resolution, such Spartan impassivity?
> It is a frenzied and chaotic age,
> Like a growth of weeds on the site of a demolished building.
> How shall we set ourselves against it,
> Imperturbable, inscrutable, in the world and yet not in it,
> Silent under the torments it inflicts upon us,
>   With a constant centre,
> With a single inspiration, foundations firm and invariable;
>   By what immense exercise of will,
> Inconceivable discipline, courage and endurance,
>   Self-purification and anti-humanity,
>   Be ourselves without interruption,
>   Adamantine and inexorable?
>
>   (1933, 151–52)

It now becomes clear that what the poet seeks is an incarnational faith nourished by a scientific intelligence. Poetic creation as praxis is an objective "manifestation of the human spirit" that approximates lithogenesis, that is, the summoning and exercise of "inconceivable discipline, courage, and endurance" that will lead to possession of the truth embodied in the stones. The susceptible mind the poet claims to have, "a mind as open as the grave," evokes the Christophanic rock of the beginning; the poet's sensibility functions as the sepulcher from which the messianic power has been resurrected. That Christophanic rock is the burden of the poem, the utterance of the truth of enduring matter that "crushes, gorgonizes all else into itself." The poet urges us to dispel the haze of bourgeois ideology, the individualism that paralyzes vision by accepting "The hard fact. The inoppugnable reality" of a world beyond our wishes or desires. We don't need a world hereafter if we can replace our romantic "infinite longing" with a resolute will deployed against the reifying force of capital. Such a will also articulates the "cunning of reason" in history, "reason" used here as a shorthand for popular-democratic praxis.

The poem arrives at the concluding stage of accepting what is at stake: secular or worldly reality. The moment comes when the poet confesses that he is "enamoured of the desert at last" where he can contemplate "spiritual issues/Made inhumanly clear." This is reminiscent of the antihumanism of Althusser's science, the passion for concrete multilayered truth devoid of ideological mystification. For MacDiarmid, the imagination corresponds to "a self-determined rhythm of life" and is tested by the "capacity for solitude." However, this does not mean that this desert inhabitant escapes from social engagement. On the contrary:

> —a question of acquiring the power
> To exercise the loneliness, the independence, of stones,
> And that only (come)s from knowing that our function remains
> However isolated we seem, fundamental to life as theirs.
>
> (1993, 154)

The poet affirms the desideratum of independence grounded on a conviction of fidelity to a just cause, founded on the rock of self-discipline. This follows from the need to reject the commodified market society of late capitalism together with the reification of vital human potential in the buying-and-selling of labor power. The poet's conception of culture hinges on the idea of lithogenesis as a process of hardening, of acquiring form as displayed by the stones, "the beginning and end of the world," in which the poet sees himself. This experience generates a sentiment of solidarity: the intelligentsia of artists needs to bring culture to the "mob," "our impossible and imperative job!"

Recalling the invocation of the Christophanic rock in the beginning (MacDiarmid thus unfolds his original name, Christopher [Murray Grieve], in a punlike way), we complete the circle of allegorizing thought. This is indeed the resurrection prefigured in the beginning, the rolling of the stone away from the tomb of the masses of people, when the artist realizes that the sublimity inscribed in matter can be found in all men since "The masses too have begged bread from stones,/From human stones, including themselves." So the poet urges detached intellectuals to share their possession of the truth with their fellow humans because it is this sharing, this communication of the cognitive and practical vision of the artist, that is the rolling of the rock from the tomb—a metaphor we can decipher as the overcoming of the forces of oppression and death in a world of inequality and injustice.

Within this hermeneutic framework, I suggest that this return of the solitary poet to the people—the lithogenesis of the spiritual power of the imagination—is what MacDiarmid is really calling for. Not to do so is to betray the artist's vocation, to welcome the stones' revenge, to allow ignorance and indifference to seal us in death, or in the miasmic lochia:

> It is not
> The reality of life that is hard to know.
> It is nearest of all and easiest to grasp,
> But you must participate in it to proclaim it.
> —I lift a stone; it is the meaning of life I clasp
> Which is death, for that is the meaning of death;
> How else does any man yet participate
> In the life of a stone,
> How else can any man yet become
> Sufficiently at one with creation, sufficiently alone,
> Till as the stone that covers him he lies dumb
> And the stone at the mouth of his grave is not overthrown?
> (1993, 155)

Each stone "covers infinite death," but the poet counsels: "let us not be afraid to die" because that is part of discovering the truth of the stone world, the infinity and permanence of matter-energy, and phase of death (the separation of the poet from the mob) as a necessary ordeal. The statement that "in death—unlike life—we lose nothing that is truly ours," affirms the continuity of matter as a moment of the circulation of energy infusing the movement of all life in the universe. At any rate, "reality," Becoming as integral to Being, is saved.

"On a Raised Beach" poses the problem of how we can tell "what is truly ours," and attempts to answer the question of the artist's connection with society and the natural world. It dramatizes the coming to a recognition that lithogenesis—a comprehension of historical reality—occurs when the poet, temporarily exiled in the desert and achieving self-recovery there, rejoins humanity and participates in the collective project of communal renewal and resurrection.

MacDiarmid once declared that he aspired to conceive of nature "in terms of human activities, being alert to the historical processes and careful to avoid the heresy of separateness" (quoted in Maxwell 1980, 204). Rivalling Lucretius' *De Rerum Naturae*, MacDiarmid's poem celebrates not a mystical glorification of minute particulars but a materialist thinking-process implying a dialectic of consciousness and matter. It projects in sensuous form a totality grounded in the historical laws of motion of society, nature, and thought interacting with each other.

Contemporary criticism has perhaps forfeited the opportunity to learn from MacDiarmid's example. For instance, David Daiches labels MacDiarmid a transhumanist—someone, I take it, who transcends the boundary of nationality and speaks for all humankind. He writes: "MacDiarmid's political vision was hardly political at all, but a vision of a society redeemed from all second-handness in living, united in an intense relishing of the reality of experience" (1979, 2329). But MacDiarmid is by no means a modernist romantic like Dylan Thomas, or a self-reflexive modernist like Wallace Stevens. Daiches' praise, though well intended, reduces the necessary and ineluctable mediations whereby MacDiarmid's rendering of his experience becomes a universal vision by first being Scottish-nationalist and therefore concretely tendentious. Alan Riach provides the necessary qualification. He scrupulously pays tribute to MacDiarmid's greatness by emphasizing the poet's repudiation of the privileged ciphers for commodity-fetishism, self-expression and egocentric lyricism, an act made possible because the poet "understood the self to be something subsidiary, secondary and changeable, and he treated his own self and others with the respect therefore due to it. . . . In the place of individualism, MacDiarmid reinstated the value of social or communal identity: a national identity, an identity defined by language, or class or political and philosophical belief" (1993, 8).

Like the works of Mayakovsky, Neruda, Brecht, Hikmet, and others, MacDiarmid's art draws its strength from its partisanship and its existential situatedness in the historical moment. This moment furnished the raw materials of experience as well as the resources of a demotic, indigenous, and electic provincialism that Robert Crawford (1992) considers the catalyzing milieu for European modernism in general. Yet I believe MacDiarmid's achievement differs from Yeats, Pound, and Eliot in its all-encompassing radicalism. What distinguishes MacDiarmid's art is precisely its genuine political inspiration—political in the sense of a profound concern with justice, liberty, and virtue in the world polis, in the community of nations fighting for equality and dignity. But because such a community characterized by justice and virtue is absent in the prevailing world system dominated by capital, by class exploitation and imperial oppression, MacDiarmid's art becomes doubly political in its critique of the ideology of individualist aesthetics and in its projection of an oppositional, subversively utopian society in his prose and poetry—an alternative that, in the spirit of the *Communist Manifesto*, only epitomizes what is already germinating in the womb of current events. MacDiarmid descants on the vicissitudes and labor of the future in genesis: "The struggle for material existence is over. It has been won./The need for repressions and disciplines has passed./The struggle for truth and that indescribable necessity,/Beauty, begins now, hampered by none of the lower needs. . . . /It is now the duty of the Scottish genius/Which has provided the economic freedom for it/To lead in the abandonment of creeds and moral compromises/Of every sort and to commence to express the unity of life" (1972, 328). In this horizon of yearning and hope, MacDiarmid's poetry acquires its ultimate strategic value and transhistorical significance. While the nationalist MacDiarmid acts as a prophet of an emergent, renewed Scotland with a world-historical destiny, the socialist MacDiarmid enables Scotland to participate in the liberation struggles of all oppressed peoples and nations in our planet. Such incommensurable energies sustain the transformative and empowering intransigence of MacDiarmid's art.

Part Three

Interventions

7

James Baldwin's Dialectical Imagination

> Be it grand or slender, burrowing, blasting or refusing to sanc-
> tify; whether it laughs out loud or is a cry without an alphabet,
> the choice word or the chosen silence, unmolested language
> surges toward knowledge, not its destruction. But who does not
> know of literature banned because it is interrogative; discredited
> because it is critical; erased because alternate? How many are
> outraged by the thought of a self-ravaged tongue?
> —Toni Morrison, *The Nobel Lecture*

> [W]hen Martin Luther King was alive and when we were try-
> ing, when we hoped to bring about some kind of revolution in
> the American conscience, which is, after all, where everything
> in some sense has to begin. . . . The problem of color in this
> country has always contained the key to all other problems. . . .
> When one is complaining about racism and fighting it, what
> you are really talking about is power.
> —James Baldwin, *A Rap on Race* (with Margaret Mead)

I

A miri Baraka once eulogized James Baldwin as "God's revolutionary mouth."
What does "revolutionary" mean here? Others considered Baldwin conservative, even a reactionary sell-out. What explains these discrepant attitudes?
Controversy has from the start dogged Baldwin's battle against "the incubus of
race." His early canonization by New Critical liberalism as "victim, witness, and
prophet" (Kinnamon 1974) of the black quest for identity has not spared him from
attacks launched by Eldridge Cleaver (1968), Harold Cruse (1968), Addison Gayle,
Jr. (1972), and others for nourishing a "racial death-wish" evidenced by his rejection of Richard Wright's paradigmatic example and of Negritude artists like Aimé
Cesaire. Baldwin's predicament involves not a death-wish but the obsession with a
dialectic of exchange where whites and blacks are positions imbricated in each
other that need to be sublated, not conflated, if racial conflict is to be resolved.[1]

---

1. New positive revaluations of Baldwin have been expressed by, among others, Bell Hooks (1992),
perhaps following the lead of C.L.R. James (1992, 331).

One manifestation of this dialectic can be seen in these lines from "Staggerlee wonders" (1985, 64–66):

> I have endured your fire
> and your whip, your rope. . . .
> yet, my love:
> You do not know
> how desperately I hoped
> that you would grow
> not so much to love me
> as to know
> that what you do to me
> you do to you.

Baldwin ascribes to white "innocence" a blindness that refuses to see and to recognize that the crime inflicted on him (synecdochically, on the collective) is ultimately a crime done to himself. This is essentially a religious, more precisely Christian, vision premised on the assumption that everyone of whatever color participates individually in the mystical body of Christ. This is Baldwin's wager. Everyone readily acknowledges that this project of transcendental reconciliation is praiseworthy. It is Baldwin's rhetorical figure of the "sublime." But unfortunately the trope of oneness fails to grapple with the complex social reality of "the politics of incarnation," with the "thickness" of collective antagonisms, whose ironies and paradoxes reproduce themselves in Baldwin's own style of humanistic compromise, a transference of a convivial "purity of heart" he once assumed lies latent in the dominant body politic.

There is a more nuanced, perhaps more incarnational, version of Baldwin's dialectic which requires that before knowledge of good and evil is grasped, humans have to change; unable to change, we compulsively repeat crimes and languish in "spiritual darkness." In the notes for *Blues for Mister Charlie*, Baldwin's powerful intervention in the "racial situation" of the sixties, he posits a "We" that disperses guilt or responsibility:

> But if it is true, and I believe it is, that all men are brothers, then we have the duty to try to understand this wretched man [the racist criminal]; and while we probably cannot hope to liberate him, begin working toward the liberation of his children. For we, the American people, have created him, he is our servant; it is we who put the cattle-prodder in his hands, and we are responsible for the crimes that he commits. It is we who have locked him in the prison of his color. It is we who have persuaded him that Negroes are worthless human beings, and that it is his sacred duty, as a white man, to protect the honor and purity of his tribe. It is we who

have forbidden him, on pain of exclusion from the tribe, to accept his beginnings, when he and black people loved each other, and rejoice in them, and use them; it is we who have made it mandatory—honorable—that white father should deny black son. These are grave crimes indeed, and we have committed them and continue to commit them in order to make money (1964, xiv-xv).

In *A Rap on Race*, Baldwin urges us to disengage ourselves from any kind of sentimentality, pointing out that the sameness that unites blacks and whites, where brotherhood exists, is human wickedness: "We've got to be as clear-headed about human beings as possible, because we are still each other's hope" (1971, 45).

In Plaguetown, U.S.A., however, we still need to ask: Who is the speaking subject here? What claim of legitimacy is registered here to assign answerability for a "We" whose all-inclusive referent is exorbitant and at best question-begging? Such a "we" is precisely the site of contradictions, a contradictory unity. If Baldwin failed to convince white America of its self-destructive "innocence," he succeeded best, I think, in settling accounts with its victims—in short, of exorcising the vision of revenge, of separatism (Afrocentrism, black nationalism) as a permanent motive force. This demanded first a "truce" with the reality of his birth. Diagnosed in *Notes of a Native Son*, the trauma of finding out what is "always already" given to him at the outset is marked by an anguished drive to reconcile the contradictions—the "bastard of the West" [or of the "Western house"] aping Shakespeare, Rembrandt, Hemingway; and Caliban's heir—lest he "would have no place in *any* scheme" (1963b, 10). The aporia of a "self-destroying limbo," in which Baldwin says that "I hated and feared the world," may be read by deconstructionists as the abysmal site where vertiginous possibilities of meaning can be discerned—the uncanny moment of "free play," the *jouissance* of becoming. But surely there is more outside the text, given the unrelenting problematization of limits and boundaries.

Baldwin of course changed the bearing of his aesthetics as he progressed in his career. In *No Name in the Street*, he compared the artist and the revolutionary, both possessed and driven by a vision, both embroiled in the mysteries of "person" and "people" (1985, 540). So I prefer to read the early position as Baldwin's ruse, a pretext, for articulating his need for a provisional "moral center" before any partisanship supervenes, a point of departure transcending the elective affinities faced by the writer. He simultaneously rejects and accepts the commonsensical doxa about the African-American artist in his time, a pragmatic stance which he could not refuse because he had committed himself then to the ethical ideal of wanting to be "an honest man and a good writer." Can one be both, wedding reality and justice, and invoke Caliban at the same time? It is not too much to say that in order to survive the madness of Plaguetown, U.S.A., Baldwin endeavored to accomplish these incommensurable tasks.

Baldwin criticized Richard Wright's protest art for its strategy of fighting the enemy on its own "self-deceived" terrain. But, as Houston Baker cogently points out, Baldwin's conceptual framework is caught in antinomies (such as the disjunction of social victims and individualistic creators) entailed by bourgeois ideology: "Baldwin elaborates a contradistinction between *individual* and *society* as though the division possesses the force of natural law, when, in fact, it carries only the reinscribed, metaphorical force of an old problematic" (1984, 142). This problematic of liberal individualism, of the monadic consciousness claiming to be free from all worldly determination, autotelic and demiurgic, operates as the fundamental premise for Baldwin's notion of the artist's autonomy.[2]

But what is striking in my view is the way the problematic itself reveals symptoms of its limitations and inadequacies. Ever sensitive to the unpredictable fusion of what helps and what hurts as he moved "from one disaster to the next," Baldwin disclaims any concern with social affairs: "it is absolutely necessary that he establish between himself and these affairs a distance that will allow, at least, for clarity, so that before he can look forward in any meaningful sense, he must first be allowed to take a long look back; but I think that the past is all that makes the present coherent, and further, that the past will remain horrible for exactly as long as we refuse to assess it honestly." In the next paragraph, however, Baldwin abandons this historical imperative and assumes a neoKantian perspective: "This is the only real concern of the artist, to recreate out of the disorder of life that order that is art." However, he confesses that this task of organizing his experience has been blocked by "the tremendous demands and the very real dangers of my social situation." So he has to "unlock" the gate called "the Negro problem in America" that requires analysis of its context: "the history, tradition, customs, the moral assumptions and preoccupations of the country; in short, the general social fabric." In effect, before artistic production can proceed, a comprehension of the social-historical totality that subtends all cultural processes and delimits the working of the imagination is required. Baldwin asserts quite peremptorily: No one escapes the effects of this structure, everyone bears responsibility for it. And so Baldwin finds himself immersed in social affairs that cannot forget him, no matter how much he may try to ignore them.

On this account, Baldwin registers all the tensions and nuances of the paradoxical situation of the subaltern artist in late capitalism: his affirmation of a privatized ethic is predicated on its impossibility. Given the reification of social life under the rule of commodity-fetishism and the domination of the market (the conversion of all use-values into exchange-value, the hegemonic cash-nexus), can

---

2. One needs to qualify this remark with the reminder that Baldwin was once acclaimed as a scourge of liberalism in the 1960s; see Loren Miller, "Farewell to Liberals: A Negro View," *The Nation* 195 (20 October 1962): 235–38.

writing achieve a zero-degree of freedom? Can the "moral center" Baldwin aspires to grasp be discovered in the absences, gaps and ruptures of a Symbolic Order governed by the "Name of the White Father"? Or is the identification of his subject-position implicated in a mirror-stage of duplicity, the regime of Sameness hiding behind the masks of difference? Part of Baldwin's difficulties is intimated by C.L.R. James's observation:

> Thus the American Negro, literate, Westernized, an American almost from the foundation of America, suffers from his humiliations and discriminations to a degree that few whites and even many non-American Negroes can ever understand. The jazz and gaiety of the American Negro are a semi-conscious reaction to the fundamental sorrow of the race. (Quoted in Buhle [1988, 58])

In the allegory of Becoming-Other exemplified by "Sonny's Blues" and the meta-narrative one can extrapolate from *The Fire Next Time*, Baldwin has, I think, demonstrated a way of mapping the antinomic predicament of the African-American artist in late capitalism and proposing an agenda for resolving it.

One discerns two strategies in *The Fire Next Time* to disentangle, if not reconcile, the binary opposition of art-centered individual freedom and socio-economic determinism that Baldwin posits in his early manifestoes, a dualism that explains much of his "savage indignation" and his compassion. In "My Dungeon Shook: Letter to My Nephew on the One Hundredth Anniversary of the Emancipation," Baldwin tells his nephew that his love for him is an emblem of the community's integrity, its weapon of survival, its Archimedean point for social transformation. This love is also what will force his white brothers to face reality and so change it. What is striking is Baldwin's trope for integration, a galactic reordering of the Copernican hierarchy where the white man's identity is a function of a hitherto fixed "pillar," a black star:

> Try to imagine how you would feel if you woke up one morning to find the sun shining and all the stars aflame. You would be frightened because it is out of the order of nature. Any upheaval in the universe is terrifying because it so profoundly attacks one's sense of one's own reality. Well, the black man has functioned in the white man's world as a fixed star, as an immovable pillar: and as he moves out of his place, heaven and earth are shaken to their foundations. (1963a, 23)

This deconstructive, more precisely prophetic, impulse finds its figural locus in the sacrifice of the Messiah in Baldwin's explosive "Down at the Cross: Letter from a Region in My Mind." In this rhetorical *tour de force,* Baldwin confronts the planetary reordering of his own life as it orbits around the geopolitics of Harlem and the plight of the whole black community. His theme is the constellation of power/knowledge. He moves out of the apocalyptic cosmos of *Go Tell it on the Mountain* where the church principles were "Blindness, Loneliness, and Terror," where the blood of the Lamb has not cleansed him because (as he writes) "I was just as black as I had been the day that I was born" (1963, 52–53)—into the antagonisms of the public sphere, the battlefields of state and civil society.

Then, in the middle of this meditation, he stages his dramatic encounter with Elijah Muhamad and the Nation of Islam. This episode represents, I think, Baldwin's exploration of separatism and the seductions of identity politics. His personal attachments and genuinely honest aversion to mercantile *Realpolitik* close that detour for him. Toward the end of this psychic cartography, he returns to history—the intertwined fates of African slaves and European settlers—and maps the point of departure: "And today, a hundred years after his technical emancipation, he remains—with the possible exception of the American Indian—the most despised creature in this country" (1963a, 98–99).

Baldwin now configures his people's situation in the context of the Cold War and the African anticolonial struggles. He identifies with the African desire for freedom, but refuses an Afrocentric transference. Here is where for Baldwin the American dream has turned into a nightmare "on the private, domestic, and international levels," where the United States has become the vindictive god of the Old Testament suppressing revolutions everywhere. Baldwin's belief in the United States as a possible utopian force is unshaken—but it is overturned by an existentialist faith that life is tragic. And this reality is for him what the black community represents. Whatever the ambiguities of Baldwin's formulations, his central argument is the fused or indivisible fate of all those caught in Du Bois' color boundary: "The price of the liberation of the white people is the liberation of the blacks—the total liberation, in the cities, in the towns, before the law, and in the mind" (1963a, 111). In this Imaginary register of the Double, Baldwin affirms the right of self-determination for all people of color as an organic part of a society-in-the-making, the New Jerusalem he envisioned arising from everyone taking responsibility for what's going on in the world. This was his utopian wager.

What I would focus on in this discourse is the cunning of the text, a kind of political unconscious that sublimates Baldwin's fierce aesthetic/artisanal individualism into an allegory for ethnogenesis. Becoming-Other is displaced into a history that is both salvational and cyclical, the myth of return metamorphosing into apocalypse and final judgment. This counters the fetish for self-healing interiority. Baldwin, the existentialist sage, celebrates the responsibility to life—"to earn one's death by confronting with passion the conundrum of life," life that is characterized by the convergence of forces immanent in history: "It is the responsibility of free men to trust and to celebrate what is constant . . . and to apprehend the nature of change, to be able and willing to change. I speak of change not on the surface but in the depths—change in the sense of renewal" (1963a, 106). This sense of renewal, the conversion of homogeneous time, the time of cyclical nature rituals, into what Walter Benjamin calls *Jetztzeit*, the time of revolutionary rupture, acquires eschatological resonance in Baldwin's imagined scene of a final accounting where art (beauty) will be salvaged and history redeemed, thanks to the slaves' vigil and their culture of resistance:

> *What will happen to all that beauty then?* I could also see that the intransigence and ignorance of the white world might make that vengeance inevitable—a vengeance that does not really depend on, and cannot really be executed by, any person or organization, and that cannot be prevented by any police or army: historical vengeance, a cosmic vengeance, based on the law that we recognize when we say, "Whatever goes up must come down." And here we are, at the center of the arc, trapped in the gaudiest, most valuable, and most improbable water wheel the world has ever seen. Everything now, we must assume, is in our hands; we have no right to assume otherwise. If we—and now I mean the relatively conscious whites and the relatively conscious blacks, who must, like lovers, insist on, or create, the consciousness of the others—do not falter in our duty now, we may be able, handful that we are, to end the racial nightmare, and achieve our country, and change the history of the world. If we do not now dare everything, the fulfillment of that prophecy, re-created from the Bible in song by a slave, is upon us: *God gave Noah the rainbow sign, No more water, the fire next time!* (1963a, 119–20)

A strange conjuncture of historical and cosmic vengeance is evoked here, together with the somewhat marginal if aleatory role of consciousness whose timely intervention, however, can save sinful humanity from Divine wrath. There is a premonition of the end of time, the endless turning of the wheel halted at last, at which point a Messianic conflagration will burst and finally reconcile man, nature, and spirit.

II

> What is important, and one of the elements that makes history, is the reaction of human beings to their situation. And that reaction, when it is a real reaction, is always excessive and always a little blind. You simply find your situation intolerable and you set about to change it, and when you do that, you place yourself in a certain kind of danger: the danger of being excessive, the

> danger of being wrong. That is the only way you ever learn
> anything, and it is also the only way the situation ever changes.
>   Everyone has been hounded all over the world, from pillar
> to post. Everyone's become an exile. . . . We're trying to
> change the past. We're trying to change the present. The price
> for that is our apprehension, our acceptance, of the past.
>   —James Baldwin, *A Rap on Race*

It would be challenging to explore how the working of this "political uncon-scious" in Baldwin's 1962 essay can retrospectively illuminate the chronotopes and heteroglossia of the major novels: *Go Tell It On the Mountain, Giovanni's Room, Another Country*, and *If Beale Street Could Talk*. That would be the project of a long treatise. My concern here is to anatomize the dialectical physiognomy or temper of Baldwin's sensibility. I would like to assess its bearing on, or what is now called its intertextuality with, one short story, "Sonny's Blues," from his 1965 collection *Going to Meet the Man*. Most interpreters tend to concentrate on the terminal scene of this story, glossing it as Baldwin's transmutation of life or emotion into art. Other readers, more ethnically oriented, place the accent on the role of the narra-tor, Sonny's brother, through whom we are supposed to understand Sonny's plight, empathize with it, and transcend it in a shared experience. Art's therapeutic grace or charisma becomes a key to resolving urgent racial conflicts as well as an emblem of the singular fate of the African-American "nation" in a late-capitalist social formation.

   This narrative is, I think, Baldwin's attempt to answer the question that obsessed him in *The Fire Next Time*: "How can the American Negro past be used?" In other words, how can ethnogenesis, a whole people's struggle for self-determi-nation, be the key to sublimating the energies moving toward "vengeance" into a more reconstructive task, the "perpetual achievement of the impossible"?

   The dialectical thrust of Baldwin's imagination springs from its apprehension of contraries and opposites. Reification in market-centered society, signalled right from the beginning in the newspaper report of Sonny's trouble with the law, engenders its opposite. The narrator sums up his self-identification via the alien-ation of the Symbolic Order that mediates kinship: "He became real to me again." Caught up in the hierarchy of status sanctioned by disciplinary regimes of educa-tional institutions, and so on, the narrator cannot admit that the "losers" can have stories to tell. Sonny's letter written after the death of the narrator's little girl, quoted in entirety, displaces the newspaper report with its message of Sonny striv-ing to "climb out of some deep, real deep and funk hole," to get outside and see the sun. In that urban jungle, a milieu of disaster, disenchanted laughter, and dan-ger which Sonny "had almost died trying to escape," the outside is shrouded with a darkness that the old folks have wrestled with and endured. This threshold con-sciousness where outside/inside becomes confused introduces the mother, the agent of popular memory, and her vivid recollection of how her husband's brother was killed by a car full of white men—the source of history as nightmare. The brother with the busted guitar, still unavenged, becomes the exemplary Orphic figure that the mother offers to her son not to forget: "You may not be able to stop nothing from happening. But you got to let him know you's *there*." So while the mother mediates the reconstruction of family solidarity, the scene of pre-Oedipal recovery is made accessible through the father's pathos: as witness of a tradition of violence and the sacrifice of his brother (the artist/performer, the pleasure-principle personified) in a moon-drenched night, he is somehow released from the codifying despotism of the racial order. This event recounted by the mother is what prepares the narrator to listen, to open up to Sonny's cry of independence from a monologic and straitjacketing authority: "I think people *ought* to do what they want to do, what else they alive for?" Indeed, it is at this moment when the narrator realizes that Sonny can be a "fixed star" moving out of its pre-assigned habitat, charting his own eccentric adventure: "it was as though he were all wrapped up in some cloud, some fire, some vision all his own; and there wasn't any way to reach him."

A symptomatic reading might be helpful in revealing the complicity of the senses of seeing and hearing in the dialectic of exchange between subject-positions. We are witnessing some kind of communicative action taking place between Sonny and his brother, between the narrative-filter and the third-person interlocutor. What enables the narrator, Baldwin's vehicle for the atomized or privatized sensibility of *l'homme moyen sensuel*, to begin to penetrate "the distant stillness in which he [Sonny] had always moved," is not any *agon* of self-reflection. Rather, it is an event in the public, secular sphere: the spectacle of an often-staged revival meeting outside, on the sidewalk of Seventh Avenue across the narrator's home. Three sisters in black, and a brother, with their voices and Bibles and a tambourine, were testifying and singing about "the old ship of Zion . . . it has rescued many a thousand!" Incongruity between appearance and reality, between ends and means, does not prevent the narrator from apprehending the process of serial entities coalescing in the lived experience of time whose fullness anticipates the end of the narrative: "As the singing filled the air the watching, listening faces underwent a change, the eyes focusing on something within; the music seemed to soothe a poison out of them; and time seemed, nearly, to fall away from the sullen, belligerent, battered faces, as though they were fleeing back to their first condition, while dreaming of their last." But the narrator resists this hallucination, this figure of synthesis that harmonizes origin and goal, beginning and ending. He believes in will power, in the ego-administered inwardness that will control "all that hatred and misery and love"—wild nomadic energies pursuing schizophrenic trajectories.

Only when the narrator enters Sonny's world, the group-in-fusion of blues-players, does he see the difference between music as "personal, private, vanishing evocations" and as order imposed on "the roar rising from the void." Sonny becomes a participant of a ritual of renewal "at the risk of ruin, destruction, madness, and death, in order to find new ways to make us listen" to the old tale "of how we suffer, and how we are delighted, and how we may triumph." At this pivotal juncture, transgressive energies find cathexis in the image of collective labor, the praxis of cooperative work, translated in the crucible of imaginative/artistic creation:

> And Sonny went all the way back, he really began with the spare, flat statement of the opening phrase of the song. Then he began to make it his. It was very beautiful because it wasn't hurried and it was no longer a lament. I seemed to hear with what burning he had made it his, with what burning we had yet to make it ours, how we could cease lamenting. Freedom lurked around us and I understood, at last, that he could help us to be free if we would listen, that he would never be free until we did. . . . And he was giving it back, as everything must be given back, so that, passing through death, it can live forever. . . . And I was yet aware that this was only a moment, that the world waited outside, as hungry as a tiger, and that trouble stretched above us, longer than the sky. (1991, 79)

What is dramatized in this epiphanic scene, a crux of the contradictory tendencies immanent in the narrative, is a recognition by the narrator of a symbolic action that is the opposite of integration: the total body of the whole is being rendered complete within each individual. What is occurring is a process in which the internal authority of a unifying logos (here the whole history of the black people) shapes Sonny's individuality, more precisely, offers him a locus in which his manifold human possibilities (*potentia*) can be expressed.

Put another way: What lives in Sonny, what is inscribed in his performance, is the complete narrative of the family's struggles, the vicissitudes of a whole people with their memories and dreams, the interruption of their lives made meaningful by their vision of their redemptive power. That is what constitutes his dignity and his vocation. In that zone of derelict space where Creole withdraws his grid of centralizing leadership, Sonny virtualizes his *potentia* (Spinoza's joy) as an act of "vengeance," as it were, against the terror of Law and Order outside. The artistic form of the blues thus becomes an occasion for grappling with catastrophe, according to Ralph Ellison, "not by the consolation of philosophy but by squeezing from it a near-tragic, near-comic lyricism. As a form, the blues is an autobiographical chronicle of a personal catastrophe expressed lyrically" (1978, 62). In this sense, Baldwin shares Ellison's will to sublimate and reconcile.

But another dimension can be glimpsed insofar as Sonny's music is not just an occasion for communion, what John Reilly calls "the discovery of self in community" (in Kinnamon 1974, 144), with the blues serving as metaphor for the black community. Charlie Parker is not necessarily the black Orpheus migrating to Harlem. Sonny has tried to communicate to his brother his need to feel in control, to manifest outside what is inside. The narrator intimates the enigmatic challenge: "I wanted to say that it was all within; but was it? or, rather, wasn't that exactly the trouble?" Assimilationism, the melting pot, cannot finally be superimposed on the closing image of "the very cup of trembling."

At this crossroad of diverse interpretations, Amiri Baraka's reminder is salutary: "The blues impulse was a psychological correlative that obscured the most extreme ideas of *assimilation* for most Negroes, and made any notion of the complete abandonment of the traditional black culture an unrealizable possibility" (1979, 54). Becoming-Other through the blues explodes the racialized subject of empire. It disintegrates the representational and fetishizing apparatus of the commodifying State not so much by deploying art (aesthetic form) but, in this example of Baldwin's discursive practice, exhibiting its limits in containing or regulating the expenditure of energy wasted in the exchange circuits of transnational capitalism. Baldwin's insight that love can annihilate racist hatred has its locus in a blindspot which cannot apprehend the incorporative power of racism. Deleuze and Guattari may shed light on the spatial enigma in the story:

> From the viewpoint of racism, there is no exterior, there are no people on the outside. There are only people who should be like us and whose crime it is not to be. The dividing line is not between inside and outside but rather is internal to simultaneous signifying chains and successive subjective choices. Racism never detects the particles of the other; it propagates waves of sameness until those who resist identification have been wiped out (or those who only allow themselves to be identified at a given degree of divergence). Its cruelty is equaled only by its incompetence and naiveté. (1987, 178)

My version of a symptomatic reading may run against the grain of Baldwin's texts, although a scrutiny of Baldwin's pronouncements in *A Rap on Race* and his massive corpus of interviews will dispel any such skepticism. Given the coexistence of demystifying and utopian tendencies in Baldwin's thought, I think this mode of appreciation does justice to the vernacular speech of the artist whose struggle for recognition depends on the other recognizing an analogous, reciprocal desire. This vernacular traces its genealogy, among other sources, to Fredrick Douglass' indignation and his clarity. But the Other is usually the bondmaster whose quest for mastery hinges on the presence and endurance of the subaltern. Here is where white and black are linked indivisibly to one universe, the turbulent cosmos of *The Fire Next Time*, a contradictory unity whose ironies and pathos Baldwin has tried to articulate in all his works.

III

> Every force creates a counterforce. . . . I am another kind of
> revolutionary now. . . . We have to assume that we are respon-
> sible for the future of this world. . . . We are meant to be wit-
> nesses to a possibility which we will not live to see, but we have
> to bring it out. . . . It has to do with what we know human
> beings have been and can become.
>   —James Baldwin, *A Rap on Race*

Toward the end of their non-moderated and improvising dialogue entitled *A Rap on Race*, Margaret Mead and James Baldwin dispute about the question of responsibility for past injustice, for the present state, and the future direction of U.S. history. Baldwin's accusing his country "of being not only my murderer but yours too" evokes a disclaimer from the celebrity, Mead, whose concept of personal responsibility acquits her (she claims) of any crimes done to African slaves and their descendants. Despite his sense of being a permanent exile, uprooted and nomadic, Baldwin's discipline of historicizing experience cannot release him from being implicated in a destiny not of his own making. He reaffirms a commitment to salvage the meaning of the black collective experience from ignominy: "I have to talk out of my beginnings, and I did begin here auctioned like a mule, bred as though I were a stallion. . . . And I have to remember that. I have to redeem that" (1971, 256). He is not only imitating Minister Meridian Henry's impassioned sermon at the end of *Blues for Mister Charlie* in which he asks, "What was that sin committed by our forefathers in the time that has vanished on the other side of the flood, which has had to be expiated by chains...on these wild shores, in this strange land? "(1964, 77) He is in effect answering it by refusing the universal price one has to pay for survival, the price of carrying another burden, that of perpetually sacrificing for the preservation of white supremacy.

Responsibility thus acquires not just a memory but also a genealogy. Baldwin returns to the radical message of Christian eschatology pivoting around the revolution led by "a disreputable Hebrew criminal," as he puts it in "White Racism or World Community?" In this 1968 address to theologians, Baldwin articulates a dialectics of the personal and the collective by locating the responsibility for the soul's salvation in the act of each individual atoning for "historical habits," specific patterns of behavior such as that evidenced in the imperial racism then rampant in South Africa and Vietnam: "I am saying that when a person, with a people, are able to persuade themselves that another group or breed of men are less than men, they themselves become less than men and have made it almost impossible for themselves to confront reality and to change it" (1985b, 440). In the same passage, Baldwin enunciates his conception of art as a form of social practice embedded in worldliness and the syncretic interaction of cultures: "the blues are not a racial creation, the blues are an historical creation produced by the confrontation precisely between the pagan, the black pagan from Africa, and the alabaster cross."

But it is in that magnificent chronicle *No Name in the Street*, composed in the middle of his career, where Baldwin finally settles accounts with aestheticism and liberal individualism, confronts Cleaver's attack, and rearticulates his necessarily antinomic view of the Afro-American who condemns U.S. civilization "out of the most passionate love, hoping to make the kingdom new, to make it honorable and worthy of life" (1972a, 194; see Campbell 1991, 255). He assumes a prophetic stance when he describes how black people, awed by their oppressors clinging to their captivity and their destruction, "have always seen, spinning above the thoughtless American head, the shape of the wrath to come." While Baldwin invokes a telos of historical becoming, a fulfillment already presaged and realized by the incarnation within a Christian philosophy of history, he also could not let go of an essentially classical notion of a cosmic logos, a law of compensation that will restore through nemesis the harmony of historico-natural forces and reinstate the rhythm of the cosmos (see Lowith 1949, 7). Hence the Old Testament warning of retribution in *The Fire Next Time.* Given the secularized calculus of pleasure and pain dominant in late capitalism with its legitimizing ideals of progress and bureaucratic rationality, and given Baldwin's disillusionment with the Church's compromise with a racist dispensation, Baldwin has to summon in some kind of ventriloquist's mimicry the cry of "Vengeance is mine!" to reinforce his diagnosis of the white psyche's need for a scapegoat. This obsession of dependency is what makes white Americans, in general, "the sickest and certainly the most dangerous people, of any color, to be found in the world today" (1985b, 478)—an observation that has aroused and continues to inflame the hostility of Establishment critics and reviewers.

In *No Name in the Street*, Baldwin attempts to resolve the dilemma of individual autonomy and social determination in his description of the Black Panther party's social program, his sensitive portrayal of Huey Newton, and his recollections of his life in exile. He registers sympathy for Bobby Seale's notion of "an indigenous socialism, formed by, and responding to, the real needs of the American people" (1985b, 541). In this connection, Henry Louis Gates opines that Baldwin's comment on Cleaver "was an exercise in perversely *willed* magnanimity" (57), and that Baldwin was trying out of character to shed his reputation of an alienated artist in order to assume the role of an organic intellectual of black America. But years after *Notes of a Native Son* and its aesthetic of distance, it is now the consensus that the deaths of Malcolm X, Martin Luther King, and Medgar Evers compelled Baldwin to return to the vocation of "witness" of the social drama of his time (Weatherby 1989). Indeed, one might ask: Was he ever really alienated from the pressures that forced him to be a writer? Baldwin's experience of writing the Malcolm X screenplay in Hollywood, and his simultaneous involvement in his friend Tony Maynard's trial in New York, among other engagements, could not but remind him of his singularly "complex fate," the circumstantiality or contingency of the categorical imperative which defined the black intellectual in the United States and separated him from Henry James, William Faulkner, and their epigones.

In my view, *No Name in the Street* marks Baldwin's emergence as unequalled prophet-historian of his generation.[3] What is significant is that in reinvoking his master-narrative of the twin fate of white and black in the production of U.S. society, Baldwin performs a revision of Hegel's phenomenology of slave and master by replacing the mediation of labor with that of culture. Black self-determination then becomes a universal allegory of virtual human potentiality becoming social power:

> Black is a tremendous spiritual condition, one of the greatest challenges anyone alive can face—this is what the blacks are saying. . . . To be liberated from the stigma of blackness by embracing it is to cease, forever, one's interior agreement and collaboration with the authors of one's degradation. It abruptly reduces the white enemy to a contest merely physical, which he can win only physically. White men have killed black men for refusing to say, "Sir": but it was the corroboration of their worth and their power that they wanted, and not the corpse, still less the staining blood. When the black man's mind is no longer controlled by the white man's fantasies, a new balance or what may be described as an unprecedented inequality begins to make itself felt: for the white man no longer knows who he is, whereas the black man knows them both. For if it is difficult to be released from the stigma of blackness, it is clearly at least equally difficult to surmount the delusion of whiteness. And as the black glories in his newfound color, which is *his* at last, and asserts, not always with the very greatest politeness, the unanswerable validity and power of his being—even in the shadow of death—the white is very often affronted and very often made afraid. . . . It was inevitable that black and white should arrive at this dizzying height of tension. Only when we have passed this moment will we know what our history has made of us. (1972a, 549–50)

The aporia of racism is thus disrupted by a transvaluation or reversal of the stigma into a virtue. Contrary to Lacan's sublimated version of Hegel, the struggle for recognition is not premised on the desire for the Other's desire but on a disintegra-

---

3. When *No Name in the Street* evoked negative reactions from the reviewers, Baldwin confided to his brother: "Have you known me to kiss ass?" His official biographer remarks: "He was trapped, he said, between the 'white fantasy' and the 'black fantasy'" (Leeming 1994, 316).

tion of the hegemonic fantasy and a grasp of the total situation. Note the "unprecedented inequality" that precedes the initiation of both protagonists into the arena
of history. Later, Baldwin would observe that white Americans "need the moral
authority of their former slaves, who are the only people in the world who know
anything about them and who may be, indeed, the only people in the world who
really care anything about them" (1985b, 554). Becoming-Other is the key to
claiming and exercising such moral authority.

This staging of the tragic *agon* of "black power" leads us inevitably to the
question of Africa in the linkage "Afro-American" and its status as a possible rally-
ing symbol. Afrocentrism is for Baldwin not yet a viable detour. For he questions
whether Africa has freed itself from domination by Europe and the United States
and become Africa-for-itself, a condition when the land and resources are controlled by, and used for, the millions of African peoples. Antagonisms of class/race
continue to plague both continents, Africa and America, both of which were "discovered . . . with devastating results for the indigenous populations, whose only
human use thereafter was the source of capital for white people" (1985b, 552).
After this passage through the vicissitudes of self-negation, inversion, and alterity,
the truce with the reality of his birth ends when Baldwin finally takes an inventory
of the inadequacies of white Eurocentric supremacy and its neocolonial syndrome.
His encounter with Arabs in France and French intellectuals during the Algerian
revolution provided the opportunity for historicizing received commonsense, a
lesson of demystification and counter-memory, that finally purges the barbarian's
shame at the gates of the polis. In contrast to his autobiographical notes, Baldwin
now foregrounds the construction of collective subject-positions, of subdued and
subduer, of those "placed within history and those dispersed outside," as a process
centering on "the root question of the possession of the land and the exploitation
of the land's resources." It is at this discovery of the time-space nexus and its ecological anchorage, the materialist moment of thought, that emancipation begins:
"At that point the cultural pretensions of history are revealed as nothing less than a
mask for power, and thus it happens that, in order to be rid of Shell, Texaco, Coca-
Cola, the Sixth Fleet, and the friendly American soldier whose mission it is to pro-
tect these investments, one finally throws Balzac and Shakespeare—and Faulkner
and Camus—out with them" (1972a, 48). It is also in this catalyzing episode of the
French reaction to the loss of empire that Baldwin, shuttling between the turmoil
at home and the anonymity of life abroad, comes to comprehend the centrality of
labor power—the praxis of multitudinous bodies, in general—in the cultural resistance of Third World peoples: "The South African coal miner, or the African dig-
ging for roots in the bush, or the Algerian mason working in Paris, not only have
no reason to bow down before Shakespeare, or Descartes, or Westminster Abbey,
or the cathedral at Chartres: they have, once these monuments intrude on their
attention, no honorable access to them. Their apprehension of this history cannot
fail to reveal to them that they have been robbed, maligned, and rejected: to bow

down before that history is to accept that history's arrogant and unjust judgment" (1972a, 47).

In reviewing Alex Haley's *Roots*, Baldwin posits the "beginning of the end of the black diaspora," the end of the history of black suffering (1985b, 554). This end also entails the triumph of black power, the incarnation of popular self-determination. By encountering the reality of African colonialism in Europe in late 1950s, Baldwin succeeded in evading the seductive detour of liberalism which he pursued during the McCarthy period. In the context of the 1970s, he equates remembering with vengeance when he recollects his life among *les misérables* in Paris. Gradually this will to revenge, a dream of empowerment, yields to a vision of judgment mediated by the Black Panther party; it is a vision of "the creation of a new people." But this prophecy of a New Jerusalem cannot be dissociated from the transformation of the whole society; for "the black and white confrontation . . . [contains] the shape of the American future and the only potential of a truly valid American identity" (1985b, 549)—a universalizing imperative that dissolves the ideology of color in the axiomatics of domination/liberation. I think this accurately exemplifies Baldwin's idea of how identity is not invented but constructed from experience. And it is how one "faces and uses his experience," he adds, that shatters the metaphysical dream of ideal form (or its postmodern mirror-image, infinite deconstruction) that once imprisoned the imagination and inaugurates Baldwin's wrestling with the specters of Richard Wright, W.E.B. Du Bois, and Frederick Douglass. Even though he proclaimed his uniqueness as an "odd quantity," he could not ignore the way the world, U.S. hegemonic society in particular, seized hold of that oddness, subsumed it in a one-dimensional stereotype, and conflated it with the embattled situation of the black community. He was conducting what he called "an astute and agile guerilla warfare with that American complacency which so inadequately masks the American panic" (1966, 213).

Because of this ethical susceptibility, Baldwin's critique of the social totality has been construed as enigmatic, inconsistent, even opportunistic. His diagnosis of the almost organically intertwined fates of whites and blacks in U.S. society has provoked much negative speculation, polarizing critics and sympathizers, and reintroducing the old dualism of assimilation versus separatism, and its mirror-image, "color-blind" liberal humanism. An early flagrant example of the latter is Irving Howe's ill-tempered harangue against Baldwin's *Tell Me How Long the Train's Been Gone* (in Kinnamon 1974, 96–108). At this juncture, I feel that I need to address briefly Baldwin's final and somewhat peremptory solution to this black/white antinomy in his blanket notion of androgyny. A transitional passage to that phase of his development, however, needs to be interposed here.

In an early pronouncement, Baldwin conceived of the human condition as constituted by our eating the fruit of the tree of knowledge and, consequently, our incessant grappling with issues of good and evil. Such a predicament signifies constant and intense vigilance. But his vision of society was not Manichean because it presupposed interaction and interdependency between the warring parties. It also involved grasping the unity of opposites—Lenin's definition of "dialectics" (1963a, 131)—at any conjuncture that impelled historical/social motion. Thus Baldwin considered the "Redskin" (indigenous) and "Paleface" (Eurocentric) traditions in American culture as "inextricably intertwined . . . in dreadful battle" (1966, 211). This principle of privileging the coalescence of opposites explains his fundamental view that the "nigger" is white America's creation (1989, 45); that racist violence is a crime committed by racists against themselves; that a relational and processual dynamics, in the ultimate analysis, characterize the lived situation of racial/ethnic groups in the United States.

One final illustration of Baldwin's dialectical strategy of imagining the fluid racial dynamics of U.S. society can be found in the 1972 scenario/script *One Day, When I Was Lost* based on Alex Haley's *The Autobiography of Malcolm X*. In mapping Malcolm's journey from his early "Babylonian captivity" to the period when the white/black conflict is sublated in global Islam, Baldwin delineates the process of nuanced qualitative change in his protagonist. Painfully straightening his hair, the young Malcolm enacted the *habitus* of the colonized subject. We see Malcolm's character develop as a convergence of slavery's "delayed effects" (in psychoanalytic parlance) and the intractable trajectory of desire. In this libidinal economy, the figure of the blond Sophia is introduced to displace the paranoid obsession with "whiteness." Baldwin's grasp of late-capitalist economy as an allegory of desire, a project of colliding wills, thus dissolves the metaphysical dualism of American "nationalism," as exemplified in a panorama of Harlem ending with this revealing montage: "Filling the screen: In God We Trust. Superimposed on this: the serial number of the bill. The Stock Exchange Board, at the end of the day. The last three figures on the Board" (1972b, 67). Baldwin brilliantly counterpoints the tensions between the Nation of Islam (personified by Luther and Sidney) and Malcolm's emergent humanitarian or cosmopolitan sensibility, his internationally oriented "horizon of expectations." In a climactic exchange between Malcolm and Sidney, Baldwin dramatizes the "unity of opposites" (demonology of the races versus transformative critique of disciplinary regimes and ideological apparatuses), a complex of contradictions that up to now serves as the site of the operations of knowledge/power in late modernity:

> *Malcolm:* I know who's in prison—and I know why. I was in prison, too, and I remember it, even though I think you think I don't. All I've been trying to say is that white people in this country are what they are not because of the color of their skins—they're what they are because of this country—because they live in a racist country. I've been trying to say that I'm beginning to see—Christianity and capitalism are the two evils which have placed us where we are—in prison.

Sidney: The white man brought us here, baby, to make money off our flesh. And now that he don't need us to make money for him no more, he's going to get rid of us. It's as cold as that. This ain't no prison. It's a dress rehearsal for a concentration camp! (1972b, 250–51).

The controversy is not easily resolved by the death of Malcolm. Here is where Baldwin proceeds from the "middle passage" of black self-negation to the crossroad of fighting the enemy in a terrain with ambiguous and shifting boundaries. (Incidentally, the crossroad metaphor used often in Baldwin's novels and essays is meant to evoke African rituals of renewal witnessed in cult practices in the Caribbean and South America [Jahn 1961].) In his interviews, Baldwin constantly refers to Malcolm X's dictum that "white is a state of mind," a moral choice (1989, 218); that black nationalism, just by affirming blackness (Afrocentrism), will not suffice: "one has to be human as well. We did not struggle for four hundred years just to become like the white man" (1989, 259). On the other hand, Baldwin subscribes deeply to Malcolm X's conviction of the need for subjugated "natives" and indigenous peoples victimized by the West's "civilizing mission" to reclaim their histories; here he echoes Amilcar Cabral, Frantz Fanon, Aimé Césaire and others whose participation in Third World cultural revolutions generated protean, all-encompassing, resourceful sensibilities. In the spirit of solidarity, Baldwin proclaimed on one occasion: "The doctrine of white supremacy on which the Western world is based has had its hour—has had its day!" (1989, 216).

Baldwin's role as "God's revolutionary mouth," to use Baraka's phrase, lies in this vocation of articulating the unity of opposites in any moment of lived experience. In his most significant works, Baldwin strove to capture the heterogeneous and mutable economy of group psyches and its inscription in the uneven, conflicted, asynchronous social formation called "United States of America." I think Baldwin accomplished this task superbly in the scenario on Malcolm X, in his sparse but electrifying theater, and in his polemical essays. His performance is essentially revolutionary not only in representing the inescapable play of contradictions but also in alluding or gesturing to the "negation of the negation," that is, the stage of transcendence (critical synthesis) of those contradictions in some utopian moment of truth or happiness. This truth or totality-in-process can be seized in the writer's act of witnessing injustice and conversion, in the testimony of contextualizing one's consciousness/conscience in quotidian affairs. Asked once what he was a witness to, Baldwin replied: "Witness to whence I came, where I am. Witness to what I've seen and the possibilities that I think I see." That response offers us the concrete substance of Baldwin's dialectic, his profoundly historicizing imagination, and his timely prophetic radicalism. That said, one last scandalous theme only touched briefly before will insist itself here even though we might want to evade it.

In one of his last essays, "Here Be Dragons," Baldwin confronted the subject of homosexuality with the same heuristic and transvaluing approach deployed in examining race and ethnic relations. His rhetorical performance foregrounded once more the opposition of freedom and necessity in the peculiar all-encompassing reflex of his sensibility. He concludes his probing inquiry into the field of sexuality in the United States with the generalization that "we are all androgynous . . . because each of us, helplessly and forever, contains the other—male in female, female in male, white in black and black in white. We are part of each other . . . and none of us can do anything about it" (1985b, 690). This statement may strike many as exorbitant, claiming too much. Or else it may alarm with the resonance of a fatality, a contagion from the Imaginary register (Lacan's mirror-stage) ordained by a supernatural force. But it contradicts his proposition offered at the outset that human possibility, energized by the confluence of imagination and desire, makes the human animal more than simply stallion or mare: "the human imagination is perpetually required to examine, control, and redefine reality, of which we must assume ourselves to be the center and the key" so that the perpetual tension between nature and revelation "is one of the keys to human history and to what is known as the human condition" (1985b, 678). The aporia of necessity and freedom is played out once more, unfolding its vicissitudes in the arena of racial relations whose logic entails making choices, "paying one's dues," as Baldwin puts it. In the context of human experience, both desire and imagination move in time, in the course of social exchange and antagonism; the trajectory of their motion (cognized as history) is what the writer seeks to track and capture in language, in the mimetic and didactic modalities of essay, drama, or narrative. In this way Baldwin configures art's sensuous energies with the overdetermined "thickness" of social complicities.

Art finally becomes historicized in the life of this African-American artist whose quest for survival and joy—potentiality become power, in Spinoza's formulation—illuminates for us the intractable course of race relations in the United States. Hegel's dialectic of master and slave, the perpetual exchange of subject-positions, is short-circuited by the message that punctuates the closure of Baldwin's story, "Previous Condition." Peter, the artist whose homelessness is symbolic of manifold varieties of alienation and estrangement in the modern world, finally finds shelter in a Harlem bar and there confesses to a woman stranger, native of the habitat: "I got no story, Ma" (1977, 572; see Porter 1989, 84–90). Lack or loss of "place" displaces paranoid syntax, the diachrony of exchange-value in commodified society, and releases the force of Becoming-Other. This telos of redemption is also inscribed in Baldwin's poems. In "Staggerlee wonders," the speaker/persona counsels us to leave History alone because she is exhausted: "She must change./Yes. History must change./A slow, syncopated/relentless music begins/suggesting her re-entry,/transformed, virginal as she was . . . before the rape which debased her/to be the whore of multitudes. . . ." For Baldwin the activist-intellectual and tribune of his people, the syncopations of art can conquer the space for equality and inaugurate the kingdom of justice—only if the rape is acknowledged, innocence unlearned, and a reckoning/revelation promised. For Baldwin's rebel conscience, the cycle of history has already been disrupted with the advent of black power and the end of white supremacy; judgment is now being fulfilled. Hence the apocalyptic tone, still prophetic and even more provocative now that the fire promised looms "always already" on the horizon, of his not wholly pacified voice.

8

History and Representation
SYMBOLIZING THE ASIAN DIASPORA
IN THE UNITED STATES

> It is therefore a source of great virtue for the practiced mind to
> learn, bit by bit, first to change about in visible and transitory
> things, so that afterwards it may be able to leave them behind
> altogether. The person who finds his homeland sweet is still a
> tender beginner; he to whom every soil is as his native one is
> already strong; but he is perfect to whom the entire world is as a
> foreign place. The tender soul has fixed his love on one spot in
> the world; the strong person has extended his love to all places;
> the perfect man has extinguished his.
> —Hugo of St. Victor, *Didascalicon*

After about four centuries of the worldwide circulation of commodities—
including the hugely profitable trade in slaves from Africa that inaugurated,
for Marx, the "rosy dawn" of capitalism—the stage was set for more intense capital
accumulation based no longer on commercial exchange and the regional discrepancies in the price of goods but on the process of production itself. "Place" gave
way to space; lived time divided into necessary, surplus, and "free" segments.
Linked by relations of exchange governed by the logic of accumulation centered in
Europe and later in North America, the trajectories of peoples of color, the "people without history" in Eric Wolf's reckoning, entered the global labor market
with the expansion of industrial capitalism, the commercialization of agriculture,
urbanization, and the concomitant dislocation and displacement of populations
from their traditional homelands.

We are still in the epoch of transnational migrations and the traffic in bodies.
The breakup of the Soviet Union and Yugoslavia, plus the exacerbated
ethnic/racial conflicts in their wake, promise mutations less tractable than the configurations of earlier boundary shifts. In the nineteenth and early twentieth centuries, the movement of the bearers of labor power, "free" workers, at first
involved mainly peasants pushed toward the industrial centers of the European
peninsula; later, 50 million people left Europe between 1800 and 1924, 32 million

of them bound for the factories and mines of the industrializing United States. (Of the 200 million migrants between 1500 to 1980, 42 million were from the continent of Asia.) Meanwhile, the victory of imperialism in China with the Opium War of 1839–42 allowed foreign entrepreneurs or brokers to establish the apparatus for the "coolie" trade that eventually facilitated the transport of 200,000 Chinese to the United States between 1852 and 1875 (Wolf 1982). In the 1860s, about 14,000 Chinese laborers were hired to build the transcontinental Central Pacific Railroad. Unlike the Chinese "pariah capitalism" in other regions (Safran 1991), the Chinese exodus to North America could only mediate between an exploitative host society and a moribund tributary formation already subjugated by Western powers.[1]

With the Native Americans resisting the conquest of their lands and alienation of their labor power, and with the majority of Africans still bound to the slave plantations, there was no alternative but the temporary implantation of the Asian "alien" into the territory of the United States; when no longer needed, they were "Driven Out"—demonized as the "Yellow Peril," then purged via the Chinese Exclusion Act of 1882 (in force until 1943). This was reinforced by the "Gentlemen's Agreement" of 1907–8 that interdicted laborers from Japan and later Korea. It was supplemented by the 1917 Immigration Act that created the Asiatic Barred Zone (all of Asia including Afghanistan and Arabia, Asiatic Russian, most Polynesian and all East Indian islands), and by other paralegal, genocidal acts of violence (Cashmore 1988; Bouvier and Gardner 1986).

I

The inaugural scene of any diaspora involves the uneven terrain of the world system I have alluded to that is simultaneously differentiated and homogenized by the logic of capital accumulation. This twofold process is concretized in the movement of peoples and nationalities at specific conjunctures where for the most part the bearers of the culture of precapitalist formations are inserted into a capitalist mode of production and forcibly undergo cataclysmic transformations. Ethnogenesis or ethnicization occurs when a consciousness of this inaugural scene is acquired by the dislocated group, a consciousness of a shared crisis signified by the terms "alienation," "uprooting," separation, exile, and isolation. Such consciousness always evolves in specific historical contexts, within definite temporal-spatial parameters, in the conjunction of inner and outer concourses of events, such that whatever strategies of resolving the crisis are forged engages structures and institutions with their more or less fixed traditions and contingent modes of representations

---

1. For a summary of the historical background of Asian immigration, see Chan (1991).

(Patterson 1983). If this shared crisis of exile and uprooting implies a removal from the time-space orientation of the homeland, the sacralized site of beginnings and endings which provides the boundaries of personal identity, in what way then (apart from the return carried out by sojourners, or the mythmaking of deferred homecoming sustained by "symbiotic" *ethnys*) have the remembering and resolution of such a crisis been explored in the writing of Asian-Americans without necessarily entailing the recovery of a literal homeland?

In essence, the crisis assumes the form of the disintegration of a way of life (its telos and its conception of a collective good) nourished in organic formations when they collide with the forces of the free market and its ethos of bureaucratic individualism. Such a collision, epitomized by the colonial subjugation of peoples of color, ultimately signifies the breakup of the intelligible meaning-producing narratives of the life of whole communities and their dispersal into monadic fragments or anomic bodies. What is lost is not only temporal-spatial continuity but, more important, the practice and vision of some collective good that informs the unity of character and life-histories of its individual members. What subtends the "liberal individualism of the market system" and its utilitarian norms is the process of reification, seriality, the instrumental rationality of means-ends, and so forth, which on the whole negates history and unity of character. Commodity fetishism subverts or undermines any impulse to construct a narrative of diaspora, of dismemberment, and its overcoming. Given this trajectory, one can outline in general the responses to this crisis of collective alienation and fragmentation inscribed in several broad symbolic configurations or genres which are not mutually exclusive and which are amenable to qualification because of the discontinuities in the migration patterns and sociohistoric backgrounds of the constituent Asian groups. Far from essentializing agency, these responses inflect the energies of "cultural nationalism" toward geopolitical and dialogical confrontations.

The first strategy is what I would call a postmodernist affirmation of heterogeneity within the thematic limits of an ideologically pluralist society. It seeks to valorize the amorphous and diverse as against the uniform (the assimilationist model of Anglo conformity), the hybrid and heteroglotic as against the predictable ethnic stereotype. One example may be found in Frank Chin's protagonist in *The Chickencoop Chinaman* who tries to exhibit the virtuosity of a bricoleur as he posits a polymorphous subject-position for his syncretic genealogy: "Chinamen are made, not born, my dear. Out of junk-imports, lies, railroad scrap iron, dirty jokes, broken bottles, cigar smoke, Cosquilla Indian blood, wino spit, and lots of milk amnesia. . . . For I am a Chinaman! A miracle synthetic. . . . I speak nothing but the mother tongues bein' born to none of my own, I talk the talk of orphans" (1991, 118, 120–21). Of course, Chin's commitment is not to his group's ability to absorb or reflect the varied surface phenomena of U.S. society but to the artist's expansive and capacious spirit, a sensibility that leaps over boundaries of nation or race. This is an elective affinity, an affiliation chosen to supersede tribal filiations. As an antidote to the Chinatown mentality, Chin's parodic pastiche refunctions the seriality of commodified humans to prove somehow that U.S. society itself is as decentered as the populist architecture of Las Vegas, a mammoth bricolage, without any nationalist marker. Whether or not this strategy of selective identification captures and resolves the existential predicament of young Chinese-Americans, what is certain is that this route of trying to beat the enemy in his language-game is filled with recuperative temptations. In other words, this verisimilitude may be a pyrrhic victory over Leviathan.

A modification of Chin's strategy is that of Jeffery Chan in his story "The Chinese in Haifa" (which I discuss below). To counter the loss of historicity in the diaspora, Chan envisages a community of all the dispossessed and disinherited, delineating the paradoxes of loyalty and betrayal in the process and also questioning linkages based on custom versus ties based on personal preference. This response characterizes the enclave micropolitics of the intellectual who rejects ethnic collectivism and opts for spiritual marginality and exile as a permanent possibility. It is possible that both Chin's and Chan's postmodernist approach, albeit with varying idiosyncracies, can nullify if not neutralize the two intellectual operations at work in theoretical racism pointed out by Etienne Balibar (1990), namely, the mode of hierarchic classification and the deployment of anthropological universals. At least, what they refuse is the obsession with purity (racial, cultural, or whatever) as an ideal or transcendent value, the metaphysical underpinning of all racisms.

In contrast, Maxine Hong Kingston combines both counter-identification (a reversal of the negative image of the alien) and dis-identification, a taking up of antagonistic positions (MacDonell 1986). In both *The Woman Warrior* and *China Men*, the damaged narratives of her family are reconstituted to thwart the racial categorization of bureaucratic individualism. Hers is a versatile approach to envisaging community as an ongoing collective project, one that posits the intelligibility of individual lives as premised on a new civic morality so that, in effect, the extended family or the ghetto sometimes functions as a surrogate for a polis that has been eroded by colonialism and racist violence. I am not saying that Kingston has simply rehabilitated Confucianism and the ideals of the old tributary, patriarchal regime in her articulation of a social good inherent in certain practices of resistance by her characters. Indeed, her feminism enables her to thwart the seductions of pragmatic relativism as she outlines the vicissitudes of a "group-in-fusion" (to use Sartre's term) and dramatizes the ruses of dis-identifications adopted by beleaguered immigrants as they test the limits of the law.

In *Jasmine*, Bharati Mukherjee (originally from India) attempts to rewrite expatriation as an allegory or montage of spiritual transmigrations. While the novel also probes the limits of patriarchal law, its strategy hinges on unfolding the narrative of a quest replete with reversals and recognitions. Mukherjee, in an interview, claims that Jyoti (reincarnated as Jase and Jane) personifies the feminist revolutionary, a love goddess or life force who gets what she wants. Unfortunately, the novel ends with Jasmine's life being embedded once again in the narrative of another person's life. Its quasi-picaresque and necessarily episodic action, while registering the crisis of modern industrial society in its architectonics, foregrounds the problematic status of an intrinsically romantic project of self-transformation (Jasmine, according to Mukherjee, "ends up being a tornado who leaves a lot of debris behind"). Paradoxically underlying the trope of a protean form of life in motion are the doctrine and institutions of the free market—a postmodern allegory, perhaps, of a "postcolonial" writer whose vision of international solidarity seems compromised in her use of the myth of the American West as an open frontier devoid of aborigines (see Mukherjee 1990, 29).

What Mukherjee's narrative seeks to achieve but fails is a goal associated with this genre: the composition of a narrative of a life whose unity and intelligibility spring from its being embedded in the history of a community which, though transplanted, continues to survive with some degree of autonomy. This objective, I think, has been masterfully attained by the Japanese-American writer Hisaye Yamamoto in her story, "Las Vegas Charley." Denarrativization (emblematized by the city and its mutabilities) is countered by practices demonstrating the residual power of certain public or civic virtues that serve to connect the segments of a character's life and redeem it from victimage. Las Vegas Charley refuses the route of Stoic self-mastery or of empty moral, categorical imperatives. Yamamoto's rendering of scenes in Charley's life suggests that its unity is not derived from his psychology or a superimposed ethical substance but from certain concrete practices whose actualization embody social goods—indeed, the subtext of this story may be the almost insurmountable difficulty of conceptualizing these goods when all sense of responsibility (personal and civic) in the majority of citizens has been been attenuated or dissolved altogether (see MacIntyre 1984). In that case, Matsumoto appropriately wears the mask of a whole city founded on the cash-nexus that extinguishes alterity and difference, a mask whose antinomic interiority may be discerned in the central character of John Okada's novel *No-No Boy*.

In stories like "Las Vegas Charley," the strategy is twofold: while the artist of the diaspora seeks to recreate a community in exile by a resumption of traditional practices with social goods internal to them, these practices in turn generate a utopian pathos because they can no longer satisfy the individual whose will and passions have become detached from any viable community. Pure becoming or absolute contingency displaces the unity of lives sharing pasts and futures. Alienation then becomes translated into an opportunity to enact a measure of autonomy and integrity. In place of the limited understanding of the character, the author interposes her will to reconstitute if not discover the migrant's life-destiny via the mediation of a symbolic causality that threads the otherwise mere contingencies of an ordinary immigrant's wanderings.

Finally, in the works of the Filipino writer Carlos Bulosan, we find a strategy of prophetic figuration that seeks to disclose the complicities between metropolis and periphery. The image of collective labor and resistance discovered in the native tradition of anticolonial revolt as it is transposed to the present becomes a kind of "objective correlative" to resolve the crisis of isolation and exilic anguish. This organon of counter-memory opposed to official history is, however, not primordial or culturalist in intent because it is anchored in anticolonialism and determined by class partisanship. (Of all Asians, the Filipinos are the only subjugated "natives" who have resisted U.S. symbolic and physical violence since their homeland was occupied in 1898 in the aftermath of the Spanish-American War.) Alternatively, Bulosan focuses on multiracial work as a social practice whose rhythm and intrinsic sociality endows it with a self-renewing *habitus*. In the struggle for recognition, the protagonists in Bulosan's fiction (see, for example, "Be American" or certain chapters in *America Is in the Heart*) learn cooperation, mutual trust, courage, sympathy, and mobilizations of latent resources as they confront the brutality of white vigilantes and the coercive ideological apparatuses of the state. This need to belong to a group in a state of siege is not fated; it is chosen, it is a commitment to a path whose unfolding is assured but unpredictable. Its goal is clearly defined as internal to its practice: not the resurrection of the homeland but the founding of a community of producers in the territory of North America where the basis of class exploitation (the commodification of racialized labor power) has been abolished.

In this sense Bulosan preempts the ethnic crisis by reinscribing alienation in the matrix of class antagonism. With this perspectival shift, the resolution to the crisis of loss of home (the colony) and ethnic alienation becomes also the resistance to imperialism founded on exploitation of class and national subalterns. Although this mode of renarrativization is not without its dangers, it is preferable because it has the power of curbing the seductiveness of ethnic chauvinism for demagogues as well as for victims who all too often spontaneously react to the racialized oppression they suffer. Bulosan tries to modulate the utopianism of a desired classless society by the symbolic validation of a fertile and beautiful land owned by no one, shared by all. Such a geopolitical site, a possible home to all citizens, is still extraterritorial insofar as goods are not shared equally and hierarchization by race still prevails. Bulosan's narratives envisage emancipation not of the human essence but of social relations; they prefigure liberations not anticipated but actualized in the struggle to break down the ethnic ghetto and root one's identity in a struggle shared with others across ethnicity, nationality, and race. Home, the primal scene of deracination, is therefore not a place but a process of unifying one's life through acts of solidarity and resistance with others dehumanized by the constructed criteria of race, class, gender, and nationality.

II

In order to dramatize the unique expressive gesture of each strategy, I focus on certain aspects of Asian diasporic texts that articulate the cultural politics of collective self-transformation in late capitalism. I begin by remarking on the forced "return" or exclusion of Asians as a racial group which I referred to earlier as an historical event that finds an inverted simulacrum in the way their entry is represented in Kingston's *China Men*.

Kingston narrates two versions of the father from China entering the fabled "Gold Mountain" (the legendary image of the United States). Of these two versions, the second is the legal way of passage through Angel Island in San Francisco Bay where "a white demon physically examined him, poked him in the ass and genitals, looked in his mouth, pulled his eyelids with a hook" and detained him until, purified by this ordeal of commodification, he passed the "American examination." The first one is, in contrast, a violation of customs law. Midwived by smugglers, the father deposits himself in a womblike crate that is stowed in the dark belly of a ship where soon he "began to lose his bearings." Caught in this self-made prison, the speaking subject becomes dispersed in a sequence of images that dissolves memory and unbalances consciousness, affording a new sensorium for the protagonist:

> Various futures raced through his mind: walking the plank, drowning, growing old in jail, being thrown overboard in chains, flogged to tell where others were hiding, hung by the neck, returned to China—all things that happened to caught chinamen. . . .
> Because of fear, he did not eat nor did he feel hungry. . . . Rocking and dozing, he felt the ocean's variety—the peaked waves that must have looked like pines; the rolling waves, round like shrubs, the occasional icy mountains; and for stretches, lulling grasslands. . . .
> He heard voices, his family talking about gems, gold, cobbles, food. . . . The villagers had to make up words for the wonders. "Something new happens every day, not the same boring farming."
> The sea invented words too. He heard a new language, which might have been English, the water's many tongues speaking and speaking. Though he could not make out words, the whispers sounded personal, intimate, talking him over, sometimes disapproving, sometimes in praise of his bravery. (1989, 50–51)

When finally a voice interrupts the cacophony of sounds, "It's me. It's me," an announcement that identifies the Other (the smuggler/outlaw) who then delivers the father from his self-fashioned captivity, Kingston's antihero is ready to "claim the Gold Mountain, his own country." Born from the ruse of the illicit Other, this subject (or subject-position) thus thwarts the normative paranoia of self-identification.[2]

The act of problematizing boundaries coincides with the refusal of one paradigmatic narrative of migration centered on the Symbolic Order authorizing racial difference. We elude the repetition compulsion of ethnic historiography epitomized by Ellis Island and the state apparatus of statistical control. Finally landing on solid ground, the stowawayed father glimpses a statue of a woman "who carried fire and a book"—the female as mythical embodiment of the civilizing mission, not so portentous a figure as the one that greeted the fictive immigrant of Kafka's *Amerika*. "'Is she a goddess of theirs?' the father asked. 'No,' said the smuggler, 'they don't have goddesses. She's a symbol of an idea.' He was glad to hear that the Americans saw the idea of Liberty so real that they made a statue of it" (1989, 52–53). The prudent father in Angel Island censored this idea: "If the U.S. government found out his thoughts on freedom, it might not let him land" (1989, 56).[3] With the fetish of the assimilating mother avoided thanks to this narrative artifice, we confront an "uncanny strangeness" in the unsettled characters and tempo of Kingston's "talk-stories." We sense "a disturbing Otherness" implicit in the recognition of that "erotic, death-bearing unconscious" which Julia Kristeva considers the basis of human solidarity; the living through of this internalized difference allegorized by the primal scene of arrival in the continent is the "ultimate condition of our being *with* others" (1991, 192). Before this condition is reached, however, the ghetto of Chinatown must be traversed first.

In establishing the practice of alterity as the condition of possibility for the Chinese fathers, the narrative disavows the doctrinaire claim that art creates authentic identity and redeems fallen reality. Although the ostensible project of *China Men* is to dramatize the negated agency of the Chinese male immanent in the pathos and waste of their experiences, what stands out is not the foundational rite of Eurocentric Americanization—adaptation to the Puritanical conquest of the wilderness, individualism, the work ethic, and so forth. Rather it is their resistance to hegemonic corporate power and the racialized nation-state. A distinctly utopian celebration of manual work on the land aims to subvert the drive of an expansive economy toward differentiation and equalization while a desire to reconstruct the genealogy of the "castrated" patriarchs substitutes for a promised return to the homeland the continuity of certain virtues tested in actual practice—such as the Brother's refusal to kill Vietnamese—integral to the preservation of the commu-

---

2. Note the analogous rite of passage in Younghill Kang's arrival in the United States recounted in *East Goes West*: "It was in New York I felt I was destined really 'to come out from the board.' The beginning of my new existence must be founded here. In Korea *to come out from the boat* is an idiom meaning to be born, as the word 'pai' for 'womb' is the same as 'pai' for 'boat'" (1974, 217–18).

3. For testimonials of how Chinese lived through their ordeal in Angel Island, see Takaki (1989, 231–39).

nity. A return is deferred, then displaced; memory induces a delayed effect, making the land of origin coeval with the present. In effect, the resistance to colonial oppression is relocated to the interior of the metropolis. This does not of course disrupt the circulation and exploitation of migrant labor power. But the evocation of a territory free from the imperial plunder of the past (the People's Republic of China), and of the resistance of the Vietnamese (whose victory ironically will provide the next reservoir of cheap labor for a deindustrializing economy), together with the suture of archaic myth and documentary testimonials in an open-ended account, suffice, I think, in neutralizing the dominant theoretical paradigm of ethnic success (via accomodation/integration) which has so effectively underwritten the racism of the past and the injustices of the present.

III

In tracking the dispersal of "Asian" bodies in the United States, it is imperative to stress one elementary proposition: that the heterogeneous cultures of both ethnic and racial minorities (in Robert Blauner's terms) are not "primordial" social relationships preserved from the past but historical effects of asymmetrical power relations between uneven formations, specifically of labor-market segmentation. This segmentation derives in turn from the shifting ratio of fixed capital (machinery) to variable capital or wage labor. What results is the phenomenon of uneven development of the world system—the spatial configuration of the margin and periphery, the core and the dependencies—that configures the way Asians, among other people of color, have been marked for the calculation of their price in the global labor market. The geography of early imperial conquest has pre-defined Asians when absolute space (feudal relations) was abolished through the universalization of wage labor; but simultaneously, various relative spaces (on the scale of the urban, the nation-state, and so on) were generated within which the bourgeoisie through the state organized the expansion and accumulation of capital, in particular the political control over the working class. As Neil Smith puts it: "The internal differentiation of national territories into identifiable regions is the geographical expression of the division of labour, both at the level of individual capitals and the particular division of labor. . . . Capital produces distinct spatial scales—absolute spaces— within which the drive toward equalization is concentrated. But it can only do this by an acute differentiation and continued redifferentiation of relative space, both within and between scales" (1984, 144, 147). This systemic process of spatial realignment underlies the allochronism of Western discourse on people of color. It also informs Eurocentric knowledge-production premised on relativism and denial of coevalness with these Others whose existence its self-identification required (Fabian 1983).

How was this hegemonic knowledge challenged by Asian writers in the United States? Since the emergence of Third World labor and its differential incorporation into the Euro-American polity are consequences of the uneven development of the capitalist mode, of the dialectic of equalization and differentiation embodied most starkly in colonial subjugation (of the Philippines, Puerto Rico, among others), how writing represents Asians transgressing the boundaries of the U.S. racial order can suggest a framework for articulating the character of the diaspora not simply as an uprooting of peoples from their homelands but also as a process of transformative critique and self-determination. Deracination thus precipitates the dream of autonomy. Instead of projecting a collective myth of return that constitutes the diverse libidinal economies of their peoples, Asian writers endeavor to dramatize the vicissitudes of ethnogenesis, opposition, and self-empowerment. If capital ingests or devours the bodies of immigrant workers, how are they able to survive this "incorporation" and preserve their integrity?

Although the syndrome of "the West and the Rest" is usually deconstructed by postmodern thinkers in order to prioritize a politics of radical difference, we might use for research purposes the attempt of schizoanalysis to explain the particularity of Asian dissemination. The first move is to refuse the claim of purity. Rejecting capital's ideals of universality identified with the self-identical subject (patriarchal, ego-centered, white) and a representative Totality, Gilles Deleuze and Felix Guattari (1987) suggest that those who are able to survive the cannibalism of the Whole belong to the tribe-race practicing nomad thought. "Deployed in a horizonless milieu that is a smooth space, steppe, desert, or sea," this "race" necessarily bastard and mixed-blood is defined "not by its purity but rather by the impurity conferred upon it by a system of domination." Instead of invoking a myth of return, the nomadic race dissolves the differentiated space engendered by capitalist modernity and invents a new habitat. Deleuze and Guattari offer this thesis: "In the same way that race is not something to be rediscovered, the Orient is not something to be imitated; it only exists in the construction of a smooth space, just as race only exists in the constitution of a tribe that peoples and traverses a smooth space" (1987, 380). Migration plays with and around fixed boundaries, soaking up heterogeneous influences and contriving new environments.[4] Schizoid thought, however, seems to flatten the map prematurely by hypothesizing a liberated "space" not hitherto codified by previous engagements where authority or some sovereign power shows its hand. Can this space of "free play" and promise of mobility be the alibi of immigrants who have mortgaged their labor (life) time beforehand?

---

4. This praxis of playing with boundaries and limits signifies, for Fredric Jameson (1991), the act of totalization which he privileges as the necessary orientation for any emancipatory or revolutionary project.

IV

The topography of the United States, however, was not smooth (literally or figuratively) when the Chinese, Japanese, Asian Indians, and Filipinos first arrived. In the West Coast from California up to Alaska, it was already demarcated by the seasonal routine of planting and harvesting that defined the itinerary of the Filipino migrant-workers chronicled by Carlos Bulosan in the classic testimony, *America Is in the Heart.*

After more than a decade of suffering and struggle, the representative persona in Bulosan's ethnobiography sums up: "The terrible truth in America shatters the Filipinos' dream of fraternity." Prohibited from marrying white women, isolated in barracks and confined to gambling halls and cabarets, target of lynching mobs and the state's coercive bureaucracy, these Filipinos reclaimed tabooed spaces and transvalued them. Circumscribed in their movements, they conducted a reconaissance of the landscape of Euro-American ambivalence and contradiction in private letters, anecdotes, photographs, and various modes of semiotic resistance other than linear print. Like Kingston, Bulosan charts the territory from a carnivalesque perspective that combines the pastoral idealization of the farmer/artisan in the homeland with the myth of America as a site of inexhaustible opportunities and resources.

In the story "Be American," for example, Bulosan celebrates the line of flight and fluctuation, "multiplicities of escape and flux," whereby the colonized "native" tries to encompass and name his predicament. Eventually the narrator anchors physical motion to an idealized perception of nature that functions as a reactive answer to the degradation of the environment by monopoly agribusiness:

> Yes, indeed, Consorcio: You have become an American, a real American. And this land that we have known too well is not yet denuded by the rapacity of men. Rolling like a beautiful woman with an overflowing abundance of fecundity and murmurous with her eternal mystery, there she lies before us like a great mother. To her we always return from our prodigal wanderings and searchings for an anchorage in the sea of life; from her we always draw our sustenance and noble thoughts, to add to her glorious history. (1983, 58)

Such nostalgia for the organic community incarnate in virgin land which is fecund but not denuded, coupled with the fact that Bulosan received generous help from white American women in a time of vicious racist attacks on Filipino workers, enables Bulosan to represent the Filipino experience as a transitional stage, a border zone of passage, from dispossession to autonomy. Unprivatized land becomes fetishized as everyone's maternal home, refuge, and haven. The Filipino resistance to Japanese colonialism, evoking those against the Spanish and the American invaders in the past, inspires a recovery of ideals that the young Bulosan originally ascribed to a mythical America and thus redeems the fallen present. This evokes a neo-Stoic ideal of human fellowship that transcends the ethnocentrism of the nation-state. In *America Is in the Heart*, the Filipino condition of exile ends when Filipinos join in the united front against world fascism to liberate the homeland and also purge their host's body of the imperial virus. But the Cold War and McCarthyism extinguished Bulosan's hope. Nearly forty years after Bulosan's death, the Filipino nationality in the United States, now in the process of comprising the largest segment in the Asian-American category, continues to inhabit an internal colony that reproduces in microcosm the dependent status of the Philippines and its caste-like role as supplier of cheap labor for U.S. multinationals.

It appears that the "New World Order" inaugurated by the war against Iraq replicates on a different scale the uneven development of capitalism in the nineteenth century. A complicating factor is this: demographically the racial minorities in the United States, soon to be the majority in the next fifty years, are bound to reconstitute the racial politics of neo–Social Darwinism and to alter the iniquitous hierarchy of power. The concept of minority, however, is not quantitative or numerical; it signifies the emergence of a new subject-position in the global ecology of permanent crisis. What characterizes the minority are multiple connections that "constitutes a line of flight . . . , a universal figure, or becoming-everybody/ everything" (Deleuze and Guattari 1987, 470). In opposition to the axiomatics of the State and the logic of the market, minorities cannot be integrated or assimilated into denumerable sets or subsets with regional, federal, or statutory autonomy because their calculus proceeds "via a pure becoming," flows, events, incorporeal transformations, "continuums of intensities or continuous variations, which go beyond constants and variables; becomings, which have neither culmination nor subject, but draw one another into zones of proximity or undecidability" (Deleuze and Guattari 1987, 507): a plane of consistency or immanence that multiplies connections. This postmodern conception of minorities may exhibit a certain excess; but it is, I think, more faithful to their metamorphic responses to the dilemma of dispossession and dislocation than either the old functionalist race-relations cycle or the prevailing ethnicity paradigm which underpins the "model minority" myth.

So far, the Chinese in Kingston's fiction and the Filipinos in Bulosan's memoirs are represented as decolonizing flows or becomings that strive to recuperate the meaning of home in cooperative work or in their precarious residence in the United States. They problematize the polarity of inside/outside. Meanwhile, two world wars intensified uneven development, ravaging the hinterlands and preventing any return for sojourners and expatriates. In the aftermath, Chinese, Japanese, and Filipinos, victimized by assorted discriminatory laws and practices, have reterritorialized their alienation via claims to property and the rights of full citizenship. Their strategies of multiplying connections were deployed for a time in a regime of signs that valorized the depths and eccentricity of singular psyches, a sacred realm of interiority that resisted conversion to the counters of exchange value. In the age of mass consumption of spectacles and simulacra, however, even the borderlands of fantasy, sexuality, and utopian desire are now subject to the surveillance of the interventionist state, a panoptic gaze reinforced by sophisticated electronic media and computerized communication. The paranoia of subjectivity attached to the cash-nexus can easily become the surrogate for ramifying connections, affiliations, solidarities until the ghetto mentality is revitalized—this time armed with a micropolitical rhetoric to match the dispersive and atomistic logic of postmodern capital (Smith 1984; Harvey 1989).[5]

V

Perhaps a telltale figuration of the postmodern mode of incorporating the Asian, specifically the Indian subject, into the crucible of flexible accumulation can be found in Mukherjee's novel *Jasmine*. Mukherjee's fiction is a protracted meditation on the plight of immigrants, refugees, expatriates, exiles in a world transfigured by the rapid consumption of space as a means of production. What the narrator apprehends is the dialectic of sameness and difference, the shifting ratio of capital and labor in racial categorizations that demarcate the zones of contact and separation:

> But we are refugees and mercenaries and guest workers; you see us sleeping in airport lounges, you watch us unwrapping the last of our native foods, unrolling our prayer rugs, reading our holy books, taking out for the hundreth time an aerogram promising a job or space to sleep, a newspaper in our language, a photo of happier times, a passport, a visa, a *laissez-passer*.
>
> We are the outcasts and deportees, strange pilgrims visiting out-landish shrines, landing at the end of tarmacs, ferried in old army trucks where we are roughly handled and taken to roped-off corners of waiting rooms where surly, barely wakened customs guards await their bribe. We are dressed in shreds of national costumes, out of season, the wilted plumage of intercontinental vagabondage. We ask only one thing: to be allowed to land; to pass through; to continue. We sneak a look at the big departure board, the one the tourists use. Our cities are there, too, our destinations are so close! . . .

---

5. Perhaps a revealing indication of this contradictory process may be illustrated by one urban policy in Britain to achieve racial integration by way of "ecological dispersal" (see Cashmore 1988, 80–81).

What country? What continent? We pass through wars, through
plagues. I am hungry for news, but the discarded papers are in characters
or languages I cannot read.

The zigzag route is straightest. (1989, 90–91)

The last statement anticipates the waning of allochronism in Western epistemology
and the realization of coevalness in affirming the cotemporality of speaking subject
and listener (more on this later), where the Other occupies the same ground and
the same time as ourselves. We suspect that the implied referent here that can only
be alluded to but not realistically described is the massive, ongoing "warm-body
export" of the Asian countries to Europe, the Middle East, and North America.
This summons up a horizon of trajectories and redundancies whose passage across
continents mocks the claims of market liberalism to underwrite and promote
equality, modernity, and progress everywhere through the principle of difference.

A new speaking subject, the "I" behind the apparatus of enunciation, is initiated into the discursive field of the internationalized Gothic novel where
diachrony collapses into synchrony. In this context, time dissolves into spatial disjunctions. Difference indeed relates, but from what point of view? We find that the
narrative releases an allegorical force from the woman's obedience to tradition, a
force that counterpoints the effects of the global shift of production and appropriation in the life of the Third World subaltern. Jasmine may be said to personify the
return of the repressed—the primal scene of deracination—so as to make it (root-
lessness) a generalized lived situation for all.

What is striking here in the light of my remarks on Kingston's *China Men* is an
analogous smuggling of the Asian, this time a woman obsessed with the past rather
than with future success, into U.S. territory via a break in the unguarded coastline
of Florida. (In both *China Men* and this novel, the Caribbean functions as a locus
for testing the vulnerability of the nation-state's closure.) She is ferried by *The Gulf
Shuttle* commanded by Half-Face, a sinister figure who "had lost an eye and ear and
most of his cheek in a paddy field in Vietnam," in what he calls "the armpit of the
universe." This deformed exemplar of the rugged individualist is a survivor of the
United States' disastrous attempt to dominate the Pacific Rim and roll back the
gains of several Asian revolutions. Jasmine's first sight of the New World undercuts
well-known literary analogues—from the Puritan evangelists to *The Great Gatsby*.
Her recollection foreshadows the suicidal agonies of the Iowa farmers and registers
the surface mutations of uneven development at the core still visible to the new-
comer:

I smelled the unrinsed water of a distant shore. Then suddenly in the
pinkening black of pre-dawn, America caromed off the horizon.

The first thing I saw were the two cones of a nuclear plant, and
smoke spreading from them in complicated but seemingly purposeful

patterns, edges lit by the rising sun, like a gray, intricate map of an unex-
plored island continent, against the pale unscratched blue of the sky. I
waded through Eden's waste: plastic bottles, floating oranges, boards,
sodden boxes, white and green plastic sacks tied shut but picked open by
birds and pulled apart by crabs....

I wonder if Bud even sees the America I do. We pass half-built,
half-deserted cinder-block structures at the edge of town, with mud-
spattered deserted cars parked in an uncleared lot, and I wonder, Who's
inside? What are they doing? Who's hiding? Empty swimming pools
and plywood panels in the window frames grip my guts. And Bud
frowns because unproductive projects give him pain. He said, "Wonder
who handled their financing?"

My first night in America was spent in a motel with plywood over
its windows, its pool bottomed with garbage sacks, and grass growing in
its parking lot. (1989, 95–97)

Retrospection insinuates the presence of Bud, the patriarch-banker, impotent
before the signs of unproductivity. Raped in a room that seemed to her like a mad-
house or prison, Jasmine performs a ritual of purification and then kills Half-Face,
agency of the Symbolic Order of laissez-faire competition, who has transported
her to the land where she has vowed to sacrifice herself according to the code of
marital obedience. Allochronism gives way to coevalness. In the borderland
between incompatible lifeworlds, "undocumented" cheap labor confronts
microchip technology; the time of suttee intersects the age of mercantile, booty
capitalism.

One can stress here how Jasmine's violation by Half-Face, symbol of the
ethos of commodification and white male supremacy, releases her from her vow
and assigns her to a new mission, a cognitive and mock-naive mapping of the
United States. Among the connections revealed by her experience—her sequence
of becomings, if you like—is the kind of commercial circuit that links her country-
man, the Professorji in Flushing, New York, with Indian women whose virgin and
innocent hair, compared to the "horrible hair of American women" ruined by
shampoos and permanents, are highly prized as an integral component of the
defense industry and high-tech business. One wonders: Is the diaspora a pretext for
recolonizing the Third World?

After a stay in New York City with a seemingly ideal couple, she ends up
temporarily in Iowa with Bud Ripplemeyer, purveyor of credit and the future,
whose body, paralyzed from a shot by a disgruntled farmer-customer, betokens the
plight of the heartland. But it is her association with their adopted Vietnamese
child Du that enables Jasmine, who has "bloomed from a diffident alien with
forged documents into adventurous Jase," to recover her sense of being "rhi-
zomatic," open to multiple transactions and intensities. She is, however, still vul-

nerable to the seductions of the stereotype: "Bud courts me because I am alien. I am darkness, mystery, inscrutability. The East plugs me into instant vitality and wisdom. I rejuvenate him simply by being who I am" (1989, 178). Gender inequity becomes romanticized under the aegis of Orientalism, a compensatory response to the indifference of cultural relativism and the mystique of American pluralism.

In contrast, it is instructive to note how, for the Korean Younghill Kang, the West taught him "rebellion against nature and fatality"; confronted by the pitiable derelicts of New York City, he invokes the Korean experience in Japanese prisons: "And yet I clutched to a new world of time, where individual disintegration was possible, as well as individual integration, where all need not perish with the social organism." (1974, 239).

In Mukherjee's novel, it is Du, however, who reconnects Jasmine to the traumatic violence of Half-Face and the whole mechanism of exchange in business society. As mysterious as her own image, Du is Jasmine's "silent ally against the bright lights, the rounded, genial landscape of Iowa." Her reading of Du's past—she has counseled herself before to "learn to read the world and everyone in it like a photographic negative of reality"—constructs a site for affirming her capacity to mobilize energies suppressed by the power of a disciplinary regime based on reification and private property. Who is this survivor of the seemingly gratuitous violence of Half-Face and the whole phallocentric machinery? Jasmine thematizes the allegory of the refugee as the typical inhabitant of the postmodern milieu:

> Considering that he has lived through five or six languages, five or six countries, two or three centuries of history; has seen his country, city, and family butchered, bargained with pirates and bureaucrats, eaten filth in order to stay alive; that he has survived every degradation known to this century, *considering all those liabilities*, isn't it amazing that he can read a Condensed and Simplified for Modern Students edition of *A Tale of Two Cities*?
>
> Du's doing well because he has always trained with live ammo, without a net, with no multiple choice. No guesswork: only certain knowledge or silence. Once upon a time, like me, he was someone else. We've been many selves. We've survived hideous times. I envy Bud the straight lines and smooth planes of his history. (1989, 189–90)

But this hermeneutics of the refugee who eludes hegemonic power by the myth of transmigration expresses not only Jasmine's intuition of difference, the "uncanny strangeness" personified by Du. It also foregrounds the hypocrisy of pluralism and the inadequacy of religion or metaphysics in helping her comprehend the geopolitics of the Vietnam War. Moreover, it reflects in general the limits of the Westernized Indian intellectual's understanding of the lived situation of other people of color: "I should have known about [Du's] friends, his sister, his community. I should have broken through, but I was afraid to test the delicate thread of the hyphenization. Vietnamese-American: don't question either half too hard" (1989, 200). The last half is scarcely interrogated—unless Half-Face, Bud, and their ilk function as synecdoches.

It is at this juncture that Mukherjee's protagonist installs the psychoanalytic figure of the lack, the absence, on which the political economy of the symbolic order of difference thrives; the lack premised on castration of the female, the absence that can only be rectified by Taylor rescuing her from the panic-stricken farmlands of Iowa and delivering her to a fabled haven in California. In this context, the Asian-Indian diaspora refunctions the syndrome of the escape/journey to the Western frontier as a vehicle for its realization of the vicissitudes of *karma.* Nevertheless we are expected to understand that the encounter between the flux of the Asian female body and the axiomatics of possessive individualism has again confirmed the perception that for capitalism, both nature and women are "objects of conquest and penetration as well as idolatry and worship" (Smith 1984, 14). The fact of Indian economic success in the United States does not detract from the truth of that perception. Based on the latest census, Indians among Asian immigrants today earn the highest income and enjoy privileges denied to the Vietnamese, Cambodians, Laotians, Hmongs, and other recent arrivals. Mukherjee's novel does not address this fact but rather allegorizes the fate of the Asian woman (especially one invested with the touristic charm of Hindu mythology) who is still conceived by mainstream U.S. society as a fetishized object of pleasure, all the more seductive because behind the docility and magical fatalism lurks an inscrutable and enigmatic power that seems to resist domestication by the liberal code of individual rights, administrative rationality, consumption goods, money, and bourgeois feminism. On the other hand, Mukherjee believes that she has once again narrativized her belief that "we murder who we were so we can rebirth ourselves in the image of our dreams" (1990, 8).[6]

In one sense, *Jasmine* is a parable of *M Butterfly* and *Miss Saigon* metamorphosed into an avenging messenger of the body, of ancestral habitats, of places wrecked by the drive for capital accumulation. Emblematic of the "combined and uneven development" of two modes of production, Jasmine's journey across the United States stages a reversal of the immigrant pattern of adjustment and adaptation, unfolding the paradox of the postmodern compression of time/space as the matrix for the return of the repressed: the Other as accident, chance, pure contingency.

---

6. For a critique of Mukherjee's temporizing responses to her Canadian and U.S. milieus, see Tapping (1992).

VI

Returning to the theme of minorities and the notion of multiple connections and deterritorializations theorized by Deleuze and Guattari, I want to comment finally on two other representations of the Asian diaspora that implicitly critique the narrative of resolved crisis exemplified by the fiction of Kingston and Bulosan and the model of aesthetic sublimation offered by Mukherjee's novel. One detects in them a fundamentalist retreat to a rich coherent tradition (Kingston), to the organic romanticism of an insurrectionary peasantry (Bulosan),[7] and the reconciling catharsis of transcendental myth (Mukherjee). These may be deemed three capitulationist tendencies immanent in the diasporic archive that still exercise some influence today.

It is possible to demonstrate that aestheticized humanism as an essentialist ideology lingers in the interiority of the characters portrayed by our three exemplars. This ideology seeks to defuse the critical-satiric force of their narratives and recuperate their vision of self-empowerment in order to legitimize commodity fetishism. It is appropriate now to propose extraterritorial (more exactly, deterritorializing) alternatives to the exorbitance of aestheticized humanism practised by celebrities like Amy Tan, Gish Jen, and others. I have in mind two texts, one by John Okada and the other by Jeffery Paul Chan, that explore horizons beyond the parameters of descent (*jus sanguinis*) and putative consent (*jus solis*) that circumscribe the apologetics of academic discourse on ethnicity and its imaginative rendering. The first exemplifies the route of negativity and the refusal of a pluralist synthesis; the second illustrates the route of interpellating the Asian subject-position via a triangulation of the family breakup, the diasporic return, and the discovery of the stranger within (the margin brought to the center).

Before proceeding to examine the texts of our two male authors, I want to enter a parenthesis here and interpose Hisaye Yamamoto's presence in order to disrupt the resurgence of phallogocentric discourse. Insurgency from the margins warrants this break. Like smuggled goods, Yamamoto's intervention may elude the Customs Officers and assorted gatekeepers—what she declares, after all, is the questionable status of nation-state borders and the artificial nature of patriarchal sovereignties.

In Yamamoto's story "Las Vegas Charley," the notion of home as the index and symbolic surrogate of property, feudal or tributary morality, and patriotism of the elite is exploded by the transgressive experience of emigration and racism. Alienated from his parents, Kazuyuki Matsumoto at twenty leaves his village for the United States where "people had green hair and red eyes and where the streets

---

7. I initiate a new approach to Bulosan in essays contributed to two volumes (San Juan 1995a; 1995b).

were paved with gold." His education begins as soon as he finds out that "Japanesee were not allowed to buy property." With the death of his wife Haru, he takes his sons to his mother in Japan. Returning to California, he becomes a seasonal worker, truly "self-sacrificing" for a while in saving his earnings but later on becoming addicted to gambling. Here, he merges with the cohorts of the workers memorialized by Bulosan in *America Is in the Heart*: "By that time Kayusuki had wandered the length of California, picking grapes in Fresno, peaches in Stockton, strawberries in Watsonville, flowers in San Fernando, cantaloupe in the Imperial Valley, always ending his day and filling his Saturdays off with the shuffling and dealing of flower cards"(77). When his father dies, he abruptly reforms his ways. A repetition of the project of settlement probes the boundaries of acceptance and rejection:

> With his sons by his side to assist him, he leased again a small farm, this time in Orange County, but somehow things did not go well. . . . The vegetables flourished, but it seemed that since the man called Rusuberuto had been elected President of the United States, there had come into being a system called prorating in which one had to go into town and get coupons which limited the boxes one could pick and send to market. This was intended to keep prices up, to help the farmer. The smaller the farm, the fewer the coupons it was allotted, so it was a struggle. (77–78)

The New Deal subsidizes the big monopolies, not the small farmer. Soon the family—together with the 110,000 Americans of Japanese descent—is forcibly moved to a concentration camp in Arizona; one of his sons is recruited and sacrifices his life for the nation-state that imprisoned his farther, brother, and thousands of compatriots born on the land he tried to cultivate.

Obsessed again by his passion for flower cards after the war, Matsumoto ends up in Las Vegas, a "smooth space" which represents for the narrator "the ultimate rebellion against the Puritan origins of this singular country." Afflicted with incurable "Las Vegas fever," an index of capital's drive to commodify illusions, he becomes a dishwasher in a Chinese restaurant, metamorphoses into "Las Vegas Charley," and promptly gets consumed by the compulsive feeding of those "insatiable mechanical monsters which swallow up large coins as though they were Necco wafers." The motif of ingestion, noted above, acquires literal import here. Routine time is transvalued, redeemed by erotic cathexis: "Each day was exciting, fraught with the promise of instant wealth." In this anti-puritanical milieu, the law of repetition underlying manual labor is suspended. The hiatus of carnival time, reminiscent of the New Year festivities of the past, supervenes: "It was like Paradise: the heavy silver dollars that were as common as pennies; the daily anticipating of getting rich overnight; the rejoicing when a fellow worker had a streak of luck and shared his good fortune with one and all, buying presents all round. . . ." (73). These frozen instants of sociality, rendered sacred by the grace of a mechanical *Fortuna*, recaptures for Matsumoto the ecstasy of repeated New Year celebrations before the war. We witness episodes of ego-cancelling conviviality when kin and friends shared in the work of preparing native food, rituals of communal activity portrayed in such a way that the sheer density of sensory detail and amount of energy expended seem to impede the flow of punctual duration and chronological sequence. Consequently the impression we cherish after reading this story centers not on the plight of the victims but around their privileged moments of worldly pleasure and spontaneous solidarity. Hobbesian individualism evaporates in subaltern carnival. What the text foregrounds are the motifs of collective work as pleasure, self-actualization, the return of what has been lost. Later on, the narrative evokes the conflict between the first generation typified by Matsumoto, adventurous and unpredictable, and their children, pragmatic and individualistic—a contrapuntal rhythm punctuating the temporal continuum of the diasporic adventure.

If we assume that the biographical design of this story attempts to integrate the fragments of Las Vegas Charley's life into an aesthetic whole, we can conclude that it fails to do so because the appearance he presents to the world and the meaning people ascribe to his life diverges from what he means to his son Noriyuki. Indeed, our sense of Kazuyuki Matsumoto's gusto, his forgiving attitude towards the racist provocateurs and his quiet acceptance of what life has to offer, all contradict the son's ambivalence and his necessarily limited knowledge of all his father's struggles and varied experiences. But what is the rationale for this model of defeat? The trope of gambling (Las Vegas) fused with the stereotypical rubric (Charley) offers an allegorical clue to the meaning of defeat as the dissolution of the "melting pot" myth and the ascendancy of Cold War racism.

Published twelve years after the end of World War II, Okada's *No-No Boy* attempts to capture the agony of self-division in the life of Ichiro, a second-generation Japanese-American, who is caught in the dilemma of claiming an identity from the nation whose government has imprisoned his parents and his racial kin. His problem replicates that of his friend Kenji while detained in the concentration camp during World War II: to prove that he is a Japanese who, in spite of or because of his descent, loves America. This predicament is only a symptom of that malaise bedevilling the *nisei* who grew up in the camps: "Was there no answer to the bigotry and meanness and smallness and ugliness of people?" Because Ichiro refused to forswear allegiance to Japan and serve in the U.S. armed forces, he was imprisoned; his nay-saying, however, does not affirm his mother's fantasy of a victorious Japan nor his father's pathetic resignation. His predicament may be intractable, given the absence of any community that reconciles natives and aliens as well as the ascendancy of a rhetoric of exchange devaluing wholeness into atomized fragments: "But I did not love enough, for you were still half my mother and I was thereby still half Japanese . . . , I was not strong enough to fight you and I was not strong enough to fight the bitterness which made the half of me which was you bigger than the half of me which was America and really the whole of me that I could not see or feel" (1974, 281). How does Okada symbolize the way out of this suspended state where difference tends to be essentialized, where an irresolvable antinomy becomes invested with libidinal affects?

The return to the "primal scene" of a repeated deracination, of life before concentration camp, adumbrates the passage beyond negativity and aporia. Okada conceives of a process of living through the contradictions and paradoxes of the whole society, a practice of negotiation associated with the chronotope of the stratified city. In the following section, the novelistic discourse intimates a mode of knowledge in which the protagonist begins to see himself in the eyes of victimized Others amid the urban decay of the Asian quarters spatially removed from, but also communicating with, the affluent district by a single street. Here class segregation qualifies the doxa of racial difference, freezing temporal motion in the landscape of a dream aborted into nightmare. In the way Ichiro's homecoming becomes transfigured by the encroachment of what U.S. nationalism/white supremacy has so effectively repressed, its racialized antithesis in the image of blacks performing a parodic carnival, we comprehend the illusory substance of pluralist democracy:

> Being on Jackson street with its familiar store fronts and taverns and restaurants, which were somehow different because the war had left its mark on them, was like trying to find one's way out of a dream that seemed real most of the time but wasn't real because it was still only a dream. The war had wrought violent changes upon the people, and the people, in turn working hard and living hard and earning a lot of money and spending it on whatever was available, had distorted the profile of Jackson Street. The street had about it the air of a carnival without quite succeeding at becoming one. A shooting gallery stood where once had been a clothing store; fish and chips had replaced a jewelry shop; and a bunch of Negroes were horsing around raucously in front of a pool parlor. Everything looked older and dirtier and shabbier.
>
> He walked past the pool parlor, picking his way gingerly among the Negroes, of whom there had been only a few at one time and of whom there seemed to be nothing but now. They were smoking and shouting and cussing and carousing and the sidewalk was slimy with their spittle.
>
> "Jap!"
>
> His pace quickened automatically, but curiosity or fear or indignation or whatever it was made him glance back at the white teeth framed in a leering dark brown which was almost black.

"Go back to Tokyo, boy." Persecution in the drawl of the persecuted.

The white teeth and brown-black leers picked up the cue and
jogged to the rhythmical chanting of "Jap-boy, To-ki-yo, Jap-boy, To-
ki-yo. . . ."

Friggin' niggers, he uttered savagely to himself and, from the same
place deep down inside where tolerance for the Negroes and the Jews
and the Mexicans and the Chinese and the too short and too fat and too
ugly abided because he was Japanese and knew what it was like better
than did those who were white and average and middle class and good
Democrats or liberal republicans, the hate which was unrelenting and
terrifying seethed up. (1974, 270–72)

Initiated in this ritual of lostness, ressentiment, and self-affirmation of one's presence as the enemy, Ichiro reaches home—a passage forecasting the diaspora's true
destination.

So here the Asian mock-prodigal son returns not to a utopian image of a tribal
hearth but to a reaffirmation of what is antithetical to exchange value, to the
bureaucratic rationality of a regime founded on racial/ethnic segmentation: the
virtue of the slave's labor (valorized by Hegel in *The Phenomenology of the Spirit*). In
this case, virtue inheres in Ichiro's courage to refuse subjection by the racial state.
But while this entails Ichiro's repudiation of his mother's fantasy (mirror-image of
imperial power), it sublates personal guilt born of an irrecusable dualism (American
nationalism versus Japanese) and ushers a condition of indeterminacy on which the
genre of the diasporic novel turns and returns. This uneven development in the
protagonist's dilemma attests to the delayed after-effects of the phenomenon of
"unprecedented   transportation"   which   John   Berger   characterizes   thus:
"Emigration does not only involve leaving behind, crossing water, living amongst
strangers, but, also, undoing the very meaning of the world and—at its most
extreme—abandoning oneself to the unreal which is the absurd. . . . To emigrate is
always to dismantle the center of the world, and so to move into a lost, disoriented
one of fragments" (1984, 56–57).

Ichiro's life may also be evaluated as a defeat, a failure of synthesis. But what is
the rationale for this denouement? One answer is: "To whisper for that which has
been lost. Not out of nostalgia, but because it is on the site of loss that hopes are
born" (Berger 1984, 55). I suspect that what we are witnessing here is the emergence of a new subject-position that interrogates what "American" signifies, just as
we perceive in the absences punctuating the life of Yamamoto's protagonist a locus
of agency whose condition of possibility is prefigured by the misrecognition and
circumstantial heterology embedded in the name "Las Vegas Charley." Is the juxtaposition of city and stereotype a ruse to frame and contain the threat of an alien

"parasite" accidentally revealing the internal corruption of the host society?[8] Isn't Ichiro's bifurcated psyche symptomatic of the return of this repressed?

VII

We are still operating within the problematic of exile and homesickness introduced by Hugo of St. Victor in the epigraph to this chapter. The home for some groups of the Asian diaspora is, as we have seen, not already predestined by the contingencies of mass dislocations; instead it is constructed by the mundane tasks of everyday life, by enduring and learning from the ordeal of racial exclusion and the problems of separation, the disintegration of the family, the surrender to the lure of reconciliation, and the ephemeral catharsis of mass consumerism. Fantasy and hallucination attend these critical moments of the passage. If the victimization of Asians in the United States is an effect of the overarching metanarrative of Enlightenment modernization and progress, a master-plot legitimized by an epistemology founded on allochronic distancing of Others, their reduction to objects of instrumentalizing knowledge and bureaucratic manipulation, then is a praxis of coevalness and dialogism[9] the solution? Chan's intriguing story, "The Chinese in Haifa," problematizes this approach and stages the nuances of its implications.

Brooding on the after-effects of his recent divorce and separation from his children, Bill Wong—the central character in Chan's story—is comforted by Mrs. Goldberg, a Jewish mother visiting her son Herb and his wife Ethel, Bill's close friends and neighbours. In answer to the question, "What are families for?" Mrs. Goldberg replies: "So when you lose one, you have more. . . . Everybody's got a family. . . . You come from one family, you make another" (1991, 88). This is the filiative solution to reification. Bill's situation of solitary freedom and anxiety to escape it enters into an ambiguous dialogue with Mrs. Goldberg's traditional view

---

8. Aside from Kristeva's speculative reflections on the function of the stranger in history, I recommend Georg Simmel's (1977) essay on "The Stranger" as one of the most provocative, seminal reconaissance of this character-type and social phenomenon.

9. For some, the scenario is that of postcolonial subaltern academics at last priming themselves up to speak to Western poststructuralists. One recent instance can be cited. Elaine Kim has taken on board the postmodernist notion that identities are "fluid and migratory," that the dominant culture is "not monolithic and unitary"; and this leads her to recycle the assimilationist paradigm in a new apologetic version: New Asian immigrants, she writes, "have moved to cities and towns where few Asian Americans had lived before and are doing things to earn their livelihoods that they could not have imagined when they were in their homelands: Cambodians are making doughnuts, Koreans are making burritos, South Asians are operating motels, Filipinos are driving airport shuttle buses" (1993, xi). Erasing the prodigious history of intervention of U.S. imperialism into the homelands of these newcomers, Kim revives the "Statue of Liberty" slogan of the United States as the home to refugees, persecuted peasants, and so on—resurrects, indeed, the ghost of Charlie Chan!

of the family, marriage, and children, as the stable, harmonizing center of society—
a view that has also characterized the tributary formation of Confucian China and
recent "politically correct" neoconservative programs of reinstituting U.S.-style
apartheid. This mentality is then syncopated with the fragmentation of life in a
world where spatiotemporal distances are compressed in order to secure a differential politics of exchange:

> Ethel winked at Bill from over her shoulder. "Maybe you can find Bill a
> nice Jewish girl, Mama, in Haifa."
>   "Are there Chinese in Haifa?" Herb asked.
>   "The Jews and the Chinese," she said, standing in the middle of the
> room and weaving her eyes back and forth from her son to his wife,
> "they're the same." She walked to the door and Herb followed. "You
> know there are Jews in China, there must be Chinese in Haifa. It's all the
> same, even in Los Angeles." (1991, 90)

But are the two diasporas the same? When Mrs. Goldberg flippantly suggests to
Ethel, "you get him married," this concern acquires a self-fulfilling resonance
when we learn later that Ethel and Bill have already begun a secret liaison, an affair
that belies Herb's claim of his successful marriage as one based on "sharing and car-
ing." But such an attempt of the narrative to establish linkages between this
anguished Chinese intellectual and his Jewish friends becomes an ironic commentary on the humanist belief in the naturalness of trust and interdependency among
beleaguered communities.

Given the unrelenting war for *Lebensraum* in Palestine, encountering the
Chinese in Haifa is less conceivable than meeting Jews in China. Amid the trials of
such dislocations both real and imaginary, Bill and Ethel offer extraterritorial compensations. Hovering over this somewhat idyllic relation between Bill and the
Goldbergs is a reported event that makes the quest for the homeland (fantasized or
documented) an occasion for a minor holocaust: three Japanese terrorists,
equipped with machine guns and grenades, opened fire on passengers getting on an
Israeli jetliner in Rome. Herb's exclamation of perplexity foregrounds the issue of
allochronism and coevalness: "And here my mother's going to Israel today. Christ
on his everlovin' crutch! What in the hell do the Japs have against us?" The ironic
pathos of Herb's question is symptomatic of a failure to make connections.
Internationalism, the "bad faith" of narcissistic nationalism, becomes a paltry apology when Herb assures Bill Wong that he can tell he's not a Japanese. On the other
hand, what is Chan's message about the adequacy of the individual Chinese male
whose *ressentiment* begins to invent a chain of signifiers that binds together incon-
gruous elements such as the Palestinian loss of their land, the Japanese Red Army's
internationalist sympathy with the Palestinians, Jewish Zionism, Israel's image as

pariah state, and Bill Wong's (and his generation's) alienation from the ancestral culture? Contrast the burden of history intimated by the opening passage: "Bill dreamed he heard the cry of starving children in Asia bundled together in a strangely familiar school yard," with the fantasy of power conjured in the last sentence: "A vague collection of swarthy Japanese in mufti crowding around Herb's station wagon at the airport grew in his mind's eye." Is this a symptom of anarchist *ressentiment* that fills up the space once occupied by Confucian virtues, or an index of "an extreme individualism" flawed (as Kristeva puts it) by "a weakness whose other name is our radical strangeness" (1991, 195)? This surmise prompts us to suggest that here, as in the other texts analyzed, the dynamic of collective envy and loathing articulates itself with the ethos of market liberalism to produce the expenditures of spirit witnessed in all diasporic testimonies.[10]

In commenting on Jean Mohr's photographs of Palestinians conducting their normal lives in abnormal circumstances, Edward Said observes that his people are "presented addressing our world as a secular place, without nostalgia for a lost transcendence" (146). And even as we look at these victims of a resolved or reversed diaspora, they are also scrutinizing, assessing, and judging us. Perhaps this is what our Asian-American writers have also accomplished in their staging of difference (cultural, sexual, racial) into dialectical contradictions; in reflexively transcoding Asian difference into a historical predicament involving the dominant group; in articulating the immigrant consciousness as sensuous practice, a body speaking and producing meaning through the materiality of language and thus constituting minds and sensibilities as co-temporal participants in the process of social interlocution. In superseding the spatial hegemony of Western culture by a temporalizing strategy of recall that disrupts the instrumental coherence of the market and the discourse of exchange, Asian-American writers have been trying to express and communicate to a world-audience the historical specificity of the Asian diaspora in the United States. They have sought to locate their ethnic and racial subjectivity in a semiotic domain hitherto ruled by a homogenizing, albeit multiculturalist, ideology where "Asian" still bears the stigmata (though now conjugated with its function as "model minority" defending private property against Latinos and blacks) of being inscrutable, devious, cunning, and exotic. This socially constructed Otherness, confirming the putative superior identity of the EuroAmerican bloc, manifests its double in an officially coded presence endowed with the miracle-inducing "wisdom of the Orient." This Orientalized subjectivity, a repeated ideological effect and a product of symbolic violence, is deeply compromised and has been gradually eclipsed by the fetishism of the "superminority" model.

---

10. In an insightful article, David Palumbo-Liu (1994) inquires into the instrumentalization of the "model minority" myth by the media apparatus to direct envy and loathing toward hegemonic ends.

We are now able to grasp the truth of this commonsense conception of the Orientalized subject as soon as it is concretely grounded in the historical events marking the expansion of U.S. monopoly capital throughout the world. The diverse and uncoordinated narratives documenting the specificities of the Asian diaspora have to contend not only with the legacy of such received notions, but also with the juridical limits established by a racial state, as attested by two unprecedented actions: the 1882 Exclusion Act and the imprisonment of 110,000 Japanese-Americans during World War II.[11] The uneven development of the world system of capital after the end of the Cold War and the dissolution of various state/bureaucratic socialisms has so far evolved to a point where the systemic crisis of capital accumulation will now conflate residual, dominant, and emergent impulses, margin and center, metropolis and periphery, in spaces where Western hegemony will take on new forms and guises. With the movement of populations in Eastern Europe and elsewhere, the primal scene of deracination returns to haunt the premature celebration of pluralist freedom, unity in diversity, and "common culture."

Here I want to enter a brief parenthesis that can only suggest the scope of further research into the aesthetics and politics of an emergent and genuinely international genre. The advent of a feminist praxis in Filipino writing (most notably in the novels of Lualhati Bautista) in the 1970s and 1980s may be explained by the phenomenon of millions of Filipino contract laborers, mostly women, sojourning in the Middle East, Europe, Japan, Hong Kong, Singapore, and elsewhere. When these migrant workers return home, they construct stories of their heterogenous experiences that assume a narrative form conflating the quest motif with the seduction/ordeal motif—a plot that violates all probabilities found in the schemas of semiotic narratology. When the female subaltern returns, the mimesis of her struggle for survival almost always implicates the diegesis of the world system as a meta-narrative of the global circulation of commodified bodies and phallocentric energies. Exchange of her labor power shortcircuits the time/space compression of the postmodern economy. Whether as household servant in Kuwait or "hospitality girl" in Tokyo, she narrates the lived experience of victimage as a reversal of the "civilizing mission." She thus repeats the whole epic of colonization—but with a difference: her gendered subject-position or agency yields not surplus value but the

---

11. Contrary to the thesis (argued by Nathan Glazer and others) that the United States was founded inter alia on the principle of free entry granted to everyone, the Chinese Exclusion Act of 1882 stands as a landmark decision in which members of a specific ethnic group for the first time in U.S. history were denied entry.

From 1910 to 1940, the Angel Island Immigration Station served to process Asian immigrants. A sample of the writings of Chinese immigrants carved on the walls of their detention barracks in Angel Island can be found in Lauter (1990, 1755–62).

hallucination of commodity fetishism when consumer goods and traumas become cargo myths for native consumption in the Philippines. In this sense, the migrant worker as "speaking subject" destabilizes the regularities of the "New World Order" and the "free market" discourse of individual self-fulfillment. Her fabula decenters the *sjuzhet* of technocratic modernization. Overall, this new genre of migrant narrative explodes the traditional definitions of the gendered subject provided by the Symbolic Order of dependent capitalism while its transgressive allegory destroys the conventional plots of immigrant success and postcolonial hybridity.

Meanwhile, the scenario in the United States may be said to vary only in its determinate historical particularities. New Asian immigrants will have to invent their own imaginative responses to changed class and race alignments that subtend U.S. political dynamics in the twenty-first century. However, the task on the whole remains the same: the reconstitution of the Asian subject-position as an agency of resistance to racist oppression and of emancipation from the bondage of globalized capital. In the words of Genny Lim, a distinguished Chinese-American playwright (in Houston 1993, 153–54): "We are living in such adverse times— ecologically, economically, morally and spiritually—that any effort made to mobilize peoples' consciousness into self-determination, self-validation, compassion, and racial, class, and sexual understanding is a step further along in the difficult journey of human survival on this planet."

9

Beyond Postmodernism

NOTES ON "THIRD WORLD" DISCOURSES OF RESISTANCE

.

> You taught me language, and my profit on 't Is, I know how to curse.
>
> —Caliban, in Shakespeare's *The Tempest*

> I am named Rigoberta Menchu and in that way my conscience was born. . . . Everything that is done today is done in memory of those who have passed on.
>
> —Rigoberta Menchu

A recent anthology of unprecedented scope entitled *The Harper Collins World Reader*, edited by Mary Ann Caws and Christopher Prendergast (1994), concludes its delightful and prodigious offering with a section called "Writing Across Boundaries." Seamus Heaney, the Irish poet, lends his authority to the idea behind it: poets "write place into existence" and unwrite it. In the wake of imperialism and its sequel, neocolonialism and postcolonialism, the editors observe that writers—among them Césaire, Nabokov, Walcott, and Rushdie—have crossed borders amid the "huge disruptions to the sense of place." Along with the painful experience of dispossession, unsettlement, and exile travelled a sense of release, of liberation. Paradoxically, these flights produced both a "heightened cosmopolitanism" and a passionate rootedness to specific locations, a tension at the heart of the "idea of world literature." Scarcely could Goethe, the eighteenth-century inventor of the rubric *Weltliteratur*, have anticipated this phenomenon in this "cataclysmic epoch that has left few native or national cultures intact" (Caws and Prendergast 1994, 2658). Amid the ruins left by the whirlwinds of this century, we find writers from the "Third World" (the term is itself a survival of the Cold War era) still writing/unwriting places, giving their habitations distinctive names and singular histories. From inside "the belly of the beast" (to evoke the great Jose Marti's sense of his displacement), I offer the following notes as homage to those kindred spirits, heirs of the rebellious Caliban, who are carrying on the struggle to map on the terrain of the imagination the space for the memories, sacrifices, and hopes of multitudes.

I

Inaugurated by the blast of Tomahawk missiles and the videotech bombing of Baghdad and the fabled bridges across the Tigris and Euphrates rivers, we enter the threshold of the twenty-first century. This "New World Order" happens to be heralded by desert storm troopers. In this transition to a post–Cold War era, we— the referent here is shadowy at the outset—confront the beginning of a strategy of U.S. military intervention in regions in the periphery where transnational capital (also called Western civilization, free enterprise, consumers' rights) has assumed a triumphalist posture. A former Sandinista foreign ministry official calls this the era of the U.S. "declaration of perpetual war" on the world. Eqbal Ahmad calls it the "recolonizing" of former colonies or dependencies, the underdeveloped South versus the industrialized North.

In any case, events transpiring in the Middle East as well as in Bosnia, Haiti, South Africa, the Philippines, or in Los Angeles—tune in to the six o'clock news—lend an ironic twist to what McLuhan (1964) once called "the concretiza- tion of human fraternity" ushered by the use of information-media technology as a weapon. McLuhan celebrated the advent of the global village and one harmonious world on the eve of the holocaust in Indo-China; the urban rebellions in Detroit, Watts, Paris; the overthrow of the Shah in Iran, the defeat of Allende's socialist experiment in Chile, and the Sandinista victory in Nicaragua. It was a celebration of postmodernity in terms of appearance, what Baudrillard today would call "si- mulacra" pervading hyperreality. For others who believed the rest of the world was just at the edge of the California suburbs, it was the end of ideology, of history or the future.

What can the writer from the margins of this "simulacra" say or do that can make a difference to the metropolitan center? Does it matter? If erstwhile exotic artists like Tagore or Ruben Dario have yielded to "boom" performers Salman Rushdie, Gabriel Garcia Marquez and Wole Soyinka, has the margin finally pene- trated the center? Have we all been pluralized, simulated, resemioticized, and tran- sculturated? Are we now all hybrid, syncretic, heterogeneous? Aren't our prejudicially classificatory terms "Third World" and "postmodernity" supplying premature answers to questions or problems still only dimly apprehended?

From what I think is the best account so far of this transition, David Harvey's *The Condition of Postmodernity*, we learn that postmodernism is a historical response to the recent crisis of overaccumulation, a crisis that manifests itself in the disori- enting compressions of time-space which have periodically occurred since the decline of the Middle Ages. The symptoms of this crisis include *inter alia*: the disin- tegration of the sovereign subject; the loss of the referent; the collapse of the link- age between moral and scientific judgments; the predominance of images over narratives, aesthetics over ethics. Ephemerality and fragmentation have displaced eternal truths and unified, organic experience. The names of Nietzsche, Marx, and

Freud mark these epochal turning points. Harvey points to the voodoo economics and image-making of Ronald Reagan as the epitome of the postmodernist temper, a frame of mind to which homelessness, unemployment, increasing poverty, and disempowerment are justified by appeals to traditional values of self-reliance, entrepreneurial individualism, the sacred family, religion, and so on. Street scenes of graffiti, urban decay, misery become "quaint and swirling backdrop" to media spectacles (as in *Blade Runner*); poverty, urban decay, hopelessness and despair become sources of aesthetic pleasure, or signs of Otherness and Difference—intimations of what what Jean-François Lyotard (1984) calls "the sublime."

Lyotard is the philosopher par excellence of the postmodern condition which he celebrates as the fulfillment of the genuine spirit of the modernist project. Arguing against Jurgen Habermas' condemnation of postmodernism as a betrayal of the Enlightenment ideals of objective science, universal morality and law, and autonomous art, Lyotard rejects the Hegelian-inspired totalizing worldview that he believes leads to a transcendental illusion of wholeness imposed by state violence. Modernity equals terrorism over the individual. Given the heterogeneous language-games of ethics, politics, and cognition, it is necessary—insists Lyotard— to do away with the notion of a self-identical subject or a unitary telos of history. Against metanarratives, we should uphold Nietzschean perspectivism, local knowledges, and ludic strategies of living. Or, better yet, a neo-Kantian aesthetic of the sublime that would induce pleasure from intuiting the unpresentable. Decentered, ironic, and parodic, the postmodern pastiche offers infinite consumption. Refusing the nostalgia for "the whole and the one, the reconciliation of the concept and the sensible," Lyotard issues a battle-cry: "Let us wage a war on totality; let us be witnesses to the unpresentable; let us activate the differences and save the honor of the name" (82). To whom is this call addressed?

While the media broadcast daily what was becoming commonplace scenes of the bombing of Iraq and experts were totalizing this spectacle of the most sophisticated electronic destruction of people on a massive scale, I happened to read an interview of Ghassan Abdullah. President of the Palestinian Writers Union, Abdullah was imprisoned by the Israeli authorities for six months in Answar III in the Negev desert. His crime: engaging in cooperative work with Israeli writers in a committee formed after the 1982 invasion of Lebanon called Writers Against Discrimination and the Occupation. Numerous Palestinian writers and artists before and after the intifada (circa 1987) have been detained for writing poems, short stories, essays, and songs. In memoirs that resemble those of George Jackson or militants of the African National Congress (ANC) in apartheid jails, Abdullah narrates the collective efforts of his fellow prisoners to continue and develop a culture of resistance in those desert camps where even prisoners praying together have been attacked with gas. He vividly describes how he would collect paper from wrappings, from cigarette packs and cartons, so that he could have something to write on; how the prisoners organized all kinds of activities to continue the teaching/learning process: lectures and discussions, carving, drawing, games, reading and writing classes, producing a rich harvest of poems, short stories, and essays. They survived, he writes, "because of our deep belief that culture is a main part of our identity and it is more easy to reach a permanent just solution with educated and cultured people than to reach it with ignorant ones" (1991, 70; see Rushdie 1988). Here it seems that the concept (autonomy) could not be reconciled with the sensible, as Lyotard hopes, simply because state terror forbids it.

What can a Filipino intellectual like myself, exiled in the metropolis, do in the face of this ongoing suppression of a whole people? In the Philippines where constitutional democracy obtains, Amnesty International reports the plight of hundreds of political prisoners, not to mention thousands of refugees in "free fire" zones, some tortured and brutalized by a military equipped and subsidized by the U.S. government. Committed writers, those conscienticized by years of combat against the Marcos dictatorship (1972–86), are silenced by fear, by the threat of vigilante or paramilitary assassination. If they cannot speak, who will speak for them?

I venture the following hypothesis: The Third World artist may be the specter of a postfeudal "Sublime" haunting the margins of the computerized supermalls only in the sense that as a group they exist in what Fanon once called "zones of occult instability": resisting the representations enforced on them by the oppressor, they are wrestling with the means of expression, how to invent them or construct them from what is given by their specific circumstances, how to wield them effectively in ways reminiscent of the beleaguered artists described in Peter Weiss's *Notes on the Cultural Life of the Democratic Republic of Vietnam*. A nation's culture is struggling to be born. There are three stages in this process, according to Franz Fanon (1963): the first is the slavish copying of the conqueror's paradigm, the mimicry of the Shakespearean sonnet, Racine's classic style, and so on. Then comes a revulsion from everything foreign leading to nativism, a worship of the indigenous and a nostalgia for origins; Negritude and the vernaculars of the Harlem Renaissance come to mind. In the third stage, the "fighting phase" associated with the revolution, a new self-aware culture rooted but not coinciding with the indigenous tradition emerges in which the artist becomes "the mouthpiece of the new reality in action," as personified by the Sandinista militants Tomas Borge, Omar Cabezas, and Sergio Ramirez. Abdullah has observed that Palestinian literature underwent a metamorphosis analogous to Fanon's schema during the intifada: after eschewing the fetish for suffering and inwardness, it retrieved from folklore the idea of sacrificing for the group's welfare until it finally discovered individual Palestinian heroes—for instance, the child hurling "the holy stone" (Murphy 1991). In the time-space compression of the intifada, the Palestinians reawakened to "the extreme importance of the cultural form of resistance" which, for Ghassan

Kanafani of the Popular Front for the Liberation of Palestine, "is no less valuable than the armed struggle itself" (Harlow 1987, 11).

Kanafani's novella, *All That's Left to You*, may be conceived as an anti-postmodern mimesis of the condition of the victims in the process of synthesizing the past (the tragedy of 1948), the present (the process of quest for the mother, the land of Palestine), and the future (the recovery of some continuity with the past mediated by the struggle). We find this theme in all texts by exiles, expatriates, uprooted migrants, exported bodies, which comprise the artifacts of the new diaspora I noted at the start. What is interesting in Kanafani's style is the montage of the consciousness of three characters (together with time and the desert as two other protagonists) where simultaneity of diverse time-segments dovetails with a relentless chronological unfolding. Fragmentation—the Palestinian deracination—is symbolized by the clock ticking in the bedroom where his sister is trapped with her lover Zakaria, and the watch which Hamid discards:

> As I did so, I came to realize how insignificant a watch is when compared to the absolutes of light and dark. In the infinite expanse of this desert night, my watch appeared to represent a temporal fetter which engendered terror and anxiety. . . . I felt more at ease when I remained alone with the night. Without the contrived semblance of time, the barrier collapsed, and we became equals in the confrontation of a real and honorable struggle, with equal weapons. The black expanse before me was a series of steps no longer measured against the two small hands of a watch. (1990, 20)

Clocktime introduced by the social division of labor at the advent of mercantile capitalism is not vanquished but sublated to the pulse of the desert's body which becomes that of a loved one, hot and exciting, mysterious and powerful. Time-space compression brought about by Israeli "postcolonialism" is defused by an act of transgressing boundaries both physical and psychic. We still find here the syndrome of interiority, not a self-referential image but a syntagmatic chain gesturing toward a lost wholeness. This reprise of the uncanny then yields to the moment of the deadly struggle between Hamid and the armed Israeli border guard—an allegory of the interlocked fates of two peoples—as Hamid seeks to cross the boundary between the occupied territories (Gaza) and Jordan. We find modernist modes of representation harnessed to convey a uniquely postmodern experience of dispossession and disinheritance.

I see the recuperation of this emancipatory project in the Chicano foundational text by Tomas Rivera (1987), *. . . y no se lo trago la tierra* (. . . and the earth did not devour him). Here in the homologous coding of dispersed time and fragmentation, the text can be charged guilty of the "imitative fallacy." Although there is a frame story to suture the acausal and syncopated episodes together, the twelve sections of the novel present the seasonal incidents in the life of a migrant child through a stream-of-consciousness mode which Ramon Saldivar (1990) calls a "chronotopic point [after Bakhtin] around which the collective experiences of Rivera's Texas-Mexican farmworkers coalesce, forming a communal oral history" (75). Unlike the Palestinians, the Chicanos encountered the shock of a military defeat (the Mexican-American War of 1848 and after); this explains the need for the learning ordeal to drain out the trauma, a catharsis which doubles as a gradual initiation into the reality of subjugation.

Saldivar asserts that Rivera's experimental technique reflects the "fragmenting effects of contemporary postmodern life" in the Texas-Mexican border just after World War II. I think Saldivar may have confused historical periods: while the novel was published in 1971, the sociohistorical milieu of Chicano labor exploitation in the Southwest has an overdetermined time-configuration to which realism (with appropriate modifications) can be deployed to register effectively the Chicano community's lived experience. While conceding that the novel's proletarian milieu resembles that of the folkloric corrido and its socially symbolic acts of resistance, Saldivar insists that the non-sequential mode puts into question the category of an unproblematic individual identity by using "the representation of personal alienation" (85). Ultimately the "subject" becomes the mystified character of *la raza* whose consciousness is the "self-consciousness of the commodity . . . the self-revelation of capitalist society founded upon the production and exchange of commodities" (Lukács 1971, 90). The Third World deconstructive critic is caught in a dilemma where the notion of the decentered subject, the subject under erasure, is projected onto the idea of an orthodox *homo economicus* that would "recuperate historical experience" by undermining the binary oppositions of bourgeois society through the "differential structure" of the Chicano narrative. Postmodernist theory has overtaken the praxis of national self-determination. It is here perhaps where Hegel's chapter on the dialectic of master and slave in *Phenomenology of the Spirit* can be useful in safeguarding us from a premature derealization of an evolving subject-position for this embattled "internal colony." It is also at this juncture where Habermas' theory of "modernity" may have residual (but qualified) resonance for activists of popular-democratic struggles whose concept still doesn't know any adequate presentation. What I am suggesting here is a more critical appropriation of theory for counter-hegemonic ends to attenuate their cooptative effects.

II

How should a subaltern intellect from the periphery view Habermas' thesis stated in his manifesto "Modernity—An Incomplete Project" and elaborated in *The*

Philosophical Discourse of Modernity? We all oppose commodification and techno-bureaucratic administration of the lifeworld now exercised by a neocapitalist cybernetic machine indissociable from modernity. Thus we are suspicious of a return to a Eurocentric ideal that, in the guise of modernization and democratic reforms, underwrites the continued exploitation of Third World multitudes.

Those of us who went through a radicalizing apprenticeship in the sixties appreciate Habermas' qualified defense of the Enlightenment project to release the cognitive potential of the domains of science, morality and art for the enrichment and "rational organization of everyday social life." To exorcise the curse of reification, Habermas invokes the imperative of "the unconstrained interaction of the cognitive with the moral-practical and the aesthetic-expressive elements" (1983, 11–12). Habermas envisions history progressing toward the synthesis of truth, beauty, and justice—substantive reason (the transmission of cultural tradition, social integration of the various specialized spheres) is recovered through communicative rationality pervading the praxis of everyday life. In other words, workers through art education can connect with the whole of European history and remedy their alienation. The bourgeois canons are useful after all. Habermas denounces the cabal of postmodern prophets from Bataille to Derrida via Foucault who apotheosize decentered subjectivity and Manicheanwise oppose to instrumental reason an archaic principle, either the will to power (Nietzsche), Being's sovereignty (Heidegger), or "the Dionysiac force of the poetical." For all those "hewers of wood and drawers of water," past and present, who have been victimized by what I would call "actually existing modernism," transnational or multinational capital as a world system, it is difficult not to suspect Habermas of "bad faith." Habermas' teachers Adorno and Horkheimer, in *Dialectics of Enlightenment*, have already demonstrated the internal contradictions in the Enlightenment project, in particular its harboring the seeds of future imperialist genocidal and fascist violence. We are still living in the terror of a neo-Hobbesian liberalism where life in the suburbs may be nasty, boring, and brutish but long.

This is not to dismiss Habermas' valid criticism of neoconservative anti-modernism. His emphasis on the historical dialectic underlying cultural practices is a desideratum for world cultural studies (see next chapter). Unlike some postmodernists suspended in the void of a self-contained "superstructure," Habermas would no doubt agree with Eric Wolf's thesis that "the construction and maintenance of a body of ideological communications is therefore a social process and cannot be explained merely as the formal working out of an internal cultural logic" (1982, 388). Culture alone is not to blame. In his article "Marxism and Postmodernism," Fredric Jameson (1989) himself has revised his early quasi-formalist view of postmodernism as "the cultural logic of late capitalism" by stressing the requisite concept of totality. He postulates "cognitive mapping" as a theoretical necessity without which it is virtually impossible to articulate the nature of decisive social transformations and their historical trajectories of which the most pivotal is the unequal exchange between Europe and "the peoples without history." Situated in this reality, the role of Third World intellectuals is to keep reminding hegemonic postmodernists of the simple truth that we live in the same world where power excludes and includes so that the quality of life and life-chances is not the same for everyone. Roberto Fernandez Retamar's *Caliban*, Walter Rodney's *How Europe Underdeveloped Africa*, and Edward Said's *Culture and Imperialism*, among many others, are such reminders.

Instead of recapitulating Alex Callinicos' (1989) well-known critique of Habermas, I would like to direct attention to a scarcely noticed but significant intervention by Enrique Dussel (1992). In his magisterial treatise, "Theology and Economy," Dussel elaborates the theory of the person as both an agent of communicative action (in Habermas' construal) and as participant in a "community of life" (*Lebensgemeinschaft*). This formulation immediately displaces the Hegelian notion of "civil society" rooted in private property, the premise of competitive liberal individualism. I want to underscore here Dussel's historical hermeneutic of "living labor" and communal praxis concealed by commodity-fetishism and the reification that vitiates all the charitable intentions of those who claim that the free market is the sole and only guarantee of civil liberties. What I would add to this is the deployment of certain concepts by Benedict Spinoza to distinguish between repressive power (*potestas*) that transforms living labor into exchange value and power (*potentia*), the constitutive and appropriative power of collectivities which Marx calls praxis. Such categories may help grasp inequities as historically differentiated modalities, interdependencies, relations of hegemony and subalternity. Given the current geopolitical insight of the lifeworld as an ecosystem, Spinoza's *Ethics* may appropriately serve as a heuristic organon for recuperating the surplus value produced by the masses since at least the dawn of Enlightenment modernity.

In an astute comment on Habermas' position, Anthony Giddens points out that the dissolution of avant-garde culture (from Baudelaire to the surrealists) was not triggered by an internal aporia. It arose from the commodification of time-space as the intrinsic logic of industrial capitalism. As Marx first explained, in capitalism time acquires its quantified form in articulating class relations within the labor-process; that is to say, surplus value is generated through the medium of quantified time because, unlike the direct appropriation of productive labor in agrarian society, this value has to be exploited through the commodity whose double existence—substance or concrete qualities/abstract form of exchange-value—spells what Lukács calls "reification" characterizing the totality of everyday life in business society. The problematic of ideology comes into play. Commodification of time and space inscribes a hiatus or difference in each; their doubling into quantified time—labor-power disciplined in the workplace; division of life into routine work and "free time," private and public spheres—and quantified space severs humans from nature, tradition, the past. Against this all-encompassing change in the experience of time-space (which Harvey attributes to the operations of ascertainable socio-economic determinants), the avant-garde project that continues to inspire postmodernism tried "to recover a rational basis for the normative character of everyday life" which has suffered the mystifying power of the commodity. It tried to sublate the object-world (commodified time-space) and resolve what Giddens calls "the asymmetry of substance and form"; the enterprise failed because it failed to grasp the historical significance óf the commodification of time and space as the fundamental reproductive logic of capital.

For peoples who are victims of the "modernist project" of mastery over nature and all "the rest," it is less a matter of figuring out whether or not postmodernist styles can signify their lived experience as one of defining first their collective predicament as non-represented or unrepresentable in the present global hierarchy of power. Subalterns have to seize the means, the occasions, to invent their own strategy of resistance and self-presentations. The key lies in the nature of the modalities of representation and their geopolitical valence. I don't have the space here—alas, we cannot escape the contagion of commodification—to elaborate on how the counter-mnemonic projects of Gabriel Garcia Marquez in *One Hundred Years of Solitude* or Salman Rushdie in *Midnight's Children*, for example, can be conceived as a version of the avant-garde attempt to demystify the doubling of time and space when colonial intervention takes place in regions overdetermined by archaic or tributary modes of production. But a glance at Garcia Marquez's post-"boom" populist novel, *Love in the Time of Cholera*, may be instructive.

In the social formation explored here, we can perceive the layering of temporal duration and calculation of spatialities in which the resistance to imperial capital (internalized in ironic ways) assumes the form of reinstating alternative existential forms of time. The formulaic style of the sentimental-popular genre mixes with aristocratic and plebeian idioms to allow for a coalition/alliance outlook to emerge. This is a variant of "magical realism" that projects the axis of diachrony onto that of synchrony, where poetic metaphor incessantly seeks to neutralize metonymy and mimesis. Suffice it to isolate one asymmetry staged by the montage of recollected events. The reader will recall how the community, including the formidable enemy of change Florentino Ariza, were all shocked when the first prize in the traditional Poetic Festival of the Antilles was awarded to a descendant of Chinese immigrants, railroad workers who fled the yellow-fever epidemic in Panama and subsequently became the "good Chinese" of the laundries, heirs of a sacred knowledge. When this Chinese prize-winner read his poem, no one understood him. In the two paragraphs Garcia Marquez devotes to this incident, we find an allegorical rendering of how European knowledge-production (as adapted in Colombia) operates to subdue and domesticate the unrepresentable, at the same time as a desublimation of aesthetic aura occurs with the flow of mass envy and loathing:

No one understood him. But when the new round of jeers and whistles was over, an impassive Fermina Daza read it again, in her hoarse, suggestive voice, and amazement reigned after the first line. It was a perfect sonnet in the purest Parnassian tradition, and through it there wafted a breath of inspiration that revealed the involvement of a master hand. The only possible explanation was that one of the great poets had devised the joke in order to ridicule the Poetic Festival, and that the Chinese had been a party to it and was determined to keep the secret until the day he died. The *Commercial Daily*, our traditional newspaper, tried to save our civic honor with an erudite and rather confused essay concerning the antiquity and cultural influence of the Chinese in the Caribbean, and the right they had earned to participate in Poetic Festivals. The author of the essay did not doubt that the writer of the sonnet was in fact who he said he was, and he defended him in a straightforward manner, beginning with the title itself: "All Chinese Are Poets." The instigators of the plot, if there was one, rotted in their graves along with the secret. For his part, the Chinese who had won died without confession at an Oriental age and was buried with the Golden Orchid in his coffin, but also with the bitterness of never having achieved the only thing he wanted in his life, which was recognition as a poet. On his death, the press recalled the forgotten incident of the Poetic Festival and reprinted the sonnet with a modernist vignette of fleshy maidens and gold cornucopias, and the guardian angels of poetry took advantage of the opportunity to clarify matters: the sonnet seemed so bad to the younger generation that no one could doubt any longer that it had, in fact, been composed by the dead Chinese. (1988, 194–95)

Ignoring the historical subtext of the migration of labor in the period of dependent modernization, this episode could be interpreted as an exemplum of either the universality of genius or the ubiquity of prejudice (insiders versus outsiders), and so forth. In effect, however, the whole incident wittily illustrates how the function of representation and its value changes in consonance with political and economic transformations.

The allusion to the "modernist vignette of fleshy maidens and gold cornucopias" which capture cultural overlayering could be to Ruben Dario's *modernismo*, a term that would be misleading if it were not historicized. Now historicizing doesn't mean relativism. To historicize is not to flatten everything so that the value of all experiences as measured by a general equivalent form of value (money, gold) can be made interchangeable (such homologous transformations are reprised by Jean-Joseph Goux in *Symbolic Economies*). Historicizing or historical specifying means providing the context for cultural production, demarcating in their motion through concrete time-space the limits and possibilities of certain forms of expression and representation. An excellent illustration can be found in the historical analysis applied by John Beverley and Marc Zimmerman (1990) to the mutations of value in the cultural production—whether Dario's modernism or Ernesto Cardenal's *exteriorismo*—of Central America where various signifying systems interpenetrate within the overdetermined totality of specific social formations.

The lesson we can gather here is that the antithesis of modernism versus postmodernism is misleading in its rigid dualism and false symmetrical opposition. It needs historical concretization (Hall 1986; Yudice 1993). This is because in the Third World context the Althusserian axiom of overdetermination (which is not reducible to syncretism or hybridity) finds its nearly perfect structural embodiment. It approximates to the materialization of a concept that sometimes reverses the stereotypes of imperial knowledge, sometimes inflects them in parodic unpredictable ways, or reworks them in mirages of affinity or resemblance, only to result in the awkward denouement that what we assumed we knew all along, something familiar and intelligible, turns out to be another of Borges' aleatory collocations of odds and ends—but this time converted into media images or information: lo and behold, another pastiche!

One signifying practice caught in the polarity of historiographic and metafictional discourses are those unforgettable photographs taken by Susan Meiselas of dead bodies, mutilated beyond recognition, piled up or scattered in the streets of Central America. Apropos of their impact, the Cuban media specialist Edmundo Desnoes (1988) reflects on the disparity between the self-referential, form-centered artifacts of the West and the historical/social reference of the photos on the basis of the incommensurable gap between core and periphery:

> The United States is a fragmented society, a society where people are encouraged to live centrifugally. The parts never make a whole. The whole is removed by the subtle mechanisms of advanced capitalism and its multiple ways of escape and dispersion. In Latin America everything is centripetal, everything is striving after unity and an axis. These discourses are in conflict due to economic and political differences; it is not a matter of temperament. (38)

In the light of the two aspects of the commodity sketched earlier, I think Desnoes' disjunctions are too clean-cut. Recall those straddling "free trade zones" in South Korea and elsewhere, the amphibious lives of people parasitic on U.S. bases, the enlargement of the public/private divide corresponding to the encroachment of the commodity into archaic and feudal spaces, and so on. But his point is unarguable. Humanity is still separated by all kinds of cleavages, ruptures, discontinuities inherited from the past and reproduced daily by the unequal division of international labor and distribution of resources. In spite of media flattening, the six o'clock news cannot conceal those discontinuities. Those bodies in Meiselas' photos contemplated by affluent viewers—*hypocrite lecteur! mon semblable!*—in the art galleries of New York City and Los Angeles seem to interrogate the bricolage of abject postmodern artifice. They do not exist in art, Desnoes insists; they "are rescued—if such a monstrous survival is possible—by society. 'If we do not believe in God, as Jose Marti wrote and lived, 'we believe in history'" (41–42). It is in this site of how history is conceived and narrated that the conflict between Third World heterogeneity and First World mastery takes place.

How trivial and disenchanting to engage in this hobby of a semiotic decoding of those bodies, Desnoes reflects. But for almost everyone conditioned by mass consumerism, the consumption of images seems to have induced temporary euphoria at the implosion of the Real. In rare moments, one can still entertain the protest of anarchists, dissident pariahs, outcasts lurking behind the props and facades. Should we, can we, abolish these images? Some cry: Free, save immediate Desire! Do away with mediations and representations! In fact, not only the images but also the bodies have been done away with in Argentina and Chile, in Haiti, East Timor, and elsewhere. As for the ethico-political implication of these "disappearances," Jean Franco observes that with the rise of the internal security state funded by the West (IMF-World Bank), all hitherto immune spaces in the underdeveloped countries—Church, family as refuge and shelter—are gone, just as affect and depth have vanished in simulations and spectacles. She notes the unprecedented sacrilege committed by U.S.-sponsored "low-intensity warfare" in the destruction of utopian space, specifically that associated with nuns, priests, women, and children. The "disappeared" no longer occupy a space that can be put "under erasure": "the smell of the cadaver will not be dispelled by the commodity culture, a debt-ridden economy and the forms of restored political democracy" (1985, 420). Compensation for such a loss cannot be made by a hundred deconstructive or schizoanalytic readings of Kipling, H. Rider Haggard, Forster, Conrad, or Malraux.

Let me enter a parenthesis here concerning Malraux, a culture-hero of European modernism. It is interesting to recall how in December 1923 Malraux was caught plundering the magnificent sculptures in Banteay Srei, part of the Angkor temples, in Kampuchea; his plea of innocence was that those treasures were not officially "protected." On this foraging expedition, Jan Myrdal comments:

> That Malraux was young and foolish is one thing. . . . What is less self-evident is why the intellectual left wing in France should have backed Malraux up. André Breton said it was absurd to send someone to prison for raping two or three stone dancers. This radical support for Malraux concealed a profound, if hidden, chauvinistic scorn for [non-Western] culture. Would they have rallied to the defense of a young Cambodian

poet who got himself arrested for collecting stone figures in the Parthenon to repair *his* finances? (1971, 44)

We are back to the issue of the postmodernist affirmation of the *differend* vis-à-vis the need to acquire a conscienticized (Paulo Freire's version of praxis) knowledge of the dynamics of the capitalist world system. Aimé Césaire, Carlos Mariategui, Che Guevarra, and others, used this knowledge for a "modernist" goal: popular mobilization. The situation of Latin American intellectuals reflects the uneven and combined development all Third World countries have experienced, thus making postmodernism (if that is the new label for dependency) almost a positivist dream of isomorphic correspondence between thought and reality (Richard 1987/88; Beverley 1991).

To be sure, not all Third World writers display solidarity against the transnational Leviathan. If Desnoes and Garcia Marquez question the universal claims of Western rationality and its metaphysics of reification, the Peruvian novelist Mario Vargas Llosa (1990), the darling of New York liberals, advocates a return to the philosophy of the Austrian Karl Popper. Llosa recycles platitudes and clichés from Popper's Cold War repertoire of the "open" versus "closed" societies. Llosa updates Popper in condemning all if not most Third World societies that have not integrated scientific rationality as closed, tribal and therefore backward, lacking the critical spirit and freedom prized in the West. Evolutionary Darwinism is resurrected from the dustbin. The source of all evil is historicism. The guilty purveyors of this evil include Plato, Hegel, Comte, Marx, Machiavelli, Vico, Spengler, Toynbee, and their disciples. They believe history has a logic that can be understood when, according to Popper's teaching, history is "a lively chaos," a "vertiginous totality of human activity that always overflows rational and intellectual attempts at apprehension"; and this activity mainly consists of power politics, "the history of international crime and mass murder" (1022–23).

Not only is history one damned thing after another, as the empiricist would have it; but it also surprisingly betrays a Nietzschean scenario: "vertigo, pandemonium, immeasurable absurdity, bottomless chaos, multiple disorder," and so on. And this frightening spectacle of freedom for Llosa can be tamed only by the artist, the novelist. So in a backhanded way, Llosa excuses art for its convivial liaison with the diabolic party of historicists, the totalitarian tyrants, the dogmatic believers. Postmodernism regresses somewhat in Llosa's praise of art's redemptive mission. He believes that Latin America's progress from the tribal swamp should proceed by way of the "third world" of spiritual creation, of culture regarded as testaments of the "sovereign individual": "These constructs, in which free will—imaginary acts of disobedience against the limits imposed by the human condition: a symbolic deicide—is radically exercised, secretly constitute (as do Herodotus' nine *Books of History*, Michelet's *History of the French Revolution*, and Gibbon's *Decline and Fall of the Roman Empire*—prodigies of erudition, ambition, good prose, and fantasy)—

testimonies to the panicked fear instilled in us by the suspicion that our fate is a 'feat of freedom' " (1024–25). In the words of Jose Garcia Villa, the Filipino avant-garde poet who disappeared in the bowels of Greenwich Village: the "Parthenogenesis of Genius" may "break, the, genetic, economy,/Springing, the, I, Absolute,/In, a, time-land, of, decimals:/Immaculate, conception,/Beyond, physiology—/The, Protagonist, of, the, age,/Mirrored, only, in, mirage" (114).

Paradoxically, Llosa's evolutionary picture based on Popper's scientism echoes the Enlightenment project endorsed by Habermas: both suppress the viewpoint of its victims, the colonized, women, and so forth. Did Llosa fail to see the "feat of freedom" in the bodies captured by Meiselas' camera? What kind of salvation has Occidentalism brought to Peru when Llosa, during his campaign for the presidency, ingratiated himself with the most reactionary forces of the native elite whose dogmatism, racist bigotry, and antidemocratic excesses would have made Popper blush in his grave?

III

The postmodern Third World intellectual looks askance at the glorious benefits supposedly granted by the West's "civilizing mission." For all its humanitarian indictment of colonialism, Joseph Conrad's *Heart of Darkness* is judged as racist by Chinua Achebe. Or consider Samir Amin's (1989) more nuanced stance when he points out how Eurocentrism, an ethnocentric ideology, reveals the fatal inadequacy of Western (Greco-Roman, Judaeo-Christian) universalism: "For Eurocentrism has brought with it the destruction of peoples and civilizations who have resisted its spread" (114). But Amin avoids privileging an essentialized identity opposed to the use of scientific technology and planning, calling this path a "nationalist culturalist retreat" that mimicks Eurocentric fundamentalism: "the affirmation of irreducible 'unique' traits that determine the course of history, or more exactly the course of individual, incommensurable histories" (135). Amin believes "culturalist nationalism" leads to an impasse. It cannot substitute for the universal vocation of Marxism, the moral-intellectual leadership of a socialist universalism signalled by "a national popular democratic advance" in the underdeveloped regions.

Like most Third World progressive thinkers, Amin upholds a totalizing approach that will negate any notion of the incommensurability of cultures and lead to what Marx calls the realization of the "species-being" in each person. This prophetic marker in Amin's treatise on Eurocentrism seems to connote a deeply rooted impulse of Enlightenment idealism that elides the fact of uneven development, scarcity, and the mediating role of the revolutionary nation-people. We see this inadequacy replicated in Aijaz Ahmad's animadversions on Fredric Jameson's "Third World Literature in the Era of Multinational Capitalism."

In that essay, Jameson initiates a contentious dialogue with Third World activists by offering a metacommentary on texts by the Chinese writer Lu Hsun and the Senegalese novelist Ousmane Sembene. Without defining exactly what he means by "national," Jameson seeks to demonstrate that all Third World writing necessarily assumes the form of national allegories: "the story of the private individual destiny is always an allegory of the embattled situation of the public third-world culture and society" (1986, 71). He takes as his point of departure the pivotal stage that Lukács alluded to in tracking the mutation of the epic into the modern novel: the separation of public and private spheres with the rise of the bourgeoisie. In Third World formations, however, the fragmentation of life has not reached the level of an all-encroaching reification experienced in the metropolis. In imperialized formations where an independent, hegemonic bourgeoisie is absent, there prevails a basically uneven, unsynchronized conjuncture that conflates a residual precapitalist (tributary) mode of production/reproduction, dominant capitalist institutions, and emergent popular-democratic consciousness. Cognizant of this, Jameson nonetheless believes that the complexity of this overdetermined formation can be, and has been, successfully registered in the form of "national allegory" in its varied manifestations.

Ahmad (1987) refuses to accept Jameson's theory of national allegory as the distinctive literary form for narratives written by Third World writers because he opts for multiplicity, not generality. Ostensibly he wants to preserve the uniqueness, the incaculable difference, of each country's mix of vernaculars, some of which may not go through a "national" phase (in Urdu literature, for Ahmad, the moment of national independence was overtaken by the "gigantic fratricide conducted by Hindu, Muslim and Sikh communalists"). Ahmad's objection to a classificatory determination of phenomena recalls the postmodernist anathema on totalization. But his insistence that one should take into account the multiple determinations at work in any text, specifying and historicizing them in order to grasp its complexity, forgets the inescapability of mediations such as the dynamics of group formation in response to imperial "divide-and-rule" schemes, racist "Bantustan" policies, and so on. How else can one read Ngugi's *Devil on the Cross* or Nadine Gordimer's *July's People*, for instance? Jameson's stress on a recurrent tendency to allegorizing in selected texts is sensitive to this doubling process in any individual act of narration as well as to the "mode of production" in which all practices are inscribed. Ahmad's caveat focuses less on the application of nonessentialist Marxism which nonetheless takes cognizance of the single conflict between capital and labor that defines the global system for Ahmad, and more on a paranoid suspicion that others will take the interlocutors (Ahmad and Jameson) as "each other's civilizational Others," that is, as stereotypical and one-dimensional representatives of each other's societies. In his book *In Theory*, Ahmad betrays a preference for an implicit socialist archetype that would judge the merits of partic-

ular nationalisms within the framework of his own historically limited understanding.

What becomes clear in the course of his argument is that Ahmad claims multiple belongingness predicated on his own will. In what sense can he "belong" to
Rigoberta Menchu's *testimonio*? His formalist stance liquidates precisely the relational dynamics of subject–position and its structural determinants (race, class, gender, etc.) for the sake of a voluntarist, arbitrary plurality of selves (Connor 231–37).
Ahmad can say anything he likes—but does it make a difference? to whom? for
whose sake? I don't see anything gained by ignoring how the dominant racializing
ethos of U.S. society, for example, has historically defined a person like Ahmad and
using that as a point of departure. This, I take it, is the rationale of Jameson's
method of "establishing radical situational difference in cultural production of
meanings" so that the categories of Identity and Difference, instead of being fixed
and eternal opposites (the way Amin postulated Eurocentrism versus cultural
nationalism), frozen in empirical duality or sheer random difference, are set in
motion "so that the inevitable starting point is ultimately transformed beyond
recognition." We graduate to another level of contradiction that sublate
(cancel/preserve) the previous stages of the argument.

On the whole, I think this encounter yields cautionary lessons. It not only
exemplifies a range of theoretical differences as to how the positionality of texts
(including practices) and their effects can be configured, and what degree of historical specification is required to formulate a hypothetical generalization. It also epitomizes the equivocal problematic of postmodernism understood and assessed by a
Third World sensibility, one symptomatic of the postcolonial mind's ambiguous
status in the diaspora. On another level of confrontation, I can contrive a parallel to
that encounter by expressing my reservation to the peremptory tone and claim of
these concluding remarks by the Australian authors of *The Empire Writes Back*:

> Post-colonial culture is inevitably a hybridized phenomenon involving a
> dialectical relationship between the "grafted" European cultural systems
> and an indigenous ontology, with its impulse to create or recreate an
> independent local identity. . . . It is not possible to return or to redis-
> cover an absolute pre-colonial cultural purity, nor is it possible to create
> national or regional formations entirely independent of their historical
> implication in the European colonial enterprise. . . . Thus the rereading
> and rewriting of the European historical and fictional record is a vital and
> inescapable task at the heart of the post-colonial enterprise. These sub-
> versive manoeuvres, rather than the construction of *essentially* national or
> regional alternatives, are the characteristic features of the post-colonial
> text. Post-colonial literatures/cultures are constituted in counter-discur-
> sive rather than homologous practices. (1989, 195–96)

Based on these exclusive stipulations, the entire research-creative program of writers like Zora Neale Hurston, N. Scott Momaday, Leslie Marmon Silko, Jan Carew, and others can be pronounced utterly misguided. Carew, for example, describes how African and Amerindian folk myths in Guyana fused and generated "homologous" texts comprising an authentically indigenous culture free from Western contamination (1988, 69–88). The African-American novelist Toni Morrison insists on the imagination's "rootedness" in "the ancestor as foundation" which guarantees black authenticity, while Silko blends oral narrative, history, and landscape in the autochtonous, wholly original expression of the Pueblo Indians (Madison 1994).

Nor can one avoid feeling that this one-sided prescription of our Australian colleagues makes a mockery of the prison writings of Abdullah and his compatriots, of Ngugi's project for a genuinely independent Kenyan creativity, of the Negritude production of texts by Aimé Césaire and others. It dismisses what Wole Soyinka (1990) calls the project of "race retrieval":

> It involves, very simply, the conscious activity of recovering what has been hidden, lost, repressed, denigrated, or indeed simply denied by ourselves—yes, by ourselves also—but definitely by the conquerors of our peoples and their Eurocentric bias of thought and relationships. . . . For a people to develop, they must have constant recourse to their own history. Not uncritical recourse but definitely a recourse. To deny them the existence of this therefore has a purpose, for it makes them neutered objects on whose tabula rasa, that clean slate of the mind, the text of the master race—cultural, economic, religious, and so on—can be inscribed. A logical resistance counterstrategy therefore develops; true nationalists find themselves, at one stage or the other and on varying levels, confronted with a need to address the recovery of their history and culture, to retrieve the fount and tributaries of their race—to plot the meanderings, drought patches, and fertile watersheds; the bewildering trick of disappearance into earth and the near-magical resurgence in a distant and differentiated epoch, potent with irrigation powers, breeding a newly aware humanity equipped with the strategies of the experience-laden journey from its beginnings to the present. (114)

Thus it is not enough simply to adduce the authority of Roland Barthes (1979) in deciphering the duplicity of "African Grammar," or cite the authority of recent self-reflexive ethnography, which is what postcolonial scholars would prescribe. What Soyinka exhorts us to undertake is "a retrieval of the authentic history of the struggle" against colonial oppression (for example, the Mau Mau uprising against the British in Kenya), a history indissociable from the geography of the land and the processes of collective labor. This program merges the second and third stages of Fanon's process of cultural liberation.

"National liberation" is the phrase I used earlier to counterpoint transnational postmodernism. Why can we in the Third World not skip this stage since "nation" and "nationalism" have acquired dangerous, pejorative implications in the West? Because it sutures the fragments of colonized lives in popular-democratic mobilization and so creates the historic agency for change. Otherwise no collective transformation, only individual conversions. Its negativity possesses a positive side: it restores what Bakhtin calls "the dialogical principle" as the matrix of social practices. Soyinka, Ngugi, Achebe, and others who share pan-Africanist ideals with such precursors as Dubois and Fanon all address the priority of national liberation (Gugelberger 1985). In praising Cesaire's poetic homage to Patrice Lumumba which captures "the rapture of the creative soul within the convulsions of nation building," Soyinka describes the song as being transmitted "through the lips, the adze, the dance motions, the textures and designs of our fabrics, the wall paintings; it is the community song of arms and feet in the organic labor of erecting shelter, planting and harvesting the earth. It is the heroic hymn of the producers of our history and culture, in the never-ending process of development" (120)—in other words, the national allegory of the African peoples.

It is impossible to sidetrack the nationalitarian or geopolitical moment in Third World cultural struggles, as the whole life of C.L.R. James would testify. The exponent of world socialist revolution and later of Pan-Africanism, James would return to the Caribbean homeland and discover the untapped revolutionary power of reggae music and the influence of the Rastafarians on the West Indian formation as well as on the diaspora in Britain as demonstrated in the 1981 urban uprisings. The Rastafari is not a hybrid or syncretic phenomenon, James avers: "They do not suffer from any form of angst. . . . The insanities of the Rastafari are consciously motivated by their acute consciousness of the filth in which they live, their conscious refusal to accept the fictions that pour in upon them from every side. . . . These passions and forces are the 'classic human virtues' " (Buhle 1988, 160). Nonetheless, this former disciple of Trotsky expressed faith in an evolving planetary culture, a socialist universality (not an eclectic, carnivalesque cosmopolitanism) such as that adumbrated by Fanon, Amin, Dussel, and others. James believed in history—literary, political—as fashioned by outsiders: Swift, Rimbaud, the proletariat. Paul Buhle, James's biographer, sums up the trajectory of the author of *The Black Jacobins*: "Without renouncing those [Marxist] insights, James followed the evidence which was thrown in relief by colonial revolution back to the point where he had begun his own creative literary and political thought. The proletariat had become the people (largely, peasants or just-removed peasants) and the great artists became those who could grasp the subject just emerging upon the horizon. Toussaint led to Lenin, but Lenin also led to Toussaint" (1988, 161). New situations, new subjects. As a liminal or threshold figure in the passage from

New World to Old, from South to North, James's career may furnish one paradigm for sublimating the antithesis of Identity and Difference to another plane, a synthesizing labor which Gramsci reserved for organic intellectuals of classes or sectors aspiring to hegemonic leadership over a whole society, articulating the particularistic interests of the masses into a revolutionary national paradigm.

IV

In surveying the revolt of the avant-garde against commodity-fetishism and the cash-nexus, Habermas made a passing reference to Walter Benjamin's notion of the Now-time, *Jetztzeit*, which designates the present as a moment of revelation, a time in which "splinters of Messianic presence are enmeshed." Seizure of this moment by art creates the break with historicism. This "Messianic" or revolutionary presence can insinuate itself into a national-popular form of organizing. To blast the continuum of Western hegemony, to free us from the nightmare of Euro-American history (which Marx discounts as "prehistory" since it is more a fatalism than a consciously guided process), is the goal of anti-imperialist artistic practice one of whose most uncompromising partisan is the Puerto Rican writer and painter Elizam Escobar, now serving a prison-term of sixty-eight years for "seditious conspiracy."

Escobar was captured on 4 April 1980 together with other men and women comrades fighting for the liberation of Puerto Rico. Accused of belonging to the FALN (Puerto Rican Armed Forces for National Liberation), they immediately declared themselves combatants in an anticolonial war against the U.S. government which they believe illegally occupies their homeland. Claiming the status of prisoners of war, they rejected the authority of U.S. courts; they refused to participate in their trials which tried to criminalize them for their struggle for self-determination. Tried in absentia, they were charged guilty in spite of the lack of substantive evidence. Classified as maximum custody prisoners, fourteen Puerto Rican prisoners of war have been subjected now to ten years of harassment, assault, isolation and castigation in spite of their exemplary conduct. At the Federal Correctional institute in Wisconsin, Escobar produced paintings that supporters in Chicago organized in a tour called "Art as an Act of Liberation" in November 1986. As a result, the Bureau of Prisons retaliated and transferred Escobar to El Reno, Oklahoma, where he was further punished by denying him materials so that he was unable to paint for a whole year. Because of massive pressure on the prison authorities by the art community and the independence movement, Escobar was permitted to paint and write again in December 1987.

In a poignant testimony entitled "Art of Liberation: A Vision of Freedom," Escobar (1990) traces four stages of his development as an artist-activist which modifies Fanon's schema: from the personal to the political, then to the professional-personal, modulated next to his fourth stage in prison, the visionary role of the artist. This role is dictated by the power of imagination to demystify and subvert the State's "structures of simulation," simulations of equal opportunity, cultural democracy, freedom of difference, and so on. To counter this culture of fear, the politics of art is needed "to bring out the real aspects of the human condition in particular and specific contexts or experiences," and also "to create a symbolic relationship between those who participate, the artwork, and the concrete world" (88–89). Following Baudrillard, Elizam rejects the formal theory of communication comprised of a linear path from transmitter to message to receiver which excludes the "ambivalence of exchange." Nonetheless, Elizam opts for a counter-hegemonic strategy of disarticulation and renegotiation of signs and meanings from within the discursive modes available: "The ironic dilemma is that we have to make use of this code though we realize that it reduces and abstracts the irreducible experience of that which we call "liberation. . . . There is a brutal difference between 'freedom' as exchange-sign-value or slogan of ideologies and abstractions, and the real freedom of experience—one that is as necessary as it is terrible" (91). Elizam invokes the inventive power of art to defy censorship, but he doesn't elevate art to the paramount cure since, for one, the reality of prison life for people of color who are also political prisoners always reminds him that the dehumanized and dehumanizing system symbolized by prison suppresses art as "the necessity of freedom." Elizam envisages the *métier* of his art as strategic in its intent of emancipating art and people "from the dictatorship of the logic, politics, and metaphysics of the sign" (93). By "sign," he means the entire network of representations and codes—the regime of reification we all have to cope with—that deceives us, preventing us from comprehending "the internal relationship between human desires and aspirations and human necessity" needed to build from the ruins of the present "transitional alternatives." Elizam's recent paintings, a fusion of stark realistic details in a surrealist, dreamlike environment, may be viewed as an effort to concretize this dialectical principle: "To me, art is the best argument for talking about freedom and about necessity when one does not separate the body from the spirit" (93).

Elizam questions the pretended rupture in the fragmented totality of U.S. society between the elite status quo and open-ended democratic pluralism effected by "first-worldist occidentalism." Behind postmodernist simulacrum behind simulacrum lies, Elizam believes, occidentalism's "moribundity, its resentment, its despair, its cultural, social, political, economic and ideological bankruptcy" whereby the ruling class projects its own decay on everyone. We should beware of being taken in by the irony and reflexiveness of postmodernism. Escobar argues that the postmodernist revolt against reification, an ambiguous one which reflects "a new historical moment" of cultural imperialism is "the last intent of occidentalist first-worldist's self-perpetuation" (1991, 28).

Like Ghassan, Fanon, and others, Escobar emphasizes the imperative of linking body and spirit in a milieu of alienation and dispersal. This is the challenge that
I think postmodernist theory evades in its guerilla war against the commodity masquerading in one aspect as simulacra, image, or spectacle. I do not know whether
to laugh or be outraged when Baudrillard, in his notorious essay "The Precession
of Simulacra," uses the Filipino tribal group known as "Tasadays" (which the
Marcos dictatorship has invented for its commercial and publicity needs) for his
virtuoso ruminations. When the Marcos government for a time supposedly
returned the Tasadays to "their primitive state," this withdrawal (according to
Baudrillard) afforded ethnology "a simulated sacrifice of its object in order to save
its reality principle." The postmodern shaman performs his own totalizing magical
number here: "The Indian thereby driven back into the ghetto, into the glass coffin of virgin forest, becomes the simulation model for all conceivable Indians *before*
ethnology. . . . Thus ethnology, now freed from its object, will no longer be circumscribed as an objective science but is applied to all living things and becomes
invisible, like an omnipresent fourth dimension, that of the simulacrum. We are all
Tasaday" (1984, 257–58). The irony here is that the hoax perpetrated by the
Marcos regime, by elite bureaucrats and the military (not by ethnologists) who
stand to gain by driving the Manobos (members of whom were forced to pose as a
Stone-Age tribe) from their mineral-rich homeland, was actually processed into a
commodity-form by the National Geographic and other Western media, plus a
gallery of spectators including Gina Lollobrigida, relatives of General Francisco
Franco invited by Elizalde and Imelda Marcos, and other celebrities to which
Baudrillard ascribes a tremendous mana-power of transforming all reality into simulation. But this item is not a simulation: one of those who testified in an international conference in 1986 to expose this hoax, Elizir Bon, was killed in September
1987 by paramilitary men near the Marcos-declared Tasaday reservation
(Berreman 3) while the rest of the "Tasadays" have been silenced by a machinery
of terror that Baudrillard would rather ignore.

At the least, postmodernist theory in complicity with Western rationality
occludes the "Indians" (the Manobos are indiscriminately dissolved into this erro-
neous generic classification) by depriving them of their history, their embeddedness in a specific sociocultural setting, in short, their integrity as humans. This is the
textualizing revenge of imperial knowledge on the world that dare claim precedence over it. How can one recognize the Other not just as a distorted projection
of all the negativity and lack in one's self? Is the Tasaday case of unconscionable
fraud reducible to pastiche, a token of hyperreal bricolage?

In the postmodernist problematic, the question of the Other—alterity conjugated and declined in infinite ways—has displaced the question of agency and now
occupies the foreground of North-South (formerly East-West) encounters. In a
critique of Said's *Orientalism*, the postmodernizing anthropologist James Clifford

(1988) faults Said's Foucauldian strategy by contending that it lacks a "developed theory of culture as a differentiating and expressive ensemble rather than as simply hegemonic and disciplinary" (263). Is the Other reducible to a field of representations produced by discourse? Is the genealogy of a discursive formation generating knowledge of the Other enough to legitimize Said's "fables of suppressed authenticity"? How does one represent the Other without totalizing control? Instead of a cosmopolitan humanism ascribed to Said, Clifford offers a concept of culture as a negotiated process with a differential plurality affording the subject with local resources to construct his or her discourse. His alternative, however, assigns the burden to the non-Western Other whom the anthropologist interrogates: "What does it mean . . . to speak like Aimé Césaire of a 'native land'? . . . Must the intellectual at least, in a literate global situation, construct a native land by writing like Césaire the notebook of a return?" (275).

Before finding out Said's response, I would like to invoke briefly two answers to the question of knowing the Other by the philosopher Emmanuel Levinas and Bakhtin. Levinas seeks to make up for the bankruptcy of liberalism's valorization of freedom and sovereign reason—Popper's and Llosa's cult objects—by accentuating "moral consciousness" before the "face of the Other" which limits the ego's freedom: "Going beyond the self, hostage to the other, responsibility is a transcendence of my freedom from above" (Davidson 1990, 45). Levinas doubts the mandate of Western liberal ideology in securing authentic dignity for the human subject. Instead he looks to an ethics founded on the "infinite transcendence of the other" which can check "Power" and discipline the spontaneous, autonomous self of Cartesian reason. This responsibility for the other, Levinas contends, "this transcendence of my self toward the other, is a movement more fundamental than freedom" (Kearney 1988, 362).

From the perspective of postmodern theory, Levinas has just proposed resuscitating a master narrative familiar to us all, the existentialist categorical imperative: concern for my brothers and sisters in the fold. But it is precisely this teleological narrative that Fanon has repudiated as so much tawdry apology for the brutalization of the colonial masses. One can raise the question here whether or not the fusion of hermeneutic horizons proposed by Gadamer and Heidegger, an orientation informing Levinas' transcendence through the other, has been able to illuminate the historical complicity of Western power in exploiting the hermeneutic circle for its benefit (see Longxi 1988). As an alternative, I would rather recommend Bakhtin's reflections on the constitutive function of alterity for a critical understanding of one's self:

I become myself only by revealing myself to another, through another and with another's help. . . . *To be* means to *communicate*. . . . To be means to be for the other, and through him, for oneself. Man has no internal sovereign territory; he is all and always on the boundary; looking within himself, he looks *in the eyes of the other* or *through the eyes of the other*. . . . I cannot do without the other; I cannot become myself without the other; I must find myself in the other, finding the other in me (in mutual reflection and perception). Justification cannot be justification of *oneself*, confession cannot be confession of *oneself*. I receive my name from the other, and this name exists for the other (to name onself is to engage in usurpation). Self-love is equally impossible. (Todorov 1984, 96)

Of course, it remains to be seen how the "I" and the "Other" are fleshed in specific circumstances where the determinants of gender, sexuality, race, class, religion, and so forth begin to complicate and disturb the lines of transnational communication.

For his part Edward Said, the engaged Palestinian critic and partisan of liberationist movements, suggests his own universalizing resolution of the Third World/postmodernism polarity: a more inclusive counter-narrative of liberation in which the antagonism between self and other can be displaced. Faulting Lyotard for separating postmodernism from the destructive consequences of European modernism in the colonized world and thus freeing it from its own history in the unequal division of labor, depoliticization of knowledge, and so on, Said diagnoses the crisis of modernism and the postmodernist impasse as one stemming from the onset of the twentieth century when Europe was being asked to take the Other (natives, women, sexual eccentrics) seriously. Albert Camus, Lyotard, Baudrillard, and Bourdieu never take into account the fact of colonialism, how the Others have been historically constituted by their imperial subjugation and exploitation. What is important is to foreground the dialectic of relations between the opposites and transgress the fixed, artificial boundary between the Self and Other.

In *Orientalism* and *Culture and Imperialism*, Said has cogently shown how the Western epistemological construction of Others in the various disciplines serves the goal of asserting its own supremacy. The modalities of the West's representation of other peoples do not furnish objective knowledge; instead they fulfill the historical agenda of confirming the ascendant identity of the British, the French, the European in general, over against non-Western/non-Christian peoples. Said elaborates the relational problematique of his approach and offers a scenario for resolving the contradictions between Habermas and Lyotard, between those who uphold difference as an unsurpassable existential condition and those who conceive it as a process of contingent and alterable relations:

Despite its bitterness and violence, the whole point of Fanon's work is to force the European metropolis to think its history *together with* the history of colonies awakening from the cruel stupor and abused immobility of imperial domination, in Aimé Césaire's phrase, "measured by the compass of suffering." . . . With Césaire and C.L.R. James, Fanon's model for the postimperial world depended on the idea of a collective as well as a plural destiny for mankind, Western and non-Western alike. . . . Cultures may then be represented as zones of control or abandonment, of recollection and of forgetting, of force or of dependence, of exclusiveness or of sharing, all taking place in the global history that is our element. (1989, 223–25)

Said's vision with its eloquent utopian-sounding promise might vindicate the truth of Abdullah's honor and possibly rescue Escobar from being trapped in "the belly of the beast"—if it did not sound like Borges' bizarre heterotopia. Meanwhile the production of Miss Saigon and new electronically sophisticated versions of Madame Butterfly will continue, Puerto Rico will continue to be the last intractable colony of the United States, and the Kurds and Palestinians will continue their struggle for a national homeland—national because, as Regis Debray explains, while the nation is a historically determined mode of existence, yet it remains a primary determinant, an invariable fact: "the cultural organization of the human collectivity in question," a materializing mediation through which the life of Homo sapiens "is rendered untouchable or sacred" (1977, 26). Whatever the status of this sacralization of life, I agree to some extent with Debray especially in his suggestion that the concept of nation curbs the voluntarism, idealism, and vanguardism that afflict intellectuals, in particular missionary postmodernists North or South. On the other hand, we should guard against the neo-nationalism of Japanese postmodernism, for example, whose basic tenet is the presumed synthesis of Western universalism and Japanese uniqueness (Mitsuhiro 1989). Again Bakhtin's principle of exotopy should warn us of the seductive route of the aesthetics of identification that offers an easy way of conflating opposites under the rubric of "human brotherhood," "colorblind folkish togetherness," either hybrid or syncretic homogenizing, only to tighten the chains around us. Neither empathy nor sentimental solidarity then. Others are needed—not the others who are simply victims of imperial conquest but the others who, though victimized, resist closure of the unfinished project of articulating their narrative of struggle for recognition, for collective affirmation, of which these remarks are mere fragments and marginalia.

V

Let me return as epilogue to a "peripheral" text now canonized by metropolitan arbiters of taste. In Borges' (1962) enigmatic fable "The Garden of Forking Paths," one will recall how the German spy Dr. Yu Tsun, a Chinese teacher of English formerly at the Tsingtao Hochschule, by a contrived happenstance, encountered his ancestor, Ts'ui Pen, the novelist of *The Garden of Forking Paths*, when he is about to kill his victim, the Sinologist Dr. Stephen Albert. Viewed retrospectively, the form of the narrative itself serves as context and symbol of the artwork discovered by this spy linking two nationalities/cultures. We can consider the narrative, the killer's testimony before his execution, as a poignant meditation on time, freedom and necessity. We do so even as we decipher its deeper logic as a warning on the hazardous quest of identity: we join our fated protagonist in mapping the labyrinth on the way to self-discovery. But what we discover ultimately is that the lines of representation and death coincide: recognition by the Other (Yu Tsun's chief, Dr. Albert) signifies death. This fatal identity, subtly dispersed in the interstices of a duplicitous text mediated by other topographers (editor, implied historian, narratee), claims at one point a racial motivation: "I carried out my plan because I felt the Chief had some fear of those my race, of those uncountable forebears whose culmination lies in me. I wished to prove to him that a yellow man could save his armies." In terms of rhetoric, it was metonymy, not syllogism, that saved Yu Tsun's "face" only to push him into that vertigo of *différance (pace* Derrida) which he calls "infinite penitence and sickness of heart."

From another perspective, what Borges has staged is less an existential allegory than a variant of the imperial theme of the East/the Asian Other unable to represent itself, thus finding its essence or authentic wholeness only through the mediation of the West. In contrast, Ludwig Wittgenstein consulted Rabindranath Tagore's *The King of the Dark Chamber* for an allegory of religious awakening (Monk 1990). It may seem that we are a long way from Hegel's judgment (delivered in 1830–31) on the character of the Chinese people: "Its distinguishing feature is, that everything which belongs to Spirit—unconstrained morality in practice and theory, Heart, inward Religion, Science and Art properly so-called—is alien to it" (1956, 138). But in a textbook like *Introduction to Comparative Literature*, François Jost (1974) improves on Hegel by attributing a self-contained, xenophobic essence to entire hybrid populations: "All the wisdom of Confucius did not enable the Chinese to discover the pineapple of the Caribbees or the girls of Baghdad. . . . In Asia, exoticism affected literature only to a very limited extent, for it did not correspond to an inner need either on the part of the public or of the poet—one further proof of the basically introverted character of Eastern peoples."

In discussing literary exoticism as a trend, Jost documents the mutations of style from Montesquieu and Voltaire to Flaubert and Durrell. He cites Paul Valery's explanation for the mirage of the Orient: "For this noun to produce in the mind its full and entire effect, it is necessary above everything else not to have been in the hazy region that it designates" (125). This is, to be sure, just one approach to the invention of what Said calls "Orientalism," a complex strategy of discourse and disciplinary practices that may in the end perhaps produce that mixing of incom-

patibilities which Nietzsche's Zarathustra needs "to give birth to a dancing star."
The crisis of First World/Western humanities of which Orientalism (vis-à-vis
Third World critiques) is a symptom, has surfaced through what we now know as
the interrogation of the self-identical Cartesian subject and its claim to apodictic
knowledge. Decentering that humanist cogito of Reason, the "masters of suspicion"—Nietzsche, Marx, and Freud, in their different and irreconcilable ways—
exposed the presumptive basis of its power and authority. But has this liberated the
Other—women, colonized subalterns, aborigines—from the perdurable effects of
this imperial logos?

Earlier I remarked on Jameson's intervention in this geopolitical comparative
field as an attempt to mediate the asymmetrical positions of Western critic (like Jost
or Valery) and Third World literary production. In a somewhat utopian gesture,
Jameson appreciates the position of the peripheral intellectual as enviable insofar as
it is organically linked to a responsive popular audience, and also at the same time
attuned to modernist forms of experience in the industrialized capitalist sectors.
Informed by a historical-materialist positioning of art in a global totality, Jameson's
reflections on Third World cultural practices evince the synthesizing power of a
Marxist critique compared to recent Anglo-American appropriations of Bakhtin
and other imports. While Jameson's risky generalization on Third World writing,
unmediated by the local indigenous traditions of China or Senegal, may be better
appraised as a cogent testimony of the dilemma of a distinguished American intellectual in search of a community and compensating for his lack by solidarity with
the insurgent victims/subalterns of the empire, it can also serve as an example of a
non-exploitative discourse which can be contraposed to Borges' fable, Jost's opinion, or to such commentaries like Karl Jaspers (1966) on Lao-tzu in his volume *The
Great Philosophers*. Faintly echoing Hegel, Jaspers faults the Chinese for never having developed an art of tragedy: ". . . great as their vision and experience of evil
have been, the tragic has remained inaccessible to them." Jaspers concludes that
Lao-tzu, and for that matter Chinese civilization as a whole, "lacks this self-clarifi-
cation [of the West], this dialogue with oneself, this eternal process of dispelling
the self-deceptions and mystifications and distortions which never cease to beset
us." Positing a Western essence, Jaspers establishes an invidious discrimination
now regarded as anachronistic and self-defeating (Schipper 1989). Compared to
this anxious, nostalgic, self-congratulatory Orientalism, how far and how remote
indeed have Jameson, Weiss, Brecht, and others travelled, taking what inscrutable
and unpredictable turns down the garden of forking paths, away from Kafka's
penal colony and its scene of "slow reading" and scrupulous, relentless writing.

10

Multiculturalism and the Challenge of World Cultural Studies

> In our genealogy, Papahanaumoku—Earth Mother—mated
> with Wakea—sky father—from whence came our islands, or
> moku. . . . As indigenous peoples, we fight for Papahanumoku,
> even as she—and we—are dying. . . . Who will protect Mother
> Earth?
>
> —Haunani Kay-Trask

Census statistics indicate that by the year 2080 the majority of the U.S. population will be composed of "minorities" (primarily Hispanics, African-Americans, Asians). Since 1991, minorities were already the majority in fifty-one of the largest cities with over 100,000 people. Such terms as "minority" and "majority" are, of course, inexact and misleading; nonetheless, the figures I cite have already frightened many, evoking in this fin-de-siècle milieu visions of a horrendous apocalypse.

The novelist Ishmael Reed paints an upbeat picture of this "twilight zone" of WASP Puritan America in his essay "What's American About America?" He opens with a citation from the *New York Times* (23 June 1983): "At the annual Lower East Side Jewish Festival yesterday, a Chinese woman ate a pizza slice in front of Ty Thuan Duc's Vietnamese Grocery store. Beside her a Spanish-speaking family patronized a cart with two signs. 'Italian Ices' and 'Kosher by Rabbi Alper.' And after the pastrami ran out, everybody ate knishes." Given the multiplicity of cultural styles in this late-modern formation, Reed questions the attitude that equates the whole society with Western civilization, an attitude that "caused the incarceration of Japanese-American citizens during World War II, the persecution of Chicanos and Chinese Americans, the near-extermination of the Indians, and the murder and lynchings of thousands of Afro-Americans." Closing his essay, Reed counters the fear and suspicion of many that alien influences are destroying the distinctive and unique American ethos with the assurance that the United States and Canada are places where the cultures of the world criss-cross, that the North American continent is unique because "The world is here." Clearly Reed's strategy of displacing the boundaries of outside and inside, or eliminating them outright, may not appease those whose identities are already psychically invested in a distinctive, unique, singular culture called "American"—a "common culture" enshrined in a hallowed set of discourses, symbolic rituals, literary canon, and other traditional practices that constitute the "American nation."

Commentators on the cultural scene like Reed have been accused of imposing a "politically correct" doctrine and charged with attempting to destroy Euro-American civilization. A whole issue of *Newsweek* (24 December 1990) entitled "Watch What You Say: Thought Police" was devoted to this controversy. Since it has already been thoroughly exploited by the commercial media, civic-spirited observers may be overexposed to this debate; but for the purpose of setting the stage for certain philosophical questions I would pose later, permit me to remap old ground.

I

All of these probably started with William Bennett's 1984 piece "To Reclaim a Legacy" and its alarming message: the irresponsibility of university administrators and their "failure of nerve and faith" have precipitated a catastrophic decline of standards. The decline of learning is ascribed to a loss of "our cultural heritage"—to wit, masterpieces from Homer, the Bible, Shakespeare to Emerson, Faulkner, and Robert Frost—so that a consensus or common culture is sacrificed. Multiculturalism threatens the destruction of Western civilization as a whole. In a famous rejoinder, Robert Scholes doubted whether U.S. society expresses any "single, durable vision" and contended that Bennett's pious clichés about sacred texts make impossible a critical engagement with them. Scholes' position represents a humanist concern shared by many liberal reformers:

> The trouble with establishing a canon—the great, insuperable problem—is that it removes the chosen texts from history and from human actualities, placing them forever behind a veil of pieties. This soulful rhetoric is guaranteed to drain the life out of the texts studied, because it permits only worship and forbids all criticism. . . . What I advocate . . . [is] the critical study of texts in their full historical context. At the heart of my belief . . . is the conviction that *no text* is so trivial as to be outside the bounds of humanistic study. The meanest graffito, if fully understood in its context, can be a treasure of human expressiveness. The purpose of humanistic study is to learn what it has meant to be human in other times and places, what it means now, and to speculate about what it ought to mean and what it might mean in the human culture. (1986, 116)

In another famous exchange, Stephen Greenblatt answers the charge of *Newsweek* commentator George Will and then chair of the National Endowment for the Humanities Lynn V. Cheney that "watery" Marxists are promoting "the political agenda of victimology" and "fighting against the conservation of the common culture that is the nation's social cement." Greenblatt argues for a historical investigation of the founding texts and ideas—like Shakespeare's *The Tempest*—which are not cement but "mobile, complex, elusive, disturbing," intertwined like any great cultural tradition "with cruelty, injustice, and pain." Greenblatt takes seriously Walter Benjamin's aphorism that "there has never been a document of culture which was not at one and the same time a document of barbarism." If the self-appointed guardians of a "common culture" want to risk collective amnesia and promote the artistic heritage as "a simple, reassuring, soporific life," they can continue to ignore "the painful, messy struggles over rights and values, the political and sexual and ethical dilemmas that great art has taken upon itself to articulate and to grapple with" (1993, 290).

While differing in their views about the function of the canon, both Scholes and Greenblatt believe that scholarly historical study of texts—where truth and art coincide—fulfills a humanistic ideal that presumably transcends partisanship. Scholes suspects canons to be instruments of a central authority bent on suppressing individual liberty, while Greenblatt conceives of literature as one that can forge community "founded on imaginative freedom, the play of language, and scholarly honesty, not on flag waving, boosterism, and conformity." While admirable in their critical stances, both scholars somehow evade the real issue underlying the origin of this debate, namely, the profoundly complex historical antagonisms articulated around the categories of race, gender, and class that define U.S. society from its very beginning. Such evasion occurs when a detour around the issue of a "national culture" is made. The key term that condenses the nuances and ambiguities in the debate, I think, is "common culture" whose seeming binary opposite, "multiculture," inaugurates a new, mine-sown field of contestation.

Even among the more liberal sympathizers of expanding the canon, one encounters sophisticated oddities: for instance, John Searle ascribes to the canon eulogized by Bloom, Bennett, and Bellow an "intellectual tradition of skeptical critical analysis" even while claiming in the same breath that "education is by its very nature 'elitist' and 'hierarchical'" (1993, 88). Or Elizabeth Fox-Genovese's (1986) opinion that the canon has "privileged the ideals of responsible individualism, rationalism, and universalism." As though attuned to the rumblings of something grievously wrong in the body politic, Alice Kessler-Harris (1992) seeks to pacify the anxiety about the fragmentation, absence, or loss of a "common culture" by dissolving the outside into the inside, analogous to Reed's move. She believes that "multiculturalism can strengthen, not undermine, a common culture" since this common culture is a perpetually constructed synthesis, a new concept of democratic culture or pluralism—a common identity that is fluid, susceptible to change, continually negotiable. Paradoxically, then, "far from undermining the search for unity, identity, and purpose, the multicultural enterprise has the potential to strengthen it." In short, *e pluribus unum.*

A year before the fires of the Los Angeles riots, a debate on multiculturalism appeared in *The American Scholar* between Molefi Asante, a proponent of the "Afrocentric Idea" and Diane Ravitch, a well-known New York educator. To Asante's proposition that "there is no common American culture as is claimed by the defenders of the status quo," Ravitch (1993) replies that the U.S. has "a common culture that is multicultural," formed by the interaction of its subsidiary cultures. Either Ravitch is just playing with words, or a performative contradiction vitiates her statement; if a common culture already prevails, why arouse suspicion by pleading for it? However, in her brief for "cultural pluralism," it turns out that the "multitextured tapestry" of American culture is dominated by Europe which occupies a "unique place" in U.S. history; the salient proof is that "our governmental institutions were created by men of British descent who had been educated in the ideas of the European Enlightenment" (292). While acknowledging the differences that have all blended into the cultural mosaic, Ravitch posits that "we are all Americans" subscribing to a Western democratic ideology, "ideas of individualism, choice, personal responsibility, the pursuit of happiness, and belief in progress." In effect, U.S. "common culture" has become universal, as proved by the Chinese students in Tiananmen Square in 1989 quoting Patrick Henry and Thomas Jefferson. But I believe no amount of triumphalist self-glorification nor astute repackaging of the canon, or rhetorical skill in shifting and deconstructing subject-positions, would necessarily guarantee that participants in the educational system would not remain ignorant of the history of U.S. race relations that has been hitherto decisive in shaping the structure and texture of current social/power relations.

II

At the 1992 MLA Convention, the keynote event of the Presidential Forum addressed the theme of "Multiculturalism: The Task of Literary Representation in the Twenty-First Century." The dominant tenor and majoritarian consensus of humanists on the "culture wars" over canon revision and curricular diversification can be gauged from the speech by Henry Louis Gates, Jr. who argues for a pluralist philosophy (Isaiah Berlin is invoked as its chief prophet) where "identities are always in dialogue," monads somehow linked by a hidden telephone switchboard. After a token acknowledgment of "leftist" critiques of late-capitalist reformism, Gates settles for a jazzy style of compromise in which individual subjects "are, like everything else, sites of contest and negotiation, self-fashioning and refashioning" (1993, 11). Sara Suleri of Yale University concurs, endorsing this refurbished liberalism as a view that captures "an enlightened dynamic that is the soul of America" (1993, 17). I comment on Gates' pluralist legitimation later. Meanwhile, in *The Chronicle of Higher Education*[1] and journals like *Academe*, multiculturalism is often celebrated as manna or talisman reconciling the competing claims of an assimilationist "common culture," a slippery American self in a continual process of construction, and the others occupying margins, ruptures, lacunae. Skeptics like William Chace, president of Wesleyan University, while conceding that multiculturalism harbors salutary impulses for change, contends that it will not provide "the basic tools of all genuine education: analysis, retention of materials, clear exposition, and intellectual seriousness"; for him, "the real pedagogical mission is to bring into association the apparently dissimilar, to reveal the commonality of all forms of discourse and taxonomy, all systems of mental discrimination" (1990, 23)—a Platonic drive for the all-encompassing integral One. At best, multiculturalism might represent a wish-fulfillment for a freewheeling social order founded on the principle of unity in multiplicity, *e pluribus unum*.

Policy conferences, seminars and workshops in teachers' conventions, publishers' marketing sessions, and curricula of schools now all target "cultural diversity," "multicultural literacy," and so forth, where once suppressed voices are allowed the chance to be heard. Without invoking the postmodern slogan of heterogeneity and *différance*, one Asian-American artist even claims that "cultural pluralism is the genuine American way" and that "multiculturalism" means "cultural affirmative action" (O'Brien and Little 1990). What's the background to this epochal trend and its attendant controversies?

Despite claims to the contrary, the national imperative to include courses on cultural diversity (non-Western material) into the General Education Core Curriculum in many colleges and universities springs from a conjunctural crisis. Multiculturalism may be conceived as the latest reincarnation of the assimilationist drive to pacify unruly subaltern groups. It can be interpreted as a strategic response to the deterioration of the social fabric of the country in the decade after the early seventies when progressive policies and institutional reforms gained by the civil rights struggles of the sixties were severely eroded or wiped out in the late seventies and throughout the eighties. One stark index of the crisis is the 1987 statistic of the gap between the poor and the rich, the largest in 40 years: the poorest fifth of all families received only 4.6 percent of the national family income while the top fifth's share was 43.7 percent (Parenti 1994; Mantsios 1992). More Americans are ill-housed, poorly educated, and without health care than ever before. The condition for the racial minorities of course is twice, even three times worse than for the general population (Franklin 1991). But the most important historical fact underlying the debate is the changing demographics of the country: by the first two

---

1. I recommend sampling articles by Rodrigues (1992), Frankel (1993), and Poston (1991).

decades of the next century, the labor force and most urban centers in the country, together with the student population in high schools and universities, will be predominantly comprised of people of color: the majority of California's population, for example, will be made up of Hispanics, African-Americans, and Asians in the next decade.

Given these realities, aside from the economic challenge of Japan and the Newly Industrializing Countries of South Korea, Taiwan, and Singapore, and perceived threats from the non-Western "Third World," as well as the sharpening global contradictions among the three spheres of transnational capitalism (the Americas dominated by the United States, Japan and Asia, and Europe), it is inevitable that the academic intelligentsia, or its "secular priesthood," should respond to make instructional programs more relevant in two ways: first, by including the representatives and agencies of traditionally neglected groups; and second, by questioning the old definition of knowledge and the disciplines as defined by a Western body of canonical texts that excluded or discounted the "Others" as insignificant. At the University of California at Berkeley, Stanford University, the Universities of Wisconsin, Minnesota, and Massachusetts, faculty and students demanded curricular reform in the wake of incidents of racially motivated harassment and violence. It was wrongly assumed before that the academy was a haven, a refuge of scholars safe from the turmoil of the worldly populace. A faculty committee at the University of Wisconsin observed that the "ethnocentric view" of the mainstream curriculum "is restricted to the Euro-American experience. Excluded and left invisible are people of color whose labor and sacrifices have been and continue to be neglected," thus making students insensitive to and intolerant of cultural and ethnic difference. One of the objectives of the cultural diversity requirement at Wisconsin is "to facilitate understanding of what it means to live in a society which may display hostility to the individual on the basis of stereotypes of fundamental, frequently unalterable characteristics of race, religion, sex or national origin" (Wald 1991, 5). The cardinal assumption behind this national crusade is that given the ethnic plurality in our society, the universities must "create an environment which will uphold, promote and instill multicultural values," premised on the notion that knowledge and information will lead toward a more enlightened, tolerant, and therefore more democratically representative society. But there were no smiles in the fierce debate that raged at the University of Texas where reactionary defenders of elite education charged that everything was being politicized: for members of the National Association of Scholars, it was a case of political correctness versus individual freedom (University of Texas Writing Group 1991). Chicano students expressed uneasiness about "multiculturalism" as a bland, catch-all phrase (connected with diversified reading lists or required courses on non-Western cultures, for example) to thwart a head-on confrontation with institutional racism, while others considered multiculturalism a new fad which signifies little more than the liberal presumption that power is dispersed evenly and you only need to realign the symbolic system to appease the disgruntled. Multiculturalism won't liberate or dignify them, students of color charge, because it does not address the issue of who has the power to determine what courses are taught, what requirements are established, and so on. In brief, it's not a question of "political correctness" but "Who controls the university"? Rebecca Rice, an African-American artist and educator, dared to pose the scandalous questions: "Who defines multiculturalism? . . . Who decides when and how various cultures will come together? Who pulls the purse strings? . . . Who really benefits from multicultural work?" (O'Brien and Little 1991, 209–10).

Such reactions have arguably precipitated a coordinated campaign in media and public forums to affirm a "common culture" against the threat of unAmerican, "politically correct" radicals, and assorted dissidents specializing in victimology and entitlements. A notorious polemicist in this camp of conformist fundamentalism is George Will, columnist of *Newsweek*, who bewailed scholars trying to "delegitimize Western civilization" and usher "collective amnesia" and social disintegration by "opposing the conservation of the common culture that is the nation's social cement"(1991, 72). Advocates of revising the Eurocentric canon thereby assume the guise of a revitalized "Yellow Peril" undermining the moral order and security of Anglo-Saxon society; they evoke a memory of all those encroaching anarchic hordes (African slaves, Jews, East European peasants, etc.) about to crush "the national mind," "the cultural patrimony," the U.S. Constitution. The theory that diversity (the new tribalism) presupposes and requires unity ("a common Americanism") is succinctly expressed by Henry Anatole Grunwald, former editor-in-chief of *Time*: "In the name of diversity and respect for various cultures— entirely praiseworthy goals—the advocates of multiculturalism seem bent on undermining the social compact that ensures diversity," a polity based on "that special American achievement: the patriotism of ideas" (1992, 19). This patriotism then serves as the foundation for a hierarchy of values and beliefs that constitutes a fixed, transcendent, and self-reproducing essence binding all Americans, a national character or signature that paradoxically guarantees the individual right to differ— up to a point, of course.

It is now clear how this revivalist quest for a common culture defining the American nation, a peculiarly American ethos binding all citizens, can be properly appraised as a symptomatic reaction to social decay (San Juan 1992). This is evidenced by, among others, the marked resurgence of racism culminating in the Los Angeles urban rebellion; and before that Bensonhurst, Virginia Beach, Howard Beach, the Miami riots, and Charles Stuart's lie which, according to Derrick Bell, "is in an American tradition that virtually defines the evil that is racism" (1990, 23). Decades after the 1968 Kerner Commission Report on Civil Disorders, we are confronted this time with an unprecedented polarization of society—not just between black and white, but across a wide range of "races," genders, classes, identity-groups, and so on. On top of this are the everyday facts of homelessness for thousands, impoverished single mothers, increasing teenage pregnancies and infant mortality rate, school dropouts; drugs, violence, and criminality (an issue now targetted by opportunist politicians); and an exploding prison population comprised mostly of racial minorities. Is everything falling apart? Alarmed by the erosion of a consensual equilibrium and its conscience aroused, Chrysler Corporation sponsored a forum on "500 Years After Columbus Rediscover America/How to Make Our Nation Better" advertised in *Money* magazine and other mass periodicals. The distinguished novelist Joyce Carol Oates was recruited for this promotional campaign; she dutifully contributed her share of "commonsense" by bewailing the loss of community and ritual which gives us our human identity. Oates' anxiety betrays a chronic predicament of the liberal mind: how can one resolve the tension between "the security of the community and the hunger for freedom in the individual"? Unfortunately, the organic and consensual community is more a myth than an archaic fantasy. Oates is aware that we inhabit "a secular, consumer-oriented society, rapidly fragmenting into sub-societies of ethnic, cultural, professional and religious diversity" (1991, 10) whose incommensurable interests can only be suspended or neutralized by media-ordained rituals like the assassination of presidents, the Gulf War, and so on.

I think what informs Oates' nostalgia for traditional life stabilized by the sense of the sacred and group-togetherness, her desire to recuperate a milieu before technological rationality and bureaucratic administration colonized the life-worlds of *l'homme moyen sensuel*, is a sentimental notion of community where contradictions between groups and individuals are dissolved in a collective faith or shared world-outlook. At the same time she intuits our sordid complicities in a Hobbesian, atomized world of actors/roles pursuing diverse interests with the use of instrumental reason to control nature and other humans. The pathos of her naive pluralism lies in its attempt to construct a discourse of community premised on primordial attachments, a discourse that claims at the same time to recognize and respect diverse others upon whose exclusion or marginalization that community is founded. Alarmed by all the changes that wrecked the self-contained pieties of her hometown, Oates cannot reconcile the truth of Watts and Harlem burning in the sixties, or Los Angeles in the nineties, with her vision of antebellum America which supposedly accommodated almost everyone.

One also recalls in this context Arthur Schlesinger's nostalgic wish to return to the "melting pot" trope (as against a divisive Tower of Babel) invented at a time when, in fact, this trope harmonized with another figure of reconciliation: "Manifest Destiny." Terrorized by the threat of a "linguistic and cultural apartheid" he attributes to the followers of the "cult of ethnicity," Schlesinger longs for the good old days when a supposed homogeneous national identity prevailed. When was this? In the time of Hector St. John de Crevecoeur two centuries ago. Schlesinger's prayer is less an echo of the Statue of Liberty's welcome than a recasting of "Manifest Destiny": "Let the new Americans forswear the cult of ghettoization and agree with Crevecoeur, as with most immigrants in the two centuries since, that in America 'individuals of all nations are melted into a new race of man'" (1994, 295). This was published before the Rodney King trial exploded in the heart of Los Angeles, reputedly the "multicultural capital of America."

III

A little historical analysis might be instructive in elucidating the dilemma of the partisans of "the common" monopoly culture. The sociologist Ferdinand Tonnies (followed by Max Weber and Emile Durkheim) was the first to schematize the disparity between the folkish community, *Gemeinschaft*, and a rationally administered system called society, *Gesellschaft*. What needs to be grasped is that those changes in human relationships, patterns of behavior, norms, and beliefs—what we now indiscriminately call "lifestyles"—did not just happen because of the wishes of individuals or the conspiracy of a few bad people. Those changes coincided and reflected transformations in the way people produced their means of existence and thereby reproduced themselves and their social networks.

My conceptualization of this historical trajectory involves a dialectical transaction of consciousness and environment, not simply a unilateral determinism. It concerns the way people associated with one another in developing circumstances, altering them, and in the process elaborating new "habits of the heart" and "structures of feeling" appropriate to the circumstances—when the horse and plow were replaced by the factory, when the factory was replaced by Ford's assembly line, and all the technological and sociocultural mutations that accompanied the periodic reconfigurings of varying modes of production. Eventually the market replaced the church as the major institution of everyday social exchange. The recurrent nostalgia for the past, for the face-to-face, more direct and immediate lives of the village folk in contrast to the formal, abstract, and instrumental relationships of a technocratic state governed by the cash-nexus and commodity-fetishism, is a familiar response with a genealogy dating back to the late eighteenth century when dispossessed peasants in England attacked the trains encroaching on their farms, all the way back to the enclosure movement in the thirteenth and fourteenth centuries in Europe. In the recent past, however, this praise of communal bond and organic solidarity easily evolved into the cult of *volkish* nationalism based on biological kinship, patrimony, blood, the virtues of the patriarchal hearth, inherited purity of the superior race with a "civilizing mission" over the "lesser breeds," and preservation of the homeland against internal and external enemies: Jewish parasites, Marxist contaminators, stigmatized aliens, and so forth. Like all representations, the notion of a "common culture" since the time of the Puritan pilgrims up to the imperialism of "Manifest Destiny" has usually been articulated to legitimate the exclusion, domination, and oppression of multitudinous others (Native Americans, African slaves, etc.) and, in effect, sanction an apartheid regime of "unity in diversity."

Not only Chrysler Corporation but media pundits, politicians, and bureaucrats all collaborate in trying to resist alternative/oppositional versions of the narrative of progress of "one nation indivisible." Civic virtue attached to citizenship require upholding and sustaining a myth of commonality so discordant with the reality of conflicts on every level of business society. Seen in this context, class, gender, and racial antagonisms expose the arbitrarily imposed grid of national belonging. Indeed, our participation in the broadcasting of this allegedly homogeneous "common culture" will be confined to that of spectators of media-packaged spectacles and other simulacra. The latest news is that we are living in a postmodern age of artifice where reality, not just the town commons or the village fair, has evaporated—"Everything solid melts into air," so proclaims *The Communist Manifesto*. Or else, it has been replaced by fragments of memory haunting us with uncanny repetitions, with our dreams and hopes now reduced to a paltry recycling of old movies, television soap operas, clichés, and stereotypes from drugstore novels and quotidian routine. Oates' vision itself comes to us in the pages of mass-produced commodities like *Money*, pastiches of the corporate machines so incompatible with her evocation of idyllic hometown uniformities. Such irony is not surprising in our age of sudden reversals, discontinuities, loss of affect, and so on that somehow parody the banal sociological diagnosis of the malaise of urban anxiety and alienation.

By this time, the call for a liberal education with a multiculturalist agenda has probably become for many observers as tiresome as the television commercial extolling the virtues of comparison shopping. But it continues to be sounded by almost everyone who tends to reduce systemic crisis to local administrative problems and acts of injustice to technical snafus remediable by the timely application of expertise and knowhow. It might be helpful to illustrate the inadequacy of this pragmatic approach by recalling what has been said of E.D. Hirsch's program for institutionalizing a "national culture." Earlier Scholes (1986) had pointed out the fallacies in Hirsch's conflation of literacy with culturally shared knowledge in which "culture" is meant to refer to the classics, the canonized monuments of "high culture." Hirsch's best-selling program of *Cultural Literacy* may be viewed as a prophylactic anodyne to a systemic crisis—in particular, the country's economic decline; the disappearance of a monolithic enemy, the Soviet Union; sharpening income disparities; widespread unemployment and homelessness; criminality, among others—by reducing it to an administrative-technical problem remediable by a timely application of expertise and knowhow. Confronting inequality and injustice, Hirsch wants to institutionalize a "national culture" based on standard written English and the fund of knowledge ascribed to the professional managerial class.

I select one other commentator, Barbara Herrnstein Smith, who has sharply criticized the notion of a transcendent American civic or national culture that can be encapsulated in one man's list. She writes: "There is . . . no single, comprehensive macroculture in which all or even most of the citizens of this nation actually participate, no numerically preponderant majority culture in relation to which any or all of the others are 'minority' cultures, and no culture that, in Hirsch's term, 'transcends' any or all other cultures. Nor do these multiplicities describe a condition of cultural 'fragmentation' except by implicit contrast to some presumed prior condition of cultural unity and uniformity [which] has never obtained in this nation at any time in its history" (1992, 77). Although Smith's theorizing of culture is fuzzy and shirks any obligation to confront the problem of "hegemony" (an idea construed by Antonio Gramsci as a consensual moral/intellectual leadership of a social bloc at specific conjunctures in history), her argument to my mind astutely exposes Hirsch's "egregiously classbound and otherwise parochial" agenda.

We do not need any gift of clairvoyance or hermeneutic of suspicion to ascertain the historically specific ideology of the professional-managerial class behind Hirsch's cult-lit scheme. Framed by the imperatives of the standardization of the work force and consuming public, Hirsch's reactive culturalism aims at a time of crisis to "shore up the ideology of equal opportunity and mask the structural inequities of the social order" (Ohmann 1992, 30). Hirsch's idea of a common culture as an autonomous realm comprised of a fixed standardized nomenclature of knowledge—shrewd enough not to exclude Marx, Malcolm X, the Black Panther Party, and the like—has a pluralist motivation and claims to appreciate heterogeneity, conflicts, negotiations of unstable and contestatory identities. Its limitation derives from the assumption that a consensus already obtains on the matter of the distribution of wealth and power. Hirsch's pluralism, however, sublimates a monolithic drive for a homogeneous mass literacy transcending family, neighborhood, and region. Hirsch insists that "literate culture is the most democratic culture in our land; it excludes nobody"—except, of course, those without full access to, and effective use of, this symbolic-cultural capital, never mind the basic necessities of food, clothing, and shelter.[2] Let me add another reservation. Analogous to schools that include, in their cultural diversity offerings, courses on sign language, Japanese silk-screen techniques, Indian cooking, African magic, and the like, the program of cultural literacy refuses any critical accounting of inequality. In effect, it denies the centrality of racism, sexism, and exploitation in what has been described as a post-Fordist, globalizing capitalism.

At this point, I hope no one accuses me of being against cultural plurality—can one be for or against what already exists? Although a totalizing comprehension of economic, political, and ideological structures constituting the U.S. social for-

---

2. For the concept of symbolic cultural capital, see Bourdieu and Passeron (1977).

mation is requisite for judging the real worth of such reforms as Hirsch's, what is primarily at issue here is cultural pluralism, a normative concept, and the corollary theory of rights and justice within the parameter of liberal ethics and jurisprudence. Why is this pluralism, translated into the pedagogical register of multiculturalism, elevated into a synthesizing formula adequate to resolve the problem of racism and ethnically motivated conflicts? Because it explains away political-economic antagonisms as effects of "natural" cultural legacies. Michael Banton points out that cultures "tend to be systems of meaning and custom" that have no clear boundaries and thus "there is no finite number of stable constituent units" that can enter such a field as "multicultural" education (1984, 69). In addition, the tendency to essentialize culture as inner, spiritual refinement (in contradistinction to the crude practices of civilization) subtly reactivates elitist, class-bound hierarchies privileging mental over manual labor, rendering inutile any demand to transform the actual circumstances of social life (Marcuse 1968; The Frankfurt Institute 1972). Thus what is needed is not mass struggle against institutional racism but individual self-improvement through a variegated reading fare.

IV

Before inquiring into the ideology of pluralism and the problems surrounding identity, difference, and community, I want to clear the ground and rehearse the competing views on multiculturalism. Manning Marable (1992) explains that multiculturalism involves two fundamental ideas: "first, the recognition that American history and this nation's accomplishments are not reflected solely in the activities of only one race (whites), one language group (English speakers), one ethnicity (Anglo-Saxons), or only one religion (Christianity). African-Americans, Latinos, Asian-Americans, Native Americans, and others have also made central contributions to our society. And secondly, beneath these differences are some underlying principles and values which bring us together, such as the ideals of human equality, democratic government, and individual liberty." There is in Marable's paradigm a dialectical process between identity and difference, the singular and the typical. Now Fred Siegel (1993), in an article on "The Cult of Multiculturalism," reduces multiculturalism to an "all-consuming politics of identity" whose chief instigator is none other than the French historian Michel Foucault. Blaming Foucault for spreading the idea that knowledge is nothing but an instrument of power, Siegel recycles clichés about the "great American hyphen" that allows Americans to be both particularists and universalists, syncretists and naturally tolerant, mixing assimilation and traditional allegiance into a homogenized if plural culture. But Siegel, nonetheless, betrays an obsessive fear of multiculturalism so that he ends his tirade with this lesson: "The future may well lie with the Stanford student who, when asked about studying important non-Western trends such as Islamic fundamentalism and Japanese capitalism, responded, "Who gives a damn about those things? I want to study myself." With such disarming naiveté, all problems indeed disappear.

In Stanford University itself, things were more complicated than this last pronouncement might suggest. As Mary Louise Pratt has recounted, the struggle to revise the Western Civilization requirement faced not only conservative resistance but also the co-optative strategy of liberalizing the canon by simple addition. Thus, the autobiography of West African Olaudah Equiano can be added to Genesis, Aquinas, and Rousseau to provide a "common intellectual experience" for all students. The center of gravity, however, still remains the monumental texts of a Europe narrowly defined to exclude Spain, Eastern Europe, and Scandinavia. The revisionists then proposed a relational or intercultural approach that would at the same time recognize the "internal fullness and integrity of particular moments and formations." Deploying the mode of examining "the complex interactions of colonialism, slavery, migration, and immigration" between Europe and people of color, the revisionists wanted to suggest an approach to Others that would not just be tokenizing nor patronizing tolerance: "It is not from Europeans that enslaved peoples have learned how to construct cultures that conserve a sense of humanity, meaningful life, and an abiding vision of freedom in the face of the West's relentless imperial expansion" (Pratt 1993, 59).

It now becomes clear that the cardinal flaw of culturalism of either the pluralist or monopolist kind lies in its disjunction of the institutional practices of intellectuals from the operations of the centralized state and the power of corporate business. Culture then becomes fetishized knowledge sealed off from contingencies dictated by state power and commercial exigencies (Chomsky 1982). In my book *Racial Formations / Critical Transformations*, I attempted to counter the essentialism and apologetics of culturalism by arguing that culture, which embraces both civilization and mental labor, must be understood within the framework of a social structure constituted by multiple contradictions, in particular from the viewpoint of the hegemonic process of struggles by multiple sectors and forces. Given the racist politics of U.S. society, the problem of subject-position or agency needs to be situated and mapped within this overarching process of antagonistic relations. Cultural practices become intelligible only when they are mediated by the categories of race, class, gender, and so forth, in concrete time-space encounters. In this way the question of identity cannot be rhetorically deferred in a putative commonality of shared experience, in a field of forces believed to be synchronized and self-equilibrating. Nor can it be displaced into a "free play of signifiers" where, for the postmodernist intelligentsia, roles circulate freely and will-power alone suffices to calculate and determine one's life-chances. In a society stratified by uneven property relations, by asymmetrical allocation of resources and of power, can there be equality of cultures and genuine toleration of differences? It is now generally agreed that culture (symbolic and cultural capital), appropriated through the educational system, functions to reproduce class relations in all spheres of civil society (particularly the job market) as well as in the technocratic institutions of the state.

To avoid the reductionist tendency of judging culture as thoroughly reified and racially interpellated groups as equivalent or surrogates of each other, we need to deploy the concept of hegemony and unfold the contradictory impulses (residual, dominant, emergent) at play in the historical dynamics of overdetermined social formations. Within this framework, Hazel Carby cogently underscores the limits of the liberal thesis of multiculturalism:

> By insisting that "culture" denotes antagonistic relations of domination and subordination, this perspective undermines the pluralistic notion of compatibility inherent in multiculturalism, the idea of a homogeneous national culture (innocent of class or gender differences) into which other equally generalized Caribbean or Asian cultures can be integrated. The paradigm of multiculturalism actually excludes the concept of dominant and subordinate cultures—either indigenous or migrant—and fails to recognize that the existence of racism relates to the possession and exercise of politico-economic control and authority and also to forms of resistance to the power of dominant social groups. (1980, 64–65)

And so therefore, in a world torn by class, gender, and racial contradictions, can any social formation plausibly claim to be democratic and organically unified, honoring equally the claims of every subject?

One reason why multiculturalism has become the ascendant strategy of liberal reformism can be located in the exorbitation of the notion of ethnicity during the Cold War. The epistemological paradigm of ethnicity worked to displace race and class as explanatory categories for dysfunctionality, for social conflict and integration. In an essay entitled "Ethnic Pluralism: The U.S. Model," Stephan Thernstrom, editor of the influential *The Harvard Encyclopedia of American Ethnic Groups*, describes the successful assimilation of European white immigrants (based on the sole index of ethnically exogamous marriages) and the dissolution of boundaries marked by national origin. This model of Americanization cannot yet be applied to Afro-Americans, Thernstrom adds, although "Black people have won full equality before the law—in some respects a favored position before the law" (1983, 253), hence the "black-white divide remains the major fault line in American society." Cognizant of this differential incorporation of "racial" groups, another authority contends that "structural pluralism" obtains in the United States, a pluralism harnessed to the ends of the functionalist metanarrative of social equilibrium (Gordon 1975). To substantiate his model of subsumption for non-European immigrants, Thernstrom asserts that "Orientals are no longer a stigmatized racial minority but a rapidly assimilating ethnic group" through marriage—which may be true for Japanese-Americans but not for other Asians. Here we discern the conflation of culture and biology, a tendency of proponents of "common culture" that warrants Paul Gilroy's criticism: "Culture is conceived along ethnically absolute lines, not as something intrinsically fluid, changing, unstable, and dynamic, but as a fixed property of social groups rather than a relational field in which they encounter one another and live out social, historical relationships. When culture is brought into contact with race it is transformed into a pseudobiological property of communal life" (1990, 266–67; see Webster 1992). Cultural racism, the latest metamorphosis of the phenomenon, is one ideological-political effect of hegemonic pluralism.

The paradigm of the U.S. as a pluralist multi-ethnic society may be said to underwrite the identity politics of self-affirmation. The constitution of identity involved here refers to the manipulation for political purposes of an ensemble of "ethnic" attributes and representations detached from their socio-historical contexts. Identity politics may be exemplified by Afrocentrism and its mirror image, the fetishism of a "common culture" championed by Establishment intellectuals. Postmodernist liberals, however, beg to differ from those parties. Proud of his eclectic cosmopolitanism, Henry Louis Gates, Jr. (1992), for example, disavows their politics and invokes the ideal of pluralism underpinned by tolerance and mastery of substantial knowledge gained from a liberal education of the kind trumpeted by Cardinal Newman.[3] Immersed in a world "fissured by nationality, ethnicity, race, and gender" ["class" is revealingly omitted], Gates exhorts us "to transcend those divisions . . . through education that seeks to comprehend the diversity of human culture." Urging us to forge a "civic culture that respects both differences and commonalities," Gates puts a high premium on the postmodern virtue of hybridity, Dewey's pluralism, individuality, and so on—all these somehow immune from corruption by the centralized state, mass consumerism, and profit-making. Ironically, while avoiding the traditional "universalistic humanism" of "melting pot" integrationists and "vulgar cultural nationalists" (like Leonard Jeffries), Gates succumbs to the pathos of the eclectic idealist so poignantly described by Frantz Fanon and George Jackson: he wishes that lived contradictions will go away by taking thought, by contemplating a dialogue among equals, by an encyclopedic inventory of differences. Granting that differences are all equal, what grounds this equivalence? Agreement to disagree—the obsession with open-mindedness—becomes a pretext for a sophisticated form of apologizing for the status quo.

Both humanists and social scientists are thus culpable in fostering the pluralist fallacy. The exorbitant focus on ethnicity and its corollary, culture, in discussions of urgent social problems has led to the virtual cancellation of the historical speci-

---

3. It is instructive to contrast Gates' position with Gerald Graff's objection to "pluralistic compromise" (1992, 70). See also Marable (1991) and Wald (1991).

ficities of the lived interaction among groups that constitute any social formation. It has mystified culture and its complex articulation with state power and civil society, the site where the public/private split is reinforced. Where multiculturalism is deployed to occlude the historical specificity of the incorporation of racialized groups into a free-market polity, ethnization results. Everyone is deemed a citizen regardless of cultural properties—provided, of course, that one stays in one's place. In Holland, for example, Philomena Essed observes that the multiculturalist agenda utilizes tolerance (or tokenization) as an instantiation of power by the dominant group to control others: "'Ethnic' minority policy in a 'multicultural' society, 'multicultural' education, 'transcultural' psychology, 'ethnic' social workers, and many more variants and concepts indicate that the dominant group manages cultural difference. Multiculturalism is the application of the norm of tolerance. . . . Therefore, cultural tolerance is inherently a form of cultural control" (1991, 210).

Assuming then that we want to move forward and tackle the problems of racism and ethnocentrism and all their institutional complexities which partisans for and against multiculturalism want to postpone or evade, let us see what the implementation of a theory of a multicultural society entails. It may be assumed that we are all committed to the principle that human beings are entitled to equal treatment regardless of their racial or ethnic category—regardless, indeed, of gender, class, race, ethnicity, and so forth; that members of any ethnic or racial constituency should be protected from derogatory stereotyping and abuse; and that all individuals should have equality of opportunity in attaining the rewards offered by society as presently constituted. Now, for some, the enjoyment of equality of opportunity requires relative or complete absorption into the dominant group, the sacrifice of what is culturally unique to one's group and therefore a denial of the right to be culturally different. Proponents of multiculturalism uphold this fundamental right—but does it guarantee equality of opportunity or access to resources for disenfranchised subalterns? Does it automatically empower the victims of liberal democracy?

Ironies and paradoxes multiply. The sociologist John Rex (1986) points out that the concept of the plural society (as used by Furnivall and others) involves the recognition of cultural difference together with the political and economic exploitation of one group by another. Not only can the right to be culturally different be conceded without allowing for equality of opportunity; cultural difference can even be used as a marker of the boundary between those enjoying legal and political rights and those who are not, leading to *de jure* or *de facto* differential incorporation. Those classified different, even deviant, are marginalized again. Consequently, if we don't address the inequality of power and of control of resources, then cultural pluralism, albeit premised on individualism and democratic freedom, will only reinforce stereotypes, racist theory, and racialist practice.

One outstanding example of multiculturalism in practice is the apartheid system in South Africa, where racist theory and racialist practice insist on the saliency of cultural differences. In this set-up, according to Rex, the various racial groups are "unequal estates differentially incorporated into the state, while the official ideology insists that the groups have their own distinctive culture," the apartheid state itself positively insisting on the recognition of cultural differences (121). This cultural separateness of whites, blacks, colored, and other racial groups is supposed to be divinely ordained. So, ironically, multiculturalism turns out to be a program for apartheid—even worse than the paternalistic slave system in the antebellum U.S. South.

Rex believes that to guarantee equality of opportunity as well as toleration or even encouragement of cultural differences that would characterize a genuine democratic polity, it is necessary to divide life into two spheres: the public and the private domains. Equality of opportunity belongs to the public domain, cultural uniqueness to the private. So in this hypothetical arrangement, every individual would enjoy equal rights before the law, in politics and in the marketplace, as well as equality of social rights provided by a welfare state, while exercising the right to conduct "private" matters (religion, family arrangements, language, culture) according to the custom of a separate ethnic or racial community. From this point of view, the United States represents a society where all groups enjoy equality before the law *de jure* side by side with *de facto* inequality in legal and political rights as well as in economic and social matters, even though this inequality may have been somewhat alleviated by civil rights programs. While the separate cultural institutions of black slaves have been abolished so that now African-Americans "share the culture of White America," Rex reminds us that "a culture of Black consciousness and Black Pride has promoted Black cultural difference."

A theoretical flaw vitiates this inquiry. Because Rex applies a functionalist methodology that tends to rigidly define public and private domains in terms of their contribution to maintaining the status quo, euphemistically labelled "Pattern Maintenance" and "Tension Management," he is unable to grasp in a more processual and integral way the contradictions in the positioning of groups in a society where scarcity (determined by private ownership of social goods, inheritance laws, etc.) spells asymmetry in the access to power and therefore the enjoyment of rights. In short, Rex assumes that the abstract moral and legal systems of the modern state suffice to insure that the old folk culture and kinship-based morality of ethnic/racial minorities function to serve the smooth operations of the system by giving psychological stability to children and performing primary socialization for all members of the family. Or, at best, these residual folkways and mores are kept neutral relative to the normal functioning of the main political, economic, and legal institutions of business society where equality of opportunity formally obtains. Community with its "primordial" sentiments has indeed given way to association, mechanical solidarity centered on kinship to organic solidarity consonant with the changing social division of labor.

V

Whatever the inadequacies of this functionalist approach employed by most scholars dealing with race relations and ethnicity, it is clear that conflicts in the political,
legal, and economic fields cannot be glossed over by postmodern language games
in a hyperreal space. The privileging of identities and cultural difference divorced
from the structural contexts, often referred to as macrostructures of inequality and
injustice, which subtend them may lead to the opposite of what is intended: a
Department of Minority Affairs or special offices are set up to deal with individuals
considered different (by ascription or self-identification) from the dominant group.
This can lead to differential incorporation of groups in plural society, surveillance,
and disciplinary regimes to enforce a specific hegemony. Conflicts between the
private and public domains—in matters relating to sex, marriage, the family, and
religion—cannot be resolved by simply theorizing what is claimed as ad-hoc,
decentered, provisional boundaries (as proposed in Fredrik Barth's influential writings), for such boundaries are subject to the forces of reification and hierarchical
determinations which condition the social practices of everyday life.

All of us share varying degrees of adherence to the ideology or civic morality
of individualism and its corollary ethos of utilitarianism transmitted by the schools,
media, and other state apparatuses. This social code of action, governed by a secular means-end rationality, is grounded in the logic of the exchangeability of values
as formal abstractions mediated through a universal measure of exchange: money.
Mainstream historians have traced the development of the industrialized nation-
state composed of "mutually substitutable atomized individuals" homogenized by
a monopoly culture, by a dominant logic of representation coalescing difference
and identity. While cultural differences have been flattened by bureaucratic
administration and technical instrumentalism, we witness simultaneously the antithetical process of increased ethnization and the valorization of assorted particularisms. Both phenomena are effects of the individualist utilitarianism that still
prevails in contemporary "postindustrial" societies.

One may argue that the possibility of divergent cultures coexisting together
harmoniously depends on all of them accepting a shared civic morality, say, an
ethics of reciprocity and mutual recognition. Rex suggests that "in an ideal multicultural society all cultures come to share a common core which prevents the
derogation of anyone because of his cultural background" (133). This "common
core," however, turns out to be the Western Enlightenment view of tolerance
based on the aforementioned ideology of liberal individualism. It often collides
with some groups' substantive religious beliefs and normative expectations. Can
this shared worldview accord people of color space for their own specific problems
and needs? Or does it simply reinscribe "Others" in a terrain of equally devalued
and marginalized lifestyles? One example of reinscription may be cited here. Frank
Wu (1991), a law student at the University of Michigan, protests that he should not

be given attention simply because he is an Asian-American; he hopes to be heard and listened to as an "individual." And yet his personal testimony was utilized by *The Chronicle of Higher Education* as a specimen of Asian-American opinion. Thus the concept of "individual" is an abstraction which is formally empty and acquires substantive import only when it circulates in the circuit of sociopolitical exchange.

We are faced with this recurrent problem: How can cultural differences be recognized without this recognition becoming an instrument of covert racist theory and racialist practice? The well-meaning advocates of multicultural diversity can become unwitting sponsors/patrons of racism if they endorse the following attitude: "They're different, so therefore they cannot be expected to have the same standards. It would not respect their specific nature, so they should be judged according to their own cultural values and norms." This is actually what British chauvinists and nationalists said in pushing for the repatriation of colored peoples from Britain (Fitzpatrick 1990). That sentiment shows affinity with the rationale of the Bantustans in apartheid South Africa. Articulated within a framework of hegemonic pluralism, a culturalist idealism becomes an apology for *de facto* differential incorporation of racial collectivities into a polity where the hegemonic ideology valorizes differences to guarantee sameness. On the other hand, those who espouse assimilation or integration and who oppose, say, arranged marriages because this contradicts a universal feminist doctrine, begin to distort the historical complexity of "minority" cultures by reducing and immobilizing them to one element and condemning that whole community as backward or even "uncivilized." Ethnicity manifests itself here in the sense of permanent heritable practices of a population of ancestors and descendants. In this case, it is necessary to make distinctions between the clear separation of public and private domains for the dominant group, and the historical fact that family and community for people of color (African-Americans, Latinos, Native Americans, Arab-Americans, and others) serve the goals of popular resistance: physical survival and affirmation of collective freedom and dignity. A pragmatic argument for the functionality of independent ethnic communities can be suggested here: in providing identity options or ideas as to who the individual is, ethnic institutions can also serve as the available social machinery that guarantees the production of the labor force and the smooth maintenance of law and order all around. Hence multiculturalism pays.

At this juncture, I want to rehearse what is ultimately at stake in the controversy surrounding multiculturalism. A binary opposition is one way of formulating it: democracy of equal groups, or the freedom of individual subjects. So far we have examined the issue of whether or not cultural pluralism, a fundamental ideal for a postmodern micropolitics of identity, requires its grounding in a "common core," a civic morality which outlaws inequality based on racist theory and racialist practice. One might speculate also on whether multiculturalism, invested with an original emancipatory charge, truly enacts a rupture of the pluralist myth by historicizing its emergence and linking it with the political economy of knowledge-power in capitalism. Whatever the merits of each case, we might be guided by Charles Taylor's insight that a politics of difference—Gates's pluralism, or "common culture" altruism— simply acquiesces to the status quo unless it has an implied ethico-political criterion of value:

> To come together on a mutual recognition of difference—that is, of the equal value of different identities—requires that we share more than a belief in this principle; we have to share also some standards of value on which the identities concerned check out as equal. There must be some substantive agreement on value, or else the formal principle of equality will be empty and a sham. We can pay lip service to equal recognition, but we won't really share an understanding of equality unless we share something more. Recognizing difference, like self-choosing, requires a horizon of significance, in this case a shared one. (1992, 51–52)

While the movement toward multicultural education originated from radical and progressive forces engaged in civil rights, women's liberation, and social change, its thrust has been blunted by several modifications (Berlowitz 1984). First, emphasis in multicultural education has been placed on a passive approach: the skills for confronting diversity in society are those of empathy, appreciation, tolerance, and smooth adjustment to variegated cultural settings. This may be due to the way culture has been operationally defined as any characteristic that identifies a group of persons: height, wearing glasses, blindness, learning disability, race, religion, sexual preference, ethnic heritage, and so forth. From this point of view, blacks are equivalent to Amish, White Southerners, the blind or visually impaired, and so on. The "high priests" of ethnicity expertise, Nathan Glazer and Daniel P. Moynihan, conceive of different groups as serially situated in "common circumstances"; what makes them unequal is that they "bring different norms to bear on common circumstances with different levels of success; hence group differences in status" (1975, 17). While appearing to ignore structural constraints and historical determinations, this functionalist epistemology actually hides them; it rejects the centrality of racism in U.S. history, the systematic assignment of people to class and status by racial categorizing and racialized politics. It clearly fails to distinguish the fundamental historical reality of the oppression of racial "minorities" in contrast to the Euro-American majority. For the disparities in status to be ascribed to the "success of the group" assumes the "circumstances" of African slaves to be the same as those of Irish and German immigrants. Liberal pluralism fails to comprehend the reality of domination and subordination in the historical continuum from colonialism to imperialism because it assumes that all groups ("interests") have equal ("veto") power, that society is a self-regulating union of competing but negotiable interests, that tolerance and cooperation prevail between capital and labor, and that inequality results from the failure of effort on the part of the disadvantaged to alter their "norms" or remedy their "cultural deficit" in order to move up the social ladder and gain wealth and prestige. Subscribing to this axiom of difference as equality, multiculturalists (whether relativists or communitarians/monopolists) proceed with "business as usual," heedless of the real suffering inflicted by either conservative expediency, the undecidability of the numbers game, or the more terrorizing "aesthetics of the sublime."

So far the most innovative and nuanced inflection of multiculturalism is John Brenkman's (1993) attempt to revive the ideal of civic republicanism or civic humanism as a substitute for the dogma of classic acquisitive individualism. Once tied to property as the enabling condition for freedom and equality among citizens (ideal-types like the medieval freeholder-warrior, or the Greek master of the household, are invoked here), civic humanism needs to be rehabilitated so that citizenship can be articulated intertextually "via several, mutable paths of social relationships and identity." Stressing the truism that "the social bases of American citizens are diverse and multiple," Brenkman repudiates Werner Sollor's semantic grid of consent and descent (elaborated in *Beyond Ethnicity*) as the grammar of the American discourse on ethnicity. I agree with Brenkman's critique of ethnicity theory established by Glazer and Moynihan, a theory founded on the axiom that given common circumstances, diverse ethnic norms produce class and status hierarchies. This hypothesis actually privileges culture (shared values, norms, practices) as the prime causal force for inequality and differential treatment. One cannot flatten in this one-dimensional grid the historical specificities of European immigrants together with African-Americans, Asians, Native Americans, and so on because "group identity responds to the institutional and discursive organization of 'consent,' that is, the prevailing consensus governing the body politic. . . . Individuals in fact participate in the polis as culturally and socially shaped agents, just as they are barred from the polis on the basis of their group belonging" (Brenkman 1993, 99). In short, the liberal synthesis refuses to take into account the complex dynamics of collective subject-positions in U.S. history.

Brenkman focuses on the western metropolis as a dynamic arena of "socially stratified and culturally differentiated practices," "a dynamic space in which citizenship is always being contested." Unless that proposition is just another postmodern aporia, it is best to take it as an expression of a wish, not of a historical fact. Citizenship within late-capitalist political economy is not a trope or discursive field susceptible of infinite permutations; juridical and ethical stratification based on class, race, and gender restricts the citizen's space for maneuvering or bargaining.

My main reservation to this Eurocentric prejudice concerns its potential to generate precisely that tendency Brenkman himself finds repressive, the tendency of triangulating social relations in terms of subject-position defined exclusively by singular categories or traits. Aside from reductively simplifying the problem of the just distribution of social goods as well as that of the pure social determinism ascribed to economistic or materialist critiques, positionality—according to

Brenkman—"misses the crucial difficult and productive tension within every position, namely, that we are always at one and the same time a member of — (or participant in —) *and* a citizen" (100). This repeats the well-known concept of ethnicity as a matter of options, given the permeability and overlapping nature of ethnic boundaries. In my judgment, the flaw of this approach lies in the displacement of the principle of contradiction by the putative freedom of the autonomous citizen and her perpetually shifting choices. Like "common culture" ideologues, Brenkman conflates ethnic self-identification with the abstract juridical taxonomy of citizenship. This error also entails overlooking the exclusion of whole nationalities by racial ascription performed by the ideological/political apparatuses of the dominant political bloc.

I register my final caveat to this updated "civic republicanism" as a heterodox version of the "common culture" revitalization movement. It seems an easy way out to attribute to the formality of citizenship—a notion circumscribed by the *Realpolitik* of the contemporary nation-state—a liberating virtue that would neutralize the danger of ethnic particularism. One also glimpses the hope that citizenship can render harmless the triumphalist strains of anarchist nihilism and retrograde dilettantism in current cultural studies. Can citizenship in an imperial polity really curb the violence of institutional racism directed at "internal colonies" and subjugated client-states? Valorizing a metaphysics of citizenship designed to supersede the narrow ethnic formula, "X is not equal to Y," Brenkman elides the question of hegemonic power grounded in the contradictions in the social relations of production and reproduction.

In general, the crucial problem obfuscated by the project of reinventing a modern civic humanism has to do with the often hidden, highly mediated, complex interaction between the centralized state and civil society, a phenomenon not encountered in pre-capitalist formations. This involves such matters as how to calculate the linkages and negotiate the transactions between the public and private domains, between the cultural (ideological) and the politico-economic spheres, between self-interpreted personal autonomy and the coercive "common culture" of the power elite. This is precisely the moment when we enter a field of warring material forces where ethnicity becomes racialized in the struggle for collective rights and political power.

A genealogy of historical themes and events may help illuminate the relationship between citizenship, race/ethnicity, and community. When the social practices and institutions of the nation-state emerged in the course of the industrial development of Europe from the Renaissance on, what became decisive was not common birth nor the sharing of native land but a specific kind of political organization connected with the market, with the exchange of commodities and the new social division of labor. In the twentieth century, the centralized nation-state cannot be conceived apart from the power of business, of transnational corporations, and the communication-propaganda agencies of civil society connected with them. So when apostles of "common culture," romantic dissidents, humanist artists like Oates, and fundamentalists bewail the disappearance of communal rituals and of "direct and directly responsible relationships" to a perceived common good, according to Raymond Williams, what they are signalling is their refusal of the "center of power" located in the apparatuses of the state and big business, "the display centre of decision and authority" (1989, 112).

Somewhat resembling apologists of "the good old days," Williams as a Welsh nationalist bewails the demise of the sense of mutual obligation and responsibility nourished by the community. But given the irreversible changes in the mode of production and all the other profound mutations in the rhythm of everyday life connected with it, Williams observes that the complexity of modern society has concealed from us certain facts which cannot be immediately grasped by the sensory apprehension of the folk. And one of these central facts is the system of ownership of productive property tied to the operations of the ideological-political machinery of state power. So despite his sympathy for the affirmative organic life of the traditional community which can no longer be restored, Williams (in contrast to Oates) warns us that a politics of community saddles us with the burden of reductions and simplifications to dogmatic complacencies. What is needed is a new articulation of community on a new foundation offering concrete sites of freedom and emancipatory resources for all peoples, not "a merely retrospective nationalist politics" of negations but a "truly prospective politics" of affirmations based on the knowledge of the limits and possibilities of the late-capitalist world system.

I interpret Williams as saying, by implication, that before we can articulate a vision of a new reconstructed society in the United States, we need to question the fiction of America as a habitat or territory possessing a "common culture," a monolithic "national" heritage. It is too easy to say that we should all live together as kind and friendly neighbors, act and think according to a uniform code, criteria, or standard in order to promote the common good. Even the Sunday church sermon today does not insist on conformity to "the American way of life." Now that the myth of the "melting pot" (updated to "salad bowl") has gone the way of such slogans as the "Manifest Destiny" of the Anglo-Saxon race so popular in the time after the Civil War up to the Spanish-American War and World War I, and almost everyone takes for granted the fact of multiple "races" and nationalities (Native Americans are made up not of tribes but of nations recognized legally by treaties and Supreme Court pronouncements) comprising the citizenry, the discourse of American community and its collective purpose/mission need to be thoroughly recast on new enlarged, popular-democratic foundations. Without the mediations needed to think our way through to a new conception of a culturally diverse polity, we shall shortcircuit our minds and arrive at a drastically foreshortened and foreclosed view of how the inequalities of race, class, and gender should be remedied. By "mediations" I am referring to the concrete historical experiences of people of color, their specific modes of incorporation into the polity, and their struggles to survive as distinct peoples and maintain their singular identities while resisting the violence of colonialism and racism. Community is no substitute for this complex, multilayered historical motion—a drama staging the contradictions of ideals and antagonisms of material interests—in which the various narratives of self-determination of people of color are unfolded. I submit that the telling of this narrative, the strategic positioning of its tellers and its audience in the process of communicative action, must be one of the prime objectives of an evolving program of popular-democratic multicultural education in our institutions of higher learning.

Since community and "common culture" have exhausted their usefulness in exploring the ambiguities of multiculturalism, can the idea of positionality (enunciated by Brenkman and Gates) in which identity can be constructed or chosen at will serve as a viable point of departure? The old categorical standpoints of class and race have been found wanting. But like the theory of shifting ethnic boundaries propounded by Barth and others, this postmodern stance is, I think, premised on an evasion. The evasion concerns the refusal to distinguish social exchange based on reciprocity and that based on complementarity. One is incompatible with the other. The distinction is of crucial importance in clarifying the relation of differentiated positions: reciprocity obtains in occasions where "giving and receiving are *mutually contingent* . . . [and] *each* party has rights *and* duties," whereas this mutuality is lacking in relations based solely upon complementarity (such as that between master and slave, or employer and worker) so that "one's rights are another's obligations, and vice versa" (Paine 1974, 9). There is also the assumption that "power differences are initial to the establishment of a fair norm of exchange, but once this norm is laid down, transactions made in conformity with it are conceived as reciprocal." In many commentaries on the Los Angeles explosion voiced by protagonists from every group and sector, one finds this positionality dramatized in the theme of the complementarity of differences (between Korean merchants and African-American consumers, for example). I should stress that in such cases of interethnic relationships, reciprocity is absent where commodity-fetishism and the ideals of "possessive individualism" (with its resonance in the work-ethic and success by personal effort) predominate. Not so long ago, William J. Wilson reaffirmed what previous studies and succeeding ones have confirmed: interethnic relations are largely influenced by group competition in the labor marketplace (Connor 1980), not the imperatives of self-centered rational choices. Such findings, however, have usually been dismissed by mainstream academics as "reductionist" even though we find the testimonies in Studs Terkel's recent survey, *Race*, all gravitating around the labor process (both manual and intellectual) and the scarcity of resources and opportunities in a milieu that some have characterized as thoroughly infected by a variant of pluralist thinking called neo–Social Darwinism.

Given the apologetic thrust of current research in ethnic relations, I urge that we focus our attention on contradictions, not on consensus, the ensemble of economic and political contradictions that underlie the racializing process in society. Because the ethnicity paradigm highlights mainly the value of group identity as functional to system integration and stabilization of consensus, academic inquiries into racism and racial conflicts tend to stress the cultural (sometimes conceived in the most anecdotal and pragmatic sense) dimensions of intergroup relations (orientations, values, goals of actors) and thus place the burden of their plight on the victims themselves. Phenomenology and assorted empiricisms may seek to foreground subjectivity but at the expense of giving functionalist positivism a blank check to underwrite everything else, including policy decisions of bureaucrats and state functionaries.

While such studies might claim to combat ethnocentrism and racialist bias, their view that ethnicity (the group's self-representation) depends on ascription from both sides of the group boundary in question results in making all parties equally complicit in identity formation and its consequences. Moreover, they occlude the matter of group categorization arising from the play of class antagonisms which are usually sublimated into racial/ethnic hostilities. This is the reason why we almost never hear of police terror or state coercion, in spite of the claim to sensitive appraisal of agency and consciousness, amid the plethora of statistics about jobs, occurrences of discrimination, illegal immigrants, and so forth.

Another example illustrates the danger of a purely culturalist/ethnicist approach. When the doxa of Asian Americans as a "model minority" is imposed by the media and neoconservative bureaucrats to establish the groundwork for gutting affirmative action, curtailing social services, and justifying "de-industrialization," aside from upholding an invidious model to instigate ethnic rivalries, then we are confronted with a process of group categorization as a part of a divide-and-rule hegemonic strategy. The implication is that African Americans and Latinos should forsake government assistance and conform to this putative ideal of individual success; we hear the familiar message that "the problem lies in the nature of these people," it has nothing to do with socioeconomic policies and programs that guarantee the normal operation of the free market and reinforce the consensus. (This consensus is aptly encapsulated in President Reagan's praise of democracy as a system where anyone can become rich.) And so the phenomenon of interethnic behavior as transactional and situationally defined needs to be inscribed in the historical dynamics of a socio-economic formation where racial politics is central to its normal routine and continuing reproduction (Miles 1989). In this contextualization far removed from the "free play" of simulations and their self-referential dialogue, we begin to understand how status, privilege, and asymmetrical distribution of power mediated through "race" as a synecdoche of class are subject to permanent political contestation. Here the state, the changing modalities of late-capitalist production and exchange, and mass political mobilization at various historical conjunctures are the major topics to be addressed in research.

Thus I would concur with critics of this mode of ethnic absolutism by proposing that we engage instead with the inescapable centrality of power relationships grounded in the history of conflicts over property (control of the means of production) and political representation when we analyze the interaction of identity groups in specific circumstances. Provided we do not succumb to a fashionable mystique of power as the absolute key to everything, Michel Foucault's questions may safeguard us from the seduction of the Multicultural Imaginary: "How are we constituted as subjects of our own knowledge? How are we constituted as subjects who exercise or submit to power relations? How are we constituted as moral subjects of our own actions?" (1992, 107)

VI

At this juncture, I would like to pursue a research agenda proposed by Fredric Jameson (1993) in the context of assessing the current status of "Cultural Studies" in the United States. He recommends that a dialectical approach to this still amorphous field of inquiry can begin by positing groups ("imaginary" totalities) and their complex relations as the primary analytic object of study. In theorizing culture as the "object" of investigation, it is necessary to articulate its position in the totality of its determinations. In other words, we need to chart the "problematic" (as Althusser once counseled) of this inquiry. Since culture is the vehicle or medium whereby the relationship between groups is transacted, we are led to reflect on how we should read the allegorical "dream-work" and logic of collective or group fantasies. "Common culture," one such fantasy or "thought of others," cannot be understood without a rigorous analysis of what and how it excludes and includes in specific historical milieus.

Like the apologias for the Establishment consensus I surveyed earlier, the desire or nostalgia called "common culture" attended by metaphors of natural blending and weaving reveals its constructed, artificial status when the "nation" is invoked. Recent inquiries into the formation of modern nation-states have shown that a nation is not just a political entity but also a symbolic community, a system of cultural representation, that enables its citizens to acquire a sense of identity and loyalty. Hence a national culture is a complex of discourses and symbolic practices that construct identities for individuals who participate in, and identifies with, the meanings of the nation produced by those discourses and practices.

Since race and class have become sublimated into the symbolic economy of national culture, we need to examine its synchronic and diachronic disposition. Stuart Hall (1992) outlines five main elements in the narrative of the national culture: (1) the narrative of events, scenarios, and landscapes which represent the shared experiences that give significance to ordinary lives; (2) the emphasis on primordial origins, continuity, and destiny; (3) the invention of tradition through rituals and public ceremonies; (4) the narrative of national culture as foundational myth; and (5) the grounding of national identity on the idea of a pure, original people or folk, such as the Puritans in the New England colonies, or the pioneers in the Western frontier.

Given the concept of the nation as an "imagined" or fabricated community that unifies and cancels/subsumes differences in a libidinal "constellation" of figures or Imaginary, we can now infer that underlying the labor of bonding and unifying is a "structure of cultural power." Behind the unity of modern nations lies a process of violent conquest, a suppression of diverse peoples with their own customs, languages, and traditions climaxed by an imposition of the conqueror's will and way of life. Alexander Saxton has pithily encapsulated this process in U.S. history:

> Already in the days of Jefferson and the "sainted Jackson" (to use Walt Whitman's phrase) the nation had assumed the form of a racially exclusive democracy—democratic in the sense that it sought to provide equal opportunities for the pursuit of happiness by its white citizens through the enslavement of Afro-Americans, extermination of Indians, and territorial expansion largely at the expense of Mexicans and Indians. (1972, 145)

In order to unify the various social classes, nationalities, and ethnic constituencies, U.S. nationalism provides alternative points of identification such as the definition of the American character as tolerant, open to diverse influence, both universalist and particularistic—all virtues of members of one family.

Via metaphoric and metonymic exfoliations, the theme of one national culture generates a kind of community that is not just instrumental or sentimental but also constitutive in the sense defined by Michael Sandel: "For [the subjects distinguished by rights], community describes not just what they *have* as fellow citizens but also what they are, not a relationship they choose (as in voluntary association) but an attachment they discover, not merely an attribute but a constituent of their identity" (1982, 150). Given the historical record, it is more accurate to think of a shared culture not as an organically unified creation but "a discursive device which represents difference as unity or identity." This is precisely what we perceive in the arguments of those anxious to project or affirm a "common culture." In thrall to an absorbing mythical identity, operating through the exercise of different forms of hegemonic power—what Sacvan Bercovitch calls "rites of assent"—they are made to speak the same language, one which harmonizes with that of the literary canon, mass media publicity, and various ideological apparatuses. This language or rhetoric of belonging is capacious enough to accommodate those resistant or deviant voices—unless they refuse the terms and rules of incorporation.

What is happening today is that an official discourse has almost succeeded in substituting the idiom of culture for the now fallacious lexicon of race as a symbolic marker of difference, positing the claim that the nation (conflated with the state) is a unified cultural entity that can weather the turbulence of political-economic crisis and the decline of its superpower ascendancy. Hence amid the current dislocations and rapid time-space compression in the political economy of transnational business, we see how the idea of a common culture—Schlesinger's theme of "the unified, democratic culture that has always been the American ideal"—only discloses the play of power behind it, together with the internal contradictions and crosscutting allegiances that presuppose it and are reproduced whenever the imperative of "national security" or "national interest" is invoked.

One example of how this play of power, the syncopation of difference into unity, can be exhibited for criticism has been offered by Toni Morrison. In her perceptive essay "Black Matter(s)," she elaborates on the topos of intertextuality, more precisely the psychic economy of the white imagination, in the foundational texts:

> I have begun to wonder whether the major, much celebrated themes of American literature—individualism, masculinity, the conflict between social engagement and historical isolation, an acute and ambiguous moral problematics, the juxtaposition of innocence with figures representing death and hell—are not in fact responses to a dark, abiding, signing Africanistic presence. . . . The literature of the United States, like its history, illustrates and represents the transformations of biological, ideological, and metaphysical concepts of racial differences. (1993, 256, 268)

This insight into the overdetermined "thickness" of American canonical literature exposes the process of how certain discursive principles—the perennial themes Morrison cites—operate to construct an unstable but reconciling artifact equivalent to the national ethos, national sensibility or character. An act of historicized deciphering is required to grasp the contradictions hidden, suppressed, or displaced in the symbolic icons of "the common culture." Especially today, when the hegemonic consensus in mediatized/commodified images has nearly colonized all spaces (including sexuality and the unconscious) under the aegis of the Simulacrum, the logic of Spectacle, the question of the democratic control of mass culture—its production, distribution, and consumption networks—deserves priority in the strategy of transformative critique.

Differences and tensions persist, allowed within the authorized framework of liberal institutions. What common-culture texts inculcate via schooling, family, and other mediations is a reconciling synthesis of competing interests, values, beliefs, and practices; a compromise sanctioning the authority of a ruling power bloc. What they provide is a sense of absolute experienced reality, not ideology in the orthodox sense but a hegemony or a "structure of feeling" that embodies "the lived dominance and subordination of particular classes." Raymond Williams defines this concept of hegemony (borrowed from Gramsci) thus: "It is the whole body of practices and expectations, over the whole of living: our senses and assignments of energy, our shaping perceptions of ourselves and our world. It is a lived system of meanings and values—constitutive and constituting—which as they are experienced as practices appear as reciprocally confirming" (1977, 110). This perspective of "the lived dominance and subordination of particular classes" explains why the fetishism of normative plurality or the seriality of autonomous instances or occasions, as advocated by such persuasive intellectuals as Gates and Brenkman, tends to contradict their avowed motive of privileging difference and multiplicity of subject-positions. Pluralism excludes by occlusion. The notion of compatibility of classes, genders, and nationalities in a more or less integrated national culture distinguished by selected key signifiers—"tolerance," "openness," and other honorific ascriptions—elides the institutional differentiation of interests and thus the question of what bloc of classes or groups exercise politico-economic control and exerts authority (consensus plus coercion). Because the axiom of "common culture" rejects the notion of hegemony, which implies a structural relation between dominant and subordinate groups, it makes impossible the asking of questions on the construction and maintenance of inequality and injustice. While I have reservations about Brenkman's attempt to revitalize the notion of civic humanism without any radical change in property relations, I think his critique of Sollors' assimilationist paradigm is salutary. His view that "literary forms, like all cultural practices, are embedded or situated in collective histories" counters the formalist and empiricist orthodoxy. It also interrogates the relativism of the "gender-race-class grid" of reflexive positionality, the laissez-faire economy of current interdisciplinary studies. It addresses the more complex dialectics of our relation to others—the scenario for enacting mass loathing and envy—explored by Bakhtin, Levinas, Cixous, by ethnologists and ecological thinkers.

One way to begin doing conventional cultural studies is to interrogate the fallacies of pluralism and its "common-culture" syndrome. Because of the fact that any society is made possible or enabled by a hegemonic process, it is appropriate to address the play of power/knowledge underlying group relations. In its genesis within the academy, cultural studies shaped an agenda for analyzing the function of discourse, texts, sexuality, and media in constituting identity. Cultural studies practitioners have focused on studying the play of power in the modes of representation and interpellation of individuals into subjects. They have conducted historical and archaeological inquiries into the ensemble of normative beliefs and practices that serve as "biotechnologies of control," the repertoire of disciplinary techniques constraining social behavior through sanctions and rewards, and so on. By eluci-dating this system of "constraint and mobility" that legitimizes differential power relations, cultural studies—in its "new historicist" version—carries out the project of demystification, of deconstructing the claims to legitimacy. One practitioner has formulated the worldly vocation of cultural criticism, its project of intervention in the political/theoretical scene, as that of listening to "the accents of Caliban." I would like to enact some implications of these somewhat commonplace ideas with a gloss on a short story by Leslie Marmon Silko (1981).

Now found in anthologies advertising a multiculturalist innovation, "Yellow Woman" is sometimes utilized to illustrate the anthropological fact about the matrilineal nature of Pueblo culture to which Silko belongs. We are told that the author is genetically multicultural (part Laguna Pueblo, part Mexican, part Anglo) and that she grew up in a reservation in the shadow of Mount Taylor in New Mexico, the legendary home of the *ka'tsina* spirits inhabiting Pueblo and Hopi mythology. The ancestral *ka'tsina* spirit who brings rain is incarnated here by a stranger named Silva whom the narrator encounters near her home. Erotically attracted to this stranger, she appears to have been seduced by his claim that he is a spirit from the mountain come to look for his mythical "yellow woman." Because of a tension between narrator and focalizer, one can detect an ambiguity as to whether the myth itself has completely possessed her. While captivated by the body and its libidinal rhythm—the sensuous imagery and tempo of the story's beginning provoke this thought—the narrator bifurcates into two personae that hover in the zone between myth and reality: "I was afraid lying there on the red blanket. All I could know was the way he felt, warm, damp, his body beside me. This is the way it happens in the stories, I was thinking, with no thought beyond the moment she meets the ka'tsina spirit and they go." She believes that when she meets another person, "then I will be certain that he [the stranger] is only a man—some man from nearby—and I will be sure that I am not Yellow Woman. Because she is from out of time past and I live now." Discriminating between narrative voice and focalizer, we are ushered into a geopolitical space of encounter with the Other: the imperial white male policing property.

Eventually, this space materializes. On the way to Marquez where the Mexicans live in order to sell Silva's stolen meat, a Texan white man with "young fat face" crosses their path. He identifies and accuses the woman's lover: "The hell you have, Indian. You've been rustling cattle. We've been looking for the thief for a long time." Employing the vernacular, the Indian "thief" tells her to go back up the mountain; she retreats, and we watch this spectacle of "mobility and con-straint":

> The white man got angry when he heard Silva speak in a language he couldn't understand. "Don't try anything, Indian. Just keep riding to Marquez. We'll call the state police from there."
>
> The rancher must have been unarmed because he was very frightened and if he had a gun he would have pulled it out then. I turned my horse around and the rancher yelled, "Stop!" I looked at Silva for an instant and there was something ancient and dark—something I could feel in my stomach—in his eyes, and when I glanced at his hand I saw his finger on the trigger of the .30-.30 that was still in the saddle scabbard. I slapped my horse across the flank and the sacks of raw meat swung against my knees as the horse leaped up the trail. It was hard to keep my balance, and once I thought I felt the saddle slipping backward; it was because of this that I could not look back. (61)

A parodic staging of phallocentrism may be glimpsed here. The "Yellow Woman" refuses the white man's interpellation and thereby thwarts the violence of property and Western secularism when she maintains her performative, mythical identity.

Later she hears four shots, "four hollow explosions that reminded me of deer hunting," but she proceeds downhill until she reaches the plain, sends the horses back, and returns to the "fallen" world of domestic routine, whereupon "I decided to tell them [husband and grandmother] that some Navajo had kidnaped me, but I was sorry that old Grandpa wasn't alive to hear my story because it was the Yellow Woman stories he liked to tell best." Here the protagonist assumes the grandfather's vocation of storyteller and thus fulfills the lover's prediction: "someday they will talk about us, and they will say, 'Those two lived long ago when things like that happened.'" Myth and reality coincide at the scene where violence occurs, evoking the past history of Indian anticolonial resistance and its continuing reinscription in the present.

With these remarks I may have committed the error of contriving another interpretation—something to be avoided in favor of theorizing the "problematic" that explains the gaps and disparities in the text, in particular what is ultimately unrepresentable because it eludes the laws of expressive-realist representation. A cultural-historicist analysis would demonstrate the production of this narrative form, both *testimonio* and allegory, by unfolding the conditions of its possibility: the displacement of Native Americans from their ancestral habitat; the residual practice of hunting as a mode of survival as well as a confirmation of male prowess; the trajectory of past wars between Anglos and Indians; the active role of women in the economy; the territorial aggrandizement of cattle-ranchers; the affinities between Indians and Mexicans in their subordinate status; and so on. All these would be enlightening in determining the raw materials—a "structure of feeling" invested in practices—of the narrative and the way they are processed and resolved by a self-reflexive, exorbitant narrator who combines the functions of witness (history) and participant (agency).

We as readers positioned by our own specific circumstances would have to attend to the operations of a mode of discourse which coincides and diverges at the same time from the prevailing convention. Readers have to make up their minds whether the woman's decision (her desire to leave the stranger was indicated twice earlier) expresses her independence, her conviction born of her attachment to the present order that it would be safer to abandon the realm of fantasy (which, revealingly, absorbs the violence of the Indian-white relation), or simply her desire to affirm the imperative priority of group survival. Earlier, of course, she didn't care about her family—"There are enough of them to handle things"—and only entertained the thought that her life would be the matrix of narrative: "they will go on like before, except that there will be a story about the day I disappeared while I was walking along the river." The narrative then stages the trope of disappearance and return, the disruption of routine and its continuation, this time haunted by the replay of memory, with the myth (or its dreamer) unable to submerge in its aura the violence of historical reality nor wish it away completely. Such a deconstructive turn in the analysis would of course stress the emancipatory value of tradition, its reconciling and healing property, its function as vehicle of release for social energies otherwise suppressed and as a means of activating the "traces" of what official history has erased. But this thematization of a rhetorical strategy, plus the threat of a transcoding closure, would only monumentalize this text and consign it to the realm of undecidability and commodity aesthetics.

VII

An alternative is possible. We can try, in an experimental mode, to deploy the method of metacommentary (symptomatic reading invested with a utopian or prophetic desire) so as to move beyond textuality as such and conduct a crossreferencing of the events in the story and their anchorage in historical contingency. In this allegorical reading, we articulate a double hermeneutic of demystification and the release of what's repressed. Here I can only sketch what needs to be done to initiate a geopolitical, historically situated reading that would give attention to the sequence of events recounted as well as to the structures underlying them, both to the circulation of "social energies" and their condensation in the ideology of the figuration itself.

Associated with the myth of the *ka'tsina* are three levels of allusion or subtexts: first, the settled agricultural mode of production of the Pueblo Indians which has something to do with the rhythm of loss and recovery; second, intersecting that is the Navajo practice of trade and social exchange involving Mexicans; and, third, the commercial society of the Anglo/Texan ranchers and its reification in a property system that exercises dominance over state and civil society. One sees at the end, from the woman's perception, how violence underlies the legitimacy of the system and how property (animal meat) becomes a metaphor for sexual power and claims to hegemony. Apart from the erotic pleasure connected with the body and its syncopation with images of the river, mountain, and undulating terrain, the evocation of the rain-bearing spirit and his consort performs that utopian gesture of negating the bourgeois individual subject—the solitary consciousness dividing time into past, present, and future—in favor of a community, a non-anthropomorphic ecosystem, which subtends the occasion of textual rendering. To rewrite this narrative as an allegory of affirming Indian resilience or their cosmology is also to suggest that such valorization is made at the expense of ignoring the creative resources of the narrator-protagonist, those heterogeneous impulses that comprise the inassimilable "otherness" we sense in this "I" who inserts herself into an interminable series of tales that now wrestle with a history that keeps repeating itself and dissolving the boundaries of fantasy and worldliness. This may be the moment of the "political unconscious" mediated by the myth where the profane and the sacramental, ideology and utopia, interpenetrate.

Contrary to Paul de Man's injunction that we defer this hermeneutic move to aestheticize the text by focusing first on the modalities whereby meaning is produced, I have followed the protocol of a geopolitical, world-cultural approach. My remarks have translated Silko's narrative to make it intelligible from one critical stance. In this process, has the text been unduly prejudged in advance? I suspect that Native Americans will say yes, I have committed the sin of colonizing Silko's text by imposing a Eurocentric paradigm of interpretation. Framed within the debate on multiculturalism which is the pretext for this exercise, I believe the deconstructive mode of valuing ironic self-referentiality above all, and the historicist mode of genealogical decipherment of the will to truth as a mask of the play of power, are both incommensurable to the project of establishing the premises for a genuinely multiculturalist or geopolitical approach. We certainly need to respect the singularity of the Pueblo Indian voice even though we, in our naive complicities, also sense the pressures of the exterior in it, its self-difference and infinite potential.

In their description of "cultural criticism," Gerald Graff and Bruce Robbins (1992) propose a concept of culture as contested space, cultures as "indeterminate sites of conflict" devoid of "a single totalized meaning" and open to challenge and contestation. They reject any totalizing or universal notion of Culture (in the Arnoldian or rational-encyclopedist sense) and particularisms that are also essentializing; however, their view that the aim of cultural studies is "to bring together, in a common democratic space of discussion, diversities that had remained unequal largely because they had remained apart" not only begs the question, but also conforms to the orthodox liberal stance on "questions of cultural identity and political strategy," inveterately compartmentalizing the discourse of inquiry from that of ethical responsibility. If cultural studies simply wants to demonstrate "hospitable inclusiveness" for low, uncanonical objects and performances, and so practice the politics of addition, then we have not learned the hard lesson of hegemony.

Our text is an event, not just a structure with a formal architectonic. This is the lesson of what I would call "world cultural studies": the embeddedness of the cultural text in the intertextual field across national boundaries, in a network of affiliations, in a configuration of complicitous discursive formations that migrate or travel around the planet. That is also the lesson of hegemony. What my sketchy gloss on "Yellow Woman" touched on is the way the power of tradition, the mythical or sacramental bond of community, enables the narrator to find meaning in what happened to her and also assert her own identity within that community, and the community's solidarity against imperial authority. This, on the surface, is what the author seeks to communicate, the Pueblo woman's refusal of the claims of "common culture," when she says: "The kinds of things that cause white upper-middle-class women to flee the home for a while to escape or get away from domination and powerlessness and inferior status, vis-à-vis the husband . . . they are not operating at all" (Silko 1986). We have a difference acknowledged here to which others are strangers. But in this process, has this difference become essentializing? In other words, has the Pueblo Indian woman acquired a substantive essence grounded in a unique experience specific to the group?

Arnold Krupat observes how Silko's articulation of *historia* and *poeisis*, mimetic transcription and symbolic expression, is a fashioning of identity in a collective vocation where role, self, and person are joined. The narrator-protagonist of our story thus participates in a collective affirmation of community, as Silko herself testifies: "Traditionally everyone, from the youngest child to the oldest person, was expected to listen and to be able to recall or tell a portion, if only a small detail, from a narrative account of story. Thus the remembering and retelling were a communal process" (Krupat 1989, 163). To quote the words of a Pueblo priest: "Time was, and is, and always will be. It flows like a river; it does not stand still like lakes. That is what we Indians know, and you have never learned" (Marriot and Rachlin 1969, 49).

Still, for most readers, history intrudes as a limit of this timeless or transcendent happening. For this communal process cannot be divorced from its conflicted relations with an outside *fabula*—the Enlightenment episteme or will to truth/power—whose presence inside, in the fold of the *shuzjet*, occasions the "Yellow Woman's" retreat from the scene of violence. Readers operating with another criteria may find the woman's return to the domestic sphere a betrayal of her capacity for *jouissance* and infringed on by her role as "Yellow Woman," a submission to patriarchal power as figured in grandfather and husband who replicate Silva's aggressive position. These readers of course mobilize a countermemory opposed to the mythical and thus identify with the protagonist's active self, or agency. This identification, however, is a fiction-effect undermined by a narrative closure that is a symptom itself of an attempt to heal the predicament of the sub-ject's fragmentation. The internal discontinuity foregrounded here is one way to elucidate the ideology of the text, its mode of ideological production.

In such a feminist reading, the text has already been inserted into history, a particular reading of the social-historical text, if you like. We may invoke for this purpose Helene Cixous' concept of writing, elaborated in "The Laugh of the Medusa," as "precisely *the very possibility of change*, the space that can serve as a springboard for subversive thought, the precursory movement of a transformation of social and cultural structures" (1989, 736). Silko is then conceived as a writer who works in the space of the in-between, the locus of the other, the dynamized and incessant process of exchange between the Same and the Other. Our narrative is not a closed, self-contained whole bounded by its beginning and end. It is part of a larger historical Imaginary.

A world-cultural-studies approach would remind all readers that the story is an episode in a larger narrative of events in the history of the struggle of Native Americans and indigenous or aboriginal peoples everywhere for survival and col-lective self-determination. Here the most eloquent witness is Michel de Certeau whose linkage of body, land, place, and resistance expresses in a profoundly urgent way what is at stake:

This history of resistance punctuated by cruel repression is *marked on the Indian's body* as much as it is recorded in transmitted accounts—or more so. This inscribing of an identity built upon pain is the equivalent of the indelible *markings* the torture of the initiation ceremony carves into the flesh of the young. In this sense, "the body is memory." It carries, in written form, the law of equality and rebelliousness that not only orga-nizes the group's relation to itself, but also its relation to the occupiers. Among the Indian ethnic groups of "Latin" America (there are about 200), this *tortured* body and another body, the *altered earth*, represent a beginning, a rebirth of the will to *construct* a *political* association. A unity born of hardship and resistance to hardship is the historical locus, the collective memory of the social body, where a will that neither confirms nor denies this writing of history originates. It deciphers the scars on the body proper—or the fallen "heroes" and "martyrs" who correspond to them in narrative—as the index of a *history* yet to be made. "Today, at the hour of our awakening, we must be our own historians." . . . [The land] was, and is, a kind of palimpsest: the gringos' writing does not erase the primary text, which remains traced there—illegible to the passersby who have manipulated the areas for four centuries—as a silent sacrament of "maternal forces," the forefathers' tomb, the indelible seal joining the members of the community together in contractual agreement. (1986, 227, 229)

Not only is our story a kind of performance of the "sacrament of maternal forces," but it is also more contingently an episode in Silko's life which includes her novel *Ceremony*, other stories in the collection *Storyteller*, and recently the epic master-piece, *Almanac of the Dead*. Silko's author-function is much more complex than I can deal with here, involving as it does the whole political-sexual subjugation of Native Americans and the internal contradictions entailed by their situation. The text is not undecidable but simply fitfully writable unless read against multilayered totalities articulated within itself. World cultural studies calls our attention to such totalities where questions of cultural identity and political power have forced us not only "to rethink the social biases and absences within the established literature programs" (Bathrick 1992, 328), but also, in Meaghan Morris's phrasing, to think "the relations between local, regional, national, and international frames of action and experience (using these terms in a sense that must be based in a politics of gen-der, race, and class)" (1992, 470). In the present U.S. conjuncture, this rethinking involves us in doing our work within the constraints of existing disciplines such as ethnic and "postcolonial" studies, feminist theory with its necessary foundational critiques of essentialism and universalism, and the study of popular/mass culture whose power of representation as it organizes public fantasy may be the decisive key to hegemony.

We also have to move outside those established disciplines and their national parochialisms (particularly British and American) if the ideal of serving as an "organic intellectual" for a popular-democratic movement is to be pursued, assuming that for us cognition is also an act or agency with effects in everyday life. Suffice it to round up these comments by recalling again the issue of a "common culture" versus, for example, the genealogist's ideal of heterogeneity and shifting, flexible subject-positions. Cultural studies is an emerging style of discourse and research program that would cross traditional boundaries and address itself to the presuppositions, nuances, and implications of this debate. In this research program, the old formalist and also recent deconstructive engagement with "literariness" acquires its valence in the contexts of specific participants and locations. In other words, as everyone has found out even without reading Roman Jakobson or his Russian-Formalist colleagues, "literariness" is more than a literary or even purely cultural question; in the present realignment of priorities, it is a world cultural issue.

In contrast to the traditional routine of literary research, the performance of geopolitical cultural critique is necessarily destabilizing. It problematizes the bor-ders of textuality where power lurks, the constitution of disciplines as well as atten-dant frames of reference and legitimation. It remaps the field of learning where knowledge is produced and organized in its questioning of institutional paradigms, epistemological models, and methodologies of representation. As Bakhtin has taught us, every verbal discourse is the scenario of events where ideological-social value judgments interact. In the same context, Bakhtin also suggested the idea that cultures may speak to but not for; you cannot fully translate and appropriate the word of the Other. Essentialism is ruled out because identity is always a dialectic of self and other, a question of conflicted and conflicting representations. In other words, the problem of cultural identity and representation cannot be separated from that of political-ideological struggle for hegemony, given the premise that the subject can be grasped only in the positionality of language and knowledge, in the articulation of discourses and practices, from which culture in its global resonance and affiliations can be properly theorized (Hall 1994).

In this period of geopolitical realignment, where the nature of the late-capitalist world system is undergoing rapid restructuring, we cannot sum up except in a provisional way. In a hegemonic process which is practically where we are always already situated, the identity and experience of others (outside and inside) become untranslatable. Or if translated, only in a way that mirrors the translator's own beliefs, norms, and judgments. Faced with strangers, we are liable to estrange ourselves; the bourgeois notion of individuality or self-identity is always the problem, hence the difficulties of reader-response neopragmatism. In the case of "Yellow Woman," can we really appropriate this text without somehow violating its integrity? What is it that I must be responsible for in interpreting this text? Is the narrator addressing me as sympathetic audience, or as an indifferent, even hostile spectator? Who is addressing whom? Is my allegorical reading a practice of epistemic violence in reducing the alterity of the woman's sensuous life to abstract concepts? Are we making fallacious fact-value inferences when we take the narrator's voice as authoritative over the experiencing protagonist? Who is that Other who makes a positive ethical demand? What register of ethical imperatives is involved when we identify that other with the alterity we discover in ourselves—an alterity that has been sacrificed by the Stanford student I quoted earlier, whose response is symptomatic of a larger dilemma in the milieu of the "common culture": "Who gives a damn about those things? I want to study myself." Indeed, only after the cacophony of multiple voices can the "self" emerge in the grand misrecognition that inaugurates what Lacan calls the adventure of paranoid subjects lost in a profound Manichean delirium. On the other hand, can the schizoid postmodern reader prove adequate in fulfilling this responsibility to the Other dissolved in the myth of community, given the regnant utilitarian ethos and its recent inflection in a neo–Social Darwinism? Or should we sustain the dialogic imagination in envisaging this scenario of encounters and confrontations without a myth such as the one privileged in Silko's story? Meanwhile Saul Bellow, proponent of and spokesman for the "common culture," can wait for the advent of the Zulu Tolstoy in some possible world where such an idea encounters the impossibility of multiculturalism, a limit-point where the Zulus will have the opportunity to judge both Bellow and Tolstoy on native ground.

In the antinomies of the "New World Order" and its disorders, we are witnessing the combined and uneven development of both the nation-state's technocratic homogenizing drive as well as an accelerated repluralization of the industrial states. It is customary to cite (for the United States) the influx of enormous numbers of Mexican migrants, legal and illegal, as well as other groups (from Indo-Chinese to Central American refugees, and now East Europeans). I think the view that an industrial nation-state requires from its citizens cultural homogeneity—everyone should conform to what people in television advertisements do, or toe the line in those rituals beloved by Oates and George Will—only helps to legitimize the hegemony of an elite minority. Culture is complicit with power and production. This is what the anthropologist Sally Falk Moore implies in her provocative essay, "The Production of Cultural Pluralism as a Process," where she demonstrates the embeddedness of cultural practices in the complex totality of a social order: "Pluralism is the *juxtaposition-in-the-world* of group cultural differences. The most important large-scale issues regarding pluralism are less about cultural content than about when and why something is *made of* cultural difference in circumstances of juxtaposition. What matters in the analysis of pluralism is not just cultural difference, but the larger system of political and economic differences into which any particular cultural difference is fitted and given consequences (1989, 37). Likewise, M.G. Smith emphasizes the point I have stated earlier that "the decisive conditions of pluralism are political and relate directly to the conditions of collective incorporation in the public domain" (1986, 195). The issue then is whether or not culturally distinct collectivities (ethnic groups) within the boundaries of a nation-state have equal access to resources and to political representation; whether or not ethnicity and race are bracketed/cancelled so that individuals alone are "equally" incorporated into a state, a power-structure which in most cases represents the hegemonic dispensation or "common culture" of the ruling bloc.

It is never too late or redundant to stress once again the distinction between two ways or paradigms of conceptualizing culture: culture as a coherent and interconnected system possessing an essence which needs to be preserved because it sustains the life of the group or community, and culture as an accidental historical product, an aggregate of separable parts. If culture is seen as a historically constructed assemblage of separable parts, then rearrangements and recompositions become occasions or stages of an inevitable and continuous process which does not destroy the integrity of the whole assemblage. "Integrity" and closure are of course debatable terms whose significations have to be investigated. Here we are addressing questions of change and continuity, whether common values are generated through social transactions (a generative model of social change through negotiation and compromise) or different cultures persist despite transactions across ethnic boundaries (culture as difference and complementarity). Is there a permanent cultural *habitus* or pattern constituting the American "national" identity? Is there a need for consensus of beliefs or shared value commitments on which to inaugurate the beginning of a genuine popular democracy? Do differences of values, symbols or practices in any setting constitute "cultural differences" that matter?

We know that the dominant culture in any society, its differential appropriation and distribution of rewards and penalties, can be used as cultural capital, an instrument of domination. A factory worker and a corporate executive can both listen to Mozart and Madonna and enjoy them, but what does that fact signify? Equality? The political meaning of cultural difference can rarely be found in the content of those differences but in how the bearers of cultural knowledge, their identities locked in conflict or alliance with others, are positioned in the structure of power. If cultural difference is a marker of class difference, then the program of multiculturalism may exert a critical transformative impact if it questions the ascendancy of one high or elite culture—a supremacy won at the expense of those who either are denied access to it for political and economic reasons, or who are silenced by it as its own condition of possibility. "Common culture" then becomes the figure or trope for suppression and domination. This is so because "social identity is defined and asserted through difference" (Bourdieu 1977). But in doing this, multiculturalism is no longer purely a "cultural" or merely ideological project of reform but one which interrogates and challenges the foundational principles of the social order itself. By then the call to grant equal social representation to groups with diverse cultures would be a call to equal participation in the exercise of substantive political power.

My brief then is for a critical analysis and transvaluation of the discourse of multiculturalism and its mirror-image, the "common culture." We need to go beyond celebrating fluid identities, hybridity, borderline or liminal bodies, uncanny deconstructive ventriloquisms setting "postcolonial" gurus as a new breed, and so on. We know that the ideal of ethnic pluralism, of multicultural democracy, can be used demagogically to legitimize existing class divisions and apologize for the systemic inequalities that enable a simulacrum of "civic humanism" to become plausible. We need to go beyond the platitudes of identity politics, however much these may provide a space for recuperating resources and renewing indigenous folk memory for nourishing the resistance. We need to wrestle with the task of historicizing the cultural symbols that construct identities and ontologies of self-representation by disclosing the constellation of power and property relationships informing them. In conclusion, if we are indeed forced to struggle on the discursive terrain of a monopolistic liberalism, we need to invent a heretical, oppositional, even utopian multiculturalism. This proposal will be generated not from arguments about citizenship, humanism, individual freedom, but from the vicissitudes and creativity of popular struggles for a broad socialist agenda, for equalizing wealth and recovering the sources of meaning and self-worth from the commodifying reach of a tendentious, patriotic "common culture" that has now almost colonized the whole planet.

BIBLIOGRAPHY

Abdullah, Ghassan. 1991. "Culture Behind the Bars." *Left Curve* 15: 68–70.

Achebe, Chinua. 1977. "An Image of Africa." *The Massachusetts Review* (Winter): 782–94.

Adorno, Theodor. 1967. *Prisms*. London: Spearman.

———— et al. 1977. *Aesthetics and Politics*. London: New Left Books.

Ahmad, Aijaz. 1987. "Jameson's Rhetoric of Otherness and the 'National Allegory.'" *Social Text* 17 (Fall): 3–27.

Althusser, Louis. 1969. *For Marx*. New York: Pantheon.

————. 1971. *Lenin and Philosophy and Other Essays*. London: New Left Books.

————. 1990. *Philosophy and the Spontaneous Philosophy of the Scientists*. London: New Left Books, 1990.

———— and Etienne Balibar. 1970. *Reading Capital*. London: New Left Books.

Amin, Samir. 1989. *Eurocentrism*. New York: Monthly Review Press.

Anderson, Perry. 1988. "Modernity and Revolution." In *Marxism and the Interpretation of Culture*, edited by Cary Nelson and Lawrence Grossberg. Urbana: University of Illinois Press.

Arvon, Henri. 1973. *Marxist Esthetics*. Ithaca: Cornell University Press.

Asante, Molefi K. 1994. "The Afrocentric Idea." In *From Different Shores*, edited by Ronald Takaki. New York: Oxford University Press.

Ashcroft, Bill, Garreth Griffiths, and Helen Tiffin. 1989. *The Empire Writes Back*. New York: Routledge.

Baker, Carlos. 1972. *Hemingway: The Writer as Artist*. 4th ed. Princeton, NJ: Princeton University Press.

Baker, Houston. 1984. *Blues, Ideology, and Afro-American Literature*. Chicago: University of Chicago Press.

Bakhtin, M. M. 1981. *The Dialogic Imagination*. Austin: University of Texas Press.

————. 1984, *Problems of Dostoevsky's Poetics*. Manchester: Manchester University Press.

————. 1986. *Speech Genres and Other Late Essays*. Austin: University of Texas Press.

————. 1993. *Toward a Philosophy of the Act*. Austin: University of Texas Press.

———— /P. Medvedev. 1978. *The Formal Method in Literary Scholarship*. Baltimore: The Johns Hopkins University Press.

———— /V. N. Voloshinov. 1973. *Marxism and the Philosophy of Language*. New York: Academic Press.

———— /V.N. Voloshinov. 1978. *Freudianism: A Marxist Critique*. New York: Academic Press.

Baldwin, James. 1961. *Nobody Knows My Name*. New York: The Dial Press.

————. 1963a. *The Fire Next Time*. New York: The Dial Press.

————. 1963b. *Notes of a Native Son*. New York: The Dial Press.

————. 1964. *Blues for Mister Charlie*. New York: The Dial Press.

————. 1966. "As Much of the Truth As One Can Bear." In *Opinions and Perspectives*, edited by Francis Brown. Baltimore: Penguin.

————. 1972a. *No Name in the Street*. New York: The Dial Press.

————. 1972b. *One Day, When I Was Lost*. New York: Dell Publishing.

————. 1977. "Previous Condition." In *Anthology*, edited by Lynn Altenbernd, 560–71. New York: Macmillan.

————. 1985a. *Jimmy's Blues*. New York: St. Martin's Press.

————. 1985b. *The Price of the Ticket*. New York: St. Martin's/Marek.

————. 1989. *Conversations*, edited by Fred Standley and Louis Pratt. Jackson: University Press of Mississippi.

————. 1991. "Sonny's Blues." In *The Story and Its Writer*, edited by Ann Charters, 55–81. Boston: Bedford Books.

———— and Margaret Mead. 1971. *A Rap on Race*. Philadelphia: J.B. Lippincott Company.

Balibar, Etienne. 1990. "Paradoxes of Universality." In *Anatomy of Racism*, edited by David Goldberg. Minneapolis: University of Minnesota Press.

Balibar, Etienne and Pierre Macherey. 1981. "On Literature as an Ideological Form." In *Untying the Text*, edited by Robert Young. New York: Routledge.

————. 1982. "Interview." *Diacritics* 12: 46–52.

Banton, Michael. 1984. "Culture." In *Dictionary of Race and Ethnic Relations*, edited by E. Ellis Cashmore. London: Routledge.

Baraka, Amiri. 1979. *Selected Plays and Prose of Amiri Baraka/Leroi Jones*. New York: William Morrow.

————. 1984. *The Autobiography of Leroi Jones*. New York: Freundlich Books.

Barth, Fredrik. 1969. *Ethnic Groups and Boundaries*. Boston: Little, Brown and Co.

Barthes, Roland. 1972. *Critical Essays*. Evanston: Northwestern University Press.

————. 1979. *The Eiffel Tower and Other Mythologies*. New York: Hill and Wang.

Bataille, Georges. 1985. *Visions of Excess: Selected Writings 1927–1939*. Minneapolis: University of Minnesota Press.

Bathrick, David. 1992. "Cultural Studies." In *Introduction to Scholarship in Modern Languages and Literatures*, edited by Joseph Gibaldi. New York: Modern Language Association of America.

Baudrillard, Jean. 1984. "The Precession of Simulacra." In *Art After Modernism*, edited by Brian Wallis. New York: The Museum of Contemporary Art.

Baxandall, Lee. 1983. "Literature." In *Dictionary of Marxist Thought*, edited by Tom Bottomore. Cambridge, Mass: Harvard University Press.

Beach, Joseph Warren. "Style in *For Whom the Bell Tolls.*" In *Ernest Hemingway: Critique of Four Major Novels*, edited by Carlos Baker, 82–89. New York: Scribners.

Bell, Derrick. 1990. "Stuart's Lie: An American Tradition." *New York Times* (14 January): 23.

Belsey, Catherine. 1980. *Critical Practice*. London: Methuen.

Benjamin, Walter. 1969. *Illuminations*. New York: Schocken.

———. 1972. *Gessamelte Schriften*, edited by Tillman Rexroth, 9–21. Volume IV, 1. Frankfurt: Suhrkamp Verlag.

———. 1978. *Reflections*. New York: Harcourt.

Bennett, Tony. 1979. *Formalism and Marxism*. New York: Methuen.

Benson, Jackson J. 1969. *Hemingway: The Writer's Art of Self-Defense*. Minneapolis: University of Minnesota Press.

Berger, John. 1984. *And Our Faces, My Heart, Brief as Photos*. New York: Pantheon.

Berlowitz, Marvin. 1984. "Multicultural Education: Fallacies and Alternatives." In *Racism and the Denial of Human Rights: Beyond Ethnicity*, edited by Marvin Berlowitz and Ronald Edari. Minneapolis: MEP Publications.

Berreman, Gerald. 1990. "The Incredible 'Tasaday': Deconstructing the Myth of the 'Stone-Age' People." *Cultural Survival Quarterly* 15: 3–25.

Bessie, Alvah. 1974. "Hemingway's *For Whom the Bell Tolls.*" In *Ernest Hemingway: Five Decades of Criticism*, edited by Linda Wagner. East Lansing: Michigan State University Press.

Beverley, John. 1994. *Against Literature*. Minneapolis: University of Minnesota Press.

Bhabha, Homi. 1992. "Postcolonial Criticism." In *Redrawing the Boundaries*, edited by Stephen Greenblatt and Giles Gunn. New York: Modern Language Association of America.

Bloch, Ernst, et al. 1977. *Aesthetics and Politics*. London: Verso.

Boal, Augusto. 1979. *Theater of the Oppressed*. New York: Urizen Books.

Boelhower, William. 1981. "Antonio Gramsci's Sociology of Literature." *Contemporary Literature* 22: 580–95.

Bold, Alan. 1988. *MacDiarmid: A Critical Biography*. Amherst: University of Massachussetts Press.

———. 1983. *The Terrible Crystal*. London: Routledge and Kegan Paul.

Booth, Wayne. 1982. "Freedom of Interpretation: Bakhtin and the Challenge of Feminist Criticism." *Critical Inquiry*, 9:1 (September 1982): 45–76.

Borges, Jorge Luis. 1962. *Ficciones*. New York: Grove Press.

———. 1981. *Borges: A Reader*, edited by Emir Rodriguez Monegal and Alastair Reid. New York: Dutton.

Bouvier, Leon and Robert Gardner. 1986. *Immigration to the U.S.: The Unfinished Story*. Washington, DC: Population Reference Bureau, Inc.

Bourdieu, Pierre and Jean Claude-Passeron. 1977. *Reproduction in Education, Society and Culture*. London: Sage.

Brecher, Jeremy, John Brown Childs, and Jill Cutler, eds. 1993. *Global Visions: Beyond the New World Order*. Boston: South End Press.

Brecht, Bertolt. 1964. *Brecht on Theater*. Translated by John Willett. New York: Hill and Wang.

———. 1967. *Gessamelte Werke, Bd. 7, Stucke 3*. Frankfurt am Main: Suhrkamp.

Brenkman, John. 1993. "Multiculturalism and Criticism." In *English Inside and Out*, edited by Susan Gubar and Jonathan Kamholtz. New York: Routledge.

Broer, Lawrence R. 1973. *Hemingway's Spanish Tragedy*. Tuscaloosa, AL: University of Alabama Press.

Buhle, Paul. 1988. *C.L.R. James: The Artist as Revolutionary*. New York: Verso.

Bulosan, Carlos. 1983. *If You Want To Know What We Are*. New Mexico: West End Press.

Burger, Peter. 1984. *Theory of the Avant-garde*. Minneapolis: University of Minnesota Press.

Burgum, Edwin Berry. 1950. "Ernest Hemingway and the Psychology of the Lost Generation." In *Ernest Hemingway: The Man and His Work*, edited by John McCaffery, 308–28.

Buthlay, Kenneth. 1982. *Hugh MacDiarmid*. Edinburgh: Scottish Academic Press.

Callinicos, Alex. 1976. *Althusser's Marxism*. London: Pluto Press.

———. 1989. *Against Postmodernism: A Marxist Critique*. New York: St. Martin's Press.

Campbell, James. 1991. *Talking at the Gates*. New York: Viking.

Carby, Hazel. 1980. "Multi-Culture." *Screen Education* 34 (Spring): 62–70.

Carew, Jan. 1988. *Fulcrums of Change*. Trenton, NJ: Africa World Press.

Cashmore, E. Ellis. 1988. *Dictionary of Race and Ethnic Relations*. London: Routledge, 1988.

Caudwell, Christopher. 1946. *Illusion and Reality*. New York: International Publishers.

———. 1971. *Studies and Further Studies in a Dying Culture*. New York: Monthly Review Press.

Caws, Mary Ann and Christopher Prendergast, eds. 1994. *The Harper Collins World Reader: The Modern World*. New York: Harper Collins.

Chace, William. 1990. "The Real Challenge of Multiculturalism (Is Yet to Come)." *Academe* (November-December): 20–23.

Chan, Jeffery Paul. 1991. "The Chinese in Haifa." In *Aiiieeeee! An Anthology of Asian American Writers*, edited by Frank Chin et al., 71–92. New York: Mentor, 1991.

Chan, Sucheng. 1991. *Asian Americans: An Interpretive History*. Boston: Twayne.

Chin, Frank. 1991. "Act I of *The Chickencoop Chinaman*." In *Aiiieeeee!* edited by Frank Chin et al., 115–47. New York: Mentor.

Chomsky, Noam. 1982. *Towards a New Cold War*. New York: Pantheon Books.

———. 1991. "The United States and Indochina: Far from an Aberration." In *Coming to Terms: Indochina, the United States, and the War*, edited by Doug Allen and Ngo Vinh Long. Boulder: Westview Press.

Cixous, Helene. 1989. "The Laugh of the Medusa." In *Literary Criticism and Theory*, edited by Robert Con Davis and L. Finke. London: Longman, 1989.

Clark, Katerina and Michael Holquist. 1984. *Mikhail Bakhtin*. Cambridge, MA: Harvard University Press.

Cleaver, Eldridge. 1968. *Soul on Ice*. New York: Delta.

Clifford, James. 1988. *The Predicament of Culture*. Berkeley: University of California Press.

Connor, Steven. 1989. *Postmodern Culture*. New York: Blackwell.

Connor, Walker. 1980. "Review Article: Ethnicity, Race and Class in the United States." *Ethnic and Racial Studies* 3.3 (July): 355–59.

Cooper, Stephen. 1987. *The Politics of Ernest Hemingway*. Ann Arbor: UMI Research Press.

Craig, David, ed. 1975. *Marxists on Literature*. London: Penguin.

Crawford, Robert. 1992. *Devolving English Literature*. Oxford: Clarendon Press.

Cruse, Harold. 1968. *Rebellion or Revolution*. New York: William Morrow.

Culler, Jonathan. 1982. *On Deconstruction*. Ithaca: Cornell University Press.

———. 1988. *Framing the Sign*. Norman: University of Oklahoma Press.

Daiches, David. 1979. *The Norton Anthology of English Literature*, edited by M.H. Abrams. Vol. 2. New York: W.W. Norton.

Davidson, Arnold. 1990. "1933–34 Thoughts on National Socialism." *Critical Inquiry* 17 (Autumn): 48–52.

Davis, Ioan. 1976. "Time, Aesthetics and Critical Theory." In *On Critical Theory*, edited by John O'Neill, 58–77. New York: Seabury.

Debray, Regis. 1970. "Notes on Gramsci." *New Left Review* (January-February): 48–52.

———. 1977. "Marxism and the National Question." *New Left Review* 105 (September-October 1977): 25–41.

De Certeau, Michel. 1989. *Heterologies: Discourse on the Other*. Minneapolis: University of Minnesota Press.

de Man, Paul. 1979. *Allegories of Reading*. New Haven: Yale University Press.

———. 1983. *Blindness and Insight*. Minneapolis: University of Minnesota Press.

———. 1986. *The Resistance to Theory.* Minneapolis: University of Minnesota Press.

Deleuze, Gilles. 1993. *The Deleuze Reader,* edited by Constantin V. Boundas. New York: Columbia University Press.

Deleuze, Gilles and Felix Guattari. 1986. *Kafka: Toward a Minor Literature.* Minneapolis: University of Minnesota Press.

———. 1987. *A Thousand Plateaus.* Minneapolis: University of Minnesota Press.

Demetz, Peter. 1967. *Marx, Engels and the Poets.* Chicago: University of Chicago Press.

Derrida, Jacques. 1981. *Positions.* Chicago: University of Chicago Press.

———. 1988. "Structure, Sign and Play in the Discourse of the Human Sciences." In *Modern Criticism and Theory,* edited by David Lodge, 108–22. New York: Longman.

Desnoes, Edmundo. 1985. "The Death System." In *On Signs,* edited by Marshall Blonsky. Baltimore: The Johns Hopkins University Press.

Dirlik, Arif. 1994. "The Postcolonial Aura: Third World Criticism in the Age of Global Capitalism." *Critical Inquiry* 20 (Winter): 328–56.

Dombroski, Robert. 1984. "Antonio Gramsci and the Politics of Literature: A Critical Introduction." *Italian Quarterly,* 30: 41–55.

———. 1989. *Antonio Gramsci.* Boston: Twayne Publishers.

Dowling, William. 1984. *Jameson, Althusser, Marx.* Ithaca: Cornell University Press.

Dunn, Allen. 1992. "The Ethics of Sublimity: The Critique of Bourgeois Morality." *The Arkansas Quarterly* 1 (Winter): 11–31.

Duparc, Jean and David Margolies, eds. 1986. *Christopher Caudwell: Scenes and Actions.* London: Routledge.

Dusell, Enrique. 1992. "Theology and Economy: The Theological Paradigm of Communicative Action and the Paradigm of Life as a Theology of Liberation." In *Development and Democratization in the Third World,* edited by Kenneth Bauzon. Washington, DC: Crane Russak.

Eagleton, Terry. 1976. *Criticism and Ideology.* London: New Left Books.

———. 1981. *Walter Benjamin or Towards a Revolutionary Criticism.* London: Verso.

———. 1986. *Against the Grain.* London: Verso.

———. 1990. *The Ideology of the Aesthetic.* New York: Basil Blackwell.

Ebert, Teresa. 1993. "Ludic Feminism, the Body, Performance, and Labor: Bringing *Materialism* Back into Feminist Cultural Studies." *Cultural Critique* (Winter): 5–50.

Ellison, Ralph. 1978. "Blues People." In *Imamu Amiri Baraka (LeRoi Jones),* edited by Kimberly Benston, 55–63. Englewood Cliffs, NJ: Prentice-Hall.

Escobar, Elizam. 1990. "Art of Liberation: A Vision of Freedom." In *Reimaging America,* edited by Mark O'Brien and Craig Little. Philadelphia: New Society Publishers.

————. 1991. "The Stealing of Nothingness." *Left Curve* 15: 23–28.

Essed, Philomena. 1991. *Understanding Everyday Racism*. London: Sage.

Fabian, Johannes. 1983. *Time and the Other: How Anthropology Makes Its Object*. New York: Columbia University Press.

Fanon, Frantz. 1963. *The Wretched of the Earth*. New York: Grove Press.

Fitzpatrick, Peter. 1990. "Racism and the Innocence of Law." In *Anatomy of Racism*, edited by David Goldberg. Minneapolis: University of Minnesota Press.

Foley, Barbara. 1985. "The Politics of Deconstruction." In *Rhetoric and Form*, edited by Robert Con Davis and Ronald Schleifer, 113–34. Norman: University of Oklahoma Press.

Forgacs, David. 1982. "Marxist Literary Theories." In *Modern Literary Theory*, edited by Ann Jefferson and David Robey. Totowa, NJ: Barnes and Noble.

Foucault, Michel. 1992. "What is Enlightenment?" In *Postmodernism*, edited by Patricia Waugh. London: Edward Arnold.

Fox-Genovese, Elizabeth. 1986. "The Claims of a Common Culture: Gender, Race, Class, and the Canon." *Salmagundi* 72 (Fall): 131–43.

Franco, Jean. 1985. "Killing Priests, Nuns, Women, Children." In *On Signs*, edited by Marshall Blonsky. Baltimore: The Johns Hopkins University Press.

Frankel, Mark S. 1993. "Multicultural Science." *The Chronicle of Higher Education* (November 10): B1–B2.

Frankfurt Institute for Social Research. 1972. *Aspects of Sociology*. Boston: Beacon Press.

Franklin, Raymond S. 1991. *Shadows of Race and Class*. Minneapolis: University of Minnesota Press.

Freedman, Carl. 1984. "Possibilities of a Political Aesthetic." *Minnesota Review* 23 (Fall): 41–69.

French, Warren. 1971. "From *The Social Novel at the End of an Era*." In *The Merrill Studies in "For Whom the Bell Tolls,"* edited by Sheldon Norman Grebstein, 56–70. Columbus, Ohio: Charles Merrill.

Frenz, Horst. 1973. "The Art of Translation." In *Comparative Literature*, edited by Newton Stallknecht and Horst Frenz, 98-121. Carbondale: Southern Illinois University Press.

Frow, John. 1986. *Marxism and Literary History*. Cambridge, MA: Harvard University Press.

Garcia Marquez, Gabriel. 1988. *Love in the Time of Cholera*. New York: Penguin.

Gates, Henry Louis, Jr. 1992. "Pluralism and Its Discontents." *Profession 92*: 35–38.

————. 1993a. "The Welcome Table." In *English Inside and Out*, edited by Susan Gubar and Jonathan Kamholtz. New York: Routledge.

————. 1993b. "Beyond the Culture Wars: Identities in Dialogue." *Profession 93*: 6–11.

Gayle, Addison, Jr. 1972. "The Function of Black Literature at the Present Time." In *The Black Aesthetic*. New York: Anchor Books.

Geismar, Maxwell. 1961. *Writers in Crisis*. Boston: Houghton Mifflin.

Geras, Norman. 1986. *Literature of Revolution*. London: Verso.

Giddens, Anthony. 1981. "Modernism and Postmodernism." *New German Critique* 22 (Winter): 15–18.

Gilroy, Paul. 1990. "One Nation Under a Groove: The Cultural Politics of 'Race' and Racism in Britain." In *Anatomy of Racism*. Minneapolis: University of Minnesota Press.

Glazer, Nathan and Patrick Moynihan, eds. 1975. *Ethnicity: Theory and Experience*. Cambridge, MA; Harvard University Press.

Glucksmann, Christine Buci. 1980. *Gramsci and the State*. London: Lawrence and Wishart.

Goldberg, David Theo. 1993. *Racist Culture*. New York: Blackwell.

Goodman, Paul. 1974. "The Sweet Style of Ernest Hemingway." In *Ernest Hemingway*, edited by Linda Wagner. East Lansing, MI: Michigan State University Press.

Gordon, Milton. 1975. "Toward a General Theory of Racial and Ethnic Group Relations." In *Ethnicity: Theory and Experience*, edited by Nathan Glazer and Patrick Moynihan. Cambridge, MA: Harvard University Press.

Gottlieb, Roger S. 1989. *An Anthology of Western Marxism*. New York: Oxford University Press.

Goux, Jean-Joseph. 1990. *Symbolic Economies After Marx and Freud*. Ithaca: Cornell University Press.

Graff, Gerald. 1992. "Teach the Conflicts." In *The Politics of Liberal Education*. Durham: Duke University Press.

Graff, Gerald and Bruce Robbins. 1992. "Cultural Criticism." In *Redrawing the Boundaries*, edited by Stephen Greenblatt and Giles Gunn. New York: The Modern Language Association of America.

Gramsci, Antonio. 1957. *The Modern Prince*. New York: International Publishers.

———. 1971. *Selections from the Prison Notebooks*. Ed. Q. Hoare and G.N. Smith. New York: International Publishers.

———. 1985. *Selections from Cultural Writings*. Cambridge, MA: Harvard University Press.

Greenblatt, Stephen. 1993. "The Politics of Culture." In *Falling Into Theory*, edited by David Richter. New York: St. Martin's Press.

Grunwald, Henry Anatole. 1992. "A Letter to My Granddaughter." *Money* (October): 19.

Gugelberger, Georg, ed. 1985. *Marxism and African Literature*. Trenton, NJ: Africa World Press.

Guttmann, Allen. 1962. "'Mechanized Doom': Ernest Hemingway and the American View of the Spanish Civil War." *Ernest Hemingway: Critiques of Four Major Novels*, edited by Carlos Baker, 95–107. New York: Scribners.

Habermas, Jurgen. 1983. "Modernity—An Incomplete Project." In *The Anti-Aesthetic*, edited by Hal Foster. Port Townsend, WA: Bay Press.

———. 1987. *The Philosophical Discourse of Modernity*. Cambridge, MA: MIT Press.

———. 1988. "Walter Benjamin: Consciousness-Raising or Rescuing Critique." In *On Walter Benjamin*, edited by Gary Smith, 90–124. Cambridge, MA: MIT Press.

Hadjor, Kofi Buenor. 1993. *Dictionary of Third World Terms*. New York: Penguin Books.

Hall, Stuart. 1986. "On Postmodernism and Articulation." *Journal of Communications Inquiry* 10: 45–60.

———. 1992. "The Question of Cultural Identity." In *Modernity and Its Futures*, edited by Stuart Hall et al. Cambridge: Polity Press.

———. 1992b. "Race, Culture, and Communications: Looking Backward and Forward at Cultural Studies." *Rethinking Marxism* 5 (Spring): 10–18.

———. 1994. "Cultural Studies: Two Paradigms." In *Contemporary Literary Criticism*, edited by Robert Con Davis and Ronald Schleifer. New York: Longman.

Harlow, Barbara. 1982. *Resistance Literature*. New York: Methuen.

Harvey, David. 1989. *The Condition of Postmodernity*. New York: Basil Blackwell.

Haug, Wolfgang Fritz. 1987. *Commodity Aesthetics, Ideology and Culture*. New York: International General.

Hawthorn, Jeremy. 1971. "Why Does Art Outlive Its Origins?" (Part One) *Marxism Today* (October): 301–7; (Part Two) *Marxism Today* (November): 332–37.

Hegel, Friedrich. 1956 [1830-31]. *The Philosophy of History*. New York: Dover.

Heller, Agnes. 1972. "Towards a Marxist Theory of Value." *Kinesis* 5 (Fall): 7–76.

———. 1984. *Radical Philosophy*. New York: Basil Blackwell Inc.

Hemingway, Ernest. 1932. *Death in the Afternoon*. New York: Charles Scribner's Sons.

———. 1932. *The Green Hills of Africa*. New York: Scribners.

———. 1940. *For Whom the Bell Tolls*. New York: Macmillan (A Scribner Classic).

Henry, Paget and Paul Buhle, eds. 1002. *C.L.R. James's Caribbean*. Durham: Duke University Press.

Hirsch, E. D. 1987. *Cultural Literacy*. Boston: Houghton Mifflin Co.

Hirst, Paul. 1979. *On Law and Ideology*. New Jersey: Humanities.

Holub, Renate. 1992. *Antonio Gramsci: Beyond Marxism and Postmodernism*. New York: Routledge.

Hooks, Bell. 1992. "Representing Whiteness in the Black Imagination." In *Cultural Studies*, edited by Lawrence Grossberg, et al., 338–46. New York: Routledge.

Houston, Velina Hasu, ed. 1993. *The Politics of Life*. Philadelphia: Temple University Press.

Howard, Dick. 1977. *The Marxian Legacy*. New York: Urizen Books.

Jackson, George. 1970. *Soledad Brother*. New York: Bantam.

Jacobs, Carol. 1978. *The Dissimulating Harmony*. Baltimore: Johns Hopkins University Press.

James, C.L.R. 1992. *The C.L.R. James Reader*. New York: Blackwell.

Jameson, Fredric. 1972. *Marxism and Form*. Princeton, NJ: Princeton University Press.

———. 1981. *The Political Unconscious*. Ithaca: Cornell University Press.

———. 1984a. "Periodizing the 60s." In *The 60s Without Apology*, edited by Sohnya Sayres, Anders Stephanson, Stanley Aronowitz, and Fredric Jameson. Minneapolis: University of Minnesota Press.

———. 1984b. "Postmodernism, or the Cultural Logic of Late Capitalism." *New Left Review* 146: 53–92.

———. 1986. "Third World Literature in the Era of Multinational Capitalism." *Social Text* 15: 65–88.

———. 1988. "Metacommentary." In *The Ideologies of Theory: Essays 1971–1986*. Vol. 1. Minneapolis: University of Minnesota Press.

———. 1989. "Marxism and Postmodernism." *New Left Review* 176 (July-August): 31–45.

———. 1991. *Postmodernism, or, The Cultural Logic of Late Capitalism*. Durham, NC: Duke University Press.

———. 1993. "On Cultural Studies." *Social Text* 34: 17–52.

Jahn, Janheinz. 1961. *Muntu*. New York: Grove Press.

Jaspers, Karl. 1966. *Anaximander Heraclitus Parmenides*. New York: Harcourt Brace.

Johnson, Barbara. 1981. "The Frame of Reference: Poe, Lacan, Derrida." In *Untying the Text*, edited by Robert Young, 225–43. Boston: Routledge.

Jost, Francois. 1974. *Introduction to Comparative Literature*. Indianapolis: Pegasus.

Jones, Leroi. 1964. *Dutchman and The Slave*. New York: Morrow Quill.

Juhl, P.D. 1984. "Playing with Texts: Can Deconstruction Account for Critical Practice?" In *Criticism and Critical Theory*, edited by Jeremy Hawthorn, 59–72. London: Edward Arnold.

Jung, Carl and Carl Kerenyi. 1963. *Essays on a Science of Mythology*. New York: Harpers.

Kafka. Franz. 1961. *The Penal Colony*. New York: Schocken Books.

Kanafani, Ghassan. 1990. *All That's Left To You*. Austin: University of Texas Press.

Kang, Younghill. 1974. "From *East Goes West*." In *Asian American Heritage*, edited by David Hsin-Fu Wand, 217–49. New York: Washington Square Press.

Kashkeen, Ivan. 1961. "Alive in the Midst of Death." In *Hemingway and His Critics: An International Anthology*, edited by Carlos Baker. New York: Hill and Wang.

Kastely, James. 1988. "Toward a Politically Responsible Ethical Criticism: Narrative in *The Political Unconscious* and *For Whom the Bell Tolls.*" *Style* 22: 535–58.

Kavanagh, James. 1982. "Marxism's Althusser: Toward a Politics of Literary Theory."

Kearney, Richard. 1988. *The Wake of Imagination*. Minneapolis: University of Minnesota Press.

Kessler-Harris, Alice. 1992. "Multiculturalism Can Strengthen, Not Undermine, a Common Culture." *The Chronicle of Higher Education* (October 21): B3, B7.

Kiernan, V. G. 1969. *The Lords of Human Kind*. London: The Cresset Library.

Kim, Elaine. 1993. "Preface." In *Charlie Chan Is Dead*, edited by Jessica Hagedorn, vii–xiv. New York: Penguin Books.

Kingston, Maxine Hong. 1989. *China Men*. New York: Vintage.

Kinnamon, Kenneth, ed. 1974. *James Baldwin*. Englewood Cliffs, NJ: Prentice Hall.

Koelb, Clayton. 1989. *Kafka's Rhetoric*. Ithaca: Cornell University Press.

Kristeva, Julia. 1980. *Desire in Language*. New York: Columbia University Press.

———. 1991. *Strangers to Ourselves*. New York: Columbia University Press.

Krupat, Arnold. 1989. *The Voice in the Margin*. Berkeley: University of California Press.

Laclau, Ernesto. 1987. "Psychoanalysis and Marxism." *Critical Inquiry* (Winter): 331–33.

Laing, David. 1978. *The Marxist Theory of Art*. Hanocks, Sussex: The Harvester Press, 1978.

Lang, Berel and Forrest Williams, ed. 1972. *Marxism and Art*. New York: David McKay.

Larsen, Neil. 1990. *Modernism and Hegemony: A Materialist Critique of Aesthetic Agencies*. Minnepolis: University of Minnesota Press.

Lauter, Paul et al., ed. 1990. *The Heath Anthology of American Literature*. Vol. 2. Lexington, MA: D.C. Heath.

Leeming, David. 1994. *James Baldwin*. New York: Alfred Knopf.

Lefebvre, Henri. 1968. *The Sociology of Marx*. New York: Vintage Books.

———. 1971. *Everyday Life in the Modern World*. New York: Harper Torchbooks.

Leitch, Vincent. 1983. *Deconstructive Criticism*. New York: Columbia University Press.

Lenin, Vladimir. 1963. "Selections from *Philosophical Notebooks.*" In *Reader in Marxist Philosophy*, edited by Howard Selsam and Harry Martel. New York: International Publishers.

———. 1967. *On Literature and Art*. Moscow: Progress Publishers.

Lifshitz, Mikhail. 1973. *The Philosophy of Art of Karl Marx*. London: Pluto Press.

Llosa, Mario Vargas. 1990. "Updating Karl Popper." *PMLA* 105 (October): 1018–25.

Lodge, David. 1987. "After Bakhtin." In *The Linguistics of Writing*, edited by Nigel Fabb et al. New York: Methuen.

Longxi, Zhang. 1988. "The Myth of the Other: China in the Eyes of the West." *Critical Inquiry* 15 (Autumn): 108–31.

Lovell, Terry. 1980. *Pictures of Reality*. London: BFI Publishing.

Lowith, Karl. 1949. *Meaning in History*. Chicago: University of Chicago Press.

Lukács, Georg. 1964. *Studies in European Realism*. New York: Grosset and Dunlap.

———. 1970a. *Lenin: A Study on the Unity of His Thought*. London: New Left Books.

———. 1970b. *Writer and Critic*. London: Merlin.

———. 1971. *History and Class Consciousness*. Cambridge, MA: MIT Press.

———. 1973. "Approximation to Life in the Novel and the Play." In *Sociology of Literature and Drama*, edited by Elizabeth and Tom Burns. London: Penguin.

———. 1980. *Essays on Realism*. Cambridge, MA: MIT Press.

Lynn, Kenneth. 1987. *Hemingway*. New York: Fawcett.

Lyotard, Jean François. 1984. *The Postmodern Condition: A Report on Knowledge*. Minneapolis: University of Minnesota Press.

Lukes, Steven. 1987. *Marxism and Morality*. New York: Oxford.

MacDiarmid, Hugh. 1967. *A Lap of Honour*. London: MacGibbon and Kees.

———. 1971. *A Drunk Man Looks at the Thistle*. Amherst: University of Massachussetts Press.

———. 1972. *Lucky Poet*. Berkeley: University of California Press.

———. 1970. *Selected Essays of Hugh MacDiarmid*, edited by Duncan Glen. Berkeley: University of California Press.

———. 1970. *Selected Poems*, edited by David Craig and John Manson. Middlesex: Penguin Books.

———. 1978. *The Socialist Poems of Hugh MacDiarmid*, edited by T.S. Law and T. Berwick. London: Routledge and Kegan Paul, 1978.

———. 1993. *Selected Poetry*, edited by Alan Riach and Michael Grieve. New York: New Directions.

MacDonnell, Diane. 1986. *Theories of Discourse*. Oxford: Blackwell.

Macherey, Pierre. 1977. "An Interview with Pierre Macherey." *Red Letters* 5: 3–9.

———. 1978. *A Theory of Literary Production*. London: Routledge.

———. and Etienne Balibar. 1981. "Literature as an Ideological Form: Some Marxist Propositions." *Praxis* 5: 43–58.

MacIntyre, Alasdair. 1981. *After Virtue*. Notre Dame, IN: University of Notre Dame Press.

———. 1990. *Three Rival Versions of Moral Enquiry*. Notre Dame, IN: Notre Dame University Press.

MacLennan, Gregor et al. 1977. *On Ideology*. London: Hutchinson.

Madison, D. Soyini, ed. 1994. *The Woman That I Am*. Boston: Bedford Books.

Malraux, Andre. 1938. *Man's Hope*. New York: Random House.

Mantsios, Gregory. 1992. "Rewards and Opportunities: The Politics and Economics of Class in the United States." In *Race, Class, and Gender in the United States*, edited by Paula S. Rothenberg. New York: St. Martin's Press.

Marable, Manning. 1991. "Multicultural Democracy." *Crossroads* (June): 2–7.

———. 1992. "Debate on Multiculturalism." *Bowling Green State University News* (March 3): 2.

Marcuse, Herbert. 1968. "The Affirmative Character of Culture." In *Negations*. Boston: Beacon Press.

———. 1978. *The Aesthetic Dimension*. Boston: Beacon.

Margolies, David N. 1969. *The Function of Literature*. New York: International Publishers.

Marriott, Alice and Carol Rachlin. 1969. *American Epic*. New York: New American Library.

Marx, Karl. 1970. *Critique of Hegel's Philosophy of Right*, edited by Joseph O'Malley. Chicago: University of Chicago Press.

———. 1973a. *Early Writings*, edited by Quintin Hoare. New York: Vintage Books.

———. 1973b. *Grundrisse*. New York: Vintage Books.

———. and Friedrich Engels. 1978. *The Marx-Engels Reader*, edited by Robert C. Tucker. New York: Norton.

Maxwell, Stephen. 1980. "The Nationalism of Hugh MacDiarmid." In *The Age of MacDiarmid*, edited by P. Scott and A. Davis. Edinburgh: Mainstream, 1980.

Mayakovsky, Vladimir. 1972. "How Verses Are Made." In *The Art and Craft of Writing*, translated by Alex Miller. Moscow: Progress Publishers.

McLuhan, Marshall. 1964. *Understanding Media*. New York: American Library.

Mercer, Colin. 1978. "Culture and Ideology in Gramsci." *Red Letters*: 19–40.

Merrington, John. 1977. "Theory and Practice in Gramsci's Marxism." In *Western Marxism*. London: New Left Books.

Meyers, Jeffrey. 1985. *Hemingway: A Biography*. New York: Harper.

———. ed. 1982. *Hemingway: The Critical Heritage*. London: Routledge.

Miles, Robert. 1989. *Racism*. London: Routledge.

Miller, J. Hillis. 1987. *The Ethics of Reading*. New York: Columbia University Press.

———. 1989. "The Search for Grounds in Literary Study." In *Literary Criticism and Theory*, edited by Robert Con Davis and Laurie Finke, 812–26. New York: Longman.

Miner, Earl. 1990. *Comparative Poetics*. Princeton, NJ: Princeton University Press.

Mitsuhiro, Yoshimoto. 1989. "The Postmodern and Mass Images in Japan." *Public Culture* 1 (Spring 1989): 8–25.

Mittenzwei, Werner. 1973. "The Brecht-Lukács Debate." In *Preserve and Create*, edited by Ursula Beitz and Gaylord Leroy. New York: Humanities.

Miyoshi, Masao. 1993. "A Borderless World? From Colonialism to Transnationalism and the Decline of the Nation-State." *Critical Inquiry* 19 (Summer): 726–51.

Monk, Ray. 1990. *Ludwig Wittgenstein*. New York: Penguin Books.

Moore, Sally Falk. 1989. "The Production of Cultural Pluralism as a Process." *Public Culture* (Spring 1989): 26–48.

Morawski, Stefan. 1973. "Introduction." In *Marx and Engels on Literature and Art*, edited by Lee Baxandall and Stefan Morawski. St. Louis: Telos Press.

———. 1974. *Inquiries into the Fundamentals of Aesthetics*. Cambridge, MA: MIT Press.

Morgan, Edwin. 1976. *Hugh MacDiarmid*. Essex: Longman.

Morris, Meaghan. 1992. "On the Beach." In *Cultural Studies*, edited by Lawrence Grossberg et al. New York: Routledge.

Morrison, Toni. 1993. "Black Matter(s)." In *Falling Into Theory*. New York: St. Martin's Press.

Morson, Gary Saul and Caryl Emerson. 1994. "M. M. Bakhtin." In *The Johns Hopkins Guide to Literary Theory and Criticism*, edited by Michael Groden and Martin Kreiswirth. Baltimore: The Johns Hopkins University Press.

Mouffe, Chantal, ed. 1979. *Gramsci and Marxist Theory*. London:

Mukherjee, Bharati. 1989. *Jasmine*. New York: Fawcett Crest.

———. 1990. "An Interview with Bharati Mukherjee." *The Iowa Review*, 30 (Fall): 7–32.

Mulhern, Francis. 1974. "The Marxist Aesthetics of Christopher Caudwell." *New Left Review* 85 (May): 37–58.

Murphy, Jay. 1991. "Ghassan Abdullah and Palestinian Culture of the Intifada." *Left Curve* 15: 66–68.

Myrdal, Jan and Gun Kesle. 1971. *Angkor*. New York: Vintage.

Neruda, Pablo. 1981. "Interview." In *Writers at Work*, edited by George Plimpton, 51-73. New York: Penguin Books.

Norris, Christopher. 1988. *Paul de Man*. New York: Routledge.

Oates, Joyce Carol. 1991. "Unless We Share, We Are Not Fully Human" [Special Advertising Section Paid by Chrysler Corporation]. *Money* (May): 10–11.

O'Brien, Mark and Craig Little. 1990. *Reimaging America: The Arts of Social Change*. Philadelphia: New Society Publishers.

Ohmann, Richard. 1992. "How To Read Cultural Literacy." *Against the Current* 36 (January/February): 27–30.

Okada, John. 1974. "From *No-No Boy*." In *Asian-American Heritage*, edited by David Wand. New York: Washington Square Press.

Palumbo-Liu, David. 1994. "Los Angeles, Asians, and Perverse Ventriloquisms: On the Functions of Asian America in the Recent American Imaginary." *Public Culture* 6 (Winter): 365–81.

Paine, Robert. 1974. *Second Thoughts About Barth's Models.* London: Royal Anthropological Institute of Great Britain and Ireland.

Parenti, Michael. 1994. *Land of Idols.* New York: St. Martin's Press.

Patterson, Orlando. 1983. "The Nature, Causes, and Implications of Ethnic Identification." In *Minorities: Community and Identity,* edited by C. Fried, 25–50. Berlin: Springer Verlag.

Paul, Elliot. 1937. *The Life and Death of a Spanish Town.* New York: Random House.

Plimpton, George. 1963. *Writers at Work: The Paris Interviews.* New York: Viking.

Porter, Horace A. 1989. *Stealing the Fire.* Middletown, CT: Wesleyan University Press.

Poston, Lawrence. 1991. "Review of *Illiberal Education* by Dinesh D'Souza. *Academe* (September-October): 53–56.

Pratt, Mary Louise. 1993. "Humanities for the Future: Reflections on the Western Culture Debate at Stanford." In *Falling Into Theory.* New York: St. Martin's Press.

Rabinbach, Anson. 1979. "Introduction to Walter Benjamin's 'Doctrine of the Similar.'" *New German Critique* 17: 60–64.

Raphael, Max. 1979. *Proudhon Marx Picasso.* New York: Humanities Press.

Ravitch, Diane. 1993. "Cultural Pluralism." In *From Different Shores.* New York: Oxford University Press.

Ray, William. 1984. *Literary Meaning.* New York: Blackwell.

Rex, John. 1986. *Race and Ethnicity.* Milton Keynes: Open University Press.

Riach, Alan. 1993. "The Mortal Memory." *Lines Review* 125 (June): 5–10.

Richard, Nelly. 1987/88. "Postmodernism and Periphery." *Third Text* (Winter): 5–12.

Ricoeur, Paul. 1978. *The Philosophy of Paul Ricoeur.* Boston: Beacon.

Rieser, Max. 1957. "The Aesthetic Theory of Social Realism." *Journal of Aesthetics and Art Criticism* 16 (December): 237–48.

Rivera, Tomas. 1987. *. . . y no se lo trago la tierra* [*. . . and the earth did not devour him*]. Houston: Arte Publico Press.

Roberts, Julian. 1983. *Walter Benjamin.* Atlantic Highlands, NJ: Humanities Press.

Rodrigues, Raymond. 1992. "Rethinking the Cultures of Disciplines." *The Chronicle of Higher Education* (April 29): B1–B2.

Rooney, Ellen. 1989. *Seductive Reasoning.* Ithaca: Cornell University Press.

Rosen, Charles. 1988. "The Ruins of Walter Benjamin." In *On Walter Benjamin,* edited by Gary Smith, 129–75. Cambridge, MA: MIT Press.

Rossi-Landi, Ferruccio. 1983. *Language as Work and Trade.* Hadley, MA: Bergin & Garvey.

Rovit, Earl and Gary Brenner. 1986. *Ernest Hemingway*. Revised edition. Boston: Twayne.

Rudich, Norman. 1965. "The Dialectics of Poesis: Literature as a Mode of Cognition." In *Boston Studies in the Philosophy of Science*, edited by Robert Cohen and Marx Wartofsky. New York: Humanities Press.

Rushdie, Salman. 1988. "Edward Said: On Palestinian Identity." *North Star Review* (Fall): 2–9.

Russo, Mary. 1986. "Female Grotesques: Carnival and Theory." In *Feminist Studies/Critical Studies*, edited by Teresa de Lauretis. Bloomington: Indiana University Press.

Said, Edward. 1985. *After the Last Sky*. New York: Pantheon.

———. 1989. "Representing the Colonized: Anthropology's Interlocutors." *Cultural Inquiry* 15 (Winter): 205–25.

Safran, William. 1991. "Diasporas in Modern Societies: Myths of Homeland and Return." *Diaspora* (Spring): 83–99.

Saldivar, Ramon. 1990. *Chicano Narrative*. Madison: University of Wisconsin Press.

San Juan, E., ed. 1973. *Marxism and Human Liberation: Essays by Georg Lukács*. New York: Delta.

———. 1989. "*Die Gewehre der Frau Carrar:* Brecht's Exemplum for the Third World?" *Communications* 18: 27-33.

———. 1991. *Writing and National Liberation*. Quezon City: University of the Philippines Press.

———. 1992a. "Critique of the New Politics of Racism/Nationalism in the United States." *Nature, Society, and Thought* 5: 307–19.

———. 1992b. *Racial Formations/Critical Transformations: Articulations of Power in Ethnic and Racial Studies in the United States*. Atlantic Highlands, NJ: Humanities International Press.

———. 1992c. *Reading the West/Writing the East*. New York: Peter Lang Publishing Inc.

———. 1994a. *Allegories of Resistance*. Quezon City: University of the Philippines Press.

———. 1995a. "Carlos Bulosan: *America Is in the Heart*." In *Teaching American Ethnic Literature*, edited by David Peck and John Maitino. Albuquerque: University of New Mexico Press.

———. 1994b. *From the Masses, to the Masses: Third World Literature and Revolution*. Minneapolis: Marxist Educational Press.

———. 1995b. "Introduction." In *On Becoming Filipino: Selected Writings by Carlos Bulosan*, edited by E. San Juan, Jr. Philadelphia: Temple University Press.

———. 1995c. *The Philippine Temptation: Dialectics of Philippines-U.S. Literary Relations*. Philadelphia: Temple University Press.

Sandel, Michael. 1982. *Liberalism and the Limits of Justice.* Cambridge: Cambridge University Press.

Sassoon, Anne Showstack. 1980. *Gramsci's Politics.* New York: St. Martin's Press.

Saxton, Alexander. 1977. "Nathan Glazer, Daniel Moynihan and the Cult of Ethnicity." *AmerAsian Journal* 4 (Summer): 141–50.

Schipper, Mineke. 1989. *Beyond the Boundaries.* London: Allison and Busby.

Schlesinger, Arthur, Jr. 1994. "The Return to the Melting Pot." In *From Different Shores.* New York: Oxford University Press.

Scholes, Robert. 1986. "Aiming a Canon at the Curriculum." *Salmagundi* 72 (Fall): 101-18.

Shcherbina, Vladimir. 1974. *Lenin and Problems of Literature.* Moscow: Progress Publishers.

Scott, Nathan A. 1966. *Ernest Hemingway.* Michigan: William Eerdmans.

Searle, John. 1993. "The Storm Over the University." In *Falling Into Theory.* New York: St. Martin's Press.

Selsam, Howard and Harry Martel, eds. 1963. *Reader in Marxist Philosophy.* New York: International Publishers.

Sender, Ramon. 1961. *Seven Red Sundays.* 1936. Reprint. New York: Collier Books.

Seung, T. K. 1982. *Structuralism and Hermeneutics.* New York: Columbia University Press.

Siegel, Fred. 1993. "The Cult of Multiculturalism." In *Race and Ethnic Relations 92/93,* edited by John Kromkowski. Guilford, CT: The Dushkin Publishing Group, Inc.

Silko, Leslie Marmon. 1981. *Storyteller.* New York: Arcade Publishing.

———. 1986. "Landscape, History, and the Pueblo Imagination." *Antaeus* 51: 83–94.

Simmel, Georg. 1977. "The Stranger." In *Race, Ethnicity, and Social Change.* North Scituate, MA: Duxbury Press.

Smith, Anthony. 1979. *Nationalism in the Twentieth Century.* New York: New York University Press.

Smith, Barbara Herrnstein. 1992. "Cult-Lit: Hirsch, Literacy, and the National Culture." In *The Politics of Liberal Education,* edited by Daryl Gless and Barbara H. Smith. Durham: Duke University Press.

Smith, Iain Crichton. 1980. "MacDiarmid and Ideas." In *The Age of MacDiarmid,* edited by P. Scott and A. Davis. Edinburgh: Mainstream.

Smith, M. G. 1986. "Pluralism, race and ethnicity in selected African countries." In *Theories of Race and Ethnic Relations,* edited by John Rex and David Mason. Cambridge, MA: Cambridge University Press.

Smith, Neil. 1984. *Uneven Development.* New York: Blackwell.

Sollors, Werner. 1986. *Beyond Ethnicity.* New York: Oxford University Press.

Solomon, Maynard, ed. 1973. *Marxism and Art.* New York: Knopf.

Soyinka, Wole. 1990. "Twice Bitten: The Fate of Africa's Culture Producers." *PMLA* 105 (January): 110-20.

Spilka, Mark. 1990. *Hemingway's Quarrel with Androgyny*. Lincoln: University of Nebraska Press.

Sprinker, Michael. 1987. *Imaginary Relations: Aesthetics and Ideology in the Theory of Historical Materialism*. London: Verso.

Stanton, Edward. 1989. *Hemingway and Spain*. Seattle: University of Washington Press.

Steiner, George. 1967. *Language and Silence*. New York: Athenaeum.

Stephens, Robert O. 1974. "Language, Magic and Reality in *For Whom the Bell Tolls*." In *Ernest Hemingway*, edited by Linda Wagner, 266–79. East Lansing: Michigan State University Press.

Sturtevant, David. 1976. *Popular Uprisings in the Philippines 1840–1940*. Ithaca: Cornell University Press.

Suleri, Sara. 1993. "Multiculturalism and Its Discontents." *Profession 1993*. New York: Modern Language Association of America.

Suvin, Darko. 1972. "The Mirror and the Dynamo." In *Brecht*, edited by Erika Munk, 80–98. New York: Bantam Books.

Sypher, Eileen. 1993. *Wisps of Violence*. London: Verso.

Takaki, Ronald, ed. 1987. *From Different Shores*. New York: Oxford University Press.

———. 1989. *Strangers from a Different Shore*. Boston: Little, Brown and Company.

Tapping, Craig. 1992. "South Asia Writes North America: Prose Fictions and Autobiographies from the Indian Diaspora." In *Reading the Literatures of Asian America*, edited by Shirley Geok-lin Lim and Amy Ling, 285–301. Philadelphia: Temple University Press.

Tatlow, Anthony. 1980. "Critical Dialectics." In *Bertolt Brecht*, edited by John Fuegi et al. Atlanta: University of Georgia Press.

Taylor, Charles. 1992. *The Ethics of Authenticity*. Cambridge, MA: Harvard University Press.

Terkel, Studs. 1992. *Race*. New York: The New Press.

Therborn, Goran. 1980. *The Ideology of Power and the Power of Ideology*. London: Verso.

Thernstrom, S. 1983. "Ethnic Pluralism: The U.S. Model." In *Minorities: Community and Identity*, edited by C. Fried. Berlin: Springer-Verlag.

Thiep, Nguyen Huy. 1992. *The General Retires and Other Stories*. Singapore: Oxford University Press.

Thompson, Robert Faris. 1983. *Flash of the Spirit*. New York: Vintage Books.

Thomson, George. 1974. *The Human Essence*. London: China Policy Study Group.

Thorne, Creath S. 1980. "The Shape of Equivocation in Ernest Hemingway's *For Whom the Bell Tolls*." *American Literature* 51: 520–35.

Thiher, Allen. 1990. *Franz Kafka: A Study of the Short Fiction*. Boston: Twayne Publishers.

Todorov, Tzvetan. 1984. *Mikhail Bakhtin: The Dialogical Principle*. Minneapolis: University of Minnesota Press.

Tomlinson, John. 1991. *Cultural Imperialism: A Critical Introduction*. Baltimore: The Johns Hopkins University Press.

Tonnies, Ferdinand. 1966 [1887]. *Community and Association*. London: Routledge and Kegan Paul.

Torres, M.L.F. 1989. "Anticipating Freedom in Theater." In *Brecht in Asia and Africa*, edited by John Fuegi et al., 134–51. Hong Kong: University of Hong Kong.

Trotsky, Leon. 1960. *Literature and Revolution*. Ann Arbor: University of Michigan Press.

Tucker, Robert, ed. 1978. *The Marx-Engels Reader*. New York: Norton.

University of Texas Writing Group. 1991. "The Realities of Multiculturalism." *Against the Current* (November-December): 5–11.

Vasquez, Adolfo Sanchez. 1977. *The Philosophy of Praxis*. London. Merlin Press

Villa, Jose Garcia. 1958. *Selected Poems and New*. New York: McDowell Obolensky.

Volosinov, V. N. 1973. *Marxism and the Philosophy of Language*. New York: Academic Press.

———. 1976. *Freudianism: A Marxist Critique*. New York: Academic Press.

Wald, Alan. 1991. *The Campaign Against 'Political Correctness': Analysis of a Frame-up and Proposals for a Socialist Response*. A Solidarity Discussion Paper. Detroit: Solidarity.

Waldhorn, Arthur. 1972. *A Reader's Guide to Ernest Hemingway*. New York: Farrar, Straus & Giroux.

Warren, Robert Penn. 1974. "Ernest Hemingway." In *Ernest Hemingway*, edited by Linda Wagner, 75-102. East Lansing: Michigan State University Press.

Weatherby, W. J. 1989. *James Baldwin: Artist on Fire*. New York: Donald Fine.

Webster, Yehudi O. 1992. *The Racialization of America*. New York: St. Martin's Press.

Webster's New Universal Unabridged Dictionary. Cleveland: OH, Dorset and Baber, 1972.

Weimann, Robert. 1989. "Text, Author-Function, and Appropriation in Modern Narrative: Toward a Sociology of Representation." In *Literature and Social Practice*, edited by Philippe Desan et al. Chicago: University of Chicago Press.

Weiss, Peter. 1970. *Notes on the Cultural Life of the Democratic Republic of Vietnam*. New York: Dell Publishing Co.

White, Hayden. 1980. "Literature and Social Action: Reflections on the Reflection Theory of Literary Art." *New Literary History* 11 (Winter): 363–80.

Wilden, Anthony. 1987. *The Rules Are No Game*. New York: Routledge and Kegan Paul.

Will, George. 1991. "Literary Politics." *Newsweek* (April 22): 72.

Willett, John. 1959. *The Theatre of Bertolt Brecht*. New York: Hill and Wang.

Williams, Raymond. 1977. *Marxism and Literature*. London: Oxford University Press.

———. 1989. *Resources of Hope*. London: Verso.

Wilson, Edmund. 1948. *The Triple Thinkers*. New York: Harcourt.

Wohlfart, Irving. 1979. "Walter Benjamin's Image of Interpretation." *New German Critique* 17: 70–98.

Wolf, Eric. 1982. *Europe and the People Without History*. Berkeley: University of California Press, 1982.

Wolff, Janet. 1983. "Aesthetics." In *A Dictionary of Marxist Thought*, edited by Tom Bottomore. Cambridge, MA: Harvard University Press.

———. 1984. *The Social Production of Art*. New York: New York University Press.

Wolin, Richard. 1982. *Walter Benjamin*. New York: Columbia University Press.

Wu, Frank. 1991. "The Trouble with Universities' Interest in Diversity Is, They've Embraced It as a Panacea for Racial Tension." *The Chronicle of Higher Education* (March 13): B2.

Yamamoto, Hisaye. 1988. *Seventeen Syllables and Other Stories*. Latham, New York: Kitchen Table Press.

Young, Philip. 1952. *Ernest Hemingway*. New York: Rinehart.

Young, Robert, ed. 1981. *Untying the Text: A Post-Structuralist Reader*. Boston: Routledge.

Yudice, George. 1994. "Postmodernism in the Periphery." *The South Atlantic Quarterly* 92 (Summer): 543–56.

INDEX

279

Rodney, Walter, 200
Romanticism, 18, 96, 111
Rooney, Ellen, 72
Rossi-Landi, Ferruccio, 49–50
Rushdie, Salman, 9, 194, 201
Russo, Mary, 43

Said, Edward, 1, 189, 200, 213–14, 215–16
Saldivar, Ramon, 198
Sandel, Michael, 245
Sandinista, 195, 196
Santayana, George, 127
Sartre, Jean–Paul, 3, 61, 168
Saussure, Ferdinand, 25
Saxton, Alexander, 245
Schizoanalysis, 174, 176, 204
Schlegel, Friedrich, 17, 18
Schlesinger, Arthur Jr., 226, 246
Scholes, Robert, 220, 228
Science, 82, 127, 139
Scotland, 121–42
Scotus, Duns, 133
Seale, Bobby, 157
Searle, John, 221
Segmentation, 173, 186
Sembene, Ousmane, 207
Semiotics, 69, 88, 95, 118
Sender, Ramon, 118
Sentence–production, 104, 106–7
Shakespeare, William, 17, 221
Silko, Leslie Marmon, 7, 209, 248–54
Simmel, Georg, 187
Simulacrum, 177, 194, 212, 228, 246
Smith, Barbara Herrnstein, 229
Smith, M.G., 256
Smith, Neil, 173
Socialism, 70, 123, 131, 142, 157, 206, 207, 210, 257
Socrates, 9
Sollors, Werner, 239, 247
"Sonny's Blues" (Baldwin), 149, 152–55
South Africa, 234–35, 237
Soviet Union, 93, 165
Soyinka, Wole, 194, 209, 210
Space, 70, 96, 109, 111, 173, 174, 183, 248–49
Spain, 93–95, 96, 98, 102, 103, 109, 111, 114, 116–17
Spanish-American War, 170
Spinoza, Benedict, 136, 154, 163, 200
Sprinker, Michael, 73, 74, 80

Stevens, Wallace, 141
Style, 86, 105, 106, 197
Surrealism, 22, 200
Symbolic exchange, 91–119
Symbolic Order, 110, 117, 149, 152, 154, 172, 179, 181, 191
Symbolism, 26, 97, 212, 213, 244, 252

Tagore, Rabindranath, 194, 217
Taine, Hippolyte, 16, 113
Tasadays, 213
Taylor, Charles, 238
Terkel, Studs, 242
Text, 38, 68, 79, 83, 85, 86, 91–119, 135, 252–53, 254
Theories of Surplus Value (Marx), 69
Thernstrom, Stephan, 232
Thiep, Nguyen, 8
"Third Hymn to Lenin" (MacDiarmid), 123
Third World, 1–4, 8, 9, 58, 65, 73, 93, 113, 116, 159, 163, 174, 178, 179, 193–218, 224
Thomas, Dylan, 141
Time-space, 109, 111–12, 178, 183, 188, 194, 197, 201–02, 252
Tolstoy, Leo, 53, 54, 61, 80, 81–82, 255
Tönnies, Ferdinand, 227
Translation, 15–33. *See also* Hermeneutics; Reading
Trilling, Lionel, 92
Trotsky, Leon, 56, 68, 210
Twain, Mark, 1

Uneven development, 4, 65, 77–78, 82, 95, 167, 173, 186, 207, 255
United States, 1, 10, 41–44, 100–103, 106, 116, 157, 158, 161, 165–91, 203, 208, 212–13, 219–22, 223–30, 232–33, 235, 238–44, 246
U.S. Civil War, 98, 101–102, 109, 117, 241
Utilitarianism, 236
Utopia, 115, 141, 150, 170, 172
Utterance, 39–40

Valery, Paul, 217
Value, 52, 56–57, 97, 98, 99, 103, 108–9, 111–12, 200, 202, 236; exchange, 177, 186. *See also* Commodification; Market
Verne, Jules, 79
Vietnam, 178–79, 180, 196
Villa, Jose Garcia, 206
Volpe, Galvano della, 54
Voloshinov, V., 23, 38, 49